D0707359

SPIRITUALITY FOR THE 21ST CENTURY

Stand at the crossroads and look; ask for the ancient paths,
ask where the good way is, and walk in it,
and you will find rest for your souls.
Jer 6:16

Pat Collins CM

Spirituality for the 21st century

Christian Living in a Secular Age

the columba press

First published in 1999 by
the columba press
55a Spruce Avenue, Stillorgan Industrial Park,
Blackrock, Co Dublin

Cover by Bill Bolger
Origination by The Columba Press
Printed in Ireland by Colour Books Ltd, Dublin

ISBN 185607 257 6

Dedicated to Fr Bill Connolly SJ of the Centre For Religious
Development, Boston, Mass., who helped his associate spiritual directors to recognise the presence and dynamics of religious experience

Contents

Foreword

The poet Tennyson wrote: 'the old order changeth, yielding place to the new; and God fulfils himself in many ways.'[1] That has never been truer than today. Like Western society, Ireland is experiencing an accelerating rate of change. There is evidence of growth in self confidence and creative expression. For many it was epitomised by *Riverdance*. The rate of change is putting pressure on all our institutions, values and beliefs. As Pope John Paul said in a prophetic way in 1979: 'Although you still live in an atmosphere where true religious and moral principles are held in honour, you have to realise that your fidelity to these principles will be tested in many ways. The religious and moral traditions of Ireland, the very soul of Ireland, will be challenged by temptations that spare no society in our age.'[2] For many years now, the Catholic Church in Ireland has in fact experienced that testing challenge. There are indications that it may not be coping very well.

Firstly, there is the problem of secularisation. According to Jan Kerhofs, it 'first appears as alienation of a large part of the population from the churches'. Instead of gaining new members, most of the mainline churches in the West are losing the members they already have. For example, there has been a drop of approximately 20% in the practice rate of Irish Catholics between 1994 and 1998. Currently, it is around 60% and the downward trend is likely to continue in urban areas, especially those that are poor and disadvantaged. In the future, practice rates may dip as low as the 15-40% figure that obtains in other Catholic countries in Europe such as France, Italy and Spain. Some time ago the *Irish Times* published the results of an MRBI poll on religion. When asked what the Catholic Church in Ireland would be like in twenty years time, 69% of the respondents said that it would be Catholic in name only.[3]

Secondly, there has been a significant drop in vocations to the priesthood and religious life in Western countries. This trend has been particularly noticeable in Ireland. Some seminaries are closing due to a lack of applicants. Others are catering for the smallest intake of candidates this century. Meanwhile, due to falling numbers, male and female religious orders are withdrawing from many of their traditional works, such as running schools and administering hospitals. A diminishing and ageing group of priests and religious is ministering to a largely youthful population. Not surprisingly, the widening generation gap often leads to communications problems.

Thirdly, a growing number of people disagree with the church's teachings, especially those to do with sexual morality. There are a number of reasons for this. In a society where traditional points of view are often called into question, there is evidence of increasing subjectivism and relativism in the realm of ethics. Self-development and happiness are the priorities in many people's lives. They are sometimes espoused at the expense of duties and commitments to the family and the wider community. One sociologist defines this process as 'the growing autonomy of individuals in developing their own norms and standards'.[4] This tendency has been reinforced by reports of clerical scandals. Not only have many lay people been shocked, they have become so disillusioned with church authority that they increasingly tend to rely on their own consciences when making decisions.

What should we make of all this? To begin with, I'm convinced that Karl Rahner was very perceptive when he wrote many years ago: 'Our present situation is one of transition from a church sustained by a homogeneously Christian society and almost identical with it, from a people's church, to a church made up of those who have struggled against the environment in order to reach a clear, explicit, and responsible personal deci-

sion of faith.'[5] Surely the issue of personal faith lies at the heart
of the matter. As Pope Paul VI once observed in words that
echoed those of the great German theologian: 'We would say
only this: today either you live your faith with devotion, depth,
vigour and joy, or that faith dies out.'[6]

It is clear that Christians are reacting in different ways to this
new and challenging state of affairs. Some of those who lapse
seem to neglect their spiritual lives by concentrating on the pleasures and worldly opportunities that the consumer society has
to offer. Others become interested in alternative forms of
Eastern and Western spirituality, such as transcendental meditation, psychosynthesis and the New Age Movement, which are
not specifically Christian. There are other disillusioned
Catholics who, instead of lapsing or leaving, become disgrun-
tled within the church. They espouse a do-it-yourself kind of
spirituality. It centres around seers and prophets who receive
private revelations, and around signs and wonders such as
weeping statues, apparitions, and other strange phenomena.
Devotees of this spirituality have a particular devotion to Padre
Pio, Our Lady of Medjugorje, and the Divine Mercy of Sr
Faustina, etc. They tend to be conservative as far as faith and
morals are concerned. Many of them are strong and even ag-
gressive supporters of the pro-life movement.

It is my belief that the popular piety movement should be
taken seriously. As traditional certainties are questioned, and
many Christian practices are changed, an increasing number of
men and women feel anxious and uneasy. Post-Vatican II liturgy
is too wordy, conceptual and abstract to meet their needs. It has
left their imaginations and hearts unnourished and unmoved.
Meanwhile, they are troubled by a disturbing decline in faith
and morals and a corresponding growth of crime in society.
What the members of the popular piety movement are looking
for is a restoration of traditional values, and forms of devotion
that will move them emotionally while giving them a sense of
the nearness of a mysterious God who answers prayer, comforts
the afflicted and transforms lives.

Within this context, the phenomenon of weeping and moving statues is instructive. I am inclined to interpret such experiences as day-dreams. Therefore I believe that they should be understood in a symbolical way as expressions of wishful thinking. For example, if one looks up the entry on 'religious statues' in Tom Chetwynd's insightful *Dictionary for Dreamers*, it says that when inanimate figures are seen to move in a life-like way it is a sign that 'what was a dead theoretical concept suddenly has new inner meaning for the dreamer' and that 'new potentialities are awakening in the dreamer'.[7] As we know, a dry doctrinal approach to religion does very little for people. Evidently, what the supporters of popular piety are looking for are doctrines that come alive with experiential meaning.

The popular piety movement is a significant presence within the church. While it professes loyalty to ecclesiastical authority, it is an ironic fact that, when members of the hierarchy question any of its cherished beliefs, the misgivings of bishops are not likely to be well received. Followers of the popular piety movement believe that, after a time of misunderstanding and opposition, God will vindicate their cause just as he vindicated the causes of people like Bernadette Soubirous and Catherine Labouré. I think that the church authorities would do well to listen to what this protest movement, which in some ways has affinities with what contemporary Pentecostalism is saying about an overly rational and masculine approach to spirituality. At the same time they need to critique its beliefs and practices from a psycho-spiritual point of view. For example, in terms of Gordon Allport's Intrinsic-Extrinsic Orientation Scale, a good deal of popular piety bears the marks of immature religion in so far as it seems to be need-centred, comfort-seeking and unwilling to come to terms with unpalatable realities that might threaten to undermine its own rigid point of view.

There are other people who have neither left the church to follow esoteric forms of spirituality, or joined the ranks of the popular piety movement. They form two groups. The first consists of many Christians who have discovered an orthodox form of spirituality within the church which satisfies them, e.g. the Charismatic Movement or Ignatian Spirituality. The second group consists of those who are loyal but dissatisfied. They are looking for a contemporary articulation of spirituality, one that combines the best of the old and the new, in a thoughtful, experiential sort of way.

While I don't suppose that too many of the followers of the popular piety movement will be interested in this book, it has been written with their aspirations in mind. It tries to steer a course between the un-devotional theology of the academy, on the one hand, and the un-theological devotion of the popular piety movement on the other. If the contents seem text-bookish at times, it is because I hope the following pages will be helpful to the increasing number of people, especially those who attend courses in spirituality, who are looking for a postmodern articulation of traditional devotion. 'Postmodern' here simply refers to the major cultural trends that have emerged in the wake of post Enlightenment modernity, as a reaction against it, a counter balance to it, or a continuation of it by other means.[8] I also hope that the following pages will put into words what many thoughtful Christians already know at a gut level, and will help them to develop such a strong inner life that they will be able to resist negative aspects of the secularising influences at work in our society.

A few words about the approach of the book. It is not an overview of contemporary spirituality. It is really a collection of loosely connected essays on spiritual topics that have interested me in recent years. Some began life as talks to the general public, others as topics for undergraduate spirituality courses in All Hallows College, while others were written as magazine articles. As a result the chapters vary in length and style. It would probably be true to say that the overall approach is more scholarly than popular; more ecumenical than rigidly Catholic; more interdisciplinary than strictly spiritual; and more eclectic than systematic. I have quoted freely, and often, from a range of authors who have influenced me over the years. Many of them are psychologists who have written about religious experience. In a culture where subjectivity and scientific knowledge are valued, the observations of these authors is particularly interesting and relevant. I should also explain that the many references to St Vincent de Paul are due to the fact that I admire him greatly and belong to a congregation which he founded in the seventeenth century. Whenever possible, I have made practical suggestions which may enable readers to grow spiritually.

I would like to express my thanks to a number of people. Firstly, I'm grateful to close friends, fellow Vincentians, and members of the charismatic and ecumenical movements who have influenced my understanding and appreciation of spirituality. Secondly, I also owe a debt of gratitude to all the men and women who have attended my lectures on spirituality over the years. Their interest and commitment has impressed me greatly. Their questions, feed-back and personal contributions have repeatedly challenged me to refine and modify my thinking. I also want to thank a number of magazine editors for permission to use previously published material.

I owe gratitude to Tom Jordan O.P. the editor of *Spirituality* magazine for permission to reproduce an altered version of an article published in January-February 1998. I also want to thank Fr Ronan Drury, the editor of *The Furrow*, for permission to reprint an article on New Age spirituality which he published in January 1998. Gratitude is due to Gerry Moloney C.Ss.R., the editor of *Reality* magazine, for permission to republish sections of an article that first appeared in September 1997 and also to Dympna Sheehan for permission to use an expanded version of an article that first appeared in the October 1998 edition of *New Creation*. Finally, I am grateful to Emeric Amyot d'Inville CM, the editor of *Vincentiana*, the international journal of the Vincentian Order, for permission to reprint, in chapter eleven, a modified version of an article that was first published by him in January-February 1998.

CHAPTER 1

Models of Spirituality

We seem to be living through a long drawn out transitional crisis in Western culture. Inevitably the Christian churches are deeply affected by this challenging state of affairs. It has led to a paradoxical situation. While many men and women are disillusioned with the institutional expressions of religion, there is a growing interest in spirituality. One philosopher has suggested why this might be so. Spiritual people feel themselves to be more at home in the universe than unspiritual persons do. They have the joy of belonging, a sense of connectedness and an inward peace which others cannot help envying and even admiring.[1]

That said, there is something ill-defined and elusive about the subject of spirituality. In an article entitled, 'Toward a Method for the Study of Spirituality' Jesuit author, Edward Kinerk maintains that, unlike most other academic disciplines, spirituality lacks both a formal definition of its content and a methodology proper to itself. While this chapter doesn't pretend to resolve these difficult issues, it does aim to throw some light on two particular points. Firstly, it will examine what the word 'spirituality' refers to and secondly, it will suggest that currently there are three models of spirituality operating in Western Christianity.

What is Spirituality?
We begin with the nature of spirituality. Here are two possible descriptions. Sandra Schneiders says, in general terms that would be applicable to any kind of spirituality theistic or non theistic, that it 'is the experience of consciously striving to integrate one's life in terms not of isolation and self-absorption but of self-transcendence toward the ultimate values one perceives.'[2] Joann Wolski Conn

offers a specifically Christian definition when she says: 'Christian spirituality involves the human capacity of self-transcending knowledge, love and commitment as it is actualised through the experience of God, in Jesus, the Christ, by the gift of the Spirit. Because God's Spirit comes to us only through experience and symbols inseparable from human community and history, Christian spirituality includes every dimension of human life.'[3] So spirituality is a life of faith, i.e. a way of trusting oneself, in a committed way, to centres of meaning and value beyond oneself, e.g. the mystery sustaining the universe, whether it is understood as the Higher Power of AA or the Blessed Trinity of Christian revelation. From a personal point of view I like to think of spirituality as a matter of being filled, guided and empowered by the Holy Spirit in one's daily life (cf. Eph 5:18; Gal 5:18; 16).

In contemporary writing there is an on-going debate which was initiated by Paul Tillich in the 1950s. It asks whether spirituality is a separate aspect of our human lives alongside other aspects such as the moral and aesthetic, or a dimension of all those aspects. Tillich himself suggested that rather than being a separate entity, spirituality is the dimension of depth and ultimate concern in all the other aspects of human life.[4] More recently Ken Wilber has revisited this debate. Writing about life in the Spirit he has observed: 'There are those who define "spiritual" as *a separate developmental line* (in which case spiritual development is alongside or parallel to psychological and emotional and interpersonal development). And there are those who define "spiritual" as the *highest reaches* of all of those lines (in which case spiritual development can only occur *after* psychological development is mostly completed).'[5] I'm inclined to believe that because grace builds on nature, it is true in a general sense that human and spiritual development are interrelated. So, for example, one could say that people will be no closer to God than they are to their true selves and their most intimate friends. The triadic relationship of self, others and God is, more or less, interdependent. So it is unlikely that a person who has very little self-awareness or interpersonal intimacy, in his or her life, will enjoy a deep personal relationship with God. Spirituality can be looked at from four points of view.

Firstly, it can be seen as an *experience* of transcendence, i.e. of the Beyond which is in the midst of everyday experience. As such it is a conscious awareness of the mediated immediacy of God, in and through nature, relationships, art, the sacraments, and so on. At this point it is worth noting that, research findings in a number of Western countries indicate that, there is a growing interest in religious experience as distinct from abstract religious truths or dogmas. It also shows that a person can be spiritual and have a spirituality without necessarily having any real church affiliation. A number of years ago, Karl Rahner anticipated this trend when he stated that, the spirituality of the future would have to live much more clearly than it had in previous generations, out of a solitary, immediate experience of God and his Spirit in the individual.[6] Some psychologists, such as Jung, Frankl and Assagioli, have maintained that true mental health and fulfilment is only possible when a person has such an experiential sense of transcendence in his or her life. In saying this they are echoing the well-known words of St Augustine in his *Confessions*, 'You have made us for yourself, and the heart of man is restless until it finds its rest in You.'[7]

Secondly, spirituality can be considered as an experience shared by large *groups* of people. In the *Catechism of the Catholic Church* we are informed that many varied spiritualities have been developed throughout the history of the churches.[8] Firstly, there is the personal charism of saintly witnesses of God's love for people, such as Ignatius of Loyola or St Francis of Assisi. Secondly, a distinct spirituality can be associated with a particular culture, e.g. Celtic spirituality. Thirdly, a spirituality can be associated with a particular movement of the Spirit in the church, e.g. the Beguines in the Middle Ages or the Charismatic and feminist movements of the late twentieth century. Fourthly, a spirituality can be associated with different churches, e.g. Orthodox or Evangelical. Although each one has a lot in common with the others, they have distinctive and defining characteristics. Spirituality tries to identify what these characteristics are, e.g. different ways of praying and relating to the world of people and nature.

Thirdly, spirituality is also a *way of living*. Some writers suggest there are three main ways of doing this, the way of devotion; the way of works; and the way of knowledge.[9] They insist that, one way or the other, the experience of relationship with God should be incarnated in all the aspects of people's everyday lives. Put briefly, it is a matter of trust in transcendental reality expressing itself through loving thoughts, feelings and choices (cf. Gal 5:6). Traditional Catholic spirituality, for example, stressed the importance of the seven spiritual and corporal works of mercy.[10] From St Paul onwards, Christian spiritual writers have warned against the dangers of dualism, a kind of spirituality that would be so heavenly minded as to be no earthly good. They stress the fact that life in the Spirit is a matter of establishing a balance between, such things as, transcendence and immanence; self-esteem and humility; psyche and spirit; individuality and community; contemplation and action; thought and feeling; pleasure and mortification; subjective conviction and openness to others, etc. Discriminating people discover that virtue stands in the middle between these polarities. As St Paul assures us: 'Those who are spiritual *discern all things*' 1 Cor 2:15. While spirituality impinges on every aspect of life in the marketplace such as aesthetics, ethics, sexuality, politics, science, sport, etc, it is not synonymous with any of them.

Fourthly, spirituality can be seen as an *academic study* of such experiences. This can be done from many different points of view such as the following.

Scriptural. The Christian experience, like its Jewish and Moslem counterparts, is expressed in the written word. As a result, Christian spirituality is firmly rooted in biblical exegesis. For example, when looking at the subject of Christian prayer one could study David M. Stanley's *Boasting in the Lord: The Phenomenon of Prayer in St Paul.*[11]

Historical. Academic spirituality also looks at the development of religious experience over the centuries. For example, when looking at the historical aspects of Christian prayer one could read Kenneth Leach's *True Prayer: An Introduction to Christian Spirituality.*[12]

Psychological. Modern psychology looks at the conscious and unconscious factors at work in religious experience. For example, Barry and Ann Ulanov's *Primary Speech: A Psychology of Prayer,*[13] looks at the subject largely from a Jungian point of view.

Phenomenological. This is a descriptive-empirical approach to religious experience. It can include an historical perspective but it concentrates its attention on the dynamics of different types of spiritual experience. For instance, German scholar Friedrich Heiler's classic 1918 investigation of *Prayer: A Study in the History and Psychology of Religion*,[14] is an outstanding example.

Liturgical. Liturgists examine religious experience from the point of view of the church's official worship such as the Divine Office and the Eucharistic Prayer. One typical book on this subject is A. Cunningham's *Prayer: Personal and Liturgical.*[15]

Professed and Operative Spiritualities

All Christians are influenced by what we call spiritual constructs. They are a combination of *professed spirituality*, i.e. what we think and feel at a conscious level, and *operative spirituality*, i.e. what our felt attitudes and gut instincts are like, largely, at an unconscious level. Dr Ana-Maria Rizutto, an Argentinian psychoanalyst, describes how a parish priest came to see her. His presenting symptoms were chronic fatigue and insomnia that compromised his ability to be available to his parishioners. A thorough examination revealed that there was nothing wrong with him physically. However, when Rizutto asked the priest about his family it became clear from his tone of voice that, although he admired his father, he also feared him because he was stern, strict and punitive. When she asked the priest about his relationship with God his reply was equally ambiguous. As Rizutto observed, the God of the priest was loving, patient and gentle (i.e. professed spirituality). The God of the man was critical, stern and demanding (i.e. operative spirituality). The God of the theologian, however, was updated (i.e. professed spirituality), but the God of the man was anachronistic and disturbing (i.e. operative spirituality).[16] Dr Rizutto went on to describe how she helped the priest to consciously recognise the conflict between his professed and operative spiritualities, and how one was the fruit of his education and the other was the result of his childhood experience of paternal authority. As soon as he became aware of these conflicting aspects of his relationship with God, he was able to revise his image of the Lord and thereby achieve peace of mind.

Because there are sometimes conflicts between professed and operative spiritualities, conversations and discussions between Christians are often confusing and unfruitful. Although we use the same spiritual vocabulary, e.g. words such as community, authority, discernment, etc., we can mean quite different things by them. In my experience, resistance to change, in individuals and groups, is sometimes due, not so much to ideological disagreements of the rational kind, as to the unacknowledged influence of pre-rational and even irrational emotional attitudes which can be rooted in the unconscious. Those who have been engaged in the work of reconciliation in the North of Ireland, for example, have encountered them, time and time again, both in themselves and in others. In recent years some theologians have used models theory, i.e. mapping of elements in the subject under consideration onto an idealised type, in order to explicate what our unconscious spiritual constructs might be.

Models of Spirituality

The notion of models is borrowed from the world of science. They are ideal cases, organising images which give a particular emphasis, enabling one to notice and interpret certain salient aspects of experience. Speaking about the models that are used in technological research, the *Encyclopaedia Britannica* says that a model is a simplified representation of the real world and, as such, includes only those variables relevant to the problem at hand. It may not include all relevant variables because a small percentage of these may account for most of the phenomenon to be explained. Many of the simplifications used, produce some error in predictions derived from the model, but these can often be kept small compared to the improvement in operations that can be extracted from them.[17]

Among theologians, Avery Dulles has shown in a number of his writings[18] how models theory can be used with helpful results.[19] Speaking specifically of religious models, Dulles says that in constructing types on the basis of the views of individual theologians one is moving from the particular to the universal, from the concrete to the abstract, from the actual to the ideal. The abstracted type does not exactly correspond to the thought of the theologians whom it includes. As an ideal case, the type may be called a model. It is a relatively simple, artificially constructed case which can be useful and illuminating when dealing with realities that are more complex and differentiated.[20]

Because spiritual models represent ideal types, an individual person or group would rarely conform exactly to any of them. However, they would belong predominantly to one or other, while incorporating characteristics of the other models in their outlook. Although different saints, such as St Vincent de Paul, adhered mainly to one model of spirituality, in his case the programmatic, there is evidence that they augmented them with elements from other models. In the course of this chapter I will illustrate each of the models – which will be described below – with relevant quotations from St Vincent's writings. It is important to stress that models are descriptive rather than evaluative. All of them are valid, and have their own distinctive strengths and weaknesses. Ideally, models should be clear and precise. It must be admitted that the way in which three different spiritualites are described in this study is a bit arbitrary, in so far as it is selective, choosing to highlight some characteristics while ignoring others. That said, you will probably see for yourself that the overall classification has a certain internal logic and cogency, which can prove illuminating and helpful.

Models in Context: Classical and Historical World Views
Like other models, spiritual ones are influenced by the world views in which they were first formulated. They are referred to nowadays as the *Classical* and the *Historical* way of looking at things, a distinction that was first suggested in the writings of Bernard Lonergan.[21] It was, indirectly adverted to in the document *The Church in the Modern World* when it observed, in paragraph five, that humankind has substituted: 'A dynamic and more evolutionary concept of nature for a static one.' In general terms we could say that we are living at the interface between the two of them.

The classical mentality is deductive. It emphasises universal principles and necessary conclusions. It tends to be abstract and *a priori*. It examines the nature of things and draws conclusions in regard to particular instances depending on whether or not they correspond to stated principles. The historical mode of thinking tends to be practical and *a posteriori*. It emphasises changing circumstances and contingent conclusions. It begins with concrete data, employs an empirical method, stresses hermeneutics, and draws its conclusions inductively from its sources. This approach is typically post-modern. Like 'The New Age' the concept of most-modernism is a very hard one to describe accurately, because its meaning can vary in different contexts. In general terms, however, it refers to a mind-set that is open-ended, and characterised by fairly sceptical attitudes that have been shaped by a great many intellectual and cultural currents such as pragmatism, existentialism, psychoanalysis, feminism, hermeneutics, deconstructionism, and the   philosophy of contemporary science, to name but a few.[22] Characteristics of the classical and historical worldviews can be outlined as follows. Clearly, a good deal of overlap is involved.

A) Static/cyclical – dynamic/evolutionary

Greek culture had a static world view. It was informed by the notion of cyclical change where the emphasis was on being rather than becoming. The modern world view is essentially dynamic. Since the advent of Darwin's theory of evolution, backed up as it is by many of the physical sciences, e.g. quantum physics and genetics, modern thought has stressed the importance of becoming. Nothing remains the same, everything is in a state of flux. So, the well known phrase, 'to live is to change, and to live well is to have changed often', is apt in this context.

B) Essentialist – existentialist

The Classical world view was primarily interested in the essential nature of things, their 'isness' so to speak. It was championed by such men as Plato, Aristotle and Aquinas. The modern world view is existentialist. It prefers to emphasize the importance of existence, i.e. the realm of the particular and the contingent. In the past two hundred years there has been a growing school of thought, both in philosophy and theology, which has reflected this changing perspective. Post-modernism believes that human knowledge is subjectively determined by a number of factors, so that objective essences, or things-in-themselves cannot be known, and so, all truths and assumptions must be continually subjected to direct testing. Pope John Paul II has acknowledged that this shift has taken place. In a number of his writings he has critiqued the weaknesses inherent in an overly subjectivist and relativist philosophy, unbridled by any objective absolutes.[23] Bryan Appleyard has adverted to the same trend in his book *Understanding the Present*. He says that in pluralistic democracies, all knowledge is, at best, relatively true. As a result, when making moral choices, many of our contemporaries inhabit a fluid, labile world. So, their decisions cannot be made by referring to an outside order or system, they can only be *their* choices, 'Given that, they will always be aware that there are different choices made by other people. They cannot argue absolutely against these different choices, they can only say that they think they are wrong.'[24]

C) Truth – self

This point follows from the last. Classical culture preferred to look at the truth in itself, whereas historical culture is interested in the way in which the truth impinges upon one's individual sense of self. Static, essentialist cultures, were confident that the truth could be known in itself. In post-modern culture, all knowledge is thought to be provisional. The claims of reason are qualified in the light of contemporary discoveries to do with hermeneutics, theories of knowledge, the role of the unconscious etc. Not surprisingly, therefore, Joann Wolski Conn says in *The New Dictionary of Theology* that: 'The issue of "the self" is the focal point of contemporary spirituality's examination of the relationship between psychology and religion between nature and grace.' She cites the writings of Thomas Merton as a typical example.

D) Objective – subjective

Because classical culture puts the emphasis on objective truth, it also has a strong sense of authority. But in modern culture many factors have conspired to change all this. Firstly, there is the accelerating rate of change which causes 'future shock' to use Toffler's well known phrase. Secondly, things such as the rise of science, universal education, travel, the mass media, feminism, etc, have called the validity of a good deal of traditional authority – the things it says and affirms – into question. In the religious sphere the situation is similar. The center of gravity has shifted from the experience of objective religious authority to the authority of subjective religious experience. This shift has been confirmed by empirical research. For example *The European Values Systems Reports* in 1984 and 1994 have indicated that across the generations, regardless of class or education there has been a shift from firm, to less firm adherence to religious authority per se.[25] John Paul II seemed to acknowledge that this is the trend when he wrote: 'people today put more trust in … experience than in doctrine.'[26]

In a chapter entitled, 'Religious and Moral Values,' Michael Hornsby-Smith and Christopher Wheelan maintain that the latest research indicates the following four points would describe so-called 'new Catholics' in Ireland. In some respects they seem to lend support to the trends we have been describing.

- They have an informed appreciation of the supernatural and sacramental life of the church, including an increasing tendency to think in terms of a spirit or life force rather than a personal God.
- They have an outlook that questions the church's right to speak with absolute authority on matters of personal morality or to speak out on Government policy while at the same time considering it appropriate that the church should be outspoken on social issues.
- They have a liberal attitude on sexual matters, which can be coupled with an adamant rejection of abortion except in circumstances where the mother's health is at risk.
- They have an optimistic interpretation of religion and of one's standing before God and the world. Beliefs and attitudes such as

hell, the Devil, sin, and fears of damnation have all taken a bad beating.[27]

Despite the evidence that secularising tendencies are at work, these authors argue that there are also clear signs of religious revitalisation and counter-secularising tendencies at work in Ireland. Anyone who knows the Irish religious scene well, knows that to be true.

Three Models of Spirituality

John C. Haughey suggests that there are good reasons for trying to design models of Christian spirituality. Firstly, having adverted to the fact that there are all kinds of disagreements and divisions in the contemporary church, he says: 'Underneath these tensions there is the key difference: how one images God, approaches him, experiences him, and articulates this experience to oneself.'[28] In other words, conflicts in theology are rooted in spirituality, in the way in which one relates to God, and how one views oneself and others as a result of that relationship. Unfortunately, this point is usually overlooked by those who write and teach academic theology. As a rule, professed theologies are the rational expressions of the operative spiritualities that inform them. Secondly, conscious awareness of models of spirituality helps people not only to grow in self-knowledge, it also increases their mutual tolerance much as a personality test like the Myers Briggs Indicator can do.[29] It can lead individuals and groups to recognise the fact that the spirituality of other individuals and groups may be influenced by alternative models that are just as valid as their own.

Haughey suggests that currently there are three models of spirituality, what he refers to as the *programmatic, pneumatic* and *autogenic.* They inform the way we live and think as Christians. By and large, the essentialist, classical world view favours programmatic spirituality, whereas the modern existentialist and historical worldview tends to favour spirituality of the autogenic and pneumatic kind. When we look at the distinctive characteristics of these spiritualities it will become apparent why this judgement can be made.

A) Programmatic spirituality

Haughey refers to his first theological model as programmatic, i.e. the Christian life is a matter of obediently following a programme of living which has been laid down in an authoritative way by the church. This spirituality has some of the following characteristics. It is one in which the person's experience of God comes in and through the church. In other words it is ecclesiocentric. Obedience, docility and loyalty are therefore the key virtues in this spirituality. Its adherents have no difficulty in finding scripture texts to support their point of view, e.g. 'Then I said, "Lo, I have come to do your will, O God," as it is written of me in the roll of the book' (Heb 10:7).

Many saints were programmatics. For example, St Vincent de Paul is supposed to have declared: 'if you keep the rules, the rules will keep you.' On another occasion he said to his companions: 'We should be completely obedient to every one of our superiors, seeing the Lord in them and them in the Lord. In the first place we should faithfully and sincerely reverence and obey our Holy Father, the pope. We should also humbly and consistently obey the most reverend bishops of the dioceses where we live. Furthermore we should not take initiatives in parishes without the approval of the parish priests.'[30] The following quote from the writings of Cardinal Newman is another, even more specific, example of the programmatic approach. It is still influential in the modern era. He says that if a person wants to become perfect he or she doesn't have to perform: '…any extraordinary service, anything out of the way, or especially heroic. He is perfect who does the work of the day perfectly, and we need not go beyond this to seek for perfection … If you ask me what you are to do in order to be perfect, I say, first – do not lie in bed beyond the due time of rising; give your first thoughts to God; make a visit to the Blessed Sacrament; say the Angelus devoutly; eat and drink to God's glory; say the Rosary well; be recollected; keep out bad thoughts; make your evening meditation well; examine yourself daily; go to bed in good time, and you are already perfect.'[31]

Programmatics read the scriptures sparingly because they are afraid of being led astray as a result of private interpretation. They welcome the notion of renewal, but they are suspicious of anything that is not initiated by, or approved of, by the church. This spirituality stresses the importance of traditional practices such as perseverance, order, and reverence for tradition, the sacraments, etc.

It would probably be true to say that programmatic spirituality has been, and in all likelihood still is, the predominant one in the Catholic Church; although it must be admitted that in recent years its influence has been declining. The Legion of Mary and *Opus Dei* would be examples of two organisations which espouse programmatic spirituality in the contemporary church. It has some obvious strengths. The fact that it stresses obedience and uniformity means that it is good at mobilising large numbers of people to achieve a specified task. As the traditional Catholic spirituality, it can embrace the masses in so far as it is not very demanding in terms of emotional integration, intelligence or learning. Mary Douglas has pointed out in her classic anthropological work, *Natural Symbols*, that rituals such as Friday abstinence and the Lenten fast were condensed symbols that enabled ordinary, theologically uneducated people to express their heartfelt faith in God in a non-conceptual way.[32] They were typical of programmatic spirituality. While this approach has contributed to the holiness of many of its members, programmatic spirituality has some obvious drawbacks.

- Firstly, it doesn't always develop the person's relationship with the Lord.
- Secondly, programmatic responses can be substitutes for heartfelt responses to the inspirations of the Holy Spirit.
- Thirdly, this spirituality is always in danger of engendering passivity and infantilism by trying to control the lives of its devotees by means of rules and regulations.

In terms of Dulles's *Models of the Church*, programmatic spirituality is best expressed in terms of the sacramental and hierarchical models of the people of God.

B) Pneumatic spirituality

The word pneumatic is coined from the Greek word *pneuma*, which means 'breath' or 'spirit'. Pneumatics claim to have a sense of the immediate presence of the Lord which only the Holy Spirit can give. Affective prayer is the context in which they experience God. Adherents of this spirituality would maintain that it is epitomised in the text which says: 'The anointing which you received from God abides in you, and you have no need that anyone should teach you; as his anointing teaches you about everything' (1 Jn 2:27). Like the other spiritualities, this one has a number of discernible characteristics.

It is historical rather than classical in nature. As such it focuses on experience rather than authority. Although pneumatics revere the church, they do not focus on it. Its teachings are markers which delineate the boundaries of orthodoxy. On a day to day basis, they are inner directed, attending in a prayerful way to the 'Beyond within'. They believe that the Risen Lord reveals his presence, his word and his will, to them, in an interior way. They would agree with the following words of St Vincent de Paul: 'An important point to which you should devote yourself, is to establish a close union between yourself and our Lord in prayer. That is the reservoir in which you will receive the instructions you need to fulfil the duties on which you are now about to enter. When in doubt, have recourse to God and say to him: "O Lord, you are the Father of lights, teach me what I ought to do in this circumstance." I give you this advice not only for those difficulties which will cause you pain, but also that you may learn from God directly what you have to teach, following the example of Moses who proclaimed to the people of Israel only that with which God had inspired him: "The Lord says this".'[33]

Like the autogenics, pneumatics believe in the importance of effective action but, unlike them, they see it as the expression of their affective sense of union with Christ. Conscience is not so much the guide about what ought to be done, as an inner discernment about where inspirations are coming from, e.g. from the self, God or the Evil one, and where they are leading, e.g. toward stronger or weaker relationship with God. In his fine book, *The Holy Spirit: Growth of a Biblical Tradition*, George Montague provides a typical example of this approach: 'One must walk by the Spirit or let one-self be led by the Spirit.' This little statement is theological dynamite. The Christian life is not a list of things to do and things to avoid. It is not virtue acquired by practice. It is a gift of being moved by the Spirit of God, and the key to life is to allow the Spirit to lead. Paul clearly speaks here of an inspired ethic and of inspired action – and it is not reserved for the holy few but is the birth-right of all who believe in Jesus. And it is readily available. A crucial point: when confronted with any moral decision, great or small, the Christian's first question should be 'Where does the Spirit lead me in this?'[34]

Haughey says that pneumatic spirituality, unlike the other two, presumes community. It believes that when two or three are gathered in the Lord's name, they can sense his presence among them. In other words, the Lord's presence is experienced in and through the community. Intimacy with God, results from intimacy with others and visa versa. Haughey points out that not all Pentecostal Christians are necessarily pneumatics. In spite of their frequent references to the Spirit, some of them can adopt a fundamentalist and programmatic approach to spirituality. He says that the criterion for judging which one is involved is to answer the question: is the experience of God in Christ experienced in an unmediated way over a sufficiently long length of time? This spirituality has obvious strengths. It is biblical, is intensely personal, stresses the role of imagination and feelings, and lends itself to ecumenical co-operation. This approach has its characteristic weaknesses.

- It can be so heavenly minded as to be of no earthly good.
- It can mistake warm feelings for genuine commitment expressed in persevering action.
- It can be experience- and, therefore, need-orientated rather than being focused on God and God's will.

In terms of Dulles's *Models of the Church*, this model of spirituality is best expressed by means of the church seen as herald and mystical communion.

C) *Autogenic spirituality*

The word autogenic is one coined by Haughey. It literally means originating in the self. This immediately suggests that this is a characteristically modern spirituality, historical rather than classical in its orientation. Haughey points out that the self involved here is not the unredeemed ego but rather the spiritual self that hungers for meaning. As such it could be referred to as Logoic spirituality because *Logos* is the Greek word for meaning. Adherents of this spirituality could quote the following verse as one that encapsulates their approach: 'Little children, let us not love in word or speech but in deed and truth' (1 Jn 3:18). This form of spirituality has a number of typical characteristics.

Because the centre of gravity in this approach has shifted from the authority of the church's teachings in themselves, to their experiential meaning, its devotees are selective in what they take seriously. They neither deny or affirm the majority of the church's teachings, they simply overlook them in everyday life. They are motivated by conviction, convictions that arise from the meanings they perceive at a personal level.

Autogenic spirituality doesn't put the primary emphasis on the affective dimension. Meaning and intelligibility are more important than feeling. They tend to spend more time discussing the legitimacy of prayer, especially the petitionary kind, than they do praying. For example, in his book *New Paths in Spirituality*, John Macquarrie includes a chapter entitled, 'Prayer as Thinking'.[35] This is the kind of approach that an autogenic would be attracted to. There is an interesting example of the autogenic attitude to prayer in Gabriel Daly's book *Asking the Father*. He writes: 'Dietrich Bonhoeffer, the Lutheran pastor and scholar martyred by the Nazis, relates how during a particularly bad air-raid a fellow prisoner who normally showed no signs of religious belief began to mutter "O God, O God". Bonhoeffer did not attempt to offer him any Christian encouragement or comfort but simply assured him that the raid would be over in ten minutes. Bonhoeffer was here putting into practice his religious and theological convictions. He believed that appeals to God to intervene directly in the world's events implied a false conception of God and that God himself is patiently teaching us "how to get along without him". The world which has now "come of age" has its rightful and God-given autonomy, and it is the duty of Christian faith to appreciate this. Bonhoeffer therefore gave his frightened companion "secular" support. He did not say, "God will protect us" or even "let us pray together", but contented himself with the down-to-earth remark that from previous experience he knew that the raid would not last much longer.'[36]

In autogenic spirituality the focus is on the immanence rather than the transcendence of God. As a result, autogenics don't spend much time praising and worshipping God. They glorify God by using their talents and graces working for others. They would agree entirely with the following sentiments of St Vincent de Paul: 'Let us love God, but let it be in the strength of our arm and in the sweat of our brow. Sentiments of love of God, of kindness, of goodwill, good as these may be, are often suspect if they do not result in good deeds ... They may be consoled by their fervent imagination or content with the sweet sentiments they experience in prayer. They may speak like angels. But when it's a matter of working for God ... Their courage fails them. We must not deceive ourselves: all our work consists in action.'[37] On an other occasion he said that if a beggar called at the door while a Daughter of Charity was attending the Eucharist, she should leave Christ on the altar and go serve him in the poor. As a result of convictions like these, autogenics are in the forefront in the fight for social justice, civil rights, environmental protection, etc. They would be inclined to join Amnesty International and Greenpeace. Autogenics are often interested in theology, and sometimes allow this penchant for thinking about God to become a substitute, albeit in an unconscious way, for relationship with God by means of contemplation and acts of faith, hope, love, etc. This kind of spirituality often predominates among the staffs and student bodies in theological colleges.

Haughey is of the opinion that the ranks of this spirituality are growing. Many educated Catholics, especially religious, are inclined to feel at home in it. Arguably this is the spirituality that informs a good deal of so-called liberation theology. Its followers are at the forefront of the church's action for justice. This spirituality has obvious strengths. Its rejection of all forms of oppression is biblical. It appeals to men and to well educated people in a way that the other two spiritualities might not. But, like its counterparts, this spirituality has its distinctive weaknesses.

- It tends to mistake what goes on in the mind or what one does in practical terms as being synonymous with the fullness of Christianity.
- It can underestimate the importance of close and intimate relationship with God and other people.
- As the faith of some of its adherents weakens, they tend to adopt a secular form of Christian lifestyle.

In terms of Dulles's *Models of the Church*, this spirituality is best expressed by means of the *servant model*.

Some aspects of the spiritualities contrasted

Having described the key characteristics of the three main models of spirituality, we can go on to describe how each of them would look at a number of important theological concepts. Obviously, this approach is very schematic and generalised. While all nuances, qualifications and explanations have been pared away, they do help to highlight essential differences in the approaches of the different spiritualities. We begin with faith as a foundational concept.

A) Concepts of faith

In an essay entitled 'The Meaning of Faith Considered in Relationship to Justice', Avery Dulles describes three models of faith. They seem to correspond to Haughey's three forms of spirituality. They are based on the fact that faith can be seen as trust, assent and action. He points out that faith includes three elements: a firm conviction regarding what is supremely important, dedication or commitment to that which one believes in, and trustful reliance on the power and goodness of that to which one stands committed. 'The three components of faith are thus conviction, commitment and trust.'[38] These complementary elements form the basis of his three models of faith. He goes on to say that in the classical tradition faith as conviction and trust were emphasised, whereas in the twentieth century faith as commitment has been highlighted.

1. Programmatic spirituality has a predominately intellectualist

conception of faith. It is largely to do with the mind. It can take two forms.

a) *The Illuminist form* aspires to contemplative union with God. It is evident in the writings of St Augustine. In the medieval period St Thomas was a great exponent of this kind of faith. He spoke frequently of belief being an inner light of the soul, between the light of natural reason and the light of glory. He also stressed things such as the gifts of wisdom and knowledge, as a connatural or instinctive awareness of God's nature and purposes.

b) *The asent to doctrine form* refers to a firm assent to the truths which the church authoritatively teaches in the name of God, whether they are understood or not. Unlike the illuminist school of thought, it equates faith with belief. This was the main kind of faith advocated by the Catholic Church in the Counter-Reformation period and Vatican I. The latter described faith in these words: 'We believe the things that God has revealed to be true, not because of their intrinsic truth perceived by the natural light of reason, but because of the authority of the revealing God himself, who can neither deceive or be deceived.'

2. Pneumatic spirituality tends to have a fiducial understanding of faith. It gives access not so much to abstract wisdom as to a person, One on whom the man or woman can totally rely thereby giving rise to a wholehearted trust, confidence and hope. In the synoptic gospels faith is practically equivalent to trust. Praise is given to those who rely on Jesus to forgive sins, heal hurts, deliver from evil, etc. This form of faith is common in the reformed tradition. It was championed by Luther and later by John Wesley, Karl Barth, etc. Nowadays, this kind of faith is common in evangelical circles and in the charismatic movement.

3. Autogenics adhere to a performative model of faith. Liberation theology describes this kind of faith as a transforming acceptance of the word, which comes as a free gift of God, breaking into human existence through the poor and oppressed, with whom Christ is seen to identify himself. Only in commitment to the liberation of the oppressed and thus only in liberating praxis, can we give the word the 'warm welcome' that constitutes faith.

As the scriptures say, 'whoever does the truth comes into the light' (Jn 3:2). The champions of this model of faith are writers such as Galilea, Gutierrez and Boff. Dulles thinks that there are no historical precedents for this model. It rejects the notion that faith is primarily either trust or assent.

B) Concepts of God
1. The programmatics see God as the Beyond above, i.e. the transcendent One who is distinct from creation, e.g. 'For who has known the mind of the Lord, or who has been his counselor?' (Rom 11:34).
2. The pneumatics see God as the Beyond within, i.e. immanent in a personal way, e.g. 'God is at work in you, both to will and to work for his good pleasure' (Phil 2:13).
3. The autogenics see God as the Beyond in the midst, i.e. immanent in the community, e.g. 'Truly I say to you, as you did it to one of the least of these my brothers or sisters, you did it to me' (Mt 25:40).

C) Concepts of time
1. Programmatics are past-orientated. Their emphasis in on the rear mirror view of history, i.e. the importance of the church's guidance being rooted in scripture and tradition.
2. Pneumatics are future-orientated. Their emphasis is mainly focused on the initiatives God will take. They are inclined to emphasise the importance of eschatology.
3. The autogenics are present-orientated. Their emphasis is upon the concrete action they intend to take, with God's help, in the here and now.

D) Concepts of community
1. According to the Programmatics, community is present when people share the same faith, worship and discipline. They do not put much emphasis on relationships of an intimate kind that involve mutual self-disclosure.
2. Pneumatics presume that community, togetherness, shared

prayer and honest communication about personal and religious matters are important in their own right and a locus for the experience of God and discernment of spirits.

3. Autogenics gather people together in order to accomplish a common task rather than to relate in a deeply personal way. It is a matter of community for mission, and autogenics tend to presume that when people work together in a co-operative or collaborative way, they are a community in virtue of that fact.

E) Concepts of authority

1. According to programmatics authority is hierarchical and vested in properly constituted superiors, e.g. the Pope, bishops and Christian leaders who act on God's behalf.
2. Pneumatics see authority in vertical terms. Ultimately it comes from God, but it can be shared by any baptised Christian who has personal experience of God and the revealed truth of God.
3. Autogenics see authority in horizontal terms. It is vested in the community and is discovered mainly in and through their co-operative efforts to discover meaning.

F) Concepts of decision making

1. Programmatics believe that decisions should be made by those who exercise rightful authority. They inform the people about what they should believe and do. When the Pope reminds the faithful that the church is not a democracy, he reinforces the programmatic point of view.
2. Although pneumatics believe that church authority is important when relevant, they believe that, by and large, day to day decisions should be made as a result of a prayerful process of discernment together.
3. Autogenics also accept church authority when it seems to be meaningful. They tend to make decisions as a result of well informed, rational discussion.

G) Concepts of sources

1. Programmatics stress the importance of the scriptures as inter-

preted by tradition and the teachings of the *magisterium* of the church.

2. Pneumatics tend to stress the importance of the inspired and inspiring word of God in scripture, as well as divine revelations which are often received in charismatic ways, e.g. by means of prophecies and visions.

3. Autogenics will rely on church teachings if and when they seem relevant and meaningful. They also rely on the power of reason and research, e.g. social analysis.

H) Concepts of prayer and worship

1. Programmatics favour liturgical and formal prayers which can be said together, usually in traditional ways, e.g. the rosary, angelus, stations of the cross, grace before and after meals, and especially the Mass.

2. Pneumatics prefer spontaneous prayer either on their own or in prayer groups of one kind or another. They are particularly attracted to the prayer of thanksgiving and praise.

3. Autogenics tend to discuss prayer from a theological point of view, e.g. the legitimacy of petitionary prayer, rather than engaging in such prayer. They see it as a potential cop out. Prayer is another word for action for justice. They would agree with Schleiermacher's observation that it is 'self-evident to every Christian that prayer necessarily includes and presupposes personal activity in bringing about what is prayed for'.

I) Concepts of spiritual direction

1. Programmatics see spiritual direction in an institutional quasi-sacramental way. Direction in this model is carried out when a director instructs the directee in the spiritual life and exercises a certain influence over the person's choices.

2. Pneumatics see spiritual direction as a charism of discernment (cf. 1 Cor 12:10) whereby the director has a graced ability to know which of the directee's inspirations are from God and which are not. Like a Russian *starets*, he or she may also have intuitive knowledge of an infused kind about God's will for the person.

3. Autogenics see spiritual direction in more incarnational terms. No aspect of the person's life is overlooked and the director uses the best insights of the human sciences, e.g. psychology, in order to help the directee to grow in relationship with God and in practical response to God's will.[39]

J) Concepts of evangelisation

1. Didactic/sacramental evangelisation is head-orientated and aims at *orthodoxy*, i.e. right doctrine, by means of catechetical instruction, reception of the sacraments and the witness of a holy life.
2. Kerygmatic/charismatic evangelisation is heart-orientated and aims at *orthokardia*, i.e. right experience, by means of inspired preaching, verbal testimony and witness, together with deeds of power such as healings and miracles.
3. Political/developmental evangelisation is hands-orientated and aims at *orthopraxis*, i.e. right action, by means of solidarity with the poor and oppressed, action for justice, human development, healing and ecology.[40]

Conclusion

Which of these models of spirituality is best suited to meet the needs of the times? We are living in a fast changing society where the centre of gravity is shifting from the experience of religious authority to the authority of religious experience. An MRBI poll in the *Irish Times* indicated that when Irish respondents were asked whether they followed the teachings of the church or their own consciences when making serious moral decisions, 78% said they followed their consciences.[41] Some commentators interpreted this statistic in negative terms as insubordination to the church. What is more likely is the fact that an increasingly well educated population is internalising values and, after mature reflection, coming to its own conscientious decisions.

Because the programmatic model of spirituality is essentialist in an existentialist culture, it is not well adapted to modern needs. It seems to me that in spite of all its undoubted merits – it has produced sanctity for centuries – the classical approach of program-

matic spirituality is less effective nowadays. Its objective, essentialist emphasis is out of step with a culture that values subjective
experience. That is why more and more people are finding it unsatisfactory. It would probably be true to say that official Catholic spirituality is still programmatic. Not surprisingly, the spirituality of
many bishops and priests is informed by this approach to divine
things. As a result, an increasing number of lay people find that
their sermons and teachings seem not so much to be wrong, as irrel-
evant and anachronistic. That is why a growing number of men and
women are deserting the programmatic approach and looking for
new, more relevant forms of spirituality such as those offered by
the pneumatic and the autogenic models. Others are seeking for
answers outside the church. To a greater or lesser extent, each of
them is pragmatic and experiential in orientation and therefore
more attuned to the modern mind.

CHAPTER 2

Religious Experience

This chapter begins with the subject of religion. Talcott Parsons (1902-1979), an eminent sociologist and scholar, has indicated that religion, in different forms, is to be found in all cultures, at all times, in all places. Religion, he says, is as universal a phenomenon as language or the incest taboo. Any conception of a merely 'natural man' who is unencumbered by such 'cultural baggage' belongs to a mistaken picture of prehistory, for which there is no solid evidence in anthropology. 'The view that such "baggage" *ought* to be dispensed with and that rational man should "face reality" without any "superstition" is a product of sophisticated culture, and in no way true of the original human condition.'[1]

The word 'religion' is derived from the Latin, *religiare*, meaning 'to bind'. So it could be said that religion binds people to God, others and to their deepest selves. The *Oxford English Dictionary* says that religion is: 'Recognition on the part of man of some higher unseen power as having control of his destiny, and as being entitled to obedience, reverence, and worship; the general mental and moral attitude resulting from this belief, with reference to its effect upon the individual or the community; personal or general acceptance of this feeling as a standard of spiritual and practical life.' In his Terry Lectures, which were delivered in Yale in 1937, Carl Jung quoted the following words from Cicero: 'Religion is that which gives reverence and worship to some higher nature which is called divine.'[2] Then Jung went on to add in a more phenomenological way: 'The term "religion" designates the attitude peculiar to a consciousness which has been changed by experience of the *numinosum*. Creeds are codified and dogmatised forms of original religious experience.'[3]

As Jung has already indicated, at the heart of religion is 'religious experience'. It is worth noting, in line with an observation already made in chapter one, that insead of talking about religious experience, we should refer, rather, to the religious dimension of human experience.[4] Implicit in this understanding is the belief that religious experience, like spirituality, is not a separate form of human experience, but rather the characteristic of subjective depth and ultimate concern, of a transcendental kind, in all the other aspects of human experience. In this chapter, I will use the term 'religious experience' with this nuanced understanding in mind. The concept itself is a difficult one to define. All religious experiences can be described in terms of three basic elements. Firstly, there are the personal concerns, attitudes, feelings, and ideas of the individual who has the experience. Secondly, there is the religious truth which is revealed in the experience. Thirdly, there are the social expressions that are due to the fact that the experience in question can be shared with others. From an experiential point of view, points one and two are inextricably linked.

The phrase 'religious experience' refers not so much to talk or thought *about* transcendental reality, as conscious, awareness *of* that reality. A religious experience, therefore, is an experience in which one senses the immediate presence of 'the divine', usually in a mediated way.[5] Although the grace of God is a supernatural reality, when it influences a human being it may have a discernible effect upon his or her experience. If and when a person is aware of the activity of grace, then that experience can be studied. As Jesuit psychiatrist, William Meissner has written: 'Whatever else we can say about religious experience, we can postulate that the form of divine intervention does not violate the nature and functioning of man's capacities – grace perfects nature – and that the form of the experience is determined significantly by the nature of the psychic organisation and functioning of the person affected.'[6] The new sense of transcendental relatedness involved in religious experiences leads to a new sense of self. That in turn is expressed in the form of religious affiliation, e.g. with a church, and by means of such things as a code of morality, rituals, sacraments, etc. Needless to say, transcendent reality can also be mediated by the church's life.

Religious Experience and the Reformed Tradition

Up to the time of the Reformation, Christians saw faith largely as assent to the truths revealed by God, i.e. an objective focus. Luther and Calvin shifted the emphasis onto faith as trust in the person of Christ, i.e. a more subjective approach. For example, Luther wrote in his *Preface to Paul's Letter to the Romans*: 'Faith is a living, daring confidence in God's grace, so sure and certain that the believer would stake his life on it a thousand times. This knowledge of and confidence in God's grace makes men glad and bold and happy in dealing with God and with all creatures. And this is the work which the Holy Spirit performs in faith. Because of it, without compulsion, a person is ready and glad to do good to everyone, and to serve everyone, to suffer everything, out of love and praise to God who has shown him this grace. Thus it is impossible to separate works from faith, quite as impossible as to separate heat and light from fire.'[7]

Ever afterwards, Protestants not only put more stress on religious experience, they were the first to study the nature of such experiences. For example, Jonathan Edwards (1703-1758) a minister in the Congregational Church in Northampton, Massachusetts, described how the Great Awakening took place in his locality. It began among members of the Dutch Reformed Church in New Jersey, and spread into New England, where it was sparked off by the preaching of Edwards and George Whitfield, a former colleague of John Wesley's. There were dramatic signs associated with the many conversions that occurred. For example, Edwards wrote: 'It was a very frequent thing to see a house full of outcries, faintings, convulsions, and such like, both with distress and also with admiration and joy. It was not the manner here to hold meetings all night, as in some places, nor was it common to continue them till very late in the night; but it was pretty often so that there were some that were so affected, and their bodies so overcome, that they would not go home, but were obliged to stay all night where they were.'[8]

Edwards was cautious about what he saw, as some of it seemed pathological and unhealthy in nature. So he wrote two classic books entitled, *The Distinguishing Marks of a Work of the True Spirit* and *The*

Religious Affections. They tried to establish criteria that would enable one to distinguish true, Spirit-inspired experiences, from those which were not genuine. This was one of the first theological studies of religious experience. Edwards wrote: 'The devil sees to it ... to endeavour to his up-most to propagate and establish a persuasion that all affections (feelings) and sensible emotions of the mind, in things of religion, are nothing at all to be regarded, but are rather to be avoided and carefully guarded against, as things of a pernicious tendency. This he knows is the way to bring all religion to a mere lifeless formality, and effectively shutting out the powers of godliness, and everything that is spiritual, and to have all true Christianity turned out of doors ... The Holy Scriptures do everywhere place religion very much in the affections, such as fear, hope, love, hatred, desire, joy, sorrow, gratitude, compassion, zeal ... He that has doctrinal knowledge and speculation only, without affection, never is engaged in the business of religion ... I am bold to assert that there was never any considerable change wrought in the mind or conversation of any person, by anything of a religious nature that he ever read, heard or saw, that had not his affections moved.'[9]

Some time later Friedrich Schleiermacher (1768-1834), possibly the greatest Protestant thinker since the Reformation, made a profound study of the religious impulse and its associated religious experiences. He did so as a philosopher examining natural religion. Instead of looking at the subject solely from an objective, dogmatic point of view, his book, *On Religion: Speeches to its Cultural Despisers*,[10] also looked at it from the point of view of subjective experience. He said that religion was based on the feeling of 'absolute dependence' and a concomitant 'thirst for the infinite'. 'Religion's essence,' he wrote, 'is neither thinking or acting, but intuition and feeling. It wishes to intuit the universe, wishes devoutly to overhear the universe's own manifestations and actions, longs to be grasped and filled by the universe's immediate influences in childlike passivity'.[11] He stressed the fact that such felt-intuitions were not entirely subjective states, they were intentional, i.e. they were about something beyond the self, what could be referred to as intimations of infinity or divinity-consciousness. Shleiermacher's perspective is reminiscent of Nicholas of Cusa's (1401-1464) coincidence of opposites. Because God is infinite, divinity embraces all things in perfect unity; God is at once the maximum and the minimum.[12] Carl Jaspers was later to echo this point of view when he referred to a sense of 'the Comprehensive', which is indirectly disclosed to consciousness. It is that mysterious Reality which embraces subject and object in a greater unity.[13] In some of his later works, Schleiermacher went so far as to say that 'Dogmas are a knowledge about feeling', i.e. notional articulations of religious experiences of a Christian kind. His attitude was, 'anyone who does not believe will not experience, and anyone who does not experience will not know'.[14]

William James (1842-1910) was a US philosopher and psychologist. He was among the first to advocate a scientific, experimental psychology. In 1902 he published his classic book, *The Varieties of Religious Experience*. It is one of the most important treatises ever written on the psychology of religious experience and was clearly influenced by Schleiermacher. James described its purpose in a letter to a friend: 'The problem I have set myself is a hard one: *first*, to defend … "experience" against "philosophy" being the real backbone of the world's religious life … and *second*, to make the hearer or reader believe, what I myself invincibly do believe, that, although all the special manifestations of religion may have been absurd, yet the life of it as a whole is mankind's most important function.'[15] He defined religious experience in the following individualistic way: 'Religion, therefore, as I ask you arbitrarily to take it, shall mean for us the feelings, acts, and experiences of individual men in their solitude, so far as they apprehend themselves to stand in relation to whatever they may consider the divine.'[16]

Rudolph Otto (1869-1937), a German scholar of religion in the early 1900s, was also an admirer of Schleiermacher. In his influential book, *The Idea of the Holy*,[17] he maintained that the 'non-rational factor in the idea of the divine' was an essential and constitutive element in every religion. People have religious experiences when they become consciously aware of the *numinous*, i.e. the holy or the 'wholly Other'. Otto says the *numinous* is mysterious, i.e. beyond the grasp of the rational mind. He writes: 'The *mysterium* is experienced in its essential, positive, and specific character, as something that bestows upon man a beatitude beyond compare, but one whose real nature he can neither proclaim in speech nor conceive in thought, but may know only by a direct and living experience.'[18] When people are aware of the mystery, it evokes two typical responses: firstly the *mysterium tremendum*, i.e. the mystery is awesome and daunting and secondly, the *mysterium fascinans*, i.e. the mystery is attractive and fascinating.

There are many things that can mediate a sense of the holiness of God such as nature, liturgy, architecture, or music. For example, one man wrote: 'A friend persuaded me to go to Ely Cathedral to hear a performance of Bach's B Minor Mass. I had heard the work before, indeed I knew Bach's choral work pretty well. I was sitting toward the back of the nave. The cathedral seemed to be very cold. The music thrilled me … until we got to the great *sanctus*. I find this experience difficult to define. It was primarily a warning. I was frightened. I was trembling from head to foot, and wanted to cry. Actually I think I did. I heard no voice except the music; I saw nothing; but the warning was very definite. I was not able to interpret this experience satisfactorily until I read – some months later – Rudolf Otto's *The Idea of the Holy*. Here I found it – the 'Numinous'. I was before the Judgement Seat. I was being weighed in the balance and found wanting. This is an experience I have never forgotten.'[19]

Religious Experience and Empirical Research
In this century a number of researchers have looked at religious experiences from a more empirical point of view. For example, Alister Hardy was born in 1896. He became a zoologist. In 1925 he went to the Antarctic to do research. Before doing so he paid an agency in England to gather quotes about religion from the papers. He would collect them when he returned. He was disappointed with the results. In 1948, when he was a professor at Oxford, Hardy gave a lecture which once again raised the religious issue. He said, 'When some of the leading biologists proclaim a mechanistic – a

materialistic – interpretation of life, they find their faith in science in conflict with an intuition which speaks to them of spiritual reality. One or other of them must be an illusion. Which is it? I am sure that the answer to that question is far more important to mankind than the discovery of atomic power.'[20] In 1951 in the course of a lecture entitled, 'Science and the quest for God,' Hardy suggested that there was need for a special institute to study religious experience. Sometime later he was invited to give two series of the Gifford Lectures. The second was entitled, 'The Divine Flame: An essay toward a Natural History of Religion.' Shortly afterwards, he retired from his professorship and decided to set up the Religious Research Unit in Manchester College, Oxford.

Hardy began to collect material by putting an ad in the paper asking for accounts of religious experience. He provided examples of what he had in mind. There was a quotation from Beatrice Webb, the co-founder of the Fabian Society: 'For my part I find it best to live as if the soul of man were in communion with a superhuman force which makes for righteousness.'[21] He included a second quotation from a Hibbert Lecture delivered by L. P. Jacks in 1922. He had said: 'All religious testimony, so far as I can interpret its meaning, converges toward a single point, namely this. There is that in the world, call it what you will, which responds to the confidence of those who trust it, declaring itself to them as a fellow worker in the pursuit of the Eternal Values, meeting their loyalty to it with reciprocal loyalty to them, and coming in at critical moments when the need of its sympathy is greatest; the conclusion being that wherever there is a soul in darkness, obstruction or misery there is also a Power which can help, deliver, illuminate and gladden the soul.'[22] In the light of these quotes, Hardy asked, had the readers ever been conscious of and perhaps influenced by, a power, whether they called it the power of God or not. This power might either appear to be beyond their individual selves, or in part outside and inside their being. If the readers had such an experience they were asked to write to Hardy about it, describing the experience and its effects. At first the responses were disappointing. There wasn't enough information to be truly representative. Hardy then sent articles to many of the papers, e.g. *The Guardian, Observer, The Times,* the BBC, and to the media in New Zealand, Australia, the US, etc. This time there were many more responses, many of them from 'non-religious' people.

When Hardy had assessed the information he received, he wrote a book about his findings entitled, *The Spiritual Nature of Man: A Study of Contemporary Religious Experience.*[23] In typical scientific fashion, he tried to classify the available material under twelve different headings. Much of the book is devoted to explaining each category, while providing concrete examples drawn from the responses. A few years ago, two women, Meg Maxwell and Verena Tschudin, went to the Alister Hardy Research Centre in Oxford where there are 5,000 testimonies on file. They gathered representative examples, under four main headings, and published them in a book entitled, *Seeing the Invisible: Modern Religious and Other Transcendent Experiences.*[24] Here are a few typical examples.

- 'I heard nothing, yet it was as if I were surrounded by golden light and as if I had only to reach out my hand to touch God himself who was so surrounding me with his compassion.'

- 'It seemed to me that, in some way, I was extending into my surroundings and was becoming one with them. At the same time I felt a sense of lightness, exhilaration and power as if I were beginning to understand the true meaning of the whole universe.'

- 'One night I suddenly had an experience as if I was buoyed up by waves of utterly sustaining power and love. The only words that came near to describing it were "underneath are the everlasting arms". Though this sounds like a picture, my experience was not a picture but a feeling, and there were the arms. This I am sure has affected my life as it has made me know the love and sustaining power of God. It came from outside and unasked.'

- 'On the first night I knelt to say my prayers, which I had now made a constant practice, I was aware of a glowing light which seemed to envelop me and which was accompanied by a sense of warmth all round me.'

- 'Suddenly I felt great joyousness sweeping over me. I use the word "sweeping" because this feeling seemed to do just that. I actually felt it as coming from my left and sweeping around and through me, completely engulfing me. I do not know how to describe it. It was not like a wind. But suddenly it was there, and I felt it move around me and through me. Great joy was in it. Exaltation might be a better word.'[25]

In the 1970s and 80s David Hay of the Alister Hardy Research Centre did similar research in England. He asked Hardy's question, 'Have you ever been conscious of a presence or power, whether you call it God or not, which is different from your everyday self?' Again 35% of the people said yes. This indicated that religious experience wasn't necessarily tied to church going. Hay, a Catholic, and later the head of the Alister Hardy Research Centre for a few years, was teaching science at Nottingham University at the time. He decided to do an in-depth survey of 172 of the students on campus. Besides using a questionnaire, he interviewed each respondent. The results were surprising because although many of the young men and women interviewed didn't go to church services, as many as 62% said they had had a religious experience.[26]

In 1973 Greely and Mc Cready of the National Opinion Research Centre, Chicago, asked a sample of people whether they ever had an ecstatic type experience. 35% responded that they had. In 1978, Princeton Religious Research Centre, a subsidiary of Gallup Polls, confirmed the Chicago figures. It asked the following question in interviews: 'How often have you felt as though you were very close to a powerful spiritual force that seemed to lift you out of yourself?' About 35% of the replies said once or more than once. When one looks at the research done on both sides of the Atlantic in recent years it indicates that about one third of the population have had a religious experience. Many of those who had such experiences were not church goers, and a surprisingly high proportion of those who reported such experiences were men, in fact in some surveys they constituted a small majority.

To the best of my knowledge this kind of research has not been done in Ireland. However the 1981 and 1990, two large surveys were done in the European Union including Ireland. The Irish results have been published in two volumes, *Irish Values and Attitudes: The Irish Report of the European Values Systems Study* [27] and *Values and Social Change in Ireland*.[28] Andrew Greely has described the latter as 'perhaps the best sociological study ever done of Ireland'. Both reports include statistics about people's religious beliefs and activities. While the surveys indicate that a significant proportion of people think that God and religion are important in their lives and subscribe to the principal Christian beliefs, we do not know what correlation there is, if any, with the incidence of religious experience. Ironically, it has been suggested in the research done in other countries that those who are not close to the institutional church may be more likely to have religious experiences than those who are.[29] There is a clear need for a research project which would establish what the true facts are.

Towards a typology of religious experience

A number of years ago I trained as a spiritual director in the Centre for Religious Development in Boston, Mass. My mentor, Fr Bill Connolly, was one of those who had been instrumental in renewing understanding of the *Spiritual Exercises* of Ignatius Loyola, in the post Vatican II era. He stressed the fact that, as Ignatius's *Autobiography* shows, the founder of the Jesuits had a profound experiential grasp of the nature and dynamics of Christian spirituality. For example, Ignatius tells us that while he was recuperating from a war wound, he experienced two desires. On the one hand, he wanted to imitate Christ and the saints, and on the other, he wanted to serve a beautiful woman at court. Ignatius noticed that the two desires had different effects upon him. While he thought of serving the lady at court he was happy, but as soon as he stopped thinking about her he was 'dry and discontented'. While he thought about our Lord and the saints he was also happy, but when he stopped thinking about them he remained 'content and happy'. As a result, 'his eyes were opened a little, and he began to marvel at the difference and to reflect upon it, realising from experience that some thoughts left him sad and others happy. Little by little he came to recognise the difference between the spirits that agitated him, one from the demon, the other from God.'[30] It was this experiential realisation that gave birth to the Ignatian form of discernment of spirits which relies upon subjective awareness of inward states of consolation and desolation for its efficacy. Ignatius believed that true spirituality needs to reach beyond notional ideas, about God and the divine will, to a contemplative awareness of the One who reveals the God-self and the divine will to the receptive human heart. That is why Ignatius encourages the person who prays, to ask for 'an intimate knowledge of our Lord,' and 'an intimate understanding and a relish of the truth'.[31]

Bill Connolly stresses the fact that what food is to cooking, religious experience is to spiritual direction.[32] He describes the art of the *anamchara*, or soul friend, in these words: 'Spiritual direction is the help given by one Christian to another which enables that person to pay attention to God's personal communication to him or her, to respond to this personally communicating God, to grow in intimacy with God, and to live out the consequences of the relationship. The *focus* of this type of spiritual direction is on experience, not ideas, and specifically on religious experience, i.e. any experience of the mysterious Other whom we call God.'[33] It would probably be true to say that in the English-speaking world, at least, spiritual direction increasingly focuses on religious experience.

Since returning from the States in 1984 I have thought a lot about the dynamics of religious experience. At this point I would like to propose a brief and tentative typology. It suggests that religious experiences usually have a fourfold structure. They begin in desire, are expressed in the form of attention, are often graced with revelation and have a number of possible knock-on effects.

A) Desire

- Desire for transcendence, meaning and God, originates in the human spirit, i.e. the *pneuma*, as distinct from the human psyche.
- These spiritual desires are prompted by the Spirit of God. To become aware of them is to become aware of the primordial movement of the Spirit within the personality. In Christian terms,

to acknowledge such 'holy desires' is to become aware of the
Father drawing the human heart into conscious relationship
with his Son. As Jesus once said: 'No one can come to me unless
the Father who sent me draws that person' (Jn 6:44). Pope St
Gregory the Great, known as the 'Doctor of Desire', argues that
desire and love are related etymologically and in fact, i.e. longing for an absent person one misses. When a person desires God
because he or she perceives God's absence, the very desire is a
form of presence: 'Whoever desires God with the whole mind
already has the one he or she loves.'[34]

The Lord prompts these desires in a number of ways.
- Firstly, he can allow a person to suffer, e.g. as a result of predictable and unpredictable crises in life.[35] Afflictions of this kind
  attack one's ego defences, thereby releasing the suppressed
  voice of the deeper, constricted self which can only be satisfied
  by numinous experience.
- Secondly, the Lord can allow one to experience moral failure,
  e.g. as a result of an addiction like alcoholism. Typically it leads
  to a situation where, in the words of Paul, 'I do not do the good I
  want, but the evil I do not want is what I do' (Rom 7:19). The
  consequent sense of disillusionment can uncover a need for God
  and God's liberating power. As Paul put it after his conversion:
  'All I want … is to know Christ and the power of his resurrection' (Phil 3:10).
- Thirdly, desires for transcendence can be evoked by the witness
  of an admired person who already enjoys a deep sense of union
  with the Lord, e.g. a happy or virtuous acquaintance or a saintly
  person like Mother Teresa.

Holy desires can be blocked or repressed in a number of predictable
ways.
- Some people are inhibited by a moralistic attitude. Because they
  are always motivated by a sense of duty – by what they 'ought,
  must, should or have to do' – they lose touch with their deeper
  spiritual yearnings. Despite the fact that they may have positive
  ideas of God at a conscious level of awareness, many people are

inhibited by the fact that, at an unconscious level of awareness, they have negative images of God as someone who is distant, hard to please and demanding. These images are often associated with negative feelings, such as fear, guilt and anger, which can cause unconscious resistance to closer relationship with God.

- Unacknowledged and unresolved negative feelings such as grief, hurt, shame, resentment, etc., which are the result of hurts and disappointments in life, can also inhibit awareness of one's deepest desires.

- A self-centred desire for physical or psychological satisfaction and fulfilment, e.g. by means of wealth, status, power and pleasure, can deafen a person to the deeper aspirations of the Spirit within. As Jesus said: 'the cares of the world and the delight in riches choke the word (in this instance, of desire) and it proves unfruitful' (Mt 13:22).

- Spiritual writers such as Pope Gregory the Great have pointed out that God prompted desires for God tend to grow when denied for a time. The Lord does this in order to strengthen, purify and deepen them. Meanwhile those which originate in the psyche, and *ipso facto* are not prompted by God, tend to wither through denial. St Gregory wrote: 'Holy desires grow with delay: if they fade through delay they are no desires at all.' Genuine desires for God are mainly associated with consolation of spirit, e.g. inner peace and joy, whereas, those which are not from God, are mainly associated with desolation of spirit, e.g. agitation and sadness of spirit.

B) Attention

- Because chapter four is devoted to this subject, its treatment here will be brief.

- If a person has a desire to have transcendental experience, it will only be satisfied when he or she decides to pay attention to reality because it can mediate the immediacy of the Lord's presence. As Simone Weil wrote: 'Attention animated by desire is the whole foundation of religious practices.'[36] The *Catholic Encyclopedia* says in similar vein: 'Attention is the very essence of prayer; as soon as attention ceases, prayer ceases.'

- The person who makes the decision to attend, needs to surrender intellectual and imaginative control over the object of attention, e.g. nature, another person or a biblical passage. He or she has to allow it to be itself, and refrain from projecting personal thoughts, symbols or memories upon it. It is also important that the person attending to reality allows it to evoke a spontaneous emotional response.
- Sustained attention to reality needs to be self-forgetful. It moves away from self-absorption by allowing its concentration to become absorbed by the object of attention. It beholds the object of contemplation in a respectful way that goes beyond appearances to reverence the unique value and worth of whatever it looks at, listens to, or touches.
- This form of contemplative attention is humble in so far as it submits to the reality of the other, the 'letting-be of being' to use John Macquarrie's phrase. As the 'isness' of the contemplated reality is revealed, it can call for a sort of cognitive conversion, a revision of previous ways of thinking, perceiving, valuing and feeling.

C) Revelation

- The scriptures make it clear in a number of places that revelation is possible. For example, in Jer 33:3 the Lord says: 'Call to me and I will answer you and tell you great and unsearchable things you do not know.' In Is 48:6-8 the Lord says: 'From now on I will tell you of new things, of hidden things unknown to you. They are created now, and not long ago; you have not heard of them before today. So you cannot say, "Yes, I knew of them." You have neither heard nor understood; from of old your ear has not been open.'
- Revelatory experiences are firstly discerned in the form of the feeling reaction that is evoked, and not willed, by the new sense of awareness. This emotional reaction can have two interrelated dimensions.
- Firstly, there is the feeling reaction which is evoked by the immediate object of attention, e.g. a beautiful lake, or a saying of Jesus in the gospel, such as awe, delight and well being.

- Secondly, there are other feelings which are evoked not so much by the lake or saying, as by a numinous sense of Presence which it mediates. It can evoke feelings of wonder, mystery, joy and peace. That is why spiritual directors ask the following three questions.

  1. When were you aware of the Lord revealing the God-self to you, e.g. enjoying nature or art, in relationship with others, praying, reading scripture, etc?

  2. How did you feel?

  3. What was it that you noticed about the Lord that evoked those feelings in you? This is the most important question. It focuses attention on the conceptual or imaginative content of the revelation which will often fail to do justice to the awareness. As St Paul says in Eph 3:18-19, 'may you have power, together with all the saints, to grasp how wide and long and high and deep is the love of Christ, and to know this love that *surpasses knowledge*.'

When directees are able to answer these questions, they are becoming consciously aware of something of the mystery of the God who has been revealed to them.

D) Effects

- In a religious experience feelings have intentionality, i.e. they are responses which are evoked by what is revealed about God, God's word, and God's will. Following the initial emotional *response* to the revelatory awareness, a secondary emotional *reaction* known as resistance can occur, e.g. a sense of apprehension to do with possible implications of the experience such as a need to change one's life.

- Genuine religious experiences lead to a new recognition of who God is and what God is like. Implicit in such experiences is the ethical imperative, 'be for others what God is for you'. For instance, if you have found God to be understanding, compassionate and accepting, be understanding, compassionate, and accepting in your daily life.

- The light of genuine experiences of God tends to expose, challenge, and displace false images of God.

- Genuine experience of God motivates the graced person to express his or her appreciation by means of thanks, praise and worship, and sometimes in the form of heartfelt sorrow for having failed in many ways to give due honour to God in the past.

- Genuine experiences of God give new life and meaning to beliefs already held, while at the same time activating the person's inner potential for a closer relationship with God. As a result of this growing intimacy, the person relates more deeply to his or her spiritual self and begins to see it as God does, i.e. in a loving, accepting way. Jesus once said: 'As the Father loves me, so I love you' Jn 15:9. Pope John Paul II has written: 'the man who wishes to understand himself thoroughly and not just in accordance with immediate, partial, often superficial, and even illusory standards and measures must... draw near to Christ. He must, so to speak, enter him with all his own self, he must 'appropriate' and assimilate the whole of the reality of the Incarnation and Redemption in order to find himself. If this profound process takes place within him, he then bears the fruit not only of adoration of God but also of deeper wonder at himself.'[37]

- This growing sense of intimacy can have positive knock-on psychosomatic repercussions also. For more on this point see chapter nine.

- As growth in wholeness and holiness occurs, the person has a growing sense of inner freedom. As St Paul put it in Gal 5:1: 'It is for freedom that Christ has set us free. Stand firm, then, and do not let yourselves be burdened again by a yoke of slavery.' He or she moves from living a dutiful life on the basis of impersonal moral imperatives to living it on the basis of inner convictions born of heartfelt relationship with God. Genuine growth in relationship with God prompts the desire and provides the power to change by means of appropriate forms of action, e.g. a preferential option to work for poor people. Religious experience, therefore, is the true source of ethics. They are a response to revelation, instead of being a substitute for it, as is often the case. This distinction captures the meaning of Paul's differentiation between living by the Spirit and living by the law. (cf. Gal 5:16-26)

- These effects elicit a new found desire to attend to reality in a more single minded way, in order to see the Lord more clearly, to love the Lord more dearly, and to follow the Lord more nearly in one's daily life. And so the dynamic cycle begins again.

A practical example

Having looked at the four points, let's examine a religious experience to see whether it illustrates them or not. This one is taken from a woman's diary. She had spoken to Dr Frank Lake, a Christian psychiatrist, about her inner turmoil. Afterwards she had gone off to pray privately. This is what happened.

I went alone into the chapel. The panic of what I would do to myself to stop the intolerable pain drove me to my knees, my tongue moving incoherently, my soul stretched tight with a weeping longing. When I was still left alone my very despair drove me to a horror and fury which was unafraid of recrimination. I was staggered by the milk-and-water apologetic God who could not calm this storm, who smiled sympathetically but abstractedly and whom I could not touch. We can bear humans to fall off their pedestals but not God himself. After the first stunning realisation of who God was, my whole mind, soul and body came into co-ordination and rose in unity to hate with entire, full-blooded, no-holds-barred hatred of the God who had so fooled mankind. Life surged back into every artery and vein, full red blood, as there streamed out from me powerful and unchecked hatred and loathing for a master whose creation had been working wrongly for centuries and who was not wise enough, strong enough or caring enough to mend it. I was livid with his apathy. Didn't he know what his carelessness had done to us? For the first time in my life I dared to demand an explanation.

When none came I was angrier than I ever remember being. I turned my eyes on the plain wooden cross and I remembered Calvary. I stood in the crowd that crucified Jesus, hating and despising him. With my own hands I drove the nails into his hands and feet, and with bursting energy I flogged him and reviled him and spat with nauseating loathing. Now he should know what it felt like – to live in the creation he had made. Every breath brought from me the words: 'Now you know! Now you know!'

And then I saw something which made my heart stand still. I saw his face, and on it twisted every familiar agony of my own soul. 'Now you know' became an awed whisper as I, motionless, watched his agony. 'Yes, now I know' was the passionate and pain-filled reply. 'Why else should I come?' Stunned, I watched his eyes search desperately for the tiniest flicker of love in mine, and as we loved one another in the bleak and the cold, forsaken by God, frightened and derelict, we loved one another and our pain became silent in the calm.

Nothing can bind us closer than common dereliction for nowhere is companionship so longed for. From that moment I was tied to Christ, knowing the rope would hold, if I fell in the climb, as I scrambled up to his side. Even the word 'love' has no meaning beside our common bond and the companionship of the climb. The debt was too great, too repeated for the ordinary courtesy of thanks. My thanks were all in the obedience with which I followed him, slowly learning to trust his commands even when they seemed crazy and perilous.

The first stage of the climb was spent in reconciling in my mind the two views I now had of God: the being I hated, who was responsible for the universe and who still had not answered my question, and the living Christ whom I relied on and adored.[38]

It is a powerful and moving experience, isn't it? Having savoured it in an empathic way, let us have a closer, more reflective look. Firstly, we can ask the question, was the woman motivated, in one way or another, by a *desire* for relationship with God? Surely she was. Why else would she have gone to the chapel. She also says at the beginning of her account that her soul was 'stretched tight with a weeping *longing*,' presumably for healing and peace. But she also says that she wanted God to explain to her why she had to endure so much suffering.

Secondly, we can ask, did she pay *attention* to external reality?

At first there is not much evidence that she did. The gravitational pull of her inner turmoil led her to be self-absorbed. She was preoccupied with her feelings and her image of God, which was a negative and distorted one. Clearly, she had been frightened by the Lord in the past, but now that she was 'unafraid of recrimination' a dam of repressed feeling broke within her and out poured a torrent of unrestrained anger and fury. Clearly her professed spirituality was very different from her operative spirituality. This passionate and even violent self-disclosure was a form of intimate prayer in so far as it published and made known what was innermost within her. It had a paradoxical effect. It enabled her to connect to her own depths, while at the same time enabling her to overcome her excessive self-reference. This happened when she paid greater attention to God as represented by the crucifix. She says in a moving way: 'and then I *saw* something which made my heart stand still. I s*aw* his face.' This is the beginning of the contemplative phase of the experience when she begins to pay sustained attention to the Crucified One. For example she says, 'I *watched* his agony,' and again, 'I *watched* his eyes.'

Thirdly, we can inquire, did the distraught woman experience any *revelation*? By her own account she did. She says that she was aware that her own agony was mirrored in the face of Christ, 'on it twisted every familiar agony of my own soul'. Jesus tells her that his incarnation was motivated by compassion. He came in order to share in the suffering of people like her. The woman tells us that she was also aware that Jesus loved her and wanted her to love him in return. Although this is the shortest part of the woman's account, it is also the most important. She revealed her deepest self to the Lord, he in turn revealed his deepest self to her.

Fourthly, we can wonder, what *effects* did her newfound awareness of God have upon her, both in the short and the long-term? It is clear from what she says that it did have an immediate effect. She says: 'we loved one another, and our pain became silent in the calm'. Not surprisingly, the awareness of God's compassion and love turned her desolation of spirit into a consoling sense of inner peace. Speaking of the long term effects, she says that she trusted that the

Lord would accompany her on her spiritual journey and give her help when she needed it. Significantly she declared: 'My *thanks* were all in the *obedience* with which I *followed* him, slowly learning to *trust* his commands even when they seemed crazy and perilous.' Evidently, she was learning to do what Prov 3:5-6 says: 'Trust the Lord with all your heart, and do not rely on your own insight. In all your ways acknowledge him, and he will make straight your paths.'

Non-theistic religious experience

In modern culture there is a growing number of people who maintain that people can have religious experiences without believing in God. This belief can be traced back to Ludwig Feuerbach's book *The Essence of Christianity*, which was published in 1841. The aim of his work, he declared, was to destroy theistic religion as an utterly pernicious illusion. He believed that God was a projection of human potential on to an imaginary supreme being. He argued that all theological concepts should therefore be translated into anthropological ones. Here are a succession of key notions from Feuerbach. 'The historical progress of religion consists in this: that which during an earlier stage religion was regarded as something objective is now recognized as something subjective, so that which was formerly viewed and worshipped as God is now recognized as something human. But that which in religion ranks first – namely God – is as I have shown, in truth and reality something second; for God is merely the projected essence of man. What therefore, ranks second in religion – namely, Man – that must be proclaimed the first and recognized as the first. If the nature of Man is man's highest being, if to be human is his highest existence, then man's love for man, must in practice become the first and highest law. Man's God is man. This is the highest law of ethics. This is the turning point of world history.'

Although Feuerbach did not believe in God, he did believe in a humanistic form of religious experience. When one reads modern sociology and psychology, it is clear that the founder of modern atheism has had many disciples. Emile Durkheim (1858-1917) was the son of a rabbi. By the time he wrote his sociologicl classic, *The Elementary Forms of Religious Life,* he was an atheist. Having make a thorough study of Australian aboriginal society, he wrote: 'Religion is a unified system of beliefs and practices relative to sacred things, that is to say, things set apart and forbidden – beliefs and practices which unite into one single moral community called a Church, all who adhere to them.'[39] He maintained that religious experience was a form of awe and effervescence which was evoked by a sense of the sacred. However, instead of believing that a transcendent God was the focus of this religious sense, he believed that God was nothing other than a symbol for people's projected feelings which are evoked by the mystery of society. God, in effect, is a symbol of society. He is an imaginary being unconsciously created by society as an instrument whereby the community exercises control over the thoughts and behaviour of its individuals. He wrote: 'The sentiment of the divine is evoked in collective ceremonial, during which, as a result of the intense emotionality and involvement which is generated, the individual feels himself swamped by the action of an entity superior to himself. Although this force *emanates from the collective assembly*, (my italics) it only realizes itself through the consciousness of the individual, who feels it to be both transcendent over him and yet immanent in him.'[40]

Sigmund Freud (1856-1939), like Durkheim an unbelieving Jew, was another of Feuerbach's disciples. Speaking about his intellectual mentor in 1875 he said: 'Among all philosophers, I worship and admire this man the most.'[41] It would probably be true to say that Freud aimed to express Feuerbach's theory in psychological terms. For him, God was nothing but a projection of one's childhood sense of paternal protection and care on to a divine Father who shields men and women from the fearful dangers of untamed nature. Not only was Freud opposed to belief in God, apparently he was opposed to non-theistic religious experiences also. He disagreed with novelist Romain Roland (1866-1944) who argued that people could rightly call themselves religious if they experienced what is sometimes referred to as 'oceanic feeling', i.e. a sense of indissoluble unity with the external world, while at the same time rejecting every religious belief and illusion. Freud thought it was yet another way of seeking false comfort in the face of harsh reality.[42] Some observers have suggested that the only experience that had any numinous quality for Freud was sexuality.[43]

In more recent times a number of well known psychologists and humanists have advocated a kind of non-theistic religious experience. Like Feuerbach, Erich Fromm (1900-1980) talks a lot about alienation, about the fact that many people seem to be separated from their true selves and their inner potential. Instead of curing this problem, authoritarian religion – which seems to be virtually synonymous to revealed religion – reinforces it. 'In authoritarian religion,' Fromm wrote, 'God becomes the sole possessor of what was originally man's: of his reason and his love. The more perfect God becomes, the more imperfect becomes man. He *projects* the best he has onto God and thus impoverishes himself. Now God has all love, all wisdom, all justice – and man is deprived of these qualities, he is empty and poor. He had begun with a feeling of smallness, but he now has become completely powerless and without strength; all his powers have been projected on to God.' In another place he describes the harmful effects of authoritarian religion: 'When man has projected his own most valuable powers onto God, what of his relationship to his own powers? They have become separated from him and in the process he has become alienated from himself. Everything he has is now God's and nothing is left in him. His only access to himself is through God. In worshipping God he tries to get in touch with that part of himself which he has lost through projection.'[44]

Unlike Freud, Fromm proposed to replace theistic religion of the authoritarian kind with a non-theistic, humanistic kind. Commenting on this form of religious experience, he wrote: 'The question is not religion or not, but what kind of religion, whether it is one furthering man's development, the unfolding of his specifically human powers, or one paralysing them …[45] Religious experience of this kind of religion is the experience of oneness with the All, based on one's relatedness to the world as it is grasped with thought and love.'[46] In another place he says: 'Not fear and submission but love and the assertion of one's own powers are the basis of mystical experience. *God is not a symbol of power over man but of man's own powers.*'[47] (my italics)

Abraham Maslow (1908-1970) was also a disciple of Feuerbach's. He found that highly actualised people were inclined to have so-called peak experiences, many of which are religious in nature. However, as a declared atheist, Maslow believed that such mystical experiences did not have to be theistic. He pointed to the fact that Buddhism, as one of the world's great religions, was not explicitly theistic. He agreed with Margharita Laski who suggested that people could have religious experiences, of an ecstatic kind, without necessarily believing in God.[48] Speaking about those who enjoyed peak experiences, Maslow said that their attitude was characterised by what he called being-cognition as opposed to deficiency-cognition. People of the latter kind were insecure, needy and mistrustful and were unlikely to have peak experiences. However, those who were secure, actualised and trusting were inclined to experience contemplative moments of heightened awareness when the usual subject-object dichotomy of everyday perception would give way to a sense of ecstatic union with the mystery of a beautiful world. 'A few centuries ago,' he wrote, 'these would all have been described as men who walk in the path of God or as godly men. A few say that they believe in God, but describe this God more as a metaphysical concept than as a personal figure. If religion is defined only in socio-behavioural terms, then these are all religious people, the atheist included. But if more conservatively we use the term religion so as to include and stress the supernatural element and institutional orthodoxy, then our answer must be quite different, for then almost none of them is religious.' It would probably be true to say that, as he grew older, Maslow himself believed in non-theistic forms of religious experience, ones he himself seemed to enjoy in later life.

Carl Jung's (1875-1961) views on this subject are interesting. Most people who are familiar with his writings would presume that he was a theist. I'm not so sure. Although he often spoke about God, there is an ambiguity in what he says. It is never quite clear whether he believed that the word God merely represents a psychic or also a metaphysical reality. Unlike Freud who believed that religious experience of the theistic kind was a form of universal obsessional neurosis, Jung believed that people were likely to become neurotic if they did not have religious experience. In his Terry Lectures on 'Psychology and Religion,' he said: 'I want to make clear that by the term "religion" I do not mean a creed. It is, however, true that every creed is originally based on the one hand upon the experience of the *numinosum* and on the other hand upon *pistis*, that is to say, trust or loyalty, faith and confidence in a certain experience of a numinous nature and in the change of consciousness that ensues ... Creeds are codified and dogmatised forms of original religious experience.'[49] Like other psychologists, Jung insisted that he wasn't looking at religious beliefs as such, rather he was examining people's experiences of them. He took a keen interest in a number of Christian doctrines such as the Trinity, the Mass, the Assumption of Mary, confession, etc. However his interest in these beliefs was psychological rather than religious. 'When psychology speaks, for instance, of the motif of the virgin birth, it is only concerned with the fact that there is such an idea, but it is not concerned whether such an idea is true or false in any other sense. The idea is psychologically true in so far as it exists.'

Jung applied much the same logic to the experience of God. God's existence is a psychological truth. Consistent with his psychological perspective, he suggested that God was an archetype of the collective unconscious, and specifically of the self. Speaking about archetypes he wrote: 'Again and again I encounter the mistaken notion that an archetype is determined by its content, in other words that it is a kind of unconscious idea. It is necessary to point out once more that archetypes are not determined as regards their content, but only as regards their form and then only to a very limited degree. A primordial image is determined as to its contents only when it has become conscious and is therefore filled out with the material of conscious experience.'[50] Apparently the God archetype represents a capacity of the collective unconscious which is open to the possibility of numinous experience. All people, in every place, have this potential.

Jung said: 'When I say as a psychologist that God is an arche-type, I mean by that the "type" in the psyche. The word "type" is, as we know, derived from *typos*, "blow" or "imprint"; thus an arche-type pre-supposes an imprinter ... We simply do not know the ulti-mate derivation of the archetype any more than we know the origin of the psyche. The competence of psychology as an empirical sci-ence only goes so far as to establish, on the basis of comparative research, whether for instance the imprint found in the psyche can or cannot reasonably be termed a "God image". Nothing positive or negative has thus been asserted about the possible existence of God, any more than the archetype of the "hero" proves the actual exist-ence of a hero.'[51] On another occasion he said: 'We know that the God-image plays a great role in psychology, but we cannot prove the metaphysical existence of God. As a responsible scientist I am not going to preach my personal and subjective convictions which I cannot prove.'

With regard to his personal convictions, Jung wrote in 1955: 'I don't *believe* but I do know of a power of a very personal nature and an irresistible influence. I call it God.'[52] Many people thought that his reply indicated belief. But not necessarily so. What he was really saying was, I have experienced the numinous power of the God archetype as a psychic event. While Jung said that religious experi-ences are 'graced' awarenesses of the 'other', it doesn't necessarily mean that he believed in a transcendent, metaphysical Other. He located the archetypal God-form in the deepest unconscious. When a person experiences the God-image as a 'graced' awareness of the 'other,' it is revealed as no more than an experience of the self that proceeds from the collective unconscious. Is it any surprise, there-fore, that Jung seemed to identify God-images with self-images? His empirical approach seemed to exclude revelation from an object-ively existing, transcendent God. In spite of his observation that the imprint of the God archetype pre-supposed an imprinter, it would appear from a number of his comments that he was Kantian in his outlook and was quite agnostic about the objective existence and attributes of God. He observed on more than one occasion: 'What God is in himself remains a question outside the competence of all psychology.'[53] He also believed, like many of the great Christian theologians and mystics, that the mystery of God was incomprehensible and therefore beyond the grasp of image and concept alike.

When reading what Jung has to say about religious experience one could be forgiven for getting the distinct impression that his subjectivist, immanentist approach to spirituality had affinities with Feuerbach's. Instead of converting theology into anthropology he seemed to transform it, in a reductionist way, into a psychic experience of the numinous kind. As Palmer points out at the end of his thoughtful and well researched book, there is reason to believe that Jung opened himself to the charge of 'psychologism,' when he implied that God had been reduced to a subjective experience.[54] Erich Fromm seemed to agree. He wrote: 'Jung reduces religion to a psychological phenomenon and at the same time elevates the unconscious to a religious phenomenon.'[55] Viktor Frankl was also critical. While he credited Jung with discovering the distinctly religious aspects of the unconscious, he felt that he overlooked or denied the personal character of the God of the unconscious. He argued that Jung placed God among the instincts – among the archetypes, explicitly defined as 'instincts capable of representation.' God is thus conceived of as an autonomous, impersonal 'power' *in* the psyche.[56] R. C. Zaehner maintained that Jung's psychology was becoming a religion in itself, an esoteric cult that is extremely individualistic. It represents he said, 'a re-emergence of some aspects of Buddhism and Taoism in modern dress; it is nature mysticism made respectable for the modern mind by the jargon of psychology.'[57] Even if some of these suspicions are incorrect, and I suspect that some of them are, many of the devotees of Jung's elitist psychology,[58] e.g. in the New Age Movement, advocate a Jungian brand of secular mysticism, without necessarily being committed to theistic belief. When they use the word God, it is meant to refer to an inner experience of the divine as a potential of the collective unconscious and not necessarily to a metaphysical reality apart from the self.

Assessment

I believe that the religious sense is natural to humans. As Catholic theology asserts, grace builds on nature. Supernatural, revealed religion builds upon a natural capacity for, and a receptivity to, transcendence. Arguably, that natural capacity can find a focus in a non-theistic form of transcendence where the mystery of the world evokes a sense of mystical awe and wonder. For example, Albert Einstein (1879-1955) did not believe in any religious creed. But he had a sense of the religious. He wrote: 'The most beautiful, the most profound emotion we can experience is the sensation of the mystical. It is the source of all true science. He to whom this emotion is a stranger, who can no longer wonder and stand rapt in awe, is as good as dead. To know that which is impenetrable to us really exists, manifesting itself as the highest wisdom and most radiant beauty which our dull faculties can comprehend only in their most primitive form – this knowledge, this feeling, is at the centre of all true religiousness.'[59] One could discuss whether the kinds of experience described by Fromm, Maslow, Laski and Einstein are merely aesthetic experiences or genuine experiences of the numinous. I tend to the view that some humanistic experiences of transcendence are aesthetic rather than religious. That said, some others are clearly numinous, but in a non-theistic way, at the level of conscious awareness. It also seems to me that New Age spirituality has been influenced by the humanistic notion of non-theistic religious experience. When it uses the word God – and it often does – it seems to do so in Fromm's sense, merely as a symbol for human potential.

Although a number of modern thinkers argue that one can have a non-theistic spirituality, two points can be made about this point of view. Firstly, one could argue that although it is non-theistic at a conceptual level, such a spirituality secretly and anonymously does acknowledge the existence of God. In his book *L'Action*, Maurice Blondel argued that people's true beliefs are discernible not just in what they say but also in what they do. Even when people consciously deny the existence of God, the intentionality of their actions may imply such a trust in absolute meaning that it would amount to an unconscious but implicit belief in God. Karl Rahner was later to refer to this kind of transcendental experience as an un-

thematic and anonymous knowledge of God.[60] Secondly, although
I can see that a person could profess a non-theistic, secular spirituality,
it would be seriously defective in so far as it had no room for prayer
or worship. As Schleiermacher once said in one of his sermons: 'To
be religious and to pray – that is one and the same thing.'[61]

Conclusion

As the previous sections have indicated, psychology can be used to
help explain religious experience. But as Gerald May points out:
'psychology and religion cannot integrate at a truly mutual level.
Psychology can in no way address the religious quest without
reducing it to some theory of personal need-meeting that at last
must be considered narcissistic.'[62] But when psychology tries to use
religion to pursue its aims, it can end up psychologising it in a
reductionist way so that it becomes a secular substitute for revealed
religion. Hence the title of Paul Vitz's book, *Psychology as Religion:
The Cult of Self-worship.*[63]

That said, there were psychologists like Carl Jung and William
James who were of the opinion that religious experience, especially
of the mystical kind, was the backbone of the world's great religions. For example, before it was ever a creed, Christianity was a
Pentecostal experience. However, those of us who are born into a
well established Christian tradition, are often catechised without
having being truly evangelised. In other words, instead of our
beliefs being the expression of heartfelt religious experiences, they
can become dry and life-denying substitutes for it. As a number of
commentators have pointed out, beliefs without experience are
dead, while experiences without beliefs are blind. In the present
day culture of experience, it is important that people would re-live
those religious experiences which first gave birth to the faiths to
which they belong.

CHAPTER 3

An Introduction to Mystical Experience

The subject of mysticism is a large and complex one. In this chapter I don't intend to offer a comprehensive survey of the topic. Others have already done so, for example Evelyn Underhill in her classic book entitled *Mysticism*, and more recently Bernard Mc Ginn in his projected four volume study, *A History of Western Christian Mysticism*. The first two volumes have already been published. The following reflections are designed to introduce interested readers to some aspects of the subject. The relatively long section on what has been referred to as the perennial philosophy or the primordial tradition, is motivated by personal interest in the possibility of a common mystical experience underpinning different religions.

Mystical experiences are religious experiences of a more intense and direct kind. William James wrote: 'I think that personal religious experience has its root and centre in mystical states of consciousness.'[1] It is very difficult to discern when a religious experience becomes a mystical one. Some writers say that while mysticism is contemplative, it is exoteric, or common, what Karl Rahner referred to as 'everyday mysticism.' Others give the impression that mysticism is esoteric, or uncommon, and sometimes associated with unusual phenomena such as visions, locutions, etc.

Because the word mysticism can mean so many different things it is difficult to define. Etymologically, it refers to a person who has been initiated into a 'mystery'. A mystic, therefore, is a person who has a certain experiential sense of what eye has not seen or ear heard (cf. 1 Cor 2:9). Here are a few definitions. Mysticism is the immediate feeling of the unity of the self with God; it is nothing, therefore, but the fundamental feeling of religion, the religious life at its very heart and centre.[2] Evelyn Underhill, one of the twentieth century's greatest students of spirituality, stated that mysticism is the direct intuition or experience of God; and a mystic is a person who has, to a greater or less degree, such a direct experience. His or her religion and life are centred, not merely on an accepted belief or practice, but on that which he or she regards as first-hand personal knowledge.[3] Irish Jesuit, William Johnston, observes that: 'Mysticism is wisdom or knowledge that is found through love, it is loving knowledge … it is the core of authentic religious experience … it is nothing but a living of the gospel at a deep level of consciousness.'[4]

A noted psychologist of religion, James Pratt, maintained, in a book entitled *Religious Consciousness*, that there were two interrelated forms of mysticism, one mild and the other extreme. He said, 'No just idea can be formed upon the subject and no sound conclusion as to the nature and place and value of mysticism can be reached unless one consistently keeps this distinction in mind.'[5] He maintained that in both kinds, people sense the presence of a being or reality through means other than the ordinary perceptive processes or the reason.[6] This immediate and intuitive feeling of presence has a compelling sense of objectivity and evokes characteristic feelings of joy and happiness. From what he says it would seem that ordinary religious experiences, the kind mentioned in the surveys, are often forms of mild mysticism, whereas the stronger, more vivid kinds, are forms of extreme mysticism. In other words, it would seem that all genuine religious experiences are mystical, either in a mild or an extreme way.

Extrovertive and introvertive forms of mysticism
Some scholars suggest that there are extrovertive and introvertive forms of mysticism. They are probably conditioned by the personality types first described by Jung in 1921. He argued that introverts are more energised by the internal world and extroverts by the external world. Introverts are orientated primarily toward an understanding of what they perceive, while extroverts naturally seek means of expression and communication. Introverts talk when they know what they think. Extroverts talk in order to discover

what they are thinking. In introverts subjectivity lies at the centre of every interest and the importance of objects lies in the way in which they affect the subject. In extroverts the factual, objective world determines the focus of interest to a large degree.[7]

Extrovertive mysticism believes that the Kingdom of God is *among* us. In this form of mysticism, sensory experiences of things such as trees, hills, rivers and seas are transfigured and transformed. The person feels that he or she is aware of an inner essence in all these things and may also feel that his or her deeper self is at one with this inner essence. Extrovertive mysticism:

1. Looks outward by means of the senses.
2. Sees the inner essence of things, an essence which appears to be alive, beautiful, and the same in all things.
3. Sense of union of one's deeper self with this inner essence.
4. Feelings that what is experienced is divine.
5. Sense of reality, that one sees things as they really are.
6. Sense of peace and bliss.
7. Timelessness, no awareness of the passage of time during the experience.

Arguably the writings of Julian of Norwich and Ignatius of Loyola are, in the main, forms of extrovertive mysticism. A quotation from an unknown author illustrates some of the characteristics involved. 'The buildings were decrepit and ugly, the ground covered with boards, rags, and debris. Suddenly, every object in my field of vision took on a curious and intense kind of existence of its own; that is, everything appeared to have an "inside" – to exist as I existed, having inwardness, a kind of individual life, and every object seen under this aspect appeared exceedingly beautiful. There was a cat out there, with its head lifted, effortlessly, watching a wasp that moved without moving just above its head. Everything was urgent with life which was the same in the cat, the wasp, the broken bottles, and merely manifested itself differently in these individuals. All things seemed to glow with a light that came from within them.'[8]

Introvertive mysticism believes that the kingdom of God is *within us*. The person is made in God's image and likeness, he or she is a temple of the Holy Spirit. In this form of mysticism God is primarily discovered within the personality. It has the following characteristics.

1. A state of consciousness devoid of its ordinary contents: sensations, images, thoughts, desires, and so forth.

2. An experience of absolute oneness, with no distinctions and divisions.

3. Sense of reality, a conviction that one is experiencing what is ultimately real.

4. Feeling that what is experienced is divine.

5. Sense of complete peace and bliss.

6. Timelessness, no awareness of the passage of time during the experience.[9]

Arguably the writings of Dionysius the Areopagite and St John of the Cross bear witness to this kind of approach. In his *Le Milieu Divin*, Teilhard de Chardin seems to illustrate some of the characteristics of introvertive mysticism in the following quote. 'For the first time in my life perhaps, I took the lamp and, leaving the zone of everyday occupations and relationships where everything seems clear, I went down into my inmost self, to the deep abyss whence I feel dimly that my power of action emanates. But as I moved further and further away from the conventional certainties by which social life is superficially illuminated, I became aware that I was losing contact with myself. At each step of the descent a new person was disclosed within me of whose name I was no longer sure, and who no longer obeyed me. And when I had to stop my exploration because the path faded from beneath my steps, I found a bottomless abyss at my feet, and out of it came – arising I know not from where – the current which I call my life ... The Kingdom of God is within us ... In order to hasten Christ's second coming, let us concentrate upon a better understanding of the process by which the holy presence is born and grows within us. In order to foster its progress more intelligently let us observe the birth and growth of the divine *milieu*, first in ourselves and then in the world that begins with us.'[10]

Mediated and un-mediated mysticism

Speaking about our availability to know God as God is, the 4th Lateran Council said in the twelfth century: 'Between the Creator and creatures no similarity can be expressed without including a greater dissimilarity.' This distinction gives rise to two types of mysticism. Firstly, there is the *kataphatic* kind, which is preferred by extroverts, and secondly, the *apophatic* kind which is preferred by introverts. Both of them were mentioned by St Thérèse of Lisieux in her autobiography. Quoting the *Imitation of Christ*, she says: 'God has two ways of revealing himself. He shows himself to some in a blaze of light, to others under a considerable veil of symbols and signs.'[11]

A) Kataphatic or mediated mysticism

The *kataphatic* approach, sometimes referred to as the *via affirmativa* (the affirmative way), stresses the knowability of God, because the divine presence is mediated by the created world and the scriptures, i.e. 'under a considerable veil of symbols'. St Paul adverts to this fact when he writes: 'Ever since the creation of the world God's eternal power and divine nature, invisible though they are, have been understood and seen through the things he has made' (Rom 1:20). Writing in his *Summa Theologica*, St Thomas said: 'The nature of man requires that he be led to the invisible by visible things. Therefore, the invisible things of God must be made manifest to man by the things that are visible.'[12] There is an example of the *kataphatic* kind of mystical experience in Hay's *Religious Experience Today: Studying the Facts*. When Estlin Carpenter was on holidays over 100 years ago he had a profound, life changing experience.

I was in a condition of religious apathy for a long time when I was at Manchester New College, then in London. I had no intellectual doubts: I do not think I am able to enter into them: that means perhaps that I had not widely departed from the philosophy in which I was trained. But though I had no doubts, I had no religion. I had no sense of personal relationship with God. I thought that I should leave the College because services were weariness to me. I never wished particularly to pray. I hoped that if I went for a time to work in some way among the poor and the ignorant, my religion might in some way be renewed in me. It was brought about not in that way. Dr Martineau persuaded me to wait in College, and one summer day I went to stay with Wickstead at his father's house in North Wales. Shall I tell you what happened to me? … I went out one afternoon for a walk alone. I was in the empty unthinking state in which one saunters along country lanes, simply yielding oneself to the casual sights around which give a town bred lad with country yearnings such intense delight. Suddenly, I became conscious of the presence of someone else. I cannot describe it, but I felt that I had as direct a perception of the being of God all about me as I have of you when we are together. It was no longer a matter of inference, it was an immediate act of spiritual apprehension. It came unsought, absolutely unexpectedly. I remember the wonderful transfiguration of the far off woods and hills as they seemed to blend in the infinite being with which I was thus brought into relation. This experience did not last long. But it sufficed to change all my feeling. I had not found God because I had never looked for him. But he had found me; he had, I could not but believe, made himself personally known to me. I had not gone in search of a satisfying emotion, I did not work myself up into this state by any artificial means. But I felt that God had come to me. I could now not only believe in him with my mind, but love him with my heart. I cannot tell you how often this has come back to me, both with thankfulness and humiliation … I am often perplexed to know why such revelations do not come to other souls. But I cannot regard this as a mere piece of romanticism, though I shall not be surprised or offended if you do. This event has never happened to me again … it was not necessary. This sense of a direct relation to God then generated in my soul has become part of my habitual thought and feeling.[13]

Like all mystical experiences, this one was self-authenticating. It was so vivid and real in an experiential way that there was no need for faith as assent to a doctrine that was accepted as true because it was taught in an authoritative way by the church. Rather, there was faith as trust in an unseen Reality which was perceived to be reliable. Chapter two suggested a typology of religious experience, one that highlighted four common characteristics, i.e. desire, attention, revelation, and effects. Why not see how many of them you can identify in Carpenter's account.

B) Apophatic or unmediated mysticism

The *apophatic* approach, sometimes known as the *via negativa* (the negative way), stresses the unknowability of God. I'm sure that William Barry is correct when he says that *apophatic* spirituality cannot avoid some mediation of the mystery of God. Perhaps the difference in the two traditions lies in the desire of the *apophatic* tradition to bypass the other dimensions, such as the symbolical and mythological, to focus on incomprehensible Mystery, and that of the *kataphatic* to try to discern the religious aspect within the other dimensions of life.[14] St Thérèse of Lisieux referred to *apophatic* mysticism in a paradoxical way when she said that God reveals himself to some people in a 'blaze of light'. In other words the human spirit, i.e. the loving will, is directly illumined by God, without the mediating role of thought or symbol. Phyllis Campbell wrote a prayer which asks for this kind of relationship with God:

Serene Light, shining in the ground of my being,

Draw me to Yourself!

Draw me past the snares of the senses,

Out of the mazes of the mind;

Free me from symbols, from words,

That I may discover

The Signified.

The Word unspoken,

In the darkness which veils the ground of my being.[15]

There is an example of what Phyllis Campbell meant in Dionysius the Areopagite's *Mystical Theology*:

Leave behind ... everything perceived and understood, everything perceptible and understandable, all that is not and all that is, and with your understanding laid aside, to strive upward as much as you can toward union with him who is beyond all being and knowledge. By an undivided and absolute abandonment of yourself and everything, shedding all, and freed from all, you will be uplifted to the ray of the divine shadow which is above everything that is.[16]

Sometimes a person on the *apophatic* way will experience what is known as the dark night of the soul. It is a form of desolation of spirit reserved for those who are already well advanced along the spiritual path. In this state, all the scaffolding of thought, image and feeling, that usually support a sense of heartfelt relationship with God, are withdrawn. Thérèse of Lisieux endured such a spiritual ordeal toward the end of her life when she was seriously ill with tuberculosis. While it didn't lead to a specific mystical experience, it did lead to a typically mystical state of purification. In her autobiography, she talks about hearing mocking voices, and how the fear of annihilation seemed to cancel all sense of inner meaning. She describes how she used to get tired of the darkness all around her and how she attempted to refresh her jaded spirits with thoughts of heaven where her hopes were fixed. But what happened? Her torment grew worse than ever; the darkness oppressing her seemed to borrow, from the sinners who lived in it, the gift of speech. She tells us how she heard it say in mocking tones: 'It is all a dream, this talk of a heavenly country, bathed in light, scented with delicious perfumes, and of a God who made it all, who is to be our possession in eternity! ... All right, all right, go on longing for death! But death will make nonsense of your hopes; it will only mean a darker night than ever, the night of mere non-existence and annihilation.'[17]

Thérèse spoke about her ordeal to some of her companions. She said to one: 'If you only knew the frightful thoughts that plague me! Pray hard for me not to listen to the Devil as he tries to make me believe his many lies. The arguments of the worst rationalists fill my mind. Why must I have such thought when I love God so much? I endure them of necessity, but even while having them, never stop renewing my acts of faith.'[18] It is not clear what rationalists Thérèse had in mind. There were many of them, such as Nietzsche, Marx and the Modernists who were writing at the time. By now Thérèse had gangrene of the intestines. Added to this, her temptations against faith could have led her to despair. She endured so much anguish that she was suicidal. 'Oh, if I didn't have the faith,' she declared, 'I could never endure all this pain. I'm amazed that atheists don't commit suicide more often ... Yes! What a mercy it is to have faith! If I didn't have faith, I should have killed myself without a moment's hesitation.'[19] Sister Augustine reported:

'She admitted something to me which surprised and confused me, "If only you knew the darkness into which I've been flung! I don't believe in eternal life; I think, after this life there will be nothing more. Everything has vanished for me".' But she added afterwards – and this is the point, 'All I have left is love.'[20] When every support had been taken away, she still believed in Love – and God is love, heaven is a place of love – beyond the evidence of sense, feeling or reason.

By June 9th 1897 it was clear that Thérèse hadn't long to live. She was moved downstairs. All the while she was receiving the barbaric and ineffective treatments of the day, e.g. blistering, cauterisation, syrup of slugs, friction with a horse hair glove, etc. She said to her companions: 'Don't be upset, dearest sisters, if I suffer a great deal and if you see no sign of happiness in me when I reach the point of death. Our Lord too died a victim of love, and see what his death agony of love was like! … Our Lord died on the cross in agony, yet this was the finest of deaths for love… The only example, indeed. Dying of love doesn't mean dying in transports of joy.'[21] All through her terrible physical and spiritual suffering, which was particularly bad during the last months of her life, i.e. from July to September 30th 1897, she never lost her trust in love. Her love was to triumph. Bernard Bro says that at the moment of death, for the space of a Credo, the darkness was torn aside. She expired saying, 'Oh, I love him. My God I love you.'[22]

Over the centuries *apophatic* mysticism has been advocated by many writers such as John Cassian, the anonymous author of *The Cloud of Unknowing*, John of the Cross, Thomas Merton and also John Main, who advocated what is known as centring prayer. For more on *apophatic* forms of spirituality see chapter five which is entitled, 'Is unceasing prayer possible?' By and large, spiritual writers would generally agree that rather than being opposed to one another these forms of mysticism are complementary. Generally speaking people who are at the beginning stage of spiritual development prefer *kataphatic* forms of mysticism. But as they mature, the Spirit can lead them to prefer *apophatic* forms. In practical terms, it means that the Benedictine and Ignatian forms of prayer are better at first. Only later should a person move to other forms such as centring prayer, using mantras and the Jesus Prayer.

Some characteristics of mystical experiences
While William James does not reduce religion to mysticism, he does claim that mystical experience is the epitome of religious experience. Instead of defining mystical states, he says that they have four identifiable characteristics.

1. Ineffability. In other words mystical experience defies expression, it cannot be adequately conveyed in language. James believed that unless the hearer has had a similar experience, the one talking would fail to convey what the felt experience was really like. Estlin Carpenter said of his experience: 'I cannot describe it.'

2. Noetic quality. Besides being states of feeling, mystical states also seem to those who have them to be states of knowledge also. They intuit depths of truth which cannot be accessed by rational, discursive thought. Estlin Carpenter: 'I felt that I had a direct perception of the being of God all round about me.'

3. Transiency. Mystical states cannot be sustained for long. At best they might last for up to a half an hour, and even less frequently for an hour. Once they are over, their intensity is hard to recapture in memory. Estlin Carpenter said: 'This experience did not last long.'

4. Passivity. Although the person may be disposed to have mystical experiences, e.g. by developing a capacity for paying sustained attention to reality, they are gratuitous. One cannot psyche oneself into a mystical awareness. 'The wind,' as scripture says, 'blows where it wills.' Estlin Carpenter said that his experience came: 'unsought, absolutely unexpectedly.'

James says that when people have mystical experiences they have predictable effects.

1. Mystical states, when well developed, usually are, and have the right to be, absolutely authoritative over the individuals to whom they come.

2. No authority emanates from them which should make it a duty

for those who stand outside of them to accept their revelations uncritically.

3. They break down the authority of the non-mystical or rationalistic consciousness, based upon the understanding and the senses alone. They show it to be only one kind of consciousness.

Is there a Perennial Philosophy?

The phrase Perennial Philosophy, was coined by Leibniz. It represented an attempt to present the highest common factor of all theologies by assembling passages from the writings of those saints and prophets who claim to have had a direct spiritual knowledge of the divine. James Pratt wrote: 'All the mystics speak *one* language and profess *one* faith.'[23] Aldous Huxley wrote a book entitled *The Perennial Philosophy*. It stated that the term refers to three interrelated points.

- It recognises a divine Reality underpinning the world of things including our own lives;
- It is the psychology that finds in the soul something similar to, or even identical with, divine Reality;
- It is the ethic that places man's final end in the knowledge of the immanent and transcendent ground of all being.[24]

He illustrated his thesis with quotations, on various subjects, from mystics of different religious traditions down the ages. Alan Watts has written that there has been a single philosophical consensus of universal extent. 'It has been held by men who report the same insights *and teach the same essential doctrine* (my italics) whether living today or six thousand years ago.'[25] More recently Ken Wilber has noted that the 'perennial,' 'primordial' or 'ancient' wisdom can have two meanings. Firstly, it can mean radically timeless, spaceless, formless Truth, the Ground of all Being. Secondly, it can refer to the particular outward forms and symbols used by cultures in the past which have led to the second widespread meaning of 'ancient wisdom' – namely, the actual doctrines, metaphors, symbols, and models used by ancient or past cultures to express and embody their own realisation of that Truth.[26]

A) Subjective Experience

There is some truth in the assertion that mystical experiences, both ancient and modern, Eastern and Western are similar in some ways, e.g. in terms of contemplative receptivity and their characteristic subjective effects. For example, following Hugh of St Victor, Wilber points out that the different traditions in the East and West share a consensus about perception. Human beings have three eyes, or faculties, of perception, namely the eye of the flesh which makes empirical knowledge possible; the eye of the mind which makes rational knowledge such as logic and philosophy possible; and the eye of contemplation which enables people to acquire spiritual knowledge and have mystical experiences.[27] All of the mystical traditions, whether in the East or West stress the importance of the spiritual eye of contemplation.

Scholars such as Mircea Eliade,[28] Joseph Campbell[29] and Carl Jung were among those who have tried to show how the archetypal symbolism of the great religions, which is expressed in myths is surprisingly similar. It is worth noting, in passing, that contrary to popular opinion, myths are not fanciful and untrue but revelations of power and symbolic articulations of absolute truths. For example, the crucifixion of Jesus is not unlike the deaths of other heroes or 'saviours' such as Osiris, Tammuz, Orpheus and Balder.[30] They were of divine or semi divine birth, were killed, and later reborn. Sir George Frazer, (1854-1941 AD) the great British anthropologist is best remembered as the author of *The Golden Bough*. He cited one non-Christian document which seemed to anticipate the passion of Jesus when it stated in mythical terms: 'They take one of the prisoners condemned to death, and seat him upon the King's throne, and give him the king's raiment, and let him lord it... But afterwards they strip and scourge and crucify him.'[31]

At the end of the last century a Canadian doctor named Richard Bucke MD drew attention to other similarities in the mystical traditions of the world. He had a life-changing religious experience which led him to take a scholarly interest in the subject of higher states of religious awareness. In his well known book *Cosmic Consciousness*, he made a number of interesting suggestions. Firstly he maintained that the majority of those men and women who broke through to cosmic consciousness were in their thirties.[32] Secondly, he described qualities they had in common. 'The prime characteristic of cosmic consciousness' he wrote, – in a way that echoed Scheiermacher – 'is, as its name implies, a consciousness of the cosmos, that is, of the life and order of the universe.'[33] Then he added: 'Along with the consciousness of the cosmos there occurs an intellectual enlightenment or illumination which alone would place the individual on a new plane of existence – would make him almost a member of a new species. To this is added a state of moral exaltation, an indescribable feeling of elevation and joyousness, and a quickening of the moral sense, which is fully as striking and more important both to the individual and to the race than is the enhanced intellectual power. With these come, what may be called a sense of immortality, a consciousness of eternal life, not a conviction he shall have this, but the consciousness that he has it already.'[34]

Later in the book he lists a number of the main characteristics of the cosmic sense. A list of them is included here without commentary.

1. Subjective light
2. Intellectual illumination
3. Sense of immortality
4. Loss of the fear of death
5. Loss of the sense of sin
6. Suddenness, instantaneousness, of the awakening.
7. Added charm of the personality so that men and women are always strongly attracted to the person.
8. Transfiguration of the subject of the change as seen by others when the cosmic sense is actually present.[35]

The rest of Bucke's book was devoted to a series of biographical studies which were arranged in accordance with a predetermined schematic list of headings. He illustrated his thesis by showing how each of those who gave evidence of cosmic consciousness did so in line with the points made above. In doing this, he tended to undervalue the rather obvious fact that the teachings of these mystics are quite different, and that those differences cannot be accounted for merely in terms of the cultural circumstances obtaining at the time they were expressed. While it is true that people seem to have a natural capacity for religious experience, what Karl Rahner referred to an 'obediential potency' for grace, or revelation, has God chosen to make a decisive and definitive revelation of the God-self and the divine will? Christians would answer, yes.

B) Objective Content

We move now to the second question. Are the contents of different mystical experiences much the same? As was noted above, Fredrich Schleiermacher, and his disciples such as William James and Rudolf Otto, tended, to a greater or lesser extent, to emphasise the importance of subjective religious experience. In more recent times a number of writers such as Huston Smith, Cantwell Smith, Aldous Huxley, Joseph Campbell and Ken Wilber have been influenced by their perspective. They have argued that while religions differ greatly at the conceptual and creedal level, they are all rooted in mystical experiences that have a lot in common. When the profound awarenesses of people like Buddha, Jesus and Mohammed were expressed in words, they were deeply affected by the cultural influences which prevailed at the time they lived. As a result, their creedal expressions of faith are manifestly different, but the intense experiences that gave rise to those creeds are surprisingly similar. The implication of this point of view is that none of the great religions is fundamentally different from the others. Despite their apparent dissimilarities, the great faiths are equally legitimate paths to God in so far as they are animated by mystical experiences which are similar in nature.

I suspect that some of Schleiermacher's disciples misunderstand his interpretation of religion. Because the great German theologian put so much emphasis on intuition and feeling, they focus on the subjective experience of religion rather than its objective content. However, in doing this they are not only mistaken, they misunderstand Schleiermacher's intent. He was well aware that, as human acts, intuition and feeling had intentionality, they focused on a tran-scendent object, namely the numinous, or the divine. He was of the opinion that, in pre-reflective religious experience, subject and object were one in a form of ecstatic knowing. In other words reli-gious people had intuitions and feelings about a reality separate from themselves, i.e. the God of religious faith. As Louis Dupre has observed: 'A closer analysis of the religious experience, as described by Schleiermacher, will show that although feeling has a subjective connotation, strictly speaking, it is not more subjective than objective because it belongs to a stage of consciousness in which subject and object are still basically identical.'[36] Theologian John Macquarrie has also pointed out that Schleiermacher did not have a subjectivist understanding of religion: 'Feeling in Schleiermacher's sense of the term,' he writes, 'is an awareness of a reality which has called forth the feeling. Feelings do not arise in our minds at random, out of our own subjectivity... It would be wrong to say that he subjectifies revelation. It has its ultimate origin in God or the universe.'[37] So, what is known in an intuitive way evokes a particular kind of emotional response.

Objective truth or revelation, mediated by the cosmos, is, there-fore, constitutive of a particular kind of subjective experience. Because all religions have access to this kind of natural revelation it isn't surprising that there would be a perennial philosophy at that level of experience. It is this kind of revelation that is studied by many philosophers of religion and by other students of religious experience such as Margharita Laski. For instance, Jacques Maritain argued in his philosophical writings, notably an essay entitled, 'The Natural Mystical Experience and the Void,' that a person can have a natural mystical experience. It reaches God indirectly insofar as God gives existence to the soul, but not directly as God is in God's own reality. He cited Indian mysticism as a prime example of this approach.[38]

But there is another kind of revelation, a trans-rational, super-natural form. Its purest expression, we believe, is contained in the bible. What is known of revealed, supernatural biblical truth has a profound and unique effect. It follows, then, that those scholars of comparative religion who overlook the distinction between natural and supernatural mysticism in order to focus on subjective experiential similarities are making an epistemological and a theological mistake.

As a result of the confusions we have cited, there is a fairly widespread view that before religions, such as Christianity, found expression in creedal form, they were pristine, religious experiences which were similar in nature. This is not accurate. It fails, as already noted, to distinguish between natural mysticism and mysticism based on supernatural revelation. Not only that, there is no such thing as virginal experiences which are unsullied by cultural influences. In reality, there is a reciprocal relationship between the two. The way in which we have experiences is influenced by the cultural paradigms prevailing at the time. Secondly the way in which we understand and express those experiences in a conceptual way is also influenced by contemporary culture. As Edward Schillebeeckx has written : 'Interpretation and experience exercise a mutual influence on one another… to experience salvation is experience *and* interpretation at the same time.'[39] So, what we know already, not only exercises a conscious and unconscious influence upon the way in which we have religious and mystical experiences, it also influences the way in which we interpret and articulate them in cognitive terms.

For example, Christianity is the only great religion to claim that its Founder was Divine. That revealed, supernatural truth, which was intimated, perhaps, in the messianic texts of the Old Testament, not only had a decisive effect on the way in which the first Christians experienced God in Christ, it also influenced the way in which they expressed that experience in their scriptures. It could also be said that, inevitably Christians, down the ages have interpreted the Old Testament in the light of the New Testament as it was experienced within the cultural ethos prevailing at the time, whether it was that of the high Middle Ages or the Enlightenment. The same epistemological principle applies to the mystical traditions of the world. Christian mysticism is different from that of other religions, not because of its receptive capacities, but because of the distinctive, divinely revealed truths that inform it. These are not accidental, but rather essential and constitutive in nature.

Teilhard de Chardin, (1881-1955) who developed his own distinctive type of creation spirituality, had interesting observations to make about the perennial philosophy. By and large, it would be true to say, that he had reservations about the legitimacy of such a concept. He felt that in all relationships there is a paradoxical issue at stake, namely, how a person can affirm his or her identity while at the same time becoming deeply united to the Other. This tension lies at the heart of mystical religion. Some, especially those in the East, solve this problem by absorbing the person into the Otherness of God. However in Christian mysticism, which is Christocentric, intensely personal, and motivated by love, personal identity is affirmed in and through ever closer union with God. Paradoxically, the more we die to self by surrendering to the love and will of God the more we possess our true individual identity.

De Chardin was surprisingly critical of some of the world's great religions because they failed to honour this paradox. He wrote: 'No one who has been deeply influenced by modern culture and the knowledge that goes with it can sincerely be a Confucian, a Buddhist or Muslim unless he is prepared to live a double interior life, or profoundly to modify for his own use the terms of his religion.'[40] De Chardin was also quite critical of Hinduism. He observed, a little unfairly perhaps, that it 'was obsessed with material forms and ritualism.' He called for a new mysticism, one that would be based upon a 'Christianity faithfully extended to its utmost limits.' He believed that the great religions were converging upon and synthesising around Christianity as the 'principal axis' of evolution, in order to bring about this new mysticism. Whether one would agree with de Chardin's particular understanding of creation spirituality or not, he seems to assert the point that the unique credo of the Christian religion is what brings about its unique experience of God and *visa versa*.

C) Assessment

Is there a perennial philosophy? While not wanting to deny that the great mystics throughout the ages have had partial but genuine revelations of God and God's will, Christians would claim that God's revelation in Christ is the fulfilment of all other revelations. Without in any way affirming that all mysticism is always and everywhere one and the same, it can be said that Christian mystics have certain experiential affinities with the mystics of other traditions in so far as their receptive faculties are the same. Arguably, the supernatural, sanctifying grace of Christian mystical experience builds upon a capacity for natural mystical experience.

On the other hand R. C. Zaehner, a respected student of mysticism, has stated that the only thing the great religions of the world have in common is the 'observed fact of human unhappiness … They are simply not starting from the same premises … The great religions are talking at cross purposes.'[41] By and large it could be said that the Eastern religions focus *on what people can do* to come into the awareness of God, while Western religions tend to emphasise *God's initiative* in revealing the God-self to people.

That said, it would seem, in one way or another, that different mythological and mystical traditions have obvious affinities. At face value it would seem that the Christian story is merely another myth among hero myths. Although it is true that Christians believed that the death and resurrection of Jesus have a mythological resonance, they are *a uniquely historical fact*. I like to believe that Christian beliefs clarify and fulfill what was intimated, to a greater or lesser degree, in the so-called perennial philosophy. As a result, while Christian mysticism fulfills the transcendental aspirations which are evident in the mythologies of different cultures, it is essentially different from the mysticism of other religions. Because revealed Christian beliefs are constitutive of the consciousness of those who experienced them, their consequent mystical epxeriences, despite some symbolical and experiential similarities, are essentially different from those of other religions.

CRITIQUE OF MYSTICAL EXPERIENCES

A) Psychological critique

Psychologists with reductionist tendencies have tried to explain mystical experiences as nothing but a cover for something else. We will look at three such explanations. The first argues that mystical experiences are a form of psychological regression, whereby an adult tries to recover the 'oceanic feeling' of early childhood. At that time the baby experienced a form of symbiotic union when, because of it's weak ego boundary, it felt blissfully merged with the all-powerful, and all-loving mother.[42] Mystics, according to this theory, are falsely trying to recover the sense of security associated with a primordial feeling of union with reality. The second argues that mystical experience is really a form of repressed or sublimated eroticism. James Leuba advocated this Freudian notion in his book *The Psychology of Religious Mysticism* (1925). He was able to cite the erotic images used by mystics to express their experiences, e.g. the Song of Songs; St Teresa of Avila saying that her heart was pene-trated by an arrow of divine love, and the erotic images in the reli-gious poetry of John of the Cross, etc. The third critique of mysti-cism argues that it is really a form of pathology, a delusional, hys-terical reaction, characterised by a certain disassociation of con-sciousness. For example, in the *Diagnostic and Statistical Manual of Mental Disorders*, used by American psychiatrists, schizophrenia is described as 'odd or bizarre ideation or magical thinking involving recurrent illusions, sensing the presence of a force or a person not actually present'. It goes on to say that the experiences of many reli-gious people, especially mystics, 'may be difficult to distinguish from delusions or hallucinations'.

B) A Protestant critique

A number of Protestant writers such as Albecht Ritschl, Adolf von Harnack, Emile Brunner, and Karl Barth have argued that there are two kinds of religion, mystical and prophetic. Friedrich Heiler describes the difference as follows: 'Mystical prayer has its roots in the yearning of the devout person for union with the Infinite, prophetic prayer arises from the profound need of the heart and longing for salvation and grace.'[43] Protestant critics argue that while prophetic forms of religion are rooted in the bible, mysticism is not really Christian. They say that historically speaking, Western mysticism was the result of linking Judeo-Christian religion of the evangelical variety, with Greek philosophy of the idealistic kind. Some of the writings of Plato and his followers would be examples of what the theologians had in mind. For example, Ritschl wrote: 'Mysticism therefore is the practice of Neoplatonic metaphysics and this is the theoretical norm of the pretended mystical delight in God. Hence the universal being viewed as God into which the mystic wishes to be mingled is a cheat.'[44] The Protestant critics also argue that the Orthodox notion of the deification of the person as a result of being united to God by means of mystical experience is subjectivist and owes more to Platonism than to the bible.

C) A Catholic critique

Those who engage in liberation theology are suspicious of mysticism. Like some Protestants, they feel that this form of religion has come into Christianity from Greek philosophy. Because of their emphasis on praxis, liberation theologians believe that the gospel is only properly understood when Christians are involved in the struggle to bring justice and liberation to the poor and the marginalised who suffer injustice and oppression. It is through such a practical engagement that the true meaning of the gospel text is illuminated. Mysticism, on the other hand, seems to withdraw from such engagement. To say that mysticism crosses over into life and practical action is mistaken. If mysticism has validity, and liberationists would question whether it has, it is because life crosses over into contemplative awareness.

Conclusion

Aldous Huxley once wrote: 'a totally unmystical world would be a world totally blind and insane.'[45] In the mid 60s F. C. Happold predicted in *Religious Faith and 20th Century Man*, that in the future 'the only acceptable religion is likely to be a "mystical" one'.[46] A few years later, Karl Rahner wrote: 'The Christian of the future will be a mystic or he or she will not exist at all, if by mysticism we mean ... a genuine experience of God emerging at the very heart of our existence.'[47] In an age when the claims of established religion are so widely questioned, the witness of the mystics is of particular importance. Another great question that confronts the present age is the relation of Christianity to other world religions. If Christianity is to embark upon truly co-operative relations with other religions, it must be deeply imbued with the insight and experience of the mystics.

St Clement of Alexandria (c. 150-215) had a strong predilection for creation spirituality. He saw God as a divine sower who spreads the seed of the *logos* word of revelation in all cultures. As a result he felt that there was a lot to be learnt from Platonic metaphysics, Stoic ethics and Aristotelian logic.[48] St Thomas Aquinas endorsed this truly catholic point of view when he wrote: 'all truth, no matter by whom it is uttered, comes from the Holy Spirit'.[49] By extension, presumably, Clement would have recognised that all the religions of the world, especially in their mystical manifestations, had, to a greater or lesser extent, an awareness of divine truth. However, he would also have maintained that revelation was at its purest and highest in God's dealings with the chosen people, and especially in God's incarnation in Jesus Christ. When all is said and done, one either believes or does not believe what Jesus asserted when he said, 'I am the way, and the truth, and the life; no one comes to the Father, but by me' (Jn 14:6). That said, however, I believe that the mystical dimension of the different religions is important as far as interfaith dialogue is concerned. Whereas there are obvious differences at the level of professed beliefs, there is much more convergence apparent at the level of experience, particularly that of mystical experience.

CHAPTER 4

Contemplative Attention

Gerald Vann opened one of his books with these memorable words: 'The heart of man is a hunger for the reality which lies about him and beyond him.'[1] This hunger is expressed in two interrelated activities, a desire to experience transcendent Reality, and the decision to attend to the reality of creation in the belief that it can mediate the presence of God (cf. Rom 1:20). Writing in his *Principles of Psychology*, William James made the significant assertion that this decision to attend is of crucial importance. 'The essential achievement of the will,' he wrote, 'is to *attend* ... Effort of attention is thus the essential phenomenon of will.'[2] The etymology of the word 'attention' is interesting. It means 'to stretch' or 'incline' the mind, in order to comprehend created and uncreated truth. Many metaphors, based on the activity of the senses, are commonly used to describe the act of attention, e.g. to look, to listen, to get in touch, etc. At this point we will examine some of the characteristics of transcendental attention.

Characteristics of the Contemplative Attitude
Firstly, it is *contemplative* in attitude. The word is derived from the Latin *contemplari* and means 'to look at, to pay sustained attention' to someone or something. It implies that this kind of mindfulness is disciplined, focused and concentrated on the object of attention. It is sometimes referred to, in a paradoxical way, as passive attention. On the one hand, it is energised by a dynamic desire to know while, on the other, it is characterised by a quiet openness and receptivity. There have been many helpful definitions of contemplation, e.g. William Mc Namara said it was: 'a long loving look at the real.'[3] St Francis de Sales wrote: 'Contemplation is simply the mind's loving, single-minded, permanent attention to the things of God.'[4]

Secondly, it is other directed and *self-forgetful*. It escapes the gravitational pull of self-absorption and excessive self-reference, by bracketing out distracting needs, memories, thoughts, images and feelings in order to pay undivided attention to the other/Other. Understood in this sense, attention is ecstatic, in that it seeks to 'stand outside' the knower in its receptivity and openness to revelation. Simone Weil described this characteristic when she wrote: 'Attention consists of suspending our thought, leaving it detached, empty and ready to be penetrated by the object ... The soul empties itself of all its own contents in order to receive into itself the being it is looking at.'[5] This kind of attention surrenders wilful control over the objects it beholds. Instead of projecting preconceived ideas or symbolisms on to objects, it is willing to let them to be themselves.[6] It is interesting to note that in Greek the word *epistrophe* can mean 'attention' or 'conversion.' In other words self-forgetful attention sometimes involves a type of cognitive crucifixion or conversion, in so far as knowledge of the new can disrupt familiar meanings that, up until then, had underpinned the security of the ego.

Thirdly when attention is focused on people it is *empathic*. The word 'empathy' is similar to the German *einfuhlung*, which literally means 'feeling into.' In his *Modern Clinical Psychiatry*, Lawrence Kolb defines empathy as a 'healthy form of identification which is limited and temporary but which enables one person to feel for and with another and to understand his experiences and feelings.'[7] Empathic knowing is made possible by paying attention to people's words and body language. If they are suffering, this kind of empathy is compassionate in nature, it is moved by their afflictions and responds spontaneously and appropriately in an affective and effective way. It is commonly impeded by such things as unresolved emotional pain, low self-awareness, moralism, prejudice, lack of good-will, countertransference and so on.[8]

Fourthly it is *intuitive*, i.e. the act or spiritual faculty of knowing directly – often by means of symbols – without the use of rational, analytical processes. The origin of this word is very interesting. It comes from the Latin *intueri*, meaning 'to look upon', 'to contemplate', and 'to see within'. In other words, by means of spiritual intuition, attention can penetrate to the mysterious essence or 'isness' of things. St Thomas says that natural and supernatural understanding (cf. Is 11:2; 1 Cor 12:8) enable a person to perceive what lies under the surface of reality. He says: 'the essences of things underlie their outer supervening qualities, meanings underlie words used to express them, truth lies behind images and figures, spiritual realities behind the images we sense, effects lie hidden in their causes; and in all cases penetrating beyond the surface is called understanding'.[9] Henri Bergson echoed St Thomas's sentiments when he wrote: 'Intuition is a sympathy whereby one carries oneself into the interior of an object to coincide with what is unique and therefore inexpressible in it.'[10] Speaking of this aspect of attention, Max Scheler wrote that it is 'not merely an activity of the knowing subject who penetrates into the already existing object, but is, at the same time, a responsive answer of the object itself; a 'self giving' and 'opening' of the object, i.e. a genuine self-revelation of the object.' Intuition, therefore, leads to an intimate, connatural rapport or sympathy with reality/Reality which publishes and makes known something of its inner nature.

Effects Of Contemplation

Having taken a brief look at some of the characteristics of transcendental attention, we go on to examine a few of its consequences. First and foremost it leads to *revelation,* whereby created reality can disclose its inner truth, much as Scheler described. As the hidden value of people and natural things is perceived, it evokes spontaneous feelings such as approval, affirmation, awe, wonder, pleasure, etc. However, this immediate experience can also indirectly disclose the presence of the Divine. As Karl Rahner has written: 'The human person's first personal partner ... cannot be God, because a mediation is always needed ... the human person and the world must be the mediator.'[11]

Speaking of human relationships, Martin Buber suggests that in modern culture human intimacy is becoming the sole form of mediation. He says that in mankind's great ages the invisible revelation of the divine outgrows old symbolisms and expresses itself in new ones. The symbol becomes ever more internalised, moves ever closer to the heart. The person who five thousand years ago saw it in the stars, sees it today in the eyes of a friend. It is not God who changes, only the manifestation of the divine in people's symbol-creating minds; until no symbol is adequate any longer, and none is needed, and life itself in the miracle of people being together, becomes a symbol – until God is actually present when one man or woman clasps the hand of another. While I think that Buber is correct when he suggests that, in modern culture, interpersonal relationships of the intimate kind are pre-eminent in their ability to mediate the divine presence, he would be mistaken if he were suggesting that they are the only way in which that presence can be mediated.

Intimations of the divine Presence and attributes evoke 'religious' feelings such as peace and joy, which are not directly evoked by the immediate object of attention. This recognition of God's value and worth is the birthplace of heartfelt praise and worship. Once again the etymologies of these words are illuminating. Praise comes from the Latin, *pretium* meaning 'to know the price or value of'. Worship comes from the Old English *weorpscipe*, meaning to know 'the worth of'. Only prayerful attention can lead to a truly experiential appreciation of God. There is a memorable example of this point in Julian of Norwich's *Revelations of Divine Love*. She says that God, 'showed me something small, no bigger than a hazel nut, lying in the palm of my hand, and I perceived that it was round as any ball. I looked at it and thought: What can this be? And I was given this general answer: It is everything that is made. I was amazed that it could last, for I thought that it was so little that it could suddenly fall into nothing. And I was answered in my understanding: It lasts and always will, because God loves it; and thus everything has being through the love of God.'[12] That is why it would be true to say that attention is the very essence of prayer, and that as soon as attention ceases, prayer ceases also.

Some eminent spiritual writers, such as John Cassian (360-435) and Gregory of Palamas (1296-1359), would have argued that while God can and does reveal the God-self in the *kataphatic* way Rahner describes, God can also reveal the divine energies,[13] if not the divine essence, in a more *apophatic* manner, without the mediation of thoughts or images, e.g. through the use of a mantra like the Jesus Prayer. More often than not, loving union with God in the cloud of unknowing may evoke very few feelings. That said, however, advocates of both *kataphatic* and *apophatic* forms of spirituality would be united in their conviction that the kind of attention described above is indispensable for an encounter with God.

The second effect of attention to reality/Reality has to do with the relationship between *inwardness* and *relatedness*. The more men and women relate to the other/Other, the deeper their awareness of their inner selves. The extent to which attention enables them to connect to the 'isness' of created things, is the extent to which the potential of their psyches is activated. The measure to which graced attention enables people to relate to the incomprehensible mystery of a loving God, is the measure to which the depths of their spiritual capacity is activated. They discover that the Transcendent One who is revealed to them without, is simultaneously the Immanent One who is present and loving them from within. As Dame Julian of Norwich (1342-1413) wrote: 'For our soul is so deeply grounded in God and so endlessly treasured that we cannot come to knowledge of it until we first have knowledge of God, who is the Creator to whom it is united ... We must necessarily be in longing ... until the time when we are led so deeply into God that we truly know our own soul.'[14]

Ways of Contemplating

God's presence can be discerned in the twin bibles of creation and the scriptures. As Galileo Galilei (1564-1642) said in a letter to the Grand Duchess Christina of Tuscany: 'From the Divine Word, nature and the sacred scriptures did alike both proceed.'[15] We will look at both forms of presence in turn, beginning with the way in which creation can reveal the Lord.

When spiritual directors discover that their directees have a rather joyless, formal way of praying, they will sometimes ask them what leisure activities they most enjoy. It might be anything, from bird watching, or gardening, to flower arranging, and appreciating good music. If, for example, a female directee said that she really loved walking on a local beach, the director might advise her to do two related things. He could begin by urging her to prayerfully tell God about her heartfelt desire for a revelation, of the divine presence, in her life. Then, ironically, he would encourage her to forget about saying any more prayers in order to pay undivided attention to sand, sea and sky. He would do this in the belief that they could be the locus, not only, of an enjoyable aesthetic experience, but also of a mediated awareness of the uncreated Origin of all created beauty.[16]

An extended quotation from Evelyn Underhill's *Mysticism* illustrates how God's presence can be mediated when a person pays contemplative attention to creation. She begins by saying that the reader should focus his or her attention on something, such as a natural scene, a flower, a burning candle, etc. 'Look then,' she says, 'at this thing which you have chosen. Wilfully yet tranquilly refuse the messages which countless other aspects of the world are sending; and so concentrate your whole attention on this one act of loving sight that all other objects are excluded from the conscious field. Do not think, but as it were pour out your personality toward it: let your soul be in your eyes. Almost at once, this new method of perception will reveal unsuspected qualities in the external world. First you will perceive about you a strange and deepening quietness; a slowing down of our feverish mental time. Next, you will become aware of a heightened significance, an intensified existence in the thing at which you look. As you, with all your consciousness, lean out toward it, an answering current will meet yours. It seems as if the barrier between its life and your own, between subject and object, had melted away. You are merged with it, in an act of true communion: and you *know* the secret of its being deeply and unforgettably, yet in a way you can never hope to express.

Seen thus, a thistle has celestial qualities: a speckled hen has a touch of the sublime. Our greater comrades the trees, the clouds, the rivers, initiate us into mighty secrets, flame out at us "like shining from shook foil". The "eye which looks upon Eternity" has been given its opportunity. We have been immersed for a moment in the

"life of the All": a deep and peaceful love unites us with the substance of all things, a "Mystic Marriage" has taken place between
the mind and some aspect of the external world. *Cor ad cor loquitur*:
Life has spoken to life, but not to the surface intelligence. That surface intelligence knows only that the message was true and beautiful: no more.'[16]

God's presence can also be discerned in a particularly profound
way in scripture. It is the primary and privileged focal point for
divine revelation. As Isaiah wrote: 'See, the former things have
taken place, and new things I declare; before they spring into being
I announce them to you' (Is 42:9). There are many ways of contemplating this inspired and inspiring word. Perhaps the best known,
historically speaking, is the Benedictine *Lectio Divina* which consists
in reading, meditating, praying, contemplating and responding to
God's word. As the Lord says in Prov 4:20-22: 'Be attentive to my
words; incline your ear to my sayings. Do not let them escape from
your sight; keep them within your heart. For they are life to those
who find them, and healing to all their flesh.'

Guigo II, the Carthusian, sometimes known as the Angelic (d.
1188), described the method in these succinct words: 'Reading is the
careful study of the scriptures, concentrating all one's powers on it.
Meditation is the busy application of the mind to seek, with the
help of one's own reason, for knowledge of the hidden truth. Prayer
is the heart's devoted turning to God to drive away evil and obtain
what is good. Contemplation is when the mind is in some sort lifted
up to God and held above itself, so that it tastes the joys of everlasting sweetness ... Reading seeks for the sweetness of a blessed life,
meditation perceives it, prayer asks for it, contemplation tastes it.
Reading, as it were, puts food whole into the mouth, meditation
chews it and breaks it up, prayer extracts its flavour, contemplation
is the sweetness itself which gladdens and refreshes. Reading
works on the outside, meditation on the path: prayer asks what we
long for, contemplation gives us delight in the sweetness which we
have found ... The first degree is proper to beginners, the second to
proficients, the third to devotees, the fourth to the blessed.'[17]

Clearly contemplation lies at the heart of the Benedictine method of scriptural prayer. As one medieval writer, John of Fecamp (990-1078) suggested in his *Theological Confessions*, contemplation occurs when the mind is lifted up in a simple gaze of the heart to God alone. The emotions are touched, the intellectual soul rejoices, the memory grows strong, the intellect shines, and the whole spirit is lit up as it is rapt into the love of things invisible.[18] Once people come into a deeper relationship with God by means of the word, it has a transforming effect as it motivates prayerful thanks, conversion of life and practical action. As St Paul says in 2 Cor 3:18: 'And all of us with unveiled faces, seeing (beholding, contemplating) the glory of the Lord (e.g. in scripture) as though reflected in a mirror, are being transformed into the same image from one degree of glory to another, for this comes from the Lord the Spirit.'

Conclusion

As contemplation is the *sine qua non* of genuine spirituality, so attention is the *sine qua non* of genuine contemplation. The primary precept, therefore, of a religious way of life is this: if you desire to know God make the decision to pay self-forgetful, undivided attention to reality/Reality. As William Blake observed in *The Marriage of Heaven and Hell*: 'If the doors of perception were cleansed, everything would be seen as it is, infinite.'

CHAPTER 5

Is Unceasing Prayer Possible?

On four separate occasions the New Testament tells us to pray continuously. Lk 18:1 says: 'Then Jesus told his disciples a parable to show them that they should always pray and not give up.' Eph 5:20 says: 'Pray at all times in the Spirit, with all prayer and supplication.' Eph 6:18 echoes this point when it says: 'And pray in the Spirit on all occasions with all kinds of prayers and requests. With this in mind, be alert and always keep on praying for all the saints.' Finally, in 1 Thess 5:18, St Paul gives this succinct injunction: 'pray continually.' Over the centuries there have been many ways of interpreting these verses.

a) The liturgy of the heart
The Holy Trinity dwells in our hearts in virtue of our baptism. As a result the Spirit constantly prays 'Abba Father' (Rom 8:15; Gal 4:6) within us whether we are consciously aware of that prayer or not. This is implied in Rom 8:26-27 when it says: 'In the same way, the Spirit helps us in our weakness. We do not know what we ought to pray for, but the Spirit himself intercedes for us with groans that words cannot express. And he who searches our hearts knows the mind of the Spirit, because the Spirit intercedes for the saints in accordance with God's will.' St Patrick bore witness to the praying voice of the Spirit within. Paradoxically, this realisation first came to him when he was asleep. 'On another occasion,' he wrote in his *Confessions*, 'I saw a person praying in me. I was as it seemed inside my body and I heard him over me, that is, over the inner man. There he was praying with great emotion. At this time I was puzzled as I wondered greatly who could possibly be praying inside me. He spoke, however, at the end of the prayer, saying that he was the Spirit. When I awoke I recalled the words of the apostle in Rom 8:26.'[1]

b) Prayer as action

There is a well known saying, *contemplata aliis tradere*, i.e. contemplation crosses over into action. This is particularly true when we make a sincere morning offering of the thoughts, words and actions of the day with this intention in mind. As a result *laborare est orare*, i.e. to work is to pray. As Origen wrote: 'He "prays without ceasing" who unites prayer to works and good works to prayer. Only in this way can we consider as realisable the principle of praying without ceasing.'[2] St Basil echoed this sentiment when he said: 'This is how to pray continually – not by offering prayer in words, but by joining yourself to God through your whole way of life, so that your life becomes one continuous and uninterrupted prayer.'[3]

c) Prayer as desire

St Augustine said 'the whole life of a good Christian is a holy desire.'[4]. In other words, spirituality and prayer are fundamentally the expression of a spiritual desire to know and to love God. During our prayer times we may acknowledge, deepen and express that desire in a conscious way. But even when we are not thinking about it, such a desire can unconsciously inform everything we do in our everyday lives, thereby making us ready to receive God's self revelation and guidance. Understood in this way, heartfelt desire whether conscious or unconscious is a form of continuous prayer. As St Augustine wrote: 'For desire never ceases to pray even though the tongue be silent. If ever desiring, then ever praying' (Sermon 80, 7). According to Mary Ann Fatula, St Thomas Aquinas discovered that 'praying always' was as easy as breathing.[5] It is simply desire and our whole life is motivated by implicit and explicit desires. Thomas wrote: 'In prayer we simply express our desires to God. When I desire something, I ask for it by praying. We pray, therefore, simply by asking suitable things from God.'[6] It would seem that the kind of prayerful desire mentioned by Sts Augustine and Thomas, is rooted in an awareness of what has been variously referred to as the sting of contingency, creature feeling and the feeling of absolute dependence. It articulates itself in the conscious acknowledgement of different forms of poverty whether material, psychological, or spiritual which are the birthplace of transcendental desire for God.

d) Prayer as love

The Christian life is essentially a loving response to the love of God. So to coin a phrase, to love is to pray and to pray is to love. The *Catechism of the Catholic Church* says: 'Against our dullness and laziness, the battle of prayer is that of humble, trusting, and persevering love. This love opens our hearts to three enlightening and life-giving facts about prayer ... prayer is a vital necessity ... prayer and Christian life are inseparable ... and it is always possible to pray' (2742).

There is merit in all of these points. From an exegetical point of view, however, the more down-to-earth, non-mystical notion of persistence in petitionary prayer seems to be the best interpretation. Jesus illustrated what he meant by such perseverance in two of his parables. Firstly there is the story of the friend who comes at midnight and continues to ask for bread until the householder gives it to him (Lk 11:5-9). Secondly there is the account of the importunate widow who keeps pestering the unjust judge who eventually gives her what she wants in order to get her off his back (Lk 18:2-9). So Jesus is saying, keep on asking and you shall receive. St Thomas's linking of the prayer of desire and petitionary prayer is the closest to the scriptural understanding of persistent prayer.

Nevertheless, over the past few years I have discovered that Western and Eastern spirituality have interpreted the relevant scripture texts in a broader, more literal way and asked the question, 'how can a person pray continuously?' I want to focus on a few well known answers, ancient and modern.

John Cassian on recollection in prayer

In his youth John Cassian (c. 360-433) had experience of monastic life in Palestine and Egypt. After spending some time in Constantinople and Rome, he moved to Gaul and began founding monasteries in 415 AD. In order to instruct the new members of his communities he gave a number of conferences on the spirituality of the desert fathers. In one of these, *Conference Ten on Prayer*, he tackled the question, how does one pray without ceasing? 'He prays too little,' he says, 'who only prays when he is on his knees. But he never prays, who while on his knees is in his heart roaming far afield.'[7]

He said that in the East the monks had discovered an effective way of praying always. They had a prayer formula or mantra which 'was given to us by a few of the oldest fathers ... They did not communicate it except to a few who were thirsty for the true way.' Apparently, the older monks thought that the entire spirituality of the bible, whether that of the Old or New Testament, could be encapsulated in one verse. 'To maintain unceasing awareness of God,' says John, 'keep this verse ever in mind: "O God, come to my assistance, O Lord, make haste to help me." (Ps 70:1). This verse has rightly been selected from the whole bible for this purpose. It fits every mood, every temptation, every circumstance. It contains a call for divine help, a humble confession of faith, a meditation upon human weakness, a confidence in God's answer, an assurance of his on-going support.'

He then goes on to show by a series of practical examples how this verse can be invoked at different times, e.g. when you can't sleep during the night; when you can't keep awake during prayer; when you are troubled by impure thoughts; when you are feeling conceited about some success; when you are worried about some future event, etc. He says that prayerful repetition of the verse 'will be a saving formula in your heart, will guard you from the attack of demons, will cleanse you of the stains of earthly life, lead you to contemplate the unseen things of heaven, and carry you up to the highest forms of prayer which very few have experienced.'

Later he says that it is better not to think about the verse or ponder its possible meaning. If perchance the mind wanders – as it often will – it is important to gently bring it back to the reverent recitation of the verse. 'This formula,' he says, 'the mind should go on grasping until it can cast away the wealth and multiplicity of other thoughts and restrict itself to the poverty of this single verse.' In this way one becomes poor in spirit. 'Such a one truly confesses himself the beggar of the Lord, like the psalmist who said, "I am a beggar and a poor man: God himself helps me" (Ps 40:17).' If one invokes the verse hundreds of times during the day, it seems to penetrate the unconscious mind so that it becomes second nature to recite it. In that sense one is praying ceaselessly even when engaged with practical, everyday tasks.

Although Cassian favours a conceptless, imageless relationship with the incomprehensible mystery of God, he does encourage people to engage in scriptural prayer. He says that the faithful recitation of the verse from Ps 70:1 prepares the mind to penetrate the spiritual meaning of scripture. As a result: 'There are times when a person understands God's scriptures with the clarity with which a surgeon understands the body when he opens up the marrow and the veins. These are the times when our experience seems to reveal the meaning before we understand it intellectually.' Then he goes on to say that the verse, 'O God, come to my assistance, O Lord, make haste to help me' sums up whatever insight one might have gleaned as a result.

Sometime later he asserts that as a result of this kind of prayer, 'The mind shall attain that purest of pure prayers: the prayer which looks to see no visual image, uses no concepts or words ... the mind is rapt upward; and devoid of the aid of the senses or of anything visible or material, pours forth its prayer to God with groanings and sighs that cannot be uttered. This explains the system of spiritual discipline,' he concludes, 'there can be nothing more sublime than to fold the recollection of God into the little space of meditation upon a single verse, to summarise all the prayerful feelings in one sentence.'

The Cloud of Unknowing

The prayer of recollection which originated in the East and was introduced to the West by Cassian, has been maintained and developed throughout European history. For example, in his medieval classic, *The Cloud of Unknowing*, the anonymous author describes another version of the prayer of recollection. He begins by saying, 'Anyone who expects to advance without having meditated often on his own sinfulness, the passion of Christ, and the kindness, goodness and dignity of God, will most certainly go astray and fail in its purpose.' Then he goes on to state: 'But a person who has long pondered these things must eventually leave them behind beneath a cloud of forgetting if he hopes to pierce the cloud of unknowing that lies between him and God. So whenever you feel drawn by grace to the contemplative work and are determined to do it, simply raise your heart to God with a gentle stirring of love. Think only of God, the God who created you, redeemed you, and guided you to this work. Allow no other ideas about God to enter your mind. Yet even this is too much. A naked intent toward God, the desire for him alone, is enough.'[8]

The unknown author – possibly Walter Hilton who died in 1396 – continues by describing in a succinct and enlightening way how this kind of prayer can be fostered by using a one word mantra. 'If you want to gather all your desire into one simple word that the mind can easily retain, choose a short word rather than a long one. A one syllable word such as 'God' or 'love' is best. But choose one that is meaningful to you. Then fix it in your mind so that it will remain there come what may. This word will be your defence in conflict and in peace. Use it to beat off the cloud of darkness above you and to subdue all distractions, consigning them to the cloud of forgetting beneath you. Should some thought go on annoying you demanding to know what you are doing, answer with the one word alone. If your mind begins to intellectualise over the meaning and connotations of this little word, remind yourself that its value lies in its simplicity. Do this and I assure you these thoughts will vanish. Why? Because you have refused to develop them with arguing.'[9] As a person gets to be proficient in this form of *apophatic* prayer, the chosen word, which encapsulates all one feels and knows about God, will begin to pray itself within the person's spirit in an unceasing way.

The Way of the Pilgrim

Perhaps the most interesting Eastern discussion of how to pray without ceasing is to be found in the anonymous book entitled, *The Way of the Pilgrim,* which was published in 1884.[10] It describes the spiritual search of a man in nineteenth-century Russia, who wanted to discover how he could carry out the scriptural injunction to pray always. He went on a spiritual pilgrimage, asking different people if they had a solution to his dilemma. At first he sought in vain; no one had an answer to his question. Then eventually he met a wise old monk. He said to him: 'Be so kind, Revered Father, as to show me what prayer without ceasing means and how it is learnt. I see you know about all these things.' The monk proceeded to teach him about the Jesus prayer. 'The continuous interior Prayer of Jesus is a constant uninterrupted calling upon the divine name of Jesus with the lips, in the spirit, in the heart; while forming a mental picture of his constant presence, and imploring his grace, during every occupation, at all times, in all places, even during sleep. The request is expressed in these terms, "Lord Jesus Christ, have mercy on me." One who accustoms himself to this appeal, experiences as a result so deep a consolation and so great a need to offer prayer always, that he can no longer live without it, and it will continue to voice itself within him of its own accord. Now do you understand what prayer without ceasing is?' 'Yes indeed, Father, and in God's name teach me how to gain the habit of it,' I cried, filled with joy.'

The monk then went on to teach him how to make this kind of prayer by quoting relevant passages from the *Philokalia*. For example, he adverted to a passage in a section by St Simeon the New Theologian who wrote: 'Sit down alone and in silence. Lower your head, shut your eyes, breathe out gently and imagine yourself looking into your own heart. As you breathe out, say "Lord Jesus Christ, have mercy on me." Try to put all other thoughts aside. Be calm, be patient, and repeat the process very frequently.'

The pilgrim went on to describe how his spiritual director instructed him to say the Jesus Prayer 6,000 times a day for the first week. This he did. When he reported to his director, he instructed him to go on to say 12,000 invocations a day, even if it meant getting up earlier and going to bed at a later time. Although he found it hard to do at first, he says that after five days he was saying the prayer 12,000 times daily, 'as I formed the habit I found at the same time pleasure and satisfaction in it'. At this point his director told the pilgrim to say the prayer constantly: 'Try to devote every moment you are awake to the prayer, call on the name of Jesus Christ without counting the number of times, and submit yourself humbly to the will of God, looking to him for help. I am sure he will not forsake you, and that he will lead you into the right path.' He says that later that summer he bought a copy of the *Philokalia* and carried it with him together with a copy of the bible. His final comment? 'And that is how I go about now, and ceaselessly repeat the Prayer of Jesus, which is more precious and sweet to me than anything in the world.'

A Modern Version

The prayer of recollection mentioned by Cassian and the anonymous author of *The Cloud of Unknowing* has been revived in our time, e.g. Thomas Keating's *Centering Prayer*. He describes his method as follows.

1. Choose a sacred word as the symbol of your intention to open and yield to God's presence and action within. The sacred word could be one of the names of God or a word that you feel comfortable with, e.g. presence, silence, peace, stillness, oneness.

2. Sitting comfortably and with eyes closed, settle briefly and silently. Introduce the sacred word as the symbol of your consent to God's presence and action within.

3. When you become aware of thoughts, return ever so gently to the sacred word. This is the only activity you initiate once the period of centring prayer has begun.

4. The term *thoughts* includes any perception at all, e.g. sense perceptions, feelings, images, memories, reflections, and commentaries. During the prayer time, avoid analysing your experience, harbouring expectations, or aiming at some specific goal, such as having no thoughts, making the mind a blank, feeling peaceful or consoled, repeating the sacred word continuously, or achieving a spiritual experience.

5. At the end of the prayer time, remain in silence with the eyes closed for a couple of minutes. This gives the psyche a brief space to readjust to the external senses and a better chance of

bringing the atmosphere of interior silence into the activities of daily life.[11]

It is recommended that a person would use this prayer exercise for twenty minutes, if possible, every morning and evening.

Praying in tongues and unceasing prayer

It is probable that some of the practitioners of centring prayer are unfamiliar with the gift of tongues. Indeed, many of those who have written about this gift, notably Morton Kelsey,[12] have failed to notice that there are many similarities between the two forms of praying. For example, just as centring prayer bypasses mind and imagination, so does the gift of tongues. Having stated that he prayed in tongues more than anyone (1 Cor 14:18) and that he would like everyone to have this, the least of the gifts (1 Cor 14:5), St Paul said in 1 Cor 14:2; 14 that those who pray in a tongue, 'do not speak to other people but to God; for nobody understands them, since they are speaking mysteries in the Spirit ... if I pray in a tongue my spirit prays but *my mind is unproductive.*' In Rom 8:27 he added: 'and God who searches the heart, knows what is the mind of the Spirit, because the Spirit prays ... according to the will of God.'

The charism of tongues, therefore, is a form of pre-rational, non-conceptual prayer of the *apophatic*, contemplative kind in so far as the human spirit prayerfully focuses its attention on God without the aid of thought or image. Eddie Ensley has indicated that throughout the ages non-conceptual prayer has been an aspect of Catholic piety in the form of jubilation. The English word is derived from the Latin *jubilatio*, meaning 'loud shouting or whooping'. He says that there were different types. Firstly, there was musical jubilation in the form of wordless singing, either personal or congregational in a liturgical setting. St Augustine described it as follows: 'What is jubilation? It means to realise that words are not enough to express what we are singing in our hearts... Joy brims over and... people give themselves up to the sheer sound of singing.'[13] For example, Thomas of Celano described how the people jubilated at the canonisation of Francis of Assisi in 1228. When the Pope had declared that Francis was enrolled among the saints he invoked the

Te Deum in a loud voice. 'Then there was raised a clamour among the many people praising God: the earth resounded with their mighty voices, the air was filled with their jubilations, and the ground was moistened with their tears. New songs were sung, and the servants of God jubilated in melody of the Spirit.'[14] Secondly, there was mystical jubilation which was a flow of wordless musical sounds, often accompanied by the laughter and gestures that accompany intense spiritual experience. Richard Rolle (1300-1349), an English mystic, described how he experienced this kind of prayer. 'Whilst I sat in the chapel at night, before supper, I sang psalms, as I might, and I heard above me the noise as it were of singers. Whilst I took heed, praying to heaven with all desire, in what manner I know not, suddenly I received a most pleasant heavenly melody dwelling within my mind. Indeed my thought was continuously changed into mirth of song.'[15]

Commenting on these non-conceptual forms of *glossolalia*, and by extension *jubilatio*, Cardinal Suenens wrote: 'praying in tongues is in relation to discursive prayer as is abstract art to figurative art.'[16] Those who regularly pray and sing in tongues know that this spiritual activity can take a number of forms such as heartfelt intercession, loud and enthusiastic praise, and quiet, reverential worship. Inevitably, when charismatic activity faded in the first three centuries, people like Cassian, and later the Hesychasts, who advocated the Jesus Prayer, had to resort to the repetitive use of a mantra in order to pray in an imageless, conceptless way. But nowadays, with the contemporary revival of the charisms, a growing number of people have an opportunity of praying in an *apophatic* way that is truly scriptural. It should be said that those who pray in tongues can easily identify two forms. In the first, one's mouth and spirit are praying, while one's mind is occupied with religious or mundane thoughts. In the second, one's mouth and spirit pray while one's mind is at rest.

Cassian argued that as a result of repeating a mantra, people could sense the ever praying voice of the Spirit within them. Those who pray in tongues have a similar kind of experience. St Isaac the Syrian wrote in the seventh century: 'When the Spirit makes its dwelling in people it does not cease to pray, because the Spirit will pray constantly in them ... When they eat or drink, when they do any work or are even immersed in sleep, the perfumes of prayer will breathe spontaneously in their hearts.'[17] Scripture scholar George Montague testifies to the truth of Isaac's statement when he says that, if he yields to the gift of praying in tongues, 'I become ever more conscious that I have stepped into a stream that was flowing long before I even approached the bank, and that as I enter the water, I am carried by a power other than my own.'[18] In other words, the gift of tongues enables one to become consciously aware of the fact that the Spirit prays within with 'sighs too deep for words' (Rom 8:26). In modern parlance it could be said that prayer in tongues is experienced as something that gratuitously emanates from the depths of the personality, i.e. from the human spirit via the unconscious mind. This explains why a person can pray in the Spirit while thinking mundane thoughts. The recognition of two simultaneous levels of interior activity, one spiritual which is expressed in the form of tongues, and the other psychic expressed in the form of thoughts and images, reveals the fact that an underground river of grace and prayer is forever flowing in the depths of people who are living in the Spirit, even when they are not consciously aware of it, e.g. when asleep. In general terms it could be argued that when scripture says: 'Awake, O sleeper' (Eph 5:14), it is a call to become consciously aware of the praying voice of the Spirit within. Understood in that sense, it is a vocation to an on-going spiritual awakening. As Andre Louf has written: 'Each and every method of prayer has but one objective: to find the heart and alert it (cf. Mt 26:41; Mk 13:33).'[19]

Cassian also states that by using a mantra the person is prepared to read the scriptures with spiritual insight. As was noted earlier in this chapter, his or her mind, like a surgeon's scalpel is enabled to cut to the most intimate meaning of God's word. Likewise, those who use the gift of praying in tongues have a similar experience. The charism ploughs the soil of the heart, making it ready to receive the seed of a revelatory word and the nourishing water of the Spirit. One is reminded here of the two kinds of prophetic experience in the Old Testament, ecstatic and classical. The earlier prophets, i.e. the *nabi*, experienced a prophetic ecstasy in the divine presence without any apparent conceptual or verbal content. For example, in 1 Sam 19:20 we read: 'they saw the community of prophets proph-esying, and Samuel there as their leader, the spirit of God came over Saul's agents, and they too fell into a frenzy.' Later in the Old Testament, the prophets could express in words what had first been revealed in a non-conceptual way to their spirits. As George Montague observes: 'In Old Testament prophecy the pendulum swings between the ecstatic, non-rational, pre-conceptual element and the intelligible, rational, spoken word. But in either case prophecy is essentially a gift of inspiration.'[20]

Having prayed in tongues, divine inspirations can come to con-temporary Christians in ordinary and extraordinary ways such as inspiring words of scripture (cf. Heb 4:12-13), prophetic messages (cf. 1 Cor 14:24-25), visions (cf. Joel 3:1), religious dreams (cf. Job 33:15), words of knowledge (cf. 1 Cor 12:8), Spirit prompted intu-itions (cf. Gal 5:16), etc. Cassian had stated that no matter what insights were gleaned from the *Lectio Divina* they could be encapsu-lated in the words, 'O God, come to my assistance, O Lord, make haste to help me.' Similarly, anyone who prays in tongues will find that whatever inspiration he or she receives can be expressed by praying, firstly, with rational understanding, and secondly, in a non-conceptual way by means of tongues. As a result there is a reci-procal relationship between non-conceptual and conceptual forms of prayer. Together, however, they can enable a person to pray always either consciously or unconsciously in the Spirit.

Conclusion
Evagrius Ponticus (346-399) stated: 'We have not been commanded to work, to keep watch and to fast constantly, but it has been laid down that we are to pray without ceasing.' We have seen that from a scriptural point of view the injunction to pray always can be understood in two ways, as perseverance in petitionary prayer, and prayer in tongues, i.e. prayer in the Spirit (Jude 1:20). As for the other interpretations, instead of contradicting one another, it is arguable that the different approaches are complementary.

CHAPTER 6

New Age Spirituality

It is hard to say when the New Age Movement originated. It could be argued that it became popular in the swinging sixties when flower power and hippie culture were at their height. At that time many people were interested in altered states of consciousness. Indeed, Professor Timothy Leary advocated the taking of psycho-active drugs, like LSD, in order to achieve new states of awareness. Some thirty years later, New Age spirituality is exerting more and more influence in Western culture. It is hard to describe because it has no fixed creed and no identifiable organisation. John Drane is correct when he says in his *What is the New Age Saying to the Church?*: 'Understanding the New Age is like trying to wrestle with a jelly. As soon as you think you have got it under control, the shape of the whole thing changes and you have to start again.'[1]

The name, New Age, has an astrological origin. According to its devotees we are leaving the age of Pisces, i.e. the Christian age, which has been characterised by a lot of violence, and are about to enter the Age of Aquarius. It will be an age of peace, harmony, wholeness and restoration. George Trevelyan, founder of the Wrekin Trust, captured something of the spirit of the New Age when he wrote: 'We face a time of change. That no one can deny. It implies breakdown and break-up of much we know, but it also implies breakthrough … The huge hope for our time is that the ocean of power and divine intelligence has actually launched an operation for the cleansing of our planet. This seems to me to be implicit in the holistic worldview. Not only is the planet a living creature of which we humans are integrally part, but the macro-system of the solar system is a Living Organic Oneness.' In this chapter we will look at some aspects of this complex subject, while noting the challenges and dangers it poses as far as orthodox forms of Christianity are concerned.

In recent centuries there has been an increasing masculinisation of culture. It was prompted by the Reformation that desacralised the world, by the rise of Western science, which studied the world in a detached, objective way, and by capitalism, which ruthlessly exploited nature by means of its new technologies. This rationalistic, materialistic process tended to sever the umbilical cord of belonging that connected people to the unity and meaning of the world. They learned to relate to the world almost entirely in terms of the left side of the brain, which favours rational analytical thought. The right side, which views things in an intuitive, affective, more holistic way, was ignored to a greater or lesser extent. This has tended to lead to a sense of absurdity, alienation, anxiety, apathy, agnosticism and even atheism. For more on this, see the following chapter. Not surprisingly, therefore, there has been a growing spiritual crisis in Western culture. Many people have left the institutional churches. Those who remain have often to put up with a rather rationalistic and unattractive version of Christianity.

New Age spirituality is a response to this cultural and spiritual crisis. It is trying to fill the vacuum in people's lives. It is opposed to two things, materialistic humanism and Judeo-Christianity. New Agers draw on a bewildering number of sources, e.g. quantum physics, astrology, Celtic druidism, alchemy, spiritualism, Eastern religions, the occult, native American religion, witchcraft and animism. It is also influenced by the writings of people like Jacob Boehme, a Protestant mystic, who had an interest in the occult; Emmanuel Swedenborg, a visionary with an interest in psychic phenomena; William Blake, an eccentric Catholic mystic who created his own mythology; Carl Jung a psychologist who was interested in dreams, alchemy and Gnostic beliefs; Joseph Campbell who explored the meaning and implications of mythology; American Transcendentalists such as Thoreau and Emerson; Madame Blavatsky, one of the founders of Theosophy; James Lovelock, originator of Gaia – the hypothesis that the planet is a living self-regulating system – Abraham Maslow, a humanistic psychologist who had an interest in Being-cognition and natural mysticism; and Ken Wilber who is interested in transpersonal psychology which studies the characteristics and dynamics of higher levels of spiritual awareness. Clearly, New Age spirituality is made up of the 'sweepings of the ages'. It has created a new, churchless religion. Although it is hard to define in any exact way, some general observations can be made about it.

Some New Age beliefs

Devotees of the New Age believe that there is an underlying unity in creation. The cosmos is a manifestation of impersonal energy which is active in both nature and human consciousness. Original sin is interpreted in developmental terms as a breakdown of that primordial sense of unity. The first stage of human evolution was characterised by what is called 'oceanic feeling', i.e. a pre-reflective sense of oneness with God and nature. But in the second stage people became reflective and developed a sense of individuality which alienated them from nature and God. Not surprisingly, New Agers see salvation in terms of restoring the original awareness of unity. Awakened, at last, from the long sleep of alienating ignorance, they will find that they possess divine attributes, and come to see the world around them holistically, not dualistically. In this way they will overcome the pernicious division between spirit and matter, self and cosmos, God and nature. As Marilyn Ferguson, author of *The Aquarian Conspiracy*, has observed: 'the mystical experience of wholeness encompasses all separation'. It is worth noting the fact that New Agers maintain that many of the world's problems are exacerbated by the institutional churches because they insist on a separation between God and humanity.

New Age spirituality is pantheistic. God is energy, and permeates all of the natural world. This partly explains why New Agers have such a concern for the environment and green issues. They believe that as the human body and soul form one single being, so God and the universe form one single being also. Russell Ackoff has pointed out that from a New Age point of view: 'God-as-the-whole cannot be individualised or personified, and cannot be thought of as the creator.' Those who are familiar with Hegel's philosophy, especially on the subject of absolute spirit, will recognise that New Age spirituality seems to have affinities with his thought. Human awareness of the interconnectedness of all things is God knowing the God-self in and through the higher levels of human consciousness. Awakened from the long sleep of ignorance, New Agers find that they possess the divine attributes, and come to see the world in a holistic way thereby overcoming the pernicious split between matter and spirit, the spirit and the self, the self and God. As a result it could be said that growth in these transpersonal levels of mystical consciousness is the actualisation of the divine potential implicit in all that exists.

New Agers would argue that in the light of the two preceding points it is important that humanity should undergo a transformation of consciousness. New Age spirituality believes that humans overcome the alienation, referred to by Ken Wilber, by achieving higher states of awareness. This is the overall aim of the wide range of techniques and therapies which are used as part of New Age spirituality. They are used with the intention of enabling people to get in touch with their higher selves, i.e. the God-self that connects them to all that exists. New Agers believe that if this is done successfully by enough people, the whole of humanity will undergo a paradigm shift as it moves on to a new level of evolutionary consciousness. This is a key to New Age spirituality. Perfection lies in higher levels of awareness rather than in ethical conversion. By and large, it's moral teaching is undemanding and subjectivist. Some of those who favour New Age thinking would even go as far as to say that victims of any kind, e.g. of South African apartheid or the Nazi holocaust, suffer as a result of their own choices and spiritual *karma*. In other words, the victim is ultimately responsible for his or her own victimisation. On the other hand, New Agers believe that changed consciousness can lead to personal, social, political and even cosmic transformation.

New Agers tend to have a strong belief in reincarnation. They maintain that it is underpinned in a number of scientific ways. They point to such things as near-death and out-of-the-body experiences as evidence. They also refer to the fact that hypnotised people, or those who have taken mind altering drugs, claim to have accessed the cosmic memory banks and to have recalled former lives. As a result, New Agers are not too worried about ethical issues such as abortion or euthanasia. They believe that the souls of the dead will be re-embodied in the future when they will have another opportunity to develop their consciousness.

Some New Age practices

Crystals as focal points of energy. New Agers generally believe that there is an energy field running through and permeating everything from rocks to people. Crystals act as transformers of energy. For example, sickness in the body is a reflection of dis-ease in the body, and healing takes place when harmony is restored through the use of an appropriate crystal and perhaps some visualisation techniques.

Contact with spirits by means of channelling. This notion was borrowed from spiritualism. New Agers consult mediums who are able to get in touch with spirit guides, e.g. they believe that Ramtha, a 35,000-year-old warrior from the lost city of Atlantis, speaks through a woman from Oregon called Knight. Some New Agers claim that they are able to tune in to their own spirit guides. This belief is akin to the Christian belief in guardian angels.

The journey inwards. All kinds of methods are used with this end in view such as Tai Chi, rebirthing, healing the inner child, the Enneagram, etc. New Age spirituality also advocates the use of meditation techniques such as yoga and transcendental meditation in order to get in touch with the God-self. As Marilyn Ferguson says: 'The myth of the Saviour out there is being replaced with the myth of the hero "in here". Its ultimate expression is the discovery of the divinity within us.'

Some characteristics of New Age spirituality

It is eclectic. It picks and chooses whatever beliefs, therapies and techniques, including aspects of Christianity, which suit its purpose. It is not committed to any particular set of religious beliefs. As Stephen Denning of the Religious Studies department of the

University of Pennsylvania has observed, the New Age is similar to catalogue shopping. Customers choose the spiritual and emotional goodies which will meet their needs.

It is syncretistic. New Age spirituality mixes elements from different systems of belief, Christian, scientific, Eastern, Jewish, Gnostic, philosophical, esoteric, etc., into a new kind of synthesis. While it can reverence Jesus as a God-intoxicated man, it cannot acknowledge him as the definitive revelation of the character of God. In the words of Kenneth Walpnick, 'he is one of God's helpers'.

It is gnostic. The early gnostics taught the redemption of the spirit from matter by means of spiritual knowledge and believed creation to be a process of emanation from the original essence or godhead. This heresy was strong at the time of the Early Church. Like its predecessor, New Age spirituality also puts a lot of emphasis on reaching higher forms of consciousness of a quasi-mystical kind. One of the reasons why Carl Jung, Joseph Campbell and Ken Wilber are so popular with New Agers is the fact that there are distinctly gnostic elements in their writings.

It is pelagian. Pelagius was a fifth century British Christian who effectively denied the doctrine of original sin and taught that people were intrinsically good. He believed that they could grow in holiness by means of their own unaided efforts. This same belief permeates the whole of New Age spirituality. As John Drane observes: 'The New age has no place for sin.'

It is anti-authoritarian and subjectivist. New Age spirituality is slow to accept any external form of divine or human authority. As the late Petra Kelly, a founder of the German Green party, wrote: 'I do not need an authoritarian male institution to help me to look for my own inner truth or search for gods or goddesses of cosmic energy and love-light.'[3] Because of its anti-rational bias and its emphasis on inner states of consciousness, New Age spirituality has a tendency to be relativist.

Implications of New Age spirituality for the church
It would seem that New Agers are correct in their rejection of mate-

rialism and their search for a new spirituality. They point to the importance of such things as personal experience, holism, respect for nature, meditation, healing, etc. However, New Age spirituality is not Christian. Indeed, many of its beliefs and practices are positively anti-Christian. But I believe that at a time when many people are disillusioned with the Christian church for one reason or another, an increasing number of them will be attracted by New Age spirituality. Just as gnosticism posed a formidable threat to the early church, so this modern version will do the same. It is important to see it for what it is, a neo-pagan spirituality, which rejects Christian revelation, and is located somewhere between pantheism and naturalism on the religious spectrum.

It could be argued that New Age spirituality, like a latter day Trojan horse, has been surreptitiously introduced into the church. Nowadays, many practising and non-practising Christians attend courses on New Age topics and use New Age techniques. Consciously or unconsciously, some of them seem to be subscribing to its gnostic worldview. Theologians and church leaders need to identify the theological and ethical implications of this new spirituality. They need to challenge its rejection of the Christian doctrines of creation, redemption and ethical discipleship. However, Christians also need to avoid a fundamentalist, *a priori* rejection of every idea and practice associated with New Age spirituality. For example, if a nurse uses aromatherapy, yoga, reflexology, or mood music in order to relax a stressed person, there is nothing necessarily wrong with her doing so. Many of these techniques are neutral in themselves and have to be evaluated in terms of the more general belief systems, Christian or New Age, that inform their use. Besides critiquing New Age spirituality, the contemporary church, like that of an earlier era, needs to learn from this influential form of gnosticism. It needs to discern what is good in this modern movement and to integrate its best insights and practices within a Christian framework.

Today's Christians need to renew and adapt their spirituality in order to meet the emerging needs of the quantum age in which we live. It could then act as a relevant and attractive alternative to New

Age spirituality. Kenneth Leach has written: 'A renewed Christian spirituality will be concerned with the recovery of the vision of God in the contemporary world. It will seek to speak of God and of the deep things of the spirit in ways which are meaningful in the present climate. It will seek, humbly and carefully, to take account of the insights presented by depth psychology, and by the secular quest for enriched consciousness, while seeking also to remain faithful to the Christian spiritual tradition.'[4] Such a spirituality could draw relevant ideas and practices from the treasury of Christian tradition, especially the teachings of Eastern and Western mystics, e.g. Cassian's use of mantras, Francis's love of nature, Nicholas of Cusa's notion of the coincidence of opposites, and Gregory of Palamas's emphasis on the energies of God. Christian pneumatology, with its emphasis on subjectivity and experience, could also have an important contribution to make. Arguably, the contemporary Charismatic Renewal is a form of orthodox Christian gnosticism in so far as it highlights such things as the activity of the Holy Spirit in inner illumination and divine guidance (cf. 1 Cor 9-16; Gal 5:25), together with the role of pre-rational charisms like tongues, visions, prophecy and healing, in everyday Christian life (cf. 1 Cor 12:8-10).

CHAPTER 7

Creation Spirituality

The subject of creation spirituality is a large one. Like some other chapters, this one doesn't try to offer a comprehensive overview. Rather it aims to concentrate, rather arbitrarily and briefly, on two points. Firstly, it examines how a right brained, intuitive outlook enables a person to have the kind of unitary worldview that mediates an awareness of God. Secondly, it will examine two different understandings of original sin or the fall.

From the Greeks onwards, there seem to have been two complementary ways of looking at the material world. One was static and essentialist in nature and stressed the primacy of being. Parmenides and Aristotle advocated this point of view. The other was dynamic and existentialist and stressed the primacy of becoming. Heraclitus was the outstanding advocate of this perspective. It tended to see everything that existed as interconnected parts in an integrated world which was governed by God-given affinities. The Pythagoreans talked of the harmony of the spheres, and the Hippocratics maintained that 'there is one common flow, one common breathing, all things are in sympathy.'

These two points of view remained in tandem in Christian Europe in the form of the medieval synthesis of philosophy, science and theology. Surely they found their most concrete expression in the life of Francis of Assisi who reverenced creation by acknowledging his kinship with animate and inanimate things. As late as 1550 Pico Mirandola could write in a rather Franciscan spirit: 'Firstly, there is the unity in things whereby each thing is at one with itself, consists of itself, and coheres with itself. Secondly, there is the unity whereby one creature is united with others and all parts of the world constitute one world.' This quotation holds together the notion that every creature asserts its own separate identity while transcending itself by means of its integrative tendencies.

Celtic Spirituality

It is worth noting that this unitary worldview was reflected in Celtic spirituality. A number of years ago, John Macquarrie wrote a couple of memorable paragraphs which are worth quoting at his point in a slightly edited form.

> Although Celtic spirituality belongs to a culture that has almost vanished it fulfils in many respects the conditions to which a contemporary spirituality would have to conform. At the very centre of this type of spirituality was an intense sense of presence. The Celt was very much a God-intoxicated person whose life was embraced on all sides by the divine Being. But this presence was always mediated through some finite this-worldly reality, so that it would be difficult to imagine a spirituality more down to earth than this one.

> The sense of God's immanence in his creation was so strong in Celtic spirituality as to amount sometimes almost to a pantheism ... But perusal of typical Celtic poems and prayers makes it clear that God's presence was even more keenly felt in the daily round of human tasks and at the important junctures of life ... The model for understanding God was the 'High King' but among the Celts the High King was never a remote figure ... The king was always among his people as well as over them. When God is conceived on such a model, he cannot become too distant and likewise his creation cannot become so profane and godless as to arouse the acquisitive and aggressive spirit of irresponsible concupiscence.[1]

This point is illustrated in the *Deer's Cry*, sometimes known as *St Patrick's Breastplate*. There are many medieval poems which unite sacred and secular, God and nature. For example, there is a fragment of four lines which reads:

> Only a fool would fail
> To praise God in his might

When the tiny mindless birds
Praise him in their flight.

Happily there have been echoes of Celtic spirituality in modern
Irish culture. One has only to remember Joseph Mary Plunkett's
christological poem 'I see his blood upon the rose,' to savour what
Macquarrie was talking about. It reads:

I see his blood upon the rose
And in the stars the glory of his eyes,
His body gleams amid the eternal snows'
His tears fall from the skies.

More recently, Patrick Kavanagh expressed the same Celtic vision
where sacred and secular intersect. Writing about local farmers he
observes:

Yet sometimes when the sun comes through a gap
These men know God the Father in a tree:
The Holy Spirit is the rising sap
And Christ will be the green leaves that will come
At Easter from the sealed and guarded tomb.

In general terms, it would be true to say that Celtic spirituality, with
its pantheistic leanings, does not separate sacred and secular. They
are interwoven, one with the other so that nature, in the words of
Gerald Manley Hopkins, is 'charged with the grandeur of God'. At
the moment Western theology recognises and approves of the secularisation and autonomy of creation as an object of human understanding and control. While Celtic spirituality can accept that distinction in theory, it tends to ignore it in practice. Ronald Stuart
Thomas, a Welsh clergyman and poet, has described how he discovered a hare's nest in the grass. He leaned down and felt the
warmth which had been generated by the creature who had been
resting there a short time before. He went on to state in a paradoxical way that creation is warm with the presence of an absent God.
That story encapsulates something of the Celtic outlook.

Breakdown of the unitary worldview
The unitary worldview was shattered by three great historical
movements, the Reformation, the rise of science and the way capi-

talism harnessed the new technologies to exploit nature. One could argue that these movements meant the triumph of right brain activity, i.e. rational, objective thinking, over left brain activity, i.e. intuitive affective thinking, and the victory of the typically detached male outlook over the more relational, feminine one. In spite of their strongly patriarchal tendencies, Catholic and Orthodox forms of Christianity had offset some of the more extreme implications of the male notion of God by incorporating the feminine principle in two ways. Firstly, they encouraged the cult of the Virgin Mary. Secondly, they believed that, just as God had become flesh in the womb of the Blessed Mother, so he is made flesh in the womb of mother nature as well.

However, all that began to change with the Reformation. As H. G. Wells has pointed out, communities of obedience, i.e. stable societies of the South, which stressed the virtues of contemplation, such as Catholicism and Orthodoxy, were challenged by communities of will, i.e. the restless nomads of the North, who stressed the importance of dynamic action, such as Calvinism and to a lesser extent Lutheranism. They focused on the male characteristics of religion and abolished Marian devotion. They maintained that revelation came solely through the word of God, while denying that mother nature could mediate the presence of the Beyond who is in its midst. In this way a masculine notion of revelation predominated over a more feminine one. God could only be mediated to rational consciousness by the conceptual *logos* or word. God could not be mediated in a more feminine way by means of pre-rational religious experiences such as dreams and sacramental symbols. Rupert Sheldrake has indicated how the disenchanted worldview of the reformers was conducive to the emergence of the mechanistic perspectives of the so-called Enlightenment

It was the rise of science in particular that shattered the unitary worldview. Men such as Bacon, Galileo and Newton replaced the medieval conviction that nature was an organism with the notion that it was an inanimate machine. At the same time, Rene Descartes became the father of modern philosophy by articulating the implications of the new worldview. Having adopted a methodology of universal doubt, he came to the conclusion that he could only be sure of one thing. Because he was conscious of being conscious he must therefore exist. As he put it, 'I think, therefore I am.' When he drew out the implications of this basic insight, Descartes began to undermine the intimate connection between mind and body. He wrote: 'I consider the human body as a machine, my thought compares a sick man to an ill made clock and a healthy man to a well made clock.' He also undermined the intimate connection between human beings and the world. With typically male detachment, scientists have aspired ever since to control and subdue mother nature with the Faustian power of objective reason. So by the end of the seventeenth century she had ceased to be feminine at all. Indeed man's conquest of nature is inseparable from sexual imagery. As one feminist writer has noted: 'By re-conceptualising reality as a machine rather than a living organism, science which was conducted by men and which reflected an exclusively male point of view, sanctioned the domination of both nature and women.'[2]

Darwin and Freud reinforced this trend. In his theory of evolution the former maintained that instead of adapting to their environments, as Lamarck had wrongly suggested, the different species were the product of random mutations and blind chance. Jacques Monand, a modern biologist, has given clear expression to this nihilistic point of view: 'Chance alone is at the source of every innovation, of all creation in the biosphere. Pure chance, absolutely free but blind, lies at the root of the stupendous edifice of evolution.'[3] Freud's theory of the influence of the unconscious mind undermined two important beliefs, namely, that humans were rational and that they were free. He indicated how apparently rational choices can be blindly influenced from the unconscious by irrational feelings and attitudes.

For their part, sociologists and historians like Weber and Tawney have shown how capitalism was able to grow and to thrive within the cultural ethos created by the Reformation and the Enlightenment. By desacralising the world of nature and stressing the importance of the work ethic, both movements paved the way for capitalism. Far from feeling scrupulous about their desire to dominate and exploit nature, capitalists saw it as an ideal in a world where nothing was holy. By applying the best technological insights of the new sciences, they learned to master, subdue and exploit the earth's resources. This became increasingly true with the advent of the industrial revolution in the nineteenth century. Not only has it tended to sever the intimate connection between people and nature, it has subordinated people, their relationships and their rights to the abstract and uncaring imperatives of market forces such as profit and loss, supply and demand, etc. Now that we are approaching the twenty-first century, we have to cope with the consequences of this form of unfettered exploitation. Not only are we facing an environmental and ecological crisis of dangerous proportions, we human beings are in trouble too. As we continue to endure the unacceptable face of capitalism, the gap between rich and poor continues to widen. In the words of Wordsworth, 'The world is too much with us; late and soon, getting and spending, we lay waste our powers.'4

Some consequences of the breakdown
As was noted already in chapter two, the word religion comes from the Latin *religiare* and it means to bind or to connect. As a result of the Reformation, science and unfettered capitalism, the umbilical cord that connected us to the realm of created and uncreated meaning has been severed with negative knock-on effects. I'd suggest that there are seven A's, those of absurdity, alienation, anxiety, anomie, apathy, agnosticism and atheism. We will take a brief look at each.

Newtonian science and Cartesian philosophy have tended to set human beings adrift in an alien world devoid of any ultimate meaning. This has given rise to the post-modern, nihilistic belief that despite all appearances to the contrary, reality is ultimately absurd. Novelist Andre Malraux has one of his characters say: 'In the depths of European man, where it dominates the great moments of his life, there resides an essential absurdity.'5 In the 60s many young adults shared that sense of meaninglessness. They found that it was reflected in works like Sartre's *Nausea*, Camus's *The*

Outsider, Beckett's *Waiting for Godot*, Kafka's *The Castle*, nearly all of Bergman's films and the apparently formless and anarchic nature of a lot of modern music and pictorial art. George Steiner has argued that the loss of a sense of ultimate meaning, in contemporary culture, has led to a form of art that is incapable of the magnanimity and sublimity which was clearly evident in Michelangelo's pictorial art, the poetry of Dante and the music of Beethoven. He quotes with approval an observation of W. B. Yeats: 'No man can create as did Shakespeare, Homer or Sophocles, who does not believe with all his blood and nerve, that man's soul is immortal.'[6]

Not surprisingly, the extent to which people lose touch with a sense of meaning, is the extent to which they will suffer from a sense of alienation. Psychologist Karen Horney described it as: 'the remoteness of the neurotic from his own feelings, wishes, beliefs, and energies. It is the loss of the feeling of being an active, determining force in his own life.'[7] Erich Fromm has written: 'Alienation as we find it in modern society is almost total; it pervades the relationship of man to his work, to the things he consumes, to his fellows, and to himself.'[8] He explains this all-pervading alienation in Marxist terms. People fail to see themselves as the active bearers of their own powers and richness, but rather as impoverished objects dependent on powers outside themselves. Then they project their living substance on to these impersonal things. Fromm shows how this form of estrangement can be reinforced by bureaucracy and consumerism.

As more and more people lose touch with the meaning of life, they experience deep down anxiety which is not necessarily neurotic in nature. In fact this phenomenon has become so widespread that the poet W. H. Auden described the twentieth century as 'the age of anxiety' and in another place says that we live in 'the Kingdom of anxiety.'[9] The word comes from the Latin *angustus* meaning to narrow. It is etymologically related to the words anguish and angina. One would be tempted to believe that as people lose a sense of meaning, their attitude to life becomes more narrow minded and defensive. Their deep down sense of anxiety can lead to psychosomatic disorders such as the widespread incidence of blood pressure and heart disease. Indeed modern medicine confirms the fact that up to 80% of people's illnesses are stress related. They often try to escape from their inner pain by an idolatrous pursuit of power, pleasure and status. As Gerald May has indicated in his book, *Addiction and Grace,* the attempted flight from anxiety can lead to all kinds of addictions and obsessions.

Emile Durkheim has said that alienation and anxiety in modern society can lead to what he calls *anomie*. He uses the word to describe a state of normlessness, the collapse of rules of conduct, the loss of belief and purpose. The concept can be understood in either psychological or social terms. Robert K. Merton has described *anomie* as the: 'breakdown in the cultural structure, occurring particularly when there is an acute disjunction between the cultural norms and goals and the ... capacities of members of the group to act in accord with them.'[10] Such people tend to become apathetic, i.e. indifferent, detached, lacking in genuine passion, feeling or enthusiasm in their responses to life and nature.

In his book, *Love and Will*, Rollo May has suggested that many apathetic people in our culture are schizoid in so far as they are out of touch with life. They avoid close relationships and suffer from an inability to feel deeply about anything. They tend to be cold, detached, and superior in their attitude. 'Apathy and lack of feeling,' May wrote, 'are defence mechanisms against anxiety. When a person is continuously facing dangers he is powerless to overcome, his final line of defence is at last to avoid even feeling the dangers.'[11] It seems to me that the contemporary famine of love, which seems to afflict affluent societies, is going to produce a generation of men and women who suppress their painful feelings of insecurity and deprivation by becoming apathetic. It is my observation that many of the mindless crimes that bedevil modern life are committed by apathetic people who are often ruthless, i.e. without care or empathy for others. For a more comprehensive treatment of this topic see chapter nine.

I have long believed that the crisis of belief in Western societies is due to the masculinisation of culture. By the way, I'm using the words masculine and feminine as metaphors for archetypal characteristics which are culturally conditioned. As the typical powers of the male ego have predominated, people have lost touch with their deeper feminine selves. In so doing, they have lost touch with the archetypal powers of the *anima* and the spiritual self which can only be fulfilled by an awareness of the transcendent Other. God's presence is mediated to the soul – which in our culture is feminine to a male God – by means of intimate relationship with the feminine principle, and through it with the rest of nature. Alienation from the *anima* has been reinforced by the fact that that cultural conditioning has separated many women from their own feminine depths. Indeed Freud said that the aim of successful analysis was a 'repudiation of femininity' in the lives of men and women. The crisis of the feminine is one of the main reasons for the religious crisis of our time. The extent to which men and women lose touch with the feminine archetype, is the extent to which they lose touch with that power of the self, which alone can bind us in an intimate way to one another, to nature, and through both to God. The decline of the feminine, contemplative dimensions of the human psyche leads almost inevitably to the virtual eclipse of God and therefore to agnosticism and even atheism.

Acknowledging God-given affinities
There is reason to believe that the worst effects of exaggerated masculinisation is coming to an end. It is being brought about by a number of modern developments which promise to bring about a paradigm shift, i.e. a fundamental change in perspective. While I intend to describe some of them, like Ken Wilber, I'm not convinced that they are either accurate or helpful.[12] Some of them owe more to new age thinking than to either mainstream science or orthodox forms of Christian theology. We can mention a number of them.

1) Changes in modern physics
In *Belonging to the Universe* Fritjof Capra offers a succinct summary of important changes that are taking place in modern science especially as a result of breakthroughs in quantum physics. The old scientific paradigm can be referred to as Cartesian, Newtonian, or Baconian, since its main characteristics were formulated by Descartes, Newton, and Bacon.

The new paradigm may be called holistic, ecological, or systemic, but none of these adjectives characterises it completely. In the old paradigm it was believed that in any complex system the dynamics of the whole could be understood in terms of the properties of the parts. In the new paradigm, the relationship is between the parts and the whole. Ultimately, there are no parts at all. In quantum physics what we call a part is merely a pattern in an inseparable web of relationships. Bede Griffiths has written: 'In physics, there has recently been the discovery that the material universe is essentially a field of energies in which the parts can only be understood in relation to the whole. A related and most profound idea which has been introduced in physics is that the whole is in some way present in every part and, further, that every part is interconnected with every other part.'[13] To illustrate his point he cites David Bohm's theory of the implicit order. According to this theory the whole universe is originally implicated, or folded up together, and what we observe in the everyday world is the explicate order, i.e. that which has been explicated or unfolded. The implicate order is continually unfolding, becoming explicate. But behind the explicate order the implicate is always present, so in that sense the whole universe is implicated behind every explicate form. Other theorists such as Michael Talbot have suggested, on the basis of Bohm's understanding of quantum theory that the universe is a giant hologram. Writing in *The Holographic Universe* he says: 'Our brains mathematically construct objective reality by interpreting frequencies that are ultimately projections from another dimension, a deeper order of existence that is beyond both space and time: The brain is a hologram enfolded in a holographic universe.'[14] A Cambridge scientist called Brian Josephson, winner of the 1973 Nobel prize for physics, has suggested in a pantheistic and Hegelian way that Bohm's implicit order may someday include the notion of God or Mind within the framework of science.

In the old paradigm it was thought that there were fundamental structures, and then there were forces and mechanisms through which these interacted, thus giving rise to processes. In the new paradigm every structure is seen as the manifestation of an underlying process. The entire web of relationships is intrinsically dynamic. In the old paradigm scientific descriptions were believed to be objective, i.e. independent of the human observer and the process of knowledge. In the new paradigm it is believed that the understanding of the process of knowledge is to be included explicitly in the description of natural phenomena. The Cartesian paradigm was based on the belief that scientific knowledge could achieve absolute and final certainty. In the new paradigm, it is recognised that all concepts, theories, and findings are limited, approximate and therefore provisional. Science can never provide any complete and definitive understanding of reality. Scientists do not deal with truth, they deal with limited and approximate descriptions of reality.[15] As Ludwig Wittgenstein once said: 'We feel that even when all possible scientific questions have been answered the problems of life remain completely untouched.'[16] Realising that this is true, many scientists are more open to the religious dimensions of reality. Many books are being written about this development, e.g. Michael Talbot's *Mysticism and the New Physics*.[17]

2) Developments in psychology and transpersonal psychology

As a human science, psychology has a role to play in the development of a modified attitude to religion. Freud and Jung explored the dynamics of the personal and collective unconscious. Jung in particular was interested in the archetypes of the unconscious. There are four main ones, the *persona*, the *shadow*, the *animus/anima*, and the *self*. The latter has a transcendental orientation to the awareness of religious meaning. He believed that a person couldn't really recover from neurosis without first recovering a sense of the divine.

In the 60s Abraham Maslow became interested in what he called 'peak experiences', i.e. intense moments of awareness, which often had religious characteristics, and which led to greater self-actualisation. In 1967 he gave a lecture in the First Unitarian Church in San Francisco. It was later published in the first edition of the *Journal of Transpersonal Psychology*. It aimed to study: 'transpersonal process, values and states, unitive consciousness, meta-needs, peak experi-

ences, ecstasy, mystical experience, being, essence, bliss, awe, wonder, transcendence of self, spirit, sacralisation of everyday life, oneness, cosmic awareness, cosmic play, individual and species wide
synergy, the theories and practices of meditation, spiritual paths,
compassion, transpersonal co-operation, transpersonal realisation
and actualisation; and related concepts, experiences and activities.'[18]

Ken Wilber is one of the better known exponents of transpersonal
psychology. He aims to describe, e.g. in his earlier books, a multi-
level spectrum of consciousness and to construct a model of
humankind's evolution towards 'integral wholeness and Spirit'. He
describes how consciousness developed over the millennia through
a series of six discernable stages. They are analogous to stages of
individual personal development. In the earlier ones, consciousness was undifferentiated, people felt themselves to be at one with
the world. Then there was the development of language, and subsequently the emergence of individual identity. He focuses, however,
on higher states of consciousness, which until recently were
neglected by Western psychology, e.g. the subtle level which is
associated with psychic powers, and also the mystical dimension of
consciousness. At this level, the sense of oneness which was characteristic of the earlier stages returns in a more self-critical way. Bede
Griffiths writes: 'It is the view of Ken Wilber and others that there
is, as it were, a spectrum of levels of consciousness, from the basic
oceanic consciousness, through all the levels right up to the
supreme consciousness. The levels are hierarchically structured in
such a way that the lower levels are integrated with the higher. At
every point of transcendence there has to be a differentiation from
the previous level and integration of it.'[19]

3) Ecological awareness

As was noted earlier, nature was desacralised as a result of the
Reformation and the Enlightenment. Instead of being a living thing
as heretofore, it was seen as something dead and inert. This has led
to the ruthless exploitation of nature, and consequently to an ecological crisis. Things such as pollution and global warming literally
threaten the future of mankind. However, in recent years a number
of scientists have challenged the Cartesian worldview.

James Lovelock. is the originator of the Gaia hypothesis, i.e. the theory that the earth's living and nonliving systems form an inseparable whole that is regulated and kept adapted for life by living organisms themselves. Scientists have long known that living things alter the environment. Plants, for example, take up carbon dioxide from the air and give off oxygen. The Gaia hypothesis goes further, suggesting that life might actually keep the environment suitable for life. According to the theory, all living things – from the tiniest cells to the largest plants and animals – interact to create the environmental conditions that they need. An example of how Gaia might work can be found in a tropical rain forest. Trees give off water through their leaves in a process called transpiration. By adding humidity to the air, the trees increase the number of rainstorms that occur. As a result, the environment necessary for a rain forest is maintained in two ways. First, the rain keeps the trees watered. Second, rain clouds block the sun to keep the forest from overheating.

The Gaia hypothesis was first presented in 1968 by James E. Lovelock, a British chemist, biologist, and inventor. He and American microbiologist, Lynn Margulis, have since refined the idea. The theory has aroused scepticism and controversy among scientists, some of whom consider aspects of it unscientific or unoriginal. Other experts think that research on Gaia may add to our understanding of serious environmental problems, such as the greenhouse effect and mass extinctions. Lovelock has written: 'Gaia theory is out of tune with the broader humanist world as it is with established science. In Gaia we are just another species, neither the owners or the stewards of this planet. Our future depends much more upon a right relationship with Gaia than with the never ending dramas of human interest.'[20]

Rupert Sheldrake is also British. He argues against the mechanistic view of the world and also against the Darwinian and neo Darwinian view that there is no purpose in evolution. He espouses a modified view of Gaia theory and argues that there are morphogenic fields regulating evolution. He says the indeterminacy and unpredictability which are evident in the material world are actually being regulated by the form of the world. In *The Rebirth of Nature* he writes: 'The hypothesis of formative causation, first proposed in my book *A New Science of Life* (1981) and further developed in *The Presence of the Past* (1988), suggests that self-organising systems at all levels of complexity, including molecules, crystals, cells, tissues, organisms and societies or organisms are organised by fields called "morphic fields." …This hypothesis is inevitably controversial, but it is testable by experiment, and there is already considerable circumstantial evidence in its favour.'[21] Commentators have suggested that Sheldrake's notion of morphic fields is similar to Plato's theory of the forms that are constitutive of being. To the best of my knowledge, there is very little empirical evidence to support his interesting theory.

CREATION SPIRITUALITY'S UNDERSTANDING OF THE FALL

The following paragraphs don't pretend to give an adequate theological understanding of the intricacies and subtleties of current Catholic thinking on the doctrine of the fall and original sin. What they do intend to do is, firstly, to give a brief outline of St Augustine's interpretation – which is the predominant Catholic view – and secondly, to look at an alternative approach, one which seems to be more congruent with creation spirituality.

a) The Augustinian interpretation of the fall

The scriptural basis of this doctrine is the teaching of St Paul. In Rom 5:12-21 he says that: 'through one man (i.e. Adam), sin entered the world,' so that 'by the trespass of one man many died'. The Genesis account of the fall expresses this theological point in an imaginative way. In his anti-Pelagian writings, especially in his *Quaestiones ad Simplicianum* (396-7), Augustine taught that original sin was transmitted to Adam's descendants by concupiscence, that is, disordered human appetites such as sexual desire. This made humanity to be a *massa damnata*, i.e. a doomed race. It enfeebled but did not destroy human freedom. It is not entirely clear whether Augustine saw concupiscence as original sin, or a consequence of it. According to the bishop, since all human beings are conceived as a result of the concupiscence of our parents, we are all born with the stain of sin already upon us. As a result we cannot please God by our own efforts. We need the help of grace to do that. For their part, the Pelagians believed that free will, aided by ascetic practices, was sufficient for the living of the Christian life and the securing of eternal salvation. In the struggle with this heresy, the main lines of the Augustinian doctrine were endorsed by a number of councils, especially the Council of Carthage (418) and the Second Council of Orange (529).

b) The evolutionary interpretation of the fall

In this section we will look at two interrelated points of view: firstly, that of St Irenaeus (130-202) and secondly, modern interpretations, such as those of Ken Wilber, modified by Bede Griffiths. Irenaeus was born at Smyrna. In his youth he was influenced by St Polycarp. He left Asia Minor as a result of persecutions. When St Pothinus was martyred, he succeeded him as bishop of Lyons. With Irenaeus Christian theology became stable and coherent. Two of his written works survive, *Presentation of the Apostolic Preaching*, and a five volume work entitled, *Refutation and Overthrow of the Knowledge so Called*, which was a polemical argument against gnostic claims, especially its pessimistic interpretation of the fall. His thinking about evil was a combination of philosophy and biblical theology, which resembled what today would be called creation spirituality. He suggested that there are two phases in creation.

By borrowing from Gen 1:26, Irenaeus proposed that in the first phase people were in the 'image of God' and in the second they were in the 'likeness of God'. The *imago* or image, which resides in our human bodily form, makes us capable as intelligent creatures of relationship with God. The 'likeness' represents what we can become through the action of the Holy Spirit. 'Human beings,' he says, 'are made spiritual and perfect because of the outpouring of the Spirit, and this is he who was made in the image and likeness of God. But if the Spirit is lacking in the soul, such a person is indeed an animal nature, and being left carnal, shall be an imperfect being, possessing indeed the image of God in his formation, but not receiving the likeness through the Spirit.'[22]

According to Irenaeus human beings were brought into existence as personal beings endowed with moral freedom and a sense
of responsibility. As such, people have a great capacity for human
and spiritual development. They were not the perfect pre-fallen
people described by Augustine. They were childlike immature people at the beginning of a long process of growth. Irenaeus said: 'God
had power at the beginning to grant perfection to human beings;
but as the latter were only recently created, they could not possibly
have received it, or even if they had received it, they could not have
contained it, or containing it, could not have retained it ... For as it
certainly is in the power of a mother to give strong food to her
infant, she does not do so, as the child is not yet able to receive more
substantial nourishment; so also it was possible for God himself to
have made humans perfect from the first, but they could not receive
this perfection, being as yet infants.'[23] In his *Proof of the Apostolic
Preaching* Irenaeus saw Adam and Eve as mere children in the
Garden of Eden. Their fall was not so much a matter of revolt as a
matter of vulnerability, weakness and immaturity. Their sin called
forth God's compassion rather than his condemnation. As St Paul
was later to say: 'God made us prisoners of disobedience in order
that he might show mercy' (Rom 11:32). There is an example of this
paradox in the life of St Peter. Jesus warned that Satan would test
him. He prayed, not that Peter would resist in the day of testing – he
knew his fall was inevitable due to his spiritual immaturity, pre-
sumption and lack of self-awareness – so he prayed rather that,
when he had fallen, he would be comforted by the Holy Spirit.
Then, strengthened and enlightened by God through bitter experiences he would be in a position to help others with the very help he
himself had received. As a result, Peter could say with Adam and
Eve, 'O happy fault, O necessary fall, that won for me such graces!'

Irenaeus's developmental approach was stated in these words:
'Now it was necessary that human beings should in the first
instance be created, should receive growth; and having received
growth, should be strengthened; and having been strengthened,
should abound; and having abounded, should recover from the disease of sin; and having recovered, should be glorified; and being

glorified, should see the Lord.'[24] His doctrine of the fall was echoed in a letter of the poet John Keats to his sister: 'The common name of this world among the misguided and superstitious is "a vale of tears," from which we can be redeemed by a certain arbitrary interposition of God and taken to heaven – What a little circumscribed straightened notion! Call the world if you please "Vale of soul-making". Do you not see how necessary a world of pains and troubles is to school an intelligence and make it a soul?'[25]

John Hick sums up the difference between the view of Augustine and Irenaeus in these words: 'Instead of the fall of Adam being presented as in the Augustinian tradition, as utterly malignant and catastrophic event, completely disrupting God's plan, Irenaeus pictures it as something that occurred in the childhood of the race, an understandable lapse due to weakness and immaturity rather than an adult crime full of malice and pregnant with perpetual guilt. And instead of the Augustinian view of the trials of life as a divine punishment for Adam's sin, Irenaeus sees the world of mingled good and evil as a divinely appointed environment for man's development towards the perfection that represents the fulfillment of God's purposes for him.'[26]

In recent years, Ken Wilber has suggested an interpretation of the fall which is in line with that of Irenaeus. He says that there are six stages of human consciousness. In the first stage, human beings live in an undifferentiated sense of unity with God, self and creation. At this stage human beings didn't know themselves as being different from God or nature. They enjoyed a sense of symbiotic union and what has been referred to as 'oceanic feeling'. Following creation came the fall. For Wilber it was an ascent rather than a descent. As the original sense of unity broke down, people developed a sense of individuality and separateness. He writes: 'This original act of severance we will call the Primary Dualism: epistemologically, it is the severance of the knower from the known; ontologically, the severance of the Infinite from the finite; theologically, it is original sin; generally, we may speak of it as the illusory split between subject and object.'[27] Bede Griffiths is correct when he says that this interpretation doesn't do justice to the biblical notion of the fall. He says: 'In the original state, body, soul and spirit were in harmony and as human beings developed consciousness, they learned to distinguish themselves from other selves, from nature and from God. As consciousness developed they became conscious of themselves as separate from the body and separate from the mother. In that state they could open themselves to the Spirit and allow the Spirit to guide them, but they could equally separate themselves from the Spirit. They could fall away from the Spirit and centre on themselves. This falling away from the Spirit into the ego, the soul, the separated self, and thereby separating from God, is the essence of original sin.'[28] In other words, while accepting Wilber's overall notion of stages, he identifies the fall with disobedience and consequent disintegration, rather than differentiation of consciousness. Speaking about the consequences of the fall, Griffiths says: 'The man and the woman would be in conflict with the world around them and with their own bodily nature. But the division goes deeper than this. It marks a fundamental split between nature and humanity and within humanity itself. The fall of humanity is the fall from the unified state of being, when humanity was in harmony with nature and God, into the state of division and duality. It is a fall from the unified or non-dualistic mind into a dualistic mind, that is, into our present mode of consciousness.'[29] It can be said in passing that while Griffiths tries to espouse an orthodox Christian point of view – whether he succeeds or not is debatable – Wilber's notion is typically Gnostic.

It is interesting to note that the *Catechism of the Catholic Church*, par 387, says: 'Only the light of Divine Revelation clarifies the reality of sin and particularly the sin committed at mankind's origins. Without the knowledge Revelation gives of God we cannot recognise sin clearly and *are tempted to explain it merely as a developmental flaw*, (my italics) a psychological weakness, a mistake, or the necessary consequence of an inadequate social structure, etc. Only in the knowledge of God's plan for man can we grasp that sin is an abuse of the freedom that God gives to created persons so that they are capable of loving him and loving one another.' While it is true that Wilber does try to explain original sin merely as a developmental flaw in the process of evolution, it strikes me that Bede Griffith's re-interpretation is in line with the teaching of the church and that of St Irenaeus. Henri de Lubac notes how Teilhard de Chardin was of the opinion that Western theology was overly influenced by the Augustinian view of original sin. Given the fact that he was so committed to an evolutionary perspective, it is not surprising to find that he preferred the approaches of Clement of Alexandria and especially St Irenaeus.[30]

Conclusion

This chapter has argued that the modern spiritual crisis is due in large part to the masculinisation of modern culture. It has severed our sense of connection with creation. As a result it no longer mediates the immediacy of God. If this process is to be reversed we need to rehabilitate the feminine dimensions of human experience. I was interested to see that at the end of his magisterial study, *The Passion of the Western Mind,* Richard Tarnas comes to a similar conclusion. He says that masculinisation has been pervasive and fundamental, in both men and women, and has affected every aspect of Western thought. It has determining its most basic conception of the human being and his or her role in the world. 'The Western mind,' he writes, 'has been founded on the repression of the feminine – on the repression of undifferentiated unitary consciousness, of the participation mystique with nature: a progressive denial of the *anima mundi*, of the soul of the world… The crisis of modern man is an essentially masculine crisis.'[31] Having diagnosed the key problem he goes on to prescribe a cure. The Western mind, he says, must be willing to open itself to a reality the nature of which could challenge and overturn its most established beliefs about itself and the world. This is the great challenge of our time, the evolutionary imperative for the masculine principle, i.e. the myopic, left brained approach to reality, is to see through and overcome its one-sidedness, to own its masculine shadow, to choose to enter into a fundamentally new relationship of mutuality with the feminine in all its forms. 'The feminine then becomes not that which must be controlled, denied, and exploited, but rather fully acknowledged, respected, and responded to for itself. It is recognised: not as the objectified "other" but rather as source, goal, and immanent presence.'[32]

Thanks to the feminist movement and many other socio-cultural changes, I believe that the age of the feminine is about to dawn. With its advent will come the re-awakening of spirituality in Western culture. Jung was well aware of the fact that the declaration of the doctrine of the assumption of Mary into heaven was not only of great religious significance to Catholics, it was also important from a psycho-spiritual point of view. To him it re-asserted the importance of the feminine archetype in Western culture, an archetype that has long been suppressed. Just as Mary gave birth to the Son of God 2,000 years ago, so the feminine will renew contemplative reverence for the created world which mediates the numinous presence of God.

CHAPTER 8

The Compassion of God

The God of many philosophers is apathetic, i.e. without feeling for suffering humanity. Their reason for asserting this is logical. If the lives of people could evoke joy or sorrow in God, it would mean that humans could affect God – in a sense, have power over the deity. But that is impossible. If God was effected by people's lives it would imply that God changed either for the better or the worse. In fact God is perfect and unchanging, therefore God is necessarily detached and unmoved by the 'still, sad music of humanity'. As Plutarch (46-120) wrote: 'He who involves God in human needs does not spare his majesty, nor does he maintain the dignity and greatness of God's excellence.'[1]

The God of revelation is quite different. Ignoring the philosophical problems faced by the Stoics, the bible simply asserts that the Lord feels for suffering human beings. For instance, Ex 34:6 tells us, God passed before Moses on one occasion and said: 'The Lord, the Lord, the compassionate and gracious God, slow to anger, abounding in love and faithfulness.' The word used for compassion in the Hebrew of the Old Testament is *rahamin*. It literally means, 'trembling movement of the womb', i.e. mother love. It is closely related in meaning to the Hebrew word *chesed*, which means 'loving kindness'. It is strong and steadfast. It is referred to throughout scripture, e.g. Ex 34:6; Neh 9:17; Ps 103:8; Jonah 4:2. In loving kindness the compassionate One longs to bring forth new life wherever there is sin, suffering or oppression.

The Compassion of Jesus
In the New Testament, Jesus was the living embodiment of the compassion of God. As Jn 3:16 tells us, the motivation for the incar-

nation was God's compassionate love for a fallen and wounded world: 'God so loved the world that he gave his only begotten Son.' While Jesus was always aware of that love, his consciousness of God's compassion reached a new level of intensity at his baptism in the Jordan (cf. Mk 1:9-111; Mt 3:13-17; Lk 3:21-22; Jn 1:30-34). At that revelatory moment, he was immersed, drenched, soaked and inundated in a heartfelt awareness of the Father's love for him, as his beloved Son in whom he was well pleased. In the light of that awareness, Jesus became clearer about his identity and mission. He was the anointed Son of man, the promised Messiah. He was not called to be the expected political messiah who would liberate the people from their Roman oppressors. Rather, his vocation was to be the suffering servant, the compassionate One, foretold by scripture (cf. Ps 2:7; Is 42:1). The spirit prompted him to manifest the incomprehensible, unconditional and unrestricted love of God for his people who were afflicted in so many ways. As Jesus declared in Jn 15:9, he loved the people with the same intensity of love with which the father loved him. He had a firm conviction that the compassion of the father, would find expression in his anointed words and deeds, but most of all his suffering and death. They would bring salvation and healing by finally overcoming the three great enemies of man, namely Satan, sin and suffering.

The word for compassion in Greek is *splanchnizomai*. It is derived from the word *splangchna* which refers to the entrails, bowels or guts. They were thought to be the source of the most intense human feelings. So when the gospels speak of Christian compassion they are using a word that connotes loving kindness and empathy of an intense kind. When we contemplate the compassion of Jesus we are contemplating the compassion of God himself. As Henri Nouwen has written: 'When Jesus was moved to compassion, the source of all life trembled, the ground of all love burst open, and the abyss of God's immense, inexhaustible and unfathomable tenderness revealed itself.'[2]

Jesus had a particularly intense compassion for the poor. As he testified himself in Lk 4:18-19: 'The Spirit of the Lord is one me, because he has anointed me to preach good news to the poor. He has sent me to proclaim freedom for the prisoners and recovery of sight for the blind, to release the oppressed, to proclaim the year of the Lord's favor.' One gospel episode epitomises the truth of this prophetic utterance. Following a period of demanding ministry, Jesus and the disciples took some time off to get a rest. But when they arrived at their destination they found that a large crowd of poor people had anticipated their arrival and were waiting for them. Although he was tired, Jesus did not show disappointment, frustration or impatience. He was unlike the bad shepherds of old. The Lord had said to them: 'You do not feed the sheep. You have not strengthened the weak, you have not healed the sick, you have not bound up the injured, you have not brought back the strayed' (Ezek 34:4). In marked contrast, Jesus was the fulfilment of the prophecy which stated: 'I myself will be the shepherd of my sheep … says the Lord' (Ezek 34:15). As the evangelist says of him: 'When he saw the crowds, he had compassion on them, because they were harassed and helpless, like sheep without a shepherd' (Mt 9:36). If I were to choose one verse in the gospels which encapsulates the spirit of Jesus' earthly and heavenly ministry, this would be it.

Jesus' contemporaries suffered in many ways. Taxes were heavy. Famines were frequent. Emigration was high. Roman rule was cruel. Physical and mental diseases were many and incurable. But the principal suffering of these poor people was shame and disgrace. The sinners of the time included most of the rural poor, e.g. those who engaged in unclean professions such as prostitutes, tax collectors, robbers, herdsmen, usurers, gamblers, those who did not pay their tithes or neglected the Sabbath day rest and ritual cleanliness, and also those who through no fault of their own didn't know the law. There was no way out for them. As a result they suffered from chronic guilt feelings which led them to fear divine punishment. Jesus had compassion for the afflicted. It was this impulse that informed his entire ministry, i.e. his lifestyle, his preaching, actions, intercessory prayer and death on the cross. We can look at each of these in turn.

Forms of Christ's compassion
Firstly, Jesus adopted a compassionate *lifestyle*. Although he was,

apparently, a member of the middle class, he became an outcast by choice, by mixing socially with the lowest of the low and identifying with them. This was so obvious that the Scribes and Pharisees accused him of being 'a friend of outcasts and sinners' (Mt 11:19; Lk 7:34). The place where this compassionate solidarity with the poor was most obvious was in table-fellowship, celebratory meals where outcasts and sinners were his companions, e.g. the meal at the home of Zacchaeus the tax collector in Lk 19:1-10. It would be impossible to overestimate the impact these meals must have had upon the poor and sinners. By accepting them as friends and equals Jesus took away their shame, humiliation and guilt. By showing them that they mattered to him as people, he gave them a sense of dignity and released them from their oppression. They were like the prodigal son being received back into their father's house to receive the cloak of honour, the ring of authority, and the shoes of freedom in a celebratory context of rejoicing.

Secondly, the *preaching* of Jesus was motivated by compassion and was often about the importance of compassion in life. For example, in Mt 9:36 we are told that when he had compassion on the crowds in the wilderness: 'he began teaching them many things' (Mk 6:34). At the core of his preaching was the proclamation of the unconditional and unrestricted mercy of God. It was expressed in many characteristic phrases such as, 'Do not cry,' 'don't worry,' and 'Don't be afraid' (e.g. Mk 5:36; 6:50; Mt 6:25-34; see also Mk 4:40; Lk 10:41). Not only was the preaching of Jesus prompted by compassion, compassion was often the subject of his teaching. For example, in three of his more memorable parables he says that the Good Samaritan (Lk 10:33), the prodigal father (Lk 15:20) and the forgiving master (Mt 18:27) were motivated by compassion.

Thirdly, the *actions* of Jesus were motivated by compassion. The evangelists tell us this on a number of occasions. Mt 20:34 states that compassion prompted Jesus to heal two blind men. Lk 7:13 says that when Jesus happened to meet a funeral cortege outside the town of Nain, he had compassion for a widow who had lost her only son. As a result he raised the young man to new life and restored him to his mother. The same was true at the tomb of

Lazarus. When Jesus saw the people weeping, he wept too. He grieved that his friend was dead and sympathised with the relatives and neighbours in their loss. He was so deeply affected that he groaned and sighed in a way that was too deep for words. 'And God, who searches the heart, knew what is the mind of the Spirit, for the Spirit interceded ... according to the will of God' (Rom 8:27). The prayerful compassion of Jesus was a participation in the compassion of God, and so he was empowered to speak a word of power and to call Lazarus forth from the tomb into new life. In many ways it was an archetypal miracle that foreshadowed his own resurrection from the dead when God the Father would speak a similar word of compassion into his Son's place of death.

Fourthly, the *death* of Jesus was his supreme act of compassionate solidarity with suffering humanity. Is 53:4 anticipates in a prophetic way how Jesus, as the suffering servant, would do this: 'Surely he took up our infirmities and carried our sorrows, yet we considered him stricken by God, smitten by him, and afflicted. But he was pierced for our transgressions, he was crushed for our iniquities; the punishment that brought us peace was upon him, and by his wounds we are healed.' That prophecy was fulfilled during Holy Week. Speaking about the compassionate high priest, Heb 5:7-8 says: 'During the days of Jesus' life on earth, he offered up prayers and petitions with loud cries and tears to the one who could save him from death, and he was heard because of his reverent submission. Although he was a son, he learned obedience from what he suffered.' Clearly, Jesus was willing, in a spirit of compassion, to drink the chalice of human suffering to the dregs.

Furthermore, the Apostles' Creed states that Jesus descended into hell. In Hebrew the word was *Sheol*.[3] It did not mean non-existence. It referred to a no-man's land which was inhabited by the living dead, people who merely existed, but in a radically disconnected way. Jesus was so compassionate upon the cross that he allowed himself to enter that world in two stages. Firstly, when he was enveloped in darkness and cried out, 'My God, my God, why have you forsaken me?' he was already entering *Sheol* in a psychological and spiritual way. This means that Jesus shared the darkness of those who feel alienated, depressed and desolate. Secondly, when he yielded his Spirit to the Father – to be donated to humanity – he slipped in a more radical way into the realm of the dead, into the valley of the dry bones mentioned by the prophet Ezek 37:1-15. The scriptures advert to this fact on more than one occasion. Eph 4:9 describes how Jesus 'descended to the lower earthly regions'. St Peter described the Lord's compassionate purpose in doing this: 'he went and preached to the spirits in prison' (1 Pet 3:19). Eph 4:8 adds that Jesus did this so that, following his glorious resurrection and ascension, he might lead forth a host of captives and give gifts to men. These texts seem to be the fulfilment of the lines in Ps 139:7-8 which say: 'Where can I go from your spirit? Or where can I flee from your presence? … if I make my bed in *Sheol*, you are there.' So when we feel that the life of grace is dead within us, or that we are facing our physical death, we can know that, motivated by compassion, Jesus has entered that reality in order to share it and to lead us forth to victory.

Fifthly, there are also clear indications that the *intercessory prayer* that Jesus offered during his ministry was motivated by compassion. There are examples of that prayer in Lk 22:31 where Jesus prays for Peter and the apostles, and the high priestly prayer for unity in Jn 17. The role of compassionate intercessor reaches its high point on the cross. Is 53:12 says: 'he bore the sin of many, and made intercession for the transgressors.' Now in heaven, Jesus continues to offer prayers of intercession for the suffering members of his body on earth. He is our compassionate High Priest who lives forever to intercede for us at the Father's right hand. As 1 Jn 2:1 says: 'we have one who speaks to the Father in our defence – Jesus Christ, the Righteous One.' Heb 7:25 adds that Jesus: 'is able to save completely those who come to God through him, because he always lives to intercede for them.' What a consoling thought. No matter how cut off, miserable and misunderstood we may feel, there is always One who prays for us, night and day, before the Father in heaven.

Three forms of compassion
Expressed in contemporary terms, compassion is empathy for people who suffer in one way or another.[4] I have suggested elsewhere

that one can discern three interrelated kinds of compassion in the ministry of Jesus.[5] Firstly, there is fellow feeling, which refers to the ability to identify with the suffering of another person because one has suffered something similar. For example, when people who were ritually unclean, or afflicted by a disease like leprosy, Jesus had fellow feeling for them in as much as he himself knew from personal experience what it was like to be marginalised and ostracised. Remember how Mk 3:21 recalled that, on one occasion, members of his extended family: 'went to take charge of him, for they said, "He is out of his mind."' St Paul probably had this type of experience in mind when he wrote in 2 Cor 1:3-4: 'Praise be to the God and Father of our Lord Jesus Christ, the Father of compassion and the God of all comfort, who comforts us in all our troubles, so that we can comfort those in any trouble with the comfort we ourselves have received from God.'

Secondly, there is wounded wonder. It goes beyond appearances to recognise and approve of the inner worth and value of another person in a wonder-full manner. However, the extent to which the person has been wounded in any way is the extent to which his or her sense of wonder is wounded. This is an important point. The person's woundedness is not the primary focus of attention. Rather it is recognised in the light of an intuitive recognition of the person's inalienable value. I can remember talking, on one occasion, to Jean Vanier, the founder of l'Arche, about the subject of compassion. I explained what I meant by the phrase 'wounded wonder,' and he said in an animated way that he not only understood what I meant, he had come up with exactly the same phrase to describe the same type of compassion. Jesus displayed this form of merciful love. When he met people he did not judge them by appearances (cf. Jn 7:24). Rather he saw them as the Father saw them, as God's children made in the divine image and likeness. This awareness evoked in him a sense of reverential wonder. But the extent to which his brothers and sisters were wounded was the extent to which his affirming sense of wonder was also wounded.

Thirdly, there is indignant compassion. When a man or woman is consciously aware of the innermost value of another, he or she resists anything that might militate against the other person's health or happiness. It is this kind of compassion that prompts him or her to bring relief in whatever way possible. When the man with the skin disease asked Jesus if he wanted to help him Jesus responded: 'Of course I want to, be clean.' Apparently in earlier versions of Mark's gospel the Greek text said that Jesus was angry with the leprosy, before reaching out to heal the disease. Joseph Schmid's translation reads, 'Then Jesus *in his anger* stretched out his hand to him, touched him, and said to him: I will – be clean.'[6] In other words, because Jesus was affirming the man's dignity as a son of God, he was angrily resisting the disease that was afflicting him in a physical and social way. Knowing in an experiential manner that his antagonism to the leprosy was a share in the heart and will of God the Father, he uttered a compassionate word of command and the man was healed. Needless to say, the same kind of indignant compassion informed his ministry of exorcism.

Albert Nolan has highlighted some of the consequences of the compassion of God in a striking and memorable way when he wrote: 'If we wish to treat Jesus as our God, we would have to conclude that our God does not want to be served by us, but wants to serve us; God does not want to be given the highest possible rank and status in our society, but wants to take the lowest place and to be without any rank and status; God does not want to be feared and obeyed, but wants to be recognised in the sufferings of the poor and the weak; God is not supremely indifferent and detached, but is irrevocably committed to the liberation of humankind, for God has chosen to be identified with all people in a spirit of solidarity and compassion. If this is not a true picture of God, then Jesus is not divine. If this is a true picture of God, God is more truly human, more thoroughly humane than any human being. God is a supremely human God.'[7] I think that Nolan is correct when he states that God has changed. In other words, the God that is revealed by Jesus Christ is in many ways different from the God of the Old Testament and the God of the philosophers. The God of compassion is a supremely human God.

In his story entitled *The Night*, Jewish writer Elie Wiesel has graphically illustrated the implications of Nolan's statement. He describes how, during the war, electrical equipment was blown up in a concentration camp. The Gestapo tortured one of the camp leaders in order to extract the names of possible perpetrators. When he refused to divulge a single name he was sent to Auschwitz where, presumably, he was gassed to death. But his youthful servant was left behind in the camp. When he, like his master, refused to divulge any names under torture, he was sentenced to die by hanging, together with two men who had been discovered with weapons.

One evening when thousands of prisoners returned from their exhausting work, they found that three gallows had been erected. They were ordered to stand in rows to witness the executions. The three victims mounted chairs. Their heads were placed in the nooses. Then the two adults cried, 'long live liberty!' The boy remained silent. A man in the crowd whispered to a companion, 'Where is God? Where is He?' As soon as he spoke the chairs were tipped over. The pathetic trio dangled between heaven and earth. The prisoners watched helplessly in silence. Many were in tears. Wiesel goes on to say that the two adults died quickly, but not the boy. 'For more than half an hour he stayed there, struggling between life and death, dying in a slow agony before our eyes. And we had to look him full in the face. He was still alive when I passed in front of him. His tongue was still red, his eyes not yet glazed. Behind me I heard the same man asking: "Where is God now?" And I heard a voice within me answer him: "Where is He? Here he is – He is hanging here on this gallows…" That night the soup tasted of corpses.'[8] As the crucified One had said, some nineteen hundred years before: 'I tell you the truth, whatever you did to one of the least of these brothers or sisters of mine, you did to me' (Mt 25:40).

Love one another as I have loved you

The Latin word for compassion is *misericordia*. It literally means 'a heart' sensitive to 'misery'. It was used by St Thomas in his writings. He says: 'Compassion (i.e. *misericordia*) is heartfelt identification with another's distress, driving us to do what we can to help …

As far as outward activity is concerned, compassion is the Christian's whole rule of life.'[9] At this point I would like to focus attention
on St Vincent de Paul, patron of all charitable works in the Catholic
Church, because, not only was compassion the rule of his life, he
had a profound understanding of its meaning and implications.

He was ordained in 1599, at the early age of nineteen. He had to
cheat a little to make it possible. In many ways he was a typical
young man. He immersed himself in the outer world at the expense
of his inner life. There is convincing evidence that he was insensi-
tive to the deeper murmerings of his own heart and the cry of the
poor around him. While he fulfilled his basic religious duties he
was mainly preoccupied with getting a good, well-paid job.

Then over a period of years, he suffered a number of painful set-
backs. They began in his mid-twenties when he was a captive in
North Africa and ended with his three year battle with temptations
against faith. These crises had a transforming effect. Vincent
became increasingly aware of his inner brokenness and the cry of
the poor about him. He began to have a deep desire for a revelation
of God in his life. God never prompts a desire to know him better
without fulfilling that desire. Bit by bit St Vincent had the power, in
the words of Eph 3:18: 'to grasp the length and breadth, the height
and depth of the love of Christ, which surpasses understanding'.
But most of all Vincent became aware of the compassion of the
Lord, whose mercy and love led him to share in the worst of our
sufferings. As a result, he began to feel that compassion was the key
to the motivation and ministry of Jesus. Speaking to some of his
priests, he said, in characteristic fashion: 'Ah! But the Son of God
was tender of heart. I cannot help constantly turning my eyes to this
model of love. He is called to visit Lazarus. He goes. Mary rises to
meet him, weeping. The Jews follow and weep as well. What does the
Lord do? He weeps with them, so loving and compassionate is he.
This tender love was the cause of his coming down from heaven.'[10]

Whenever the Lord is revealed to a person as he really is, that
person has an inner desire to become for others what God has
become for him or her. God was revealed to Vincent as compassion,
so he had a growing desire to become 'compassionate as the Father

is compassionate' (Lk 6:36). He wanted to imitate the Saviour by proclaiming and demonstrating the love of God, especially to the poor. This he began to do. But the dreams of his heart far exceeded his ability to fulfil them unaided. So he founded the Congregation of the Mission, known in English-speaking countries as the Vincentians, to preach the good news to the poor of neglected parishes in rural areas. Among other things, he told his priests that they were to preach the good news in a spirit of compassion. On one occasion he said: 'St Vincent Ferrer maintains that there is no way of profiting from preaching if one does not preach from the depths of compassion.'[11]

Together with his friend St Louise de Marillac, Vincent founded the Ladies of Charity, a part-time lay group, and the Daughters of Charity, who were committed full time to the evangelisation of the poor. These women were to demonstrate the compassion of God, principally by means of works of mercy for the poor. Speaking to the Daughters of Charity on one occasion, Vincent said: 'You are destined to represent God's goodness towards these poor sick people. Now, since this goodness deals gently and lovingly with the afflicted, you too must behave towards the poor invalids just as God's goodness teaches you, that is with gentleness, compassion and love; for they are your masters, and mine too.'[12]

Vincent's life and teaching were informed by two interrelated insights. The compassion of Christ, the good shepherd, is expressed by those who show affective and effective empathy for those who suffer. But by entering into the pain of others in this way, compassionate people encounter Christ, the Lamb who was slain, in those who suffer in body, mind or spirit. As Vincent de Paul once wrote: 'We must open our hearts so that they become responsive to the sufferings and miseries of the neighbour. We should pray God to give us a true spirit of mercy and compassion, which is in truth the Spirit of God.'[13] On another occasion he told some Daughters of Charity that if they ministered in a spirit of compassion, 'In serving the poor you are serving Jesus Christ. A sister may go to the sick ten times a day, and ten times a day she will find God there. Visit the poor convicts in the chain gangs and there you will find God. Oh

Daughters, how gratifying it is! You go into poor homes and you find God there.'

What might St Vincent de Paul say if he were alive today? I suspect that he would indicate how the poverty of the late twentieth century is very different from that of seventeenth-century France. I'm sure he would have agreed with Mother Teresa of Calcutta when she said that there are two famines in the contemporary world. In the underdeveloped nations there is often a famine of the stomach, due to lack of food. In the developed nations like ours, there is often a famine of the heart due to a lack of self-forgetful love. Mother Teresa referred to its victims as the 'new poor' of our day.

Compassion for today's poor

When I travel around Ireland I meet the new poor everywhere I go. From the middle class suburbs of Cork to the travellers' official and unofficial sites in Dublin, the story is the same. Besides anxiety about such things as the drug problem, the rising crime rate, high levels of stress and the like, many people suffer from lack of self-esteem and unresolved feelings of unworthiness and inadequacy. These painful feelings, the inner toothache of the heart, can lead to anger and aggression. In my experience this situation is linked to Ireland's three greatest problems, family breakdown, addictions, and depression which quenches the flame of feeling in the heart. Tragically, as love is eclipsed, so is the face of the living God. As a result, many of our people are in a state of spiritual desolation.

How can we help the poor of our day? One thing is for sure, it won't be easy. As Mother Teresa said, it is relatively easy to end the famine of the stomach. All its victims need is a bowl of rice, bandages for their wounds and a good hug. The problems associated with the famine of love go much deeper. In most cases they are psycho-spiritual rather than material. As such they are much harder to cope with. To become credible witnesses to the God of compassion we will have to encounter that God, as Vincent de Paul did, in a prayerful way in the depths of our hearts. It begins by facing our own poverty and listening not only to the still sad music of our own lives, but also to that of the people around us. As we express our feelings and desires to the Lord, Jesus will come to our aid. Not only will the God of compassion be revealed to us in this kind of prayer, but like Vincent we will have both the desire and the power to show compassion to the new poor of our day.

The victims of the famine of love need us to spend time with them, to offer them a listening ear and an understanding heart. It won't be easy. Hurt people are often demanding, self-absorbed and unpredictable. But if we listen, if we stay with their sufferings while allowing ourselves to respond in a spirit of acceptance and love, great things can happen. Famine victims begin to accept and love themselves in a new and therapeutic manner. Some time ago I saw this happen in a memorable way.

A few years ago I attended a conference in Wales. After a long day's work I was taking a welcome rest. Suddenly my peace was disturbed by urgent knocking on the door. As soon as I said 'enter', a worried looking man called Frank came in. He said that a nun named Sr Monica had brought a gypsy to the conference. He was homeless, a non-believer and emotionally disturbed. He asked if I would talk to him. In a weary voice I said that I was willing to do so, and asked where he was. Frank said that he was in the bar. So we headed off to meet him.

I was introduced to the gypsy who told me his name was Ed. Then he poured out his story. He was an only child. His father was a violent drunk, who had often beaten his wife. On one occasion, when Ed was about seven or eight years of age, he saw his father fling his mother through a caravan window. The breaking glass severed an artery in her neck. She fell to the ground, and quickly bled to death in front of her terrified son. Subsequently, the father was tried, found guilty of murder, and sent to prison where he died some years later. Meantime, Ed was sent to live with some of his Gypsy relatives. He was very unhappy with them and, although it was against their social code, he ran away.

He lived in a boiler house next to a clergyman's home. Ed used to rob bread and vegetables in order to feed himself. After a few years he met a teenage Gypsy girl. She ran away from her family and lived with Ed in an abandoned railway carriage. Eventually they married. Meantime, Ed got involved with motor trade and set up a business that did well. Then his wife had their only child, a daughter. Ed wanted to give his wife and daughter all the love that he himself had never received. For a time his life was happy. But then tragedy struck. His beloved wife got cancer, and after a long, lingering illness she died. A few weeks later his daughter was walking along the pavement when a car went out of control, mounted the kerb and killed her. Ed was absolutely distraught. He said that he hadn't really undressed in two years because he couldn't sleep. As a result he was always tired, depressed and angry. His business went down hill and finally he was declared bankrupt. He lost everything, his premises, house and car. He was living rough when Sr Monica asked him to come to the conference.

He explained that he wasn't a Christian. He didn't believe in God, had never read the Bible or prayed, and had only been in a church on two occasions in his life. Then he contradicted himself when he said that he hated God. Although I was very tired at the time, I tried to listen as carefully and empathically as I could. I was deeply moved by the tragic story Ed had recounted. I felt powerless to help him. Instead of being upset, as I often am in those situations, I experienced a surprising sense of calm. It was evoked by a deep interior awareness of God's love and compassion for Ed, a disposition in which I myself shared. Inexplicably I also had a certain conviction that sooner or later the Lord would be revealed in a saving and healing way in his life. I suspect that, at that moment of undoubting certainty, I was granted the gift of expectant or charismatic faith, spoken about by Jesus in Mk 11:24, and by Paul in 1 Cor 12:9.[14] As a result I was able to encourage Ed not to worry, because I was quite sure that something good was going to happen in his life.

The following day I was having my evening meal in the cafeteria when Frank came rushing in. 'No one has seen Ed since last night,' he said anxiously. 'We are afraid that he may have done something rash.' 'Have you tried his room?' I asked. 'Yes,' Frank replied, but there was no answer. 'Why not try again?' I said. 'Break the lock if necessary.' He headed off. Some time later Frank returned and told

me what had happened. He and another man had broken the lock
and burst into the room. They found Ed, undressed, and fast asleep
in his bed. When they woke him up he told them what had happened. Having returned to his room the previous evening he had
taken of his clothes and got into bed. He dozed for a while. Then a
radiant man, dressed in white, came into his room. He asked Ed
what he wanted. He spontaneously responded, 'I want to sleep.'
The man in white touched his brow and gently said, 'now you will
have a deep sleep.' Sometime during the night Ed had a vivid
dream. Three doves flew into his room. One landed on his fore-
head, another on his chest and another on his stomach. Ed knew
that the doves represented the souls of his mother, wife and daughter. He slept soundly for about twenty hours. When he woke up, Ed
had a nascent sense of God and a feeling of inner peace.

The next day was the last of the conference. I had been appointed
the celebrant at the concluding eucharist. Some time before it was
due to begin, Ed asked me if he could speak briefly after the gospel
reading. I was reluctant at first, because I wasn't sure what he
would say. But some inner impulse led me to say yes. So after the
reading of the good news Ed came forward to the microphone. He
began to tell his story in a quiet, unemotional tone of voice. Even so,
it was rivetting. He recounted many of the facts that he had already
shared with Frank and myself in the bar. He spoke about his experience in the bedroom, two nights before. He added that since then,
Jesus had appeared to him in a vision. He went on to say, 'When I
came here, I hated God because of all the suffering in my life. In fact
I didn't believe in him. But now your God is my God. The God you
love is the God I love. The God you serve is the God I serve. I am
prepared to go anywhere, and to do anything on his behalf. In fact,
many of you would find that a hard thing to do because you have
so many attachments. But I have none. So I will be able to serve him
with all my heart.' It was an extraordinarily eloquent and moving
testimony. Ed was as good as his word. Some months later he
became a Christian. And although he suffered a good deal of ill
health he married again. That was a truly Vincentian experience. I
had tried to respond to Ed's suffering in a compassionate way. God

did the rest by pouring out his grace. It enabled a contemporary victim of the famine of love to hear the gospel for the first time and to respond to it with generosity and faith.

Conclusion

As far as I know it was Brian Moore who wrote the ironic words: 'In the beginning was the word and the word was no!' That is the experience of many of the poor and the new poor. But if we proclaim and demonstrate the love of God in a spirit of compassion, perhaps we will be able to say: 'In the beginning was the word, and the word was yes!' a big, affirming yes of love and affirmation from Almighty God, one that will evoke an answering yes of love from them. Compassion may not be enough. Many of the poor and the new poor need action for justice and practical help. Compassion without appropriate action is sentimentality, while action without compassion is condescension. But compassion expressed in appropriate action is Emmanuel, God-with-us.

CHAPTER 9

Praying for Healing

Jesus demonstrated the good news in a number of characteristic ways: by means of loving relationships, action of liberation, and deeds of power such as healing, exorcisms and miracles. Speaking of the healings and exorcisms, scripture scholar David Stanley has written, in an article entitled 'Salvation and Healing': 'All the evangelists regard the healings ... as an integral part of the message itself ... they are presented simply as the good news in action.' We are told in Mt 14:14: 'When Jesus landed and saw a large crowd, he had compassion on them and healed their sick.' As was noted in chapter eight, there are many instances of compassionate ministry in the public life of Jesus, e.g. in Mt 20:34 it prompted him to heal two blind men, and in Lk 7:13 it led him to raise the dead son of the widow of Nain.

Jesus commissioned his disciples to heal. For example, in Lk 9:1-3 we read: 'Jesus called the twelve disciples together and gave them the power and the authority to cast out all demons and to cure diseases. Then he sent them to preach the kingdom of God and to heal the sick.' Before his ascension into heaven, we are told in Mk 16:17-19: 'Believers will be given the power to perform miracles, they will drive out demons in my name; they will speak in strange tongues; if they pick up snakes or drink any poison they will not be harmed; they will place their hands on sick people who will get well.' We know that in the New Testament church the apostles healed many sick people. For example, in Acts 28:8 Paul healed the father of Publius, 'When this had happened,' we are told in the following verse, 'the rest of the sick on the island came and were cured.'

As the centuries passed the charism of healing tended to die out. St Augustine echoed a common view in one of his earlier writings when he said that the charisms were given in order to help the early church get off the ground. However, once it was established, the charisms were no longer needed so they faded away. I may say in passing that, later in his life, Augustine retracted this view when he said that healing was a perennial gift in the church. The fact that so many healings were reported in his own diocese led him to change his mind.[1] So Christ continues to offer salvation and healing to the church of our day. They are two sides of the same coin of God's love. Healing can be experienced as a result of:

- Prayers of petition and intercession for healing.
- The charism of faith expressed by means of the laying on of hands, or anointing with oil. (cf. Mk 16:14; 1 Cor 12:9)
- The administration of the sacraments, especially the eucharist and the anointing of the sick.
- Visiting shrines such as Lourdes and Knock.

In Greco-Roman thought a person is made up of body and mind. In biblical theology, however, a person is made up of body, mind and spirit. This distinctive point of view is expressed in 1 Thess 5:23: 'May God himself, the God of peace, sanctify you through and through. May your whole spirit (*pneuma*), mind (*psyche*), and body (*soma*) be kept blameless at the coming of our Lord Jesus Christ.' The body, or *soma*, is the material, flesh and bone part of us. It connects us to the earth, to other people and to fellow members of the body of Christ. The mind, or *psyche*, includes reason, memory, will and emotion. The spirit, or *pneuma*, is that part of us which cannot be satisfied by created, finite realities. Scripture scholar George Montague says: 'If *psyche* is the inward principle of life which animates me, *pneuma* is my self as born from above and facing upward, my openness to self-transcendence, to movement beyond where I now stand.'[2] Rudolf Otto referred to the human spirit as 'a God-shaped blank'. In other words, it is that part of us which can only be filled and fulfilled when it is touched by the Holy Spirit.

It follows from this threefold understanding of the human person that there are three main forms of healing:

- Spiritual healing, i.e. releasing and liberating what has been referred to as the 'underdeveloped, constricted, or frustrated self'.

- Inner healing, i.e. healing of hurting memories, troubled emotions and psychological problems thereby enabling troubled people to experience peace.
- Physical healing, i.e. healing injuries, diseases, and infections.

Spiritual healing

Two of the founders of twentieth-century psychology have had an important discussions about the relationship between religious experience and mental health. Freud was an atheist. In 1913 he wrote: 'The analysis of individual human beings teaches us in no uncertain terms that the god of each of them is formed in the likeness of his father, that his personal relation to God depends on his relation to his father in the flesh, and changes along with that relation. *At bottom God is nothing other than an exalted father.*'[3] As we noted in a previous chapter, Freud believed that religion was a form of universal, obsessional neurosis. So if people wanted to become psychologically healthy, they had to abandon their childish God projection, take responsibility for their lives and learn to live without the aid of this emotional crutch.

Jung came to the opposite conclusion. He said that unless people had religious experience they would be neurotic. He felt that the decline in religion in the modern era had, in fact, led to widespread neurosis. He wrote: 'I am sure that everywhere the mental state of European man shows an alarming lack of balance. We are living undeniably in a period of the greatest restlessness, nervous tension, confusion, and disorientation of outlook.'[4] Jung said that the human psyche could only be fulfilled when the self – his word for the human spirit – enjoyed a conscious sense of the numinous. In *Modern Man in Search of a Soul* he wrote: 'In thirty years I have treated many patients in the second half of life. Every one of them became ill because he or she had lost that which the living religions in every age have given their followers (i.e. religious experience) and none of them was fully healed who did not regain his religious outlook.'[5] It is interesting to note that many of his patients were practising Christians, indeed some of them were clergymen. He argued that they got ill because, although they were committed to Christian doctrines and rituals, they were starved of conscious experience of God.

There are other psychologists who agree with Jung. For example, Viktor Frankl, a Jewish psychiatrist, was imprisoned in a number of concentration camps during the second World War, including Auschwitz, Dachau, and Theresienstadt. He noticed that, all things being equal, some prisoners were much better able to survive than others. He discovered that it was the prisoners who had a sense of higher meaning who could endure great hardship, whereas those who hadn't such a sense of meaning lost the will to live and died. Frankl described how this important realisation dawned on him in the camp. He tried to introduce into psychotherapy a point of view that saw in human existence not only a will to pleasure, in the sense of the Freudian pleasure principle, and a will to power, in the Adlerian sense of striving for superiority, but also what he referred to as the will to meaning. 'In the camp,' he relates, 'psychotherapy depended on appealing precisely to this will to meaning. But in the extreme marginal state in which the human being found himself in the camp, this meaning had to be an unconditional meaning, it had to include not merely living but also suffering and dying. And perhaps the deepest experience which I myself had in the concentration camp was that, while the concern of most people was summed up by the question, "Will we survive the camp?" – for if not, then this suffering has no sense – the question which in contrast beset me was, "has this whole suffering, this dying a meaning?" – for if not, then ultimately there is no sense in surviving. For a life whose meaning stands or falls upon whether one survives or not, a life, that is, whose meaning depends upon such a happenstance, such a life would not really be worth living at all.'[6] As a result of this experience, Frankl came to the conclusion that man's basic drive was a not a desire for pleasure or power, as some psychologists had suggested, but rather a desire for meaning, and ultimately a desire for God. He was the originator of logotherapy, i.e. a method of achieving mental health by discovering spiritual meaning in one's life.

Like Jung, Fankl felt that in modern culture this religious sense is often ignored. The consequent lack of meaning leads people to suffer from a vacuum, an emptiness at the centre of their lives, what he called existential frustration. It can lead to boredom, depression and neurosis. He felt that if people suppressed the religious sense, they would end up in a kind of idolatry by making things like pleasure, power, and reputation into unsatisfactory substitutes for meaning. He maintained that this existential vacuum can also result in neurotic illness. In other words, when the human spirit is deprived of the oxygen of meaning the person becomes dysfunctional. This kind of spiritual neurosis is not rooted in conflicts between different drives, or clashes of psychic components such as the so-called *id, ego* and *superego*. Rather, it is rooted in a conflict between different values, or in the unsatisfied longing for an ultimate meaning to life. The belief informing logotherapy is that spiritual neurosis can only be cured through an experience of ultimate meaning, i.e. God. It is interesting to note that, speaking as a theologian, Karl Rahner echoed Frankl's point. He stated that the extent to which people try to synthesise worldly and gospel values is the extent to which they will tend to suffer from neurosis.[7]

In his fine book *Riding the Wind*, George Montague indicates why religious experience leads to mental health. Because of the unity of spirit, mind and body in the scriptures, the different forms of Christian healing are interrelated. He says: 'If the *psyche* has such an influence on the body, might not the spirit in turn have a powerful influence on the *psyche* and through the *psyche* on the body as well? If we can speak of psychosomatic diseases, might we not also speak of pneuma-psychosomatic diseases? Such diseases have psychic and somatic effects but their roots are really in the underdeveloped or constricted *pneuma*.'[8] When praying for healing it is important, therefore, to go beyond the presenting problem, to discern what the underlying dysfunction might be. For example a person might have a diseases of the colon. Could it be, that it is due, in part at least, to suppressed anger? Could that anger, in turn, be rooted in the fact that the person is afflicted by anxiety which is the result of the lack of a heartfelt sense of meaning? Paul was praying for a healing of that kind of fundamental alienation when he said: 'I pray that out of his glorious riches he may strengthen you with power through his Spirit in your inner being' (Eph 3:16).

In chapter seven we noted how we live in the age of anxiety. Conscious relationship with God is the only really effective antidote to the sting of contingency and a constricted, underdeveloped self. It occurs as a result of a spiritual awakening, whether dramatic or gradual in nature. There are many graphic accounts of how people have had this experience. For example, one of the founders of Alcoholics Anonymous, Bill Wilson, described how, at the age of thirty nine, he was delivered from his destructive addiction. 'Suddenly my room blazed with an indescribable white light. I was seized with an ecstasy beyond description ... Then, seen in the mind's eye, there was a mountain. I stood upon its summit, where a great wind blew. A wind, not of air, but of spirit. In great, clean strength, it blew right through me. Then came the blazing thought, "You are a free man." ...a great peace stole over me... I became acutely conscious of a Presence which seemed like a veritable sea of living spirit ... "This," I thought, "must be the great reality. The God of the preachers." I seemed to be possessed by the absolute, and the curious conviction deepened that no matter how wrong things seemed to be, there could be no question of the ultimate rightness of God's universe. For the first time I felt I really belonged. I knew that I was loved and could not love in return.'[9] Commenting on liberating spiritual experiences of this kind, a book entitled *Twelve Steps and Twelve Traditions*, says: 'When a man or woman has a spiritual awakening, the most important meaning of it is that he has now become able to do, feel, and believe that which he could not do before on his unaided strength and resources alone. He has been granted a gift which amounts to a new state of consciousness and being ... What he has received is a free gift, and yet usually, at least in some small part, he has made himself ready to receive it.'[10] Having experienced a spiritual awakening, the AA programme encourages recovering alcoholics and by extension, all addicted people, to consolidate, clarify and deepen their spiritual lives.

I'm convinced that there are many people in modern society

who are suffering from psychological problems that are spiritual in origin. They need a spiritual awakening in order to recover. Although it might not be as dramatic as Bill Wilson's, it would lead to a therapeutic sense of God's presence, love and providence in their lives. In my experience, what is variously referred to as 'baptism in the Spirit,' being 'filled with the Spirit,' and the 'release of the Spirit' has not only a transforming effect, it also has a healing dimension. It could be described as a religious experience which inaugurates a new and decisive awareness of God's presence and action in a person's life, thereby enabling the constricted, underdeveloped, and frustrated self to grow strong in the Spirit (cf. Eph 3:16).

The need for inner healing

Pope John Paul II talks about the desirability of a civilisation of love. To build it, Christians will have to have the willingness and the power to carry out the great commandment, 'to love the neighbour as oneself' (Mt 19:19; Rom 13:9). A modern psychologist called Rollo May defined love as: 'A delight in the presence of the other person and an affirming of his or her value and development as much as one's own.'[11] The truth is, many people find it hard to love others because they cannot love themselves. As Meister Eckhart (1260-1327) stated in a surprisingly modern way: 'If you love yourself, you love everybody else as you do yourself. As long as you love another person less than you love yourself, you will not succeed in loving yourself; but if you love all alike, including yourself, you will love them as one person and that person is both God and man. Thus he is a great and righteous person who, loving himself, loves all others equally.'[12] The inability to love others in this way is often due to the fact that many people are suffering from unresolved inner pain.

Many modern psychologists would argue that although there are different psychological problems, ranging from eating disorders, addictions, obsessions, depression, etc., they have a common root, the inner conflict between the acceptable and unacceptable self. For example, Jung wrote: 'Neurosis is an inner cleavage – the state of being at war with oneself. Everything that accentuates this cleavage makes the patient worse, and everything that mitigates it tends to heal him. What drives people to war with themselves is the suspicion that they consist of two persons in opposition to one another. The conflict may be between the sensual and the spiritual, between the ego and the shadow … Neurosis is a splitting of personality.'[13] To be healed, neurotic people need to experience the unconditional mercy and love of God. It can happen in two ways. Firstly, by experiencing the unconditional love of a committed Christian. Secondly, the person can have a direct experience of the merciful love of God, so that he or she has the grace to accept that he or she is accepted. What do we learn from this? It is love that heals, human and divine love. It ends the civil war of the heart. Once the human spirit is in real relationship with God, inner healing can take place.

When it comes to inner healing, I have found that there are two recurring problems, low self-esteem and the effect of traumatic experiences.

1) Low self-esteem

Low self-esteem is a common complaint which is mainly due to shortcomings in the nurturing of children, such as, separation, conditional love, lack of physical affection, and different forms of emotional, physical and sexual abuse. As a result, the growing youngster can suffer from a lack of self-acceptance and inner worth. Instead, he or she has a feeling of inferiority and insecurity. Here are some of the predictable signs of low self-esteem which I have dealt with more fully elsewhere.[14]

- Lack of self-confidence and shyness.
- Difficulties in trusting others or sharing one's most intimate thoughts, feelings and memories with them.
- Difficulties in accepting gratitude or praise.
- Difficulties in asking for or accepting help from others.
- An exaggerated fear of failure, often associated with a tendency to brag.
- Feelings of jealousy and envy which are rooted in insecurity.

- Sexual difficulties of all kinds which are often rooted in anxiety rather than lust.
- Co-dependency and addictions of all kinds, such as substance addictions, e.g. alcoholism, and process addictions, e.g. compulsive masturbation.
- A tendency to judge and condemn others in a harsh way.
- Over sensitivity so that one is easily hurt and prone to negative emotions and anti-social behaviour.
- Unhealthy levels of emotional and physical stress.

2) The experience of trauma

All of us can be traumatised by the slings and arrows of outrageous fortune. Unfortunately bad things can, and do, happen to good people. Often, they suffer at the hands of others, as for example, when men and women are robbed, beaten up, or ruthlessly exploited in one way or another. At other times it seems as if blind chance takes a hand, as for example, when an accident or a natural disaster occurs. Some young people are traumatised by witnessing violence in the home, e.g. an angry and drunken father beating up his wife. Others are badly affected by such things as betrayal, or finding the corpse of someone who committed suicide by hanging. While the list of potential hurts is almost endless, the effects are often similar.

Clearly, people are wounded psychologically and emotionally. In the more extreme cases of hurt, such as child sex abuse, the pain is so bad that the person completely represses the memory and its associated feelings in the unconscious mind. From there it has a negative effect on conscious attitudes, feelings and behaviours. Needless to say, relationships suffer. Depression is common. In other cases, memory of the trauma is not completely repressed. But for one reason or another the unfortunate victim is unable to cope with the consequences. Arguably, vulnerabilities of the unconscious or conscious kind can leave the afflicted person open to the malign influence of the evil one. Satan can exploit negative memories, attitudes and feelings to separate a person from the loving presence of God. *Satan* in Hebrew means 'the accuser'. The evil one can exploit hurts and their associated negative feelings by tempting people to judge and condemn themselves so that they feel that God could not love them as they are. The minister of inner healing aims to bring the power of God's healing love to bear on problems such as low self-esteem and its consequences, and on traumas together with their negative effects on the personality. In this way he or she hopes to release people from the negative effects of hurting memories in order to set them free to love.

PRAYING FOR INNER HEALING

There are at least six steps in praying for inner healing.

a) Praying in the right spirit

One has to ask God to help one to pray in the right spirit, i.e. in a spirit of gentleness, compassion and reverence for the person.

- One needs to be *gentle*, i.e. sensitive, when dealing with people in their vulnerability and weakness. As Cardinal Newman once remarked, a gentle person is one who avoids inflicting unnecessary pain.
- When faced with the inner suffering of another human being one needs *compassion*, i.e. an empathic ability to recognise the hurt in another person's life and to be moved by it.
- *Reverence* is also needed. It is an ability to go beyond appearances to become aware of the sanctity of another person's inner life. After all, he or she is made in the image and likeness of God and is a temple of the Holy Spirit in virtue of baptism.

b) Praying for wisdom and knowledge

The one who prays for inner healing needs to ask God for the wisdom and knowledge which are mentioned in Is 11:2 and 1 Cor 12:8. The Lord can answer such a prayer in a number of ways.

1. Firstly, the healer is enabled by means of perceptive questioning and discussion, to go beyond a presenting problem, to discover what its root cause might be, e.g. a traumatic experience in the past.
2. Secondly, as a result of an intuitive hunch, which is often influenced by past experience and a knowledge of the human heart, the healer might sense what the key issue really is.

3. Thirdly, by means of a word of knowledge, in the form of a men-
    tal picture or an intuitive thought, one might be enabled to have
    an inspired awareness of some forgotten or repressed memory.
4. Fourthly, by means of discernment of spirits the healer might be
    able to identify whether the afflicted person was in need of
    deliverance, because an aspect of his or her personality was
    being oppressed by a spirit of evil.

Sometimes a person will ask for prayer for some physical problem,
e.g. arthritis. As the healer talks and discerns, he or she senses that
the arthritic problem is the presenting one, whereas repressed
anger to do with past hurts is the real one. So the focus quickly
switches from physical to emotional healing. Other people will be
well aware from the word go that their problem is an emotional
one, and will ask for inner healing.

c) Self-disclosure and inner healing

The most common methods of ministering inner healing are as follows. To begin with, if people suffer from low self-esteem it is
advisable to encourage them to talk about their problems. One
urges them to tell the truth, the whole truth and nothing but the
truth about their past memories and feelings, especially those
which are shameful and embarrassing. As Jas 5:16 advises: 'Confess
your sins to one another, and pray for one another, so that you may
be healed.' Over the years a number of recovering alcoholics have
asked if they could do step five, with me, by admitting their wrong-
doings and hurts in an open and honest way.

I believe, as Carl Rogers discovered, that there is great wisdom
in this step. It enables the recovering person to move from being
merely dry, to enjoying genuine sobriety. This is so because it tack-
les the problem of a lack of self-acceptance which is one of the main
underlying causes of addiction. I have been deeply impressed by
the honesty of recovering alcoholics as a courageous desire to be
honest struggled with an understandable fear of talking about the
shameful side of their lives. Their emotional fear of rejection mirrored their own attitude to themselves, i.e. the lack of self-esteem
that led them to drink in the first place. If the would-be healers listen

with unconditional positive regard and acceptance, recovering addicts begin to accept and love themselves as they are and not as they could be. At graced moments like these, one could imagine that the fiery dove of the Spirit is alighting in people's hearts to bring healing and peace. To paraphrase Eph 2:14-17, the dividing wall of rejection breaks down between the acceptable and the unacceptable self in a liberating way. As a result of getting back in touch with the true self, new energy is made available to the personality. It is this strength that makes possible true sobriety and growth. Over the years I have found that the sacrament of reconciliation and/or a non-sacramental form of self-disclosure, like that involved in step five of AA, can be used with beneficial results by anyone struggling with low self-esteem.

If people have suffered some kind of trauma, healers can assist the victims, in whatever way they can, to remember the damaging experiences and their associated feelings. There are a number of points to be kept in mind here. Often people will feel anger against those who hurt them and possibly against God who allowed the hurts to be inflicted in the first place. Often those negative feelings will be repressed, for one reason or another. Some men and women have been brought up to feel that anger is sinful; others are fearful of expressing their anger to God, because they might be punished for doing so. Repressed anger doesn't go away. It is simply buried alive in the unconscious where it attacks the person. It tends to turn into feelings of insecurity and even depression. So the healer encourages people who can recall hurting memories, to recover their sense of hurt and loss and its accompanying anger and to express it openly and honestly.

d) Forgiveness and inner healing

Unforgiveness and resentment against the people who hurt them and against an uncaring God is another common problem. In psychological and spiritual terms there is only one way forward, and that is by means of forgiveness. While it is true that divine forgiveness is freely available to us sinners at all times, we can only experience it to the extent that we are willing to extend it, with no strings attached, to those who have hurt or injured us. The scriptures make this abundantly clear. We can take a brief look at two representative texts. In Eccles 2:1-5 we are told, in words that foreshadow the teaching of the New Testament, that God will treat us as we treat others. 'Whoever exacts vengeance will experience the vengeance of the Lord, who keeps strict account of sin. Pardon your neighbour any wrongs done to you, and when you pray, your sins will be forgiven. If anyone nurses anger against another, can one then demand compassion from the Lord? Showing no pity for someone like oneself, can one then plead for one's own sins?' In Lk 6:36-39 Jesus says: 'Do not judge and you will not be judged; do not condemn and you will not be condemned. Forgive and you will be forgiven ... for the measure you give will be the measure you will get back.'

At this point I would like to cite two examples of merciful love that have inspired me deeply. As you know millions of Jews were unjustly murdered by the Nazis. A prayer redolent with mercy was found at the Ravensbruck concentration camp. It was scrawled on a piece of wrapping paper which lay near the body of a dead child. It read:

> 'Lord remember not only the men and women of good will but also those of ill will. As well as remembering the suffering they have inflicted on us, remember also the fruits we have produced, thanks to this suffering, – our comradeship, our loyalty, our humility, the courage, the generosity, the greatness of heart which have grown from all this. And when they come to judgement, let all the fruits we have borne be their forgiveness.'

More recently, a terrible civil war has been raging in Algeria. It has already claimed the lives of over 60,000 people. In 1996 a Trappist monk named Fr Christian de Cherge realised that he could be murdered by a Muslim extremist. Shortly before he was actually killed in May 1996, he wrote these moving words:

> My life has no more value than any other, nor any less value. In any case, it has not the innocence of childhood. I have lived long enough to know that I share in the evil which seems, alas, to pre-

vail in the world, even in that act of aggression that may strike me down. I should like when the time comes, to have a clear space which would allow me to beg forgiveness from God and from all my fellow human beings, and at the same time to forgive with all my heart the one who would strike me down … Friend of my final moment, who will not be aware of what you are doing. Yes, for you also I wish to say, *thank you* – and, *adieu* – and to commend you to the God whose face I see in yours. And may we, happy 'good thieves,' find each other in Paradise, if it pleases God, the Father of us both.

If there is someone who needs your forgiveness you could react in three possible ways:

- 'I won't.' Be aware that such a response threatens to cut you off from the grace of God.
- 'I can't.' Strictly speaking, this is true. As Shakespeare reminds us 'to err is human, to forgive divine.'
- 'I will with God's help.' This is the way forward into Christian peace. We can be assured that what we want to do is so conformed to the will of our merciful God that he will pour out his Spirit of forgiveness into us, thereby empowering us to do what otherwise would be impossible. At this point you might like to pray: 'Father in heaven, in the name of Jesus your divine and merciful Son, help me to worship you in spirit and in truth. Take away my heart of stone and grant me, instead, a merciful heart like yours. Forgive me for the many times I have hurt you and other people. Help me, in my turn, to remember if there is any person, living or dead, who stands in need of my forgiveness. (Pause for prayerful reflection) Lord, grant me both the desire and the power to forgive that person from my heart. I thank you that even now you are granting me the grace of forgiveness, taking away my bitterness, and blessing the person who hurt me in the past. Now Lord, let a tidal wave of your mercy engulf us so that we may truly experience your peace. Amen'

A cautionary note needs to be registered here. It is admirable when people who have suffered a terrible loss say in the immediate after-math that they forgive those responsible. After all, the scriptures say we shouldn't let the sun go down on our anger (Eph 4:26). Nevertheless, experience teaches that it takes time for the full implications of a major trauma to sink in. When it does, it will be normally associated with feelings such as loss, grief, anger and resentment. These feelings need to be fully acknowledged. If they are suppressed in the name of a premature and dutiful act of for-giveness, there is a danger that the forgiveness will be superficial and lacking depth and credibility. As the book of Ecclesiastes chap-ter three reminds us, there is a time for everything, including, we could add, a time for being angry and a time for forgiving. As the onion of pain is progressively peeled, new layers of hurt and anger will be exposed, hence the scriptural injunction that we keep on for-giving (Mt 18:22) until no anger or resentment remains.

In my experience, forgiveness lies at the heart of inner healing. Once resentment is gone, hurt feelings are freed to surface at a con-scious level of awareness. At this point the healer can explain that even if the sufferer felt deserted by God at the time of the traumatic experiences, God was there, nevertheless, suffering with and for the person. Then one explains that to the Lord 'a day is as a thousand years and a thousand years is a day' (2 Pt 3:8). Divine grace is avail-able to touch the hurting memories as if they were occurring just now and not long ago. Then he or she prays that the compassionate love of God will enter the hurting memories to bring them healing and peace.

e) Deliverance and inner healing

Sometimes, the healer will discern that besides suffering from psy-chological and emotional problems, there is reason to believe that spiritual oppression may be involved as well. In other words, the evil one, the accuser, the liar and opponent of God's kingdom may be exploiting the person's psycho-spiritual vulnerability in some way or other, e.g. by prompting a compulsive and irrational desire to commit suicide. In that case, the healer would pray silently but confidently in the name of Jesus, either asking God to deliver the person from the evil, or even commanding the oppressive spirit to go. It should be noted in passing that we are not talking about possession or solemn exorcism. In my experience they are very rare, and should only be dealt with by someone appointed by the local bishop. It is important to believe, as scripture tells us: 'Although we live in the world, we do not wage war as the world does. The weapons we fight with are not the weapons of the world. On the contrary, they have divine power to demolish strongholds (of Satan). We demolish arguments and every pretension that sets itself up against the knowledge of God, and we take captive every thought to make it obedient to Christ' (2 Cor 10:3-5). By and large it is better to say nothing about evil spirits to the person being prayed with. It is also better to pray quietly, and not out loud, that the person would be freed from spiritual oppression.

f) Aftercare is important
To pray for inner healing is to form a relationship with a person. It is important therefore that afterwards one keeps in touch with the person who has been prayed with to see how he or she is getting on. This acts as an encouragement. It will often happen that one level of inner healing reveals another layer of need and so it may be necessary to have on-going prayer for inner healing. In my experience it is also important to encourage the afflicted person to strengthen his or her spiritual life, e.g. by prayer, reading of scripture, reception of the sacraments, etc., because the closer one is to God, the better one is able to cope with inner vulnerability. I am convinced that it is a mistake to believe that all inner hurts can and will be healed in this life. Quite often, the Lord leaves us to endure them. They are our thorn in the flesh. What we can learn to do is to befriend and manage our problems, e.g. a propensity to anxiety or depression, while believing that God's power 'will be made perfect in our weakness' (2 Cor 12:9). Vulnerabilities of this kind, which Jung referred to as 'sacred woundedness', can school us in many virtues, such as reliance on God, patience and forbearance, humility and above all compassion (cf. Rom 5:5:3-4). St Paul said that God: 'comforts us in all our afflictions, so that we may be able to comfort those who are

in any affliction, with the comfort with which we ourselves are comforted by God' (2 Cor 1:4). It is significant surely that Paul does not speak here of either healing or consolation. Rather he speaks about comfort. The word comes from the Latin, *con fortis,* which means, 'with strength'. The Lord strengthens the afflicted, by his Spirit, to endure in a faithful and persevering way.

Physical healing

Like inner healing, the subject of physical healing is a big one. Here are a few comments about it. They don't pretend to be comprehensive. Firstly many of the points that were made in connection with inner healing are relevant here, also.

Prayer for physical healing has to be conducted within a context of peace. So healers try to be as relaxed as possible when praying. They encourage the person who is being prayed with, to be relaxed as well. There is no need for anxious effort. The Lord says, 'the battle is not yours but mine' (2 Chron 20:15). Indeed research has shown that, typically, the brainwaves of many healers change from alpha rhythms, i.e. 14 to 20 cycles per second, to the beta rhythms characteristic of the sleeping state, i.e. 4 to 7 cycles per second. They are contagious in the sense that often the brainwaves of the person being prayed with also change to beta rhythms.[15] It is within this context of peace that one is open to divine inspiration, such as an appropriate scripture text, an image, a word of knowledge, or discernment. The latter is needed in order to see if the presenting physical problem, e.g. arthritis, has a psychological or spiritual dimension, as it often has. For example, it is now thought that most physical sickness is stress related. But stress can be rooted in the psychological fact that a person is very insecure, and in the spiritual fact that the person has a constricted self which isn't sufficiently open to the felt awareness of God and God's love.

Secondly, when praying it is important to do so within the measure of faith that one has been given by God (cf. Rom 12:3). There are two forms of this kind of trust, hesitant and expectant. A person with hesitant trust accepts God's promises at a notional level, believing them to be true. However, when faced by a particular problem such as an illness, he or she may not be quite sure whether God is going to act, right now, in these particular circumstances. Typically the person prays a prayer of *petition* in the hope that God may do something in the future, if what is asked is in accordance with God's will, e.g. 'Lord I know that nothing is impossible to you. I ask you, if it is your will, to heal this person whom you love.' A person with expectant or charismatic faith accepts that the promises of God are true at a notional level. But as a result of a divine inspiration, in a particular situation of need, he or she has no inner doubt about them (cf. Mk 11:22), and confidently believes that God is acting, or soon will act, in the here and now. Typically such a person prays a prayer of *command*. Instead of having to see evidence in order to believe, this kind of confident faith believes in order to see, e.g. 'Lord, nothing is impossible to you. In your name I say to this sickness, yield to the healing power of God at work within you, and I thank you Lord, that even now that your Spirit is hastening to fulfil your loving will.' The future hope of a prayer of command like this is rooted in present conviction. As the letter to the Hebrews 11:1 puts it: 'Faith is the assurance (in the present) of things hoped for (in the future), the conviction (in the present) of things not seen (in the future).

Here is an example of what can be involved. A few years ago I was a speaker at a conference in Wales. I was due to give a talk on the gifts of the Holy Spirit, one of which is the word of knowledge, i.e. an inspired intuition about some unknown fact. Before going out on stage, I asked the Lord if he wished to give me such a word, so that I would be able to illustrate the section on the charism of knowledge with a concrete example. With that, the image of a woman came to mind. It seemed as if something was wrong with one of her eyes and that it was causing her a good deal of pain. In the course of my talk some time later, I referred to this mental image. When the talk was over a woman came forward. She said that the moment I mentioned the symptoms, she knew that she was the person in question. Apparently, two assailants had attacked her a year before. They had beaten her up and thrown acid in her face. The sight in one eye had been badly damaged and the other eye was causing her a lot of pain. A number of us gathered round and prayed for her. Because of the word of knowledge we were convinced that we were praying within the will of God and that the Spirit was acting. Well, a few hours later the painful eye was restored, the pain was gone, never to return, and the woman had no further need of medication. Not only that, the traumatic effects of the attack, such as panicky fear and apprehension, melted away over a period of a few hours, so that the woman was filled with an inner sense of peace.

Thirdly, many people involved in the healing ministry stress the importance of creative imagination. They try to imagine the person getting better. Because grace builds upon nature, I focus my imagination on the immune system of the person. It is his or her God given defence mechanism. It tries to ward off illness and disease, e.g. cancer. If perchance the person does pick up an infection, the immune system tries to overcome it. The same is true of physical injuries. For example, if a person breaks a bone or is wounded in some way or another, the natural healing powers of the body are mobilised in an effort to repair the damage. I find that it can be helpful to imagine, in an affirming way, that the Holy Spirit, the Lord and *giver of life*, is focusing divine energy on the immune system and the self-repairing powers of the body as it accelerates and directs their defensive and therapeutic activities. In her book *The Healing Light*, Agnes Sanford suggests that it is good to imagine what you are convinced is happening.[16] You can see the afflicted part of the body bathed in the light of the Spirit, and also see it recovering, e.g. the disks in an injured spine growing stronger, more subtle and flexible, while thanking God that the Lord's healing love is at work in and through the recuperative powers of the body (cf. Phil 4:6; Thess 5:18).

Fourthly, when the prayer is over, its better not to claim too much. A tentative approach is more suitable, e.g. 'The Lord was truly present as we prayed. I wouldn't be a bit surprised if you began to improve. Let's wait and see what happens.' If the person does seem to improve, be slow to publicise the fact for a while. Some apparent healings are due to the placebo effect which tends to wear off over a week or two. Sometimes the person prayed with will experience a partial improvement. That may be an indication that he or she needs further soaking prayer. Incidentally, it is unwise to advise people to give up their medication as a sign of faith, unless a doctor has verified that fact that they don't need it anymore. As Sir 38:1-16 tells us, medicine is part of God's provision for healing. 'The Lord created medicines out of the earth, and the sensible will not despise them ... by them the physician heals and takes away pain; the pharmacist makes a mixture from them. God's works will never be finished; and from him health spreads over all the earth. My child, when you are ill, do not delay, but pray to the Lord, and he will heal you ... Then give the physician his place, for the Lord created him; do not let him leave you, for you need him. There may come a time when recovery lies in the hands of physicians, for they too pray to the Lord that he grant them success in diagnosis and in healing, for the sake of preserving life.' My father was a veterinary surgeon. I can remember how he echoed the words of scripture when he said that while doctors and vets can assist the healing process, ultimately healing comes from God in and through the body's own recuperative powers.

Conclusion

In this chapter we have only taken a brief look at some points to do with healing of body, mind and spirit. Over the years I have found that when the sacraments, e.g. of eucharist, reconciliation and anointing of the sick, are administered and received in faith, they can be powerful instruments of healing grace. Because I have dealt with this aspect of healing elsewhere, I will not dwell on it here.[17] Suffice it to say that healing, as a sign and pledge of the future restoration of all things in Christ's second coming, is an important aspect of the Christian life.

CHAPTER 10

Spiritual Warfare

It is clear in the gospels and the other New Testament writings that Jesus and his disciples espoused a worldview in which they saw two kingdoms in contention, the kingdom of God and the kingdom of this world. Indeed Satan, the father of lies, the accuser of the brethren, the divider and murderer, is described as prince of this world (Jn 12:31; 14:30; 16:11). This framework of understanding is presumed in Eph 6:1-17, and is the focus of attention in this chapter. It assumes that through his death, resurrection and ascension, Jesus has broken the power of Satan in principle in the heavenly realm, and is progressively breaking that power, in fact, in the earthly realm.

By and large this worldview is not accepted any more. The devil is seen by many as a myth, a personification of human sin and weakness. As a result, this passage doesn't seem relevant to them. For example, I looked at a commentary on Ephesians, by Lionel Swain, a Catholic scripture scholar, which was published in 1980. In the section on Eph 6:10-17 he says: 'Warfare – even spiritual warfare – is not a metaphor that is very congenial to our modern mentality, especially when we realise that belligerent spiritual forces outside man are part of an outmoded cosmology.' As a result, he says little or nothing about the spiritual armour mentioned in chapter six. This raises an important question. Does the church still teach that the devil exists? The answer is yes, with certain qualifications.

For example, Pope Paul VI said in an address, 'The question of the devil and the influence he can have on individual persons as well as communities, whole societies or events, is a very important chapter of Catholic doctrine … It is a departure from the picture provided by biblical and church teaching to refer to the devil's existence … as a pseudo reality, a conceptual and fanciful personification of the unknown causes of our misfortunes.' The Pope's views were echoed in *Christian Faith and Demonology*, published by the Vatican in 1975. It states: 'We repeat … that though still emphasising in our day the real existence of the demonic, the Church has no intention … of proposing an alternative explanation which would be more acceptable to reason. Its desire is simply to remain faithful to the gospel and its requirements.'

Raymond Brown was one of the greatest biblical scholars writing in English. In two of his later books *Responses to 101 Questions on the Bible* and *An Introduction to New Testament Christology*, he clearly stated that he believed that the devil exists and that Jesus was an exorcist. Albert Nolan, another Catholic scholar, has stated that 'Jesus saw his liberating activity as a kind of power struggle with Satan, a warfare against the power of evil in all its shapes and forms.'[1] Karl Rahner, the greatest Catholic theologian of the century, has written: 'It will be firmly maintained that the existence of angels and demons is affirmed in scripture and not merely assumed as a hypothesis which can be dropped today.' While Catholic theology believes that the devil and evil spirits exist, it would not be committed to the largely mythological cosmology of Paul's day which believed that there were sovereignties, rulers, powers and principalities in the heavenly realm. While being agnostic and non-committal about those entities, it would say Jesus is Lord over whatever spirits exist. It also avoids exaggerating the importance of the devil's role in a fundamentalist and simplistic way that overlooks the influence of sinful human nature as a primary source of temptation and wrong doing.

Spiritual writers, especially those who are interested in discernment of spirits, acknowledge that the evil spirit can impinge in different ways upon the human spirit. St Ignatius of Loyola is the best known guide in this area. In his *Spiritual Exercises* he says that there are three possible sources of the inspirations that motivate people, the human spirit, the Holy Spirit and the evil spirit. Discernment of spirits is necessary in order to work out which spirit it is. Ignatius described his well known guidelines for testing the spirits as 'rules for understanding to some extent the different movements produced in the soul, and for recognising those that are good, to admit them, and those that are bad, to reject them.'[2] Ignatius says that, typically, the devil seeks to separate people from God in three different ways. Firstly, he can tempt them in such a bullying and intimidating manner that they feel that effective resistance is not possible. This bluff can be exposed when temptation is resisted with courage and energy. Secondly, the devil can act like a seducer. He can encourage those he seeks to influence to keep their temptations private and secret. This tactic can be overcome by revealing one's temptations to a trusted confidant, confessor or spiritual director. Thirdly, the evil one can act like a military commander who assesses the principal weaknesses of a person in order to ruthlessly exploit them. Ignatius says that the devil will be outmanoeuvred if the person is aware of his or her principal vulnerabilities while trusting in God's power to strengthen and protect.

This chapter does not intend to take a comprehensive look at the different ways in which a person can defend him or herself against the temptations, illusions and false inspirations of the evil one. Like other authors,[3] I have dealt with this topic elsewhere.[4] Here we will restrict ourselves to a brief exegetical study of the most important passage on the subject of spiritual warfare in Eph 6:10-20.

Paul begins by saying 'Be strong in the Lord and in the strength of his might' (Eph 6:10). This verse finds an echo in 1 Cor 16:13, 'Keep alert, stand firm in your faith, be courageous, be strong'; and 2 Tim 2:1, 'Be strong in the grace that is in Christ Jesus.' These verses remind one of passages in the Old Testament where the Jewish people had to face the armies of their enemies which were often larger and better equipped. Time and time again the Lord said things like: 'Remember I have commanded you to be determined and confident! Don't be afraid or discouraged, for I, the Lord your God, am with you' (Jos 1:9); And in another place, 'Do not be afraid! Stand by and see the salvation of the Lord which he will accomplish for you today ... The Lord will fight for you while you remain silent' (Ex 14:13); and finally, 'The Lord says that you must not be discouraged or be afraid ... the battle depends on God, not on you' (2 Chron 20:15). In all these passages, unwavering reliance on the Lord invariably leads to victory.

Spiritual armour

St Paul says that we need to 'put on the full armour of the Lord.' A number of comments can be made about this verse. Firstly, in the Old Testament we are told that God is a warrior who himself wears this armour. Speaking of the Lord Is 11:5 says: 'Righteousness will be his belt and faithfulness the sash around his waist.' In Is 59:17 we are told that God 'put on righteousness as his breastplate, and the helmet of salvation on his head; he put on the garments of vengeance and wrapped himself in zeal as in a cloak.' These points are reiterated in Wis 5:17-20: 'The Lord will take his zeal as his whole armour, and will arm all creation to repel his enemies; he will put on righteousness as a breastplate and wear impartial justice as a helmet; he will take holiness as an invincible shield, and sharpen stern wrath for a sword.' To put on the armour of the Lord is to be clothed in his strength and protection.

Secondly, when St Paul spoke about armour in Eph 6:10-20 he was probably thinking about the six pieces that were worn by Roman soldiers. When he was under house arrest he would have had a Roman soldier guarding him. He would have had a good opportunity to see the armour at close quarters and to ask questions about it. The first three items, the belt, breastplate and footwear were commonly worn when soldiers were at work during peacetime. The second three, the shield, sword and helmet were worn in times of danger and battle. Lets look at each piece in turn.

a) The belt of truth

Is 11:5 is probably the Old Testament origin of Paul's reference here. Speaking of God it says: 'Righteousness will be his belt and faithfulness the sash around his waist.' What had Paul in mind? Mention of the belt involves three possibilities. Firstly, a Roman soldier used to wear a leather apron to protect his lower abdomen. Secondly he wore a leather belt which would tuck in his tunic and carry his dagger and sword. Thirdly, if he were an officer he would wear a special sash or belt. It is probable that Paul had this last type in mind. The Christian is girded with a sign of great dignity and authority. The truth here does not refer to doctrinal orthodoxy, but rather to integrity, dependability and trustworthiness. By living in this way the Christian reflects divine attributes. As Paul says in Eph 5:9: 'the effects of the light are seen in complete goodness and uprightness in truth.' Unfortunately many of us lack that integrity of life to the extent that we try to create a false synthesis of gospel and worldly values. For instance, in sexual and financial matters we can adopt a worldly lifestyle that is clearly at odds with the teachings of scripture. These compromises leave a person very vulnerable to the influence of the spirit of evil, especially in the day of testing.

b) The breastplate of righteousness

The breastplate protected the soldier's body. There were different forms. Originally it was a sleeveless jacket made of many layers of linen or leather and which was worn like a corset. But it is thought that Paul had a frontal piece of metal in mind – the kind worn by the infantrymen of his day – and also chain mail that covered the chest and hips. For Paul it is a metaphor for the righteousness that justifies a person by grace alone (cf. Rom 3:21-31). It is expressed by means of the obedience of faith, i.e. leading an upright life and having, as a result, a good conscience. Arguably, because this piece of armour protects the body, it is a metaphor for protection against the sins of the body such as intemperate use of food, drink, sex, drugs, etc. As a Christian develops strength of character by donning the breastplate of right relationship with God, his or her heart is protected from sin and evil.

c) The gospel of peace

It is probable that Is 40:3, 9, and 52:7 provide the Old Testament background to this verse. Apparently, Roman soldiers wore distinctive footwear which was firm, gave them leg support and enabled them to conduct long marches. The Christian's footwear is the gospel of peace. The peace mentioned here refers to the peace made and proclaimed by the Messiah. As Paul says in Eph 2:14, Jesus is our peace, he breaks down the dividing wall of division between different groups, e.g. Catholics and Protestants. This peace which unites, and will continue to unite all who believe in the Lord, will give them strength to resist non-human, demonic attacks of whatever kind. As Jesus said in Mk 3:25: 'If a house is divided against itself, that house cannot stand.' It is possible that two other points are implicit here. Firstly, there is a willingness to bring the gospel of peace to others. As Is 52:9 and Rom 10:15 says: 'How lovely on the mountains are the feet of the one who brings good news.' Secondly, there is a need for firmness and at the same time adaptability in the service of the good news.

d) The shield of faith

Roman soldiers had two types of shield. The one referred to here was the larger of the two. It was oval shaped, four and a half feet high and two and a half feet wide. It consisted of two layers of wood and was covered with leather. When the enemy were firing arrows, tipped with burning pitch, in the earlier phase of a battle, the soldiers would douse their shields with water, form a phalanx, and crouch behind them for protection. St Paul says that the shield of faith will put out all the fiery darts of the evil one, just as the shields of the Roman soldiers would do. Scripture repeatedly makes it clear that the Lord is our spiritual shield. For example, in Prov 30:5 we read: 'He (God) is a shield to those who take refuge in him', and in Ps 144:2: 'He is my loving God, my fortress, my stronghold and my deliverer, my shield in whom I take refuge.'

This is an important assurance. We can deal with *all* the fiery darts of greed, lust, jealousy, envy, unbelief, resentment, etc., by raising the shield of faith. In other words, although St Peter says: 'resist the devil firm in your faith' (1 Pt 5:9), and St James says: 'resist the devil and he will flee from you' (Jas 4:7), we don't do so directly. Rather we take refuge in the One who is greater than our adversary. When asked how she had survived the evils of life in a concentration camp, the late Corrie Ten Boom replied, 'I learned to nestle and not to wrestle.' In other words, when she was confronted by evil from either within or without her personality, she nestled in the Lord through faith instead of wrestling directly with it. As St Paul assures us in 1 Cor 10:13: 'God is faithful, he will not let you be tempted beyond what you can bear. But when you are tempted, he will also provide a way out so that you can stand up under it.'

Over the years I have found that I can best express my faith by invoking the holy name of Jesus. As Paul says in Phil 2:9-11: 'God exalted him to the highest place and gave him the name that is above every name, that at the name of Jesus every knee should bow, in heaven and on earth and under the earth, and every tongue confess that Jesus Christ is Lord, to the glory of God the Father.' In other words, no matter what kind of spirit one has to contend with, it has to submit to the greater authority of the holy name. Over the years a number of people have told me that in the past they used to have a recurring nightmare in which they were terrified by a shadowy presence of evil which used to insinuate itself into their bed rooms. At first they would be so paralysed by fear that they could neither scream or speak. Then it occurred to them, 'if I could only utter the holy name of Jesus, this evil would leave me.' At first they could only manage to whisper it with difficulty. Then they could say it quietly. But as their defiant confidence grew, they could shout out the name of the Lord. As soon as they did, the sense of evil would evaporate like dew before the rising sun and their inner peace returned. So when faced with evil from either within or without your personality, raise the shield of faith by invoking the name of Jesus with reverence and trust.

e) The helmet of salvation

Is 59:17; 11:4 and 49:2 are the Old Testament background to this item of armour. Roman helmets were usually made of bronze or iron alloy. They often had a hinged visor added so that there would be extra protection for the face. The head is the centre of thoughts and attitudes. Confidence of our salvation in Christ, the assurance that in him we have all the graces we need is our best protection against the negative thoughts and feelings that might assail us. For example, I have often been tempted to feel that God couldn't work through me because of my past sins and failures. But as the saying goes, feelings are not facts. Scripture tells us what the objective truth really is when it says: 'For those who are in Christ Jesus there is now no condemnation' (Rom 8:1), and consequently 'God *is* at work within you to will and to work for his good pleasure' (Phil 2:13).

f) The sword of the Spirit

What Paul has in mind here is not a heavy broad sword, the kind one sees in most pictures, but rather the short double-edged dagger used for close fighting. This is the only piece of equipment that was used specifically for attack. The Christian's sword is the word of God. As Heb 4:12 tells us: 'The word of God is alive and active. Sharper than any double-edged sword, it penetrates even to dividing soul and spirit, joints and marrow, it judges the thoughts and attitudes of the heart.' A hymn in the *Divine Office* says: 'Bright as fire in darkness, sharper than a sword, lives throughout the ages God's eternal word.' As such, it has power to ward off the attacks of the evil one. It is a striking fact that when Jesus was tempted by Satan in the wilderness he counteracted his lies and false promises by quoting inspired *rhema* words from scripture. For example, when the devil tempted him to turn stones into bread, Jesus replied by quoting these words from Deut 8:3: 'Human beings live not on bread alone but on every word that comes from the mouth of God' (Mt 4:4).

In the Greek language there are two ways of describing God's word, i.e. either as the *logos* word or the *rhema* word. As a generalisation, it is more or less true to say that the *logos* word is the objective truth in itself. The *rhema* word, on the other hand, is the spoken word that is revealed by God in a particular situation.[5] It may be a text that is spontaneously remembered at the time, or one that a person is led to in the scriptures. That inspired word has the Spirit given power to effect what it says. As Is 55:11 says, it will not return to the Lord without achieving the purpose for which it was sent.

Over the years I have found that in moments of need and temptation, the Lord has caused many scripture texts to jump alive off the page into my heart. It was those words that enabled me to cope and to overcome. For example, if I was tempted by a spirit of fear, I would recall the words of 2 Tim 1:7: 'The spirit you received from God is *not* a spirit of fear.' This verse enabled me to discern that my temptation to fear was not from the Lord. It may have come from either my unconscious or from the evil one. Then I'd recall a reassuring promise from scripture: 'So do not fear, for I am with you; do not be dismayed, for I am your God. I will strengthen you and help you; I will uphold you with my righteous right hand' (Is 41:10). When I was tempted by sinful desires I'd often recall the words: 'The Spirit you received is a spirit of love and power and soundmindedness, i.e. *self-control*' (2 Tim 1:7), and the reassuring verse: 'He who is within you (i.e. the Holy Spirit) is greater than he who is in the world (i.e. Satan)' (1 Jn 4:4). Armed with the sword of truths like these I could ward of the attacks of the adversary. As Luther put it in his hymn, *A Mighty Fortress*:

> And through this world, with devils filled, should threaten to undo us;
> We will not fear, for God has willed his truth to triumph through us.
> The prince of darkness grim, we tremble not for him;
> His rage we can endure; for lo! his doom is sure;
> *One little word shall fell him.*
> *That word above all earthly powers, no thanks to them, abideth.*
> The Spirit and the gifts are ours, through him with us abideth.

Conclusion

In the Lord's prayer we say, 'deliver us from the evil', i.e. from Satan, the evil one. In Eph 6:10-17 Paul has shown us how the Lord can deliver us. As he says in Heb 2:14-15, Jesus died that he might destroy him who has the power of death, that is, the devil; and again in Col 2:15: 'And having disarmed the powers and authorities, he made a public spectacle of them, triumphing over them by the cross.' To do battle with the forces of evil we need to be strong in the Spirit that Jesus poured out on the cross (cf. Jn 19:34). In other words, we need to be baptised in the Spirit and to renew and deepen that anointing on a daily basis by means of prayer in the Spirit. As Jesus said to the apostles in Gethsemene, 'Watch and pray so that you will not fall into temptation. The spirit is willing, but the body is weak' (Mk 14:38). Paul echoed these words when he said: 'Never get tired of staying awake to pray … keep praying in the Spirit on every possible occasion' (Eph 6:18).

Finally, it is interesting to note that in his letter to Polycarp, St Ignatius of Antioch, one of the early Fathers of the Church, wrote: 'Make every effort to satisfy the Commander under whom you serve, and from whom you will draw your pay; and be sure that no deserter is found in your ranks. For a shield take your baptism, for a helmet your faith, for a spear your love, and for body-armour your patient endurance; and lay up a store of good works as a soldier deposits his savings, so that one day you may draw the credits that will be due to you. And be patient and gentle with one another, as God is with you.'[6]

CHAPTER 11

Friendship and Evangelisation

The link between friendship and evangelisation is biblical. In this chapter we will explore St Vincent de Paul's understanding of the nature of the connection, together with the motives and means that modern day Christians have of fostering it. Originally these reflections were written with Vincentian priests and brothers in mind. They have been adapted, however, to include men and women of the wider Vincentian family. It embraces people like the Daughters of Charity of St Vincent de Paul, members of the St Vincent de Paul Society, the Holy Faith Sisters, and the many lay men and women who, animated by the spirit of St Vincent, work alongside the Vincentians in different situations. Briefly put it is a spirit of gentleness, compassion and reverence for the individual, especially for the poor and the marginalised. Hopefully the following thoughts will not only prove helpful to them but, to all Christians who are committed to the urgent task of evangelisation. The final section, of this chapter has been written with their needs in mind.

Friendship and Evangelisation in the New Testament Church
New Testament Christians believed that there was a close connection between friendship in the community and evangelisation. St Luke described the link in these words in Acts 4:32: 'All the believers were one in heart and mind. No one claimed that any of his possessions was his own, but they shared everything they had. With great power the apostles continued to testify to the resurrection of the Lord Jesus, and much grace was upon them all. There were no needy persons among them. For from time to time those who owned lands or houses sold them, brought the money from the sales and put it at the apostle's feet, and it was distributed to anyone as he had need.'

A number of comments can be made about these verses. Firstly, the opening one echoes the teaching of the Greeks, Jews and Romans on the nature of friendship. For example, in the fifth century BC Pythagoras founded a community of friends. It had four guidelines:

- Friends share in the perfect communion of a single spirit.
  Later the phrase 'friendship is one soul dwelling in two bodies' was attributed to Aristotle.
- Friends share everything in common.
- Friends are equals, and friendship is an indication of equality.
- A friend is a second self.[1]

Perhaps the outstanding Old Testament passage on friendship, in Sir 6:14-18, was influenced by Greek thinking after the conquest of Palestine by Alexander.[2] It reads: 'Faithful friends are a sturdy shelter; whoever finds one has found a treasure. Faithful friends are life-saving medicine; and those who fear the Lord will find them. Those who fear the Lord direct their friendship aright, for as they are so are their neighbours also.' The friendship between David and Jonathan in 1 Sam 18:1-5 epitomised this ideal: 'Jonathan became one spirit with David and loved him as himself ... he swore eternal friendship for him. He took off the robe he was wearing and gave it to David, together with his armour and also his sword and his belt.' The relationship between David and Jonathan prefigured the friendship between Jesus and the apostles. Jesus told the twelve that they were his friends, he shared his most intimate secrets with them and saw his death as an act of sacrificial love for them.

In the Roman era Cicero echoed the Greco-Jewish ideal to a certain extent when he wrote: 'All I myself can do is to urge you to place friendship above every other human concern that can be imagined! Nothing else in the whole world is so completely in harmony with our nature ... Real friendship is more powerful than kinship; for the latter may exist without goowill, whereas friendship can do no such thing ... It may be defined as a complete identity of feeling about all things in heaven and earth, an identity which is strengthened by mutual goodwill and affection. With the single exception of wisdom, I am inclined to regard it as the greatest of all the gifts the gods have bestowed upon mankind … Moreover, it is to moral goodness that friendship owes its entire origin and character. Without goodness, it cannot even exist.'[3]

It would probably be accurate to say that Luke was consciously and deliberately saying that, thanks to the transforming power of grace, the early Christians fulfilled these ancient ideals of friendship, i.e. unity of mind and heart expressed in a community of goods.[4] Although some members of the early Christian church may have been intimate friends, I don't think that Luke was implying that all the members were necessarily sharing their inmost thoughts and feelings with one another. They were one in mind and heart in so far as they were conformed to the mind and heart of Christ. St Paul seemed to endorse this interpretation when he said in Phil 2:2; 5: 'Be of the same mind, having the same love, being in full accord and of one mind … Let the same mind be in you that was in Christ.' This ideal was echoed in many other New Testament epistles, e.g. Rom 15:5-6: 'May the God who gives endurance and encouragement give you a spirit of unity among yourselves as you follow Christ Jesus so that with one heart and mouth you may glorify the God and Father of our Lord Jesus Christ;' and 1 Cor 1:10: 'I appeal to you, brothers and sisters, in the name of our Lord Jesus Christ, that all of you agree with one another so that there may be no divisions among you and that you may be perfectly united in mind and thought;' and 1 Pt 3:8: 'Finally, all of you, live in harmony with one another; be sympathetic, love as brothers and sisters, be compassionate and humble.'

What is really significant in the passage, adverted to in the Acts, is the fact that Luke inserted a verse about evangelisation into the middle of a passage on community relationships, i.e. 'With great power the apostles continued to testify to the resurrection of the Lord Jesus, and much grace was upon them.' What he seemed to be saying was this: friendly, loving relationships in the community, and effective evangelisation in the world, are inextricably linked. This was true for a number of reasons.

- As the story of the two disciples on the road to Emmaus shows, the risen Jesus is experienced in the eucharistic community where the members share their lives in the context of God's word and the breaking of bread (cf. Lk 24:13-36; Acts 2:42).

- As members of this community, the apostles – like the disciples on the road to Emmaus – had the desire and the power to witness to the resurrection of the Lord in an effective way. Their preaching of the *kerygma* was energised by the loving mercy they themselves experienced on a daily basis in the Christian fellowship.

- Not only that, the loving Christian community – the body of Christ on earth – was a living embodiment of the apostle's inspired preaching of the Good News, so that the hearts of those who heard it burned within them (cf. Lk 24:32) and enabled them to exclaim, 'God is really among you' (1 Cor 14:25). As a result, more and more people joined the Christian community.

St Vincent de Paul on friendship in community and evangelisation
Friendship has been valued throughout Christian history. In his book, *Friendship and Community: The Monastic Experience 350-1250*, Brian Mc Guire has shown, in a fascinating and well researched study, how the ideal of Christian friendship was cultivated, from the Fathers of the Church to the high middle ages.[5] For example, St Thomas Aquinas enjoyed spiritual friendships with Reginald of Piperno and Albert the Great who were fellow Dominicans. Indeed when Thomas died, Albert the Great could never hear Thomas's name without shedding tears. In his writings the angelic doctor used his experience of Christian friendship as a key theological construct to understand many subjects such as the Trinity, grace, contemplation, etc.[6] Around the same time, Sts Bernard and Aelred of Rievaulx articulated the monastic ideal. In his classic work, *Spiritual Friendship*, which was a Christianised version of Cicero's *De Amictitia*, Aelred said: 'God is friendship, it does sound strange doesn't it? And there is no authority for it in scripture, but I wouldn't hesitate to attribute to friendship anything associated with charity, as for instance. "he who abides in friendship abides in God and God abides in him".'[7]

Heterosexual friendships have their place in the Christian life.

Rosemary Radar has shown, in a well researched study, how friendship, whether same-sex or hetrosexual, was esteemed in the first few centuries of Christianity. For example, in the *Book of the Angel*, which was written in 8th century Ireland, we read: 'Between holy Patrick and Brigid, pillars of the Irish, there existed so great a friendship of charity that they were of one heart and one mind.'[8] Richard Rolle (1300-1349) acknowledged that friendship between men and women 'is apt to turn to virtue's disadvantage,' but nevertheless he wrote: 'there is a certain love that man has for woman and woman for man which none of us is without, not even the saint. It is both natural and 'instituted of God' in origin, and through it we exist, and fit in with each other, and enjoy instinctively each other's company. Indeed this delightful thing has its own pleasures, as for example in mutual conversation, or seemly contact, or a happy marriage.'[9] There were celebrated friendships around the time Rolle wrote, e.g. those between Sts Francis and Clare, and Jordan of Saxony, St Dominic's successor, and Diana of Andalo.[10] Jordan and Diana exchanged letters from 1222-1237. In one of them the Superior General of the Dominicans wrote: 'You are so deeply engraved on my heart that the more I realise how truly you love me from the depths of your soul, the more incapable I am of forgetting you and the more constantly you are in my thoughts, for your love of me moves me profoundly and makes my love for you burn more strongly.'[11]

There was a flowering of the ideal of Christian friendship in seventeenth- century France. A number of post-Tridentine reformers, established long-lasting heterosexual friendships. For example, Jean Eudes was a friend of two women, Madame de Camilly and Marie des Vallees. Pierre de Berulle maintained a long relationship with Madame Acarie, while Francis de Sales was a close friend of Jane de Chantal, founder of the Visitation order.[12] His affectionate relationship with the latter influenced the sections of the *Introduction to the Devout Life*[13] and the *Treatise On the Love of God*,[14] which are devoted to the subject of friendship love. The love shared by the bishop and the widow expressed itself in many fruitful forms of evangelisation. St Vincent was aware of all this. It is significant that his only recorded vision affirmed and encapsulated his understanding of the bond that simultaneously united Francis and Jane, to one another and to God. 'There appeared to him a small globe of fire which rose from the earth to the upper regions of the air to be united with another globe which was larger and more luminous, and these two became one, mounting even higher, entering and being incorporated into yet another globe which was infinitely greater and more resplendent than the others.'[15]

Viewed in the light of this experience, it is not surprising that Vincent formed a close if not an intimate friendship with Louise de Marillac. Wendy Wright says that his friendship with Mademoiselle Le Gras, Louise's married name, was 'coloured by a certain austere reserve reflective of his personality.'[16] That said, their collaboration was generative to an extraordinary degree. Together, they and their followers served and evangelised tens of thousands of poor people, both at home and abroad.

Vincent on community as friendship

Vincent's spiritual friendship with Louise taught him many things which he might not, otherwise, have learned. There is good reason to believe that it highlighted, in an experiential way, the important link between loving friendship in community and inspired and inspiring evangelisation in society. In 1655 he said in an experimental version of the *Common Rules* for his newly founded congregation: 'Brotherly love should always be present among us, as well as the bond of holiness, and these should be safeguarded in every possible way. For this reason there should be great mutual respect, and we should get along as *good friends*, always living in community. We should particularly avoid exclusive friendships, as well as any sort of ostracism, as experience has shown that these give rise to factions and destroy Congregations.'[17]

This ideal later found its definitive expression in chapter eight, paragraph two, of the *Common Rules* of the Vincentian Fathers in 1658. Although Vincent was aware that individual members of the community could form intimate friendships of the non-exclusive kind, he didn't think that they would be the norm. What he had in mind was a oneness which was based on conformity to the mind and heart of Christ. For example, he said to eight Vincentians who were being sent to Ireland: 'Be united together and God will bless you. But let it be in the love of Jesus Christ, for any other union will never be cemented by the blood of this Divine Saviour, and cannot last. It is therefore in Jesus Christ, by Jesus Christ, and for Jesus Christ, that you should be united to one another. The Spirit of Jesus Christ is a spirit of union and peace.'[18]

Vincent said that friendships in the community would have a number of typical characteristics:

- *Friendliness or cordiality.* The two words seem to be virtually synonymous in Vincent's writings. By cordiality he meant emotional warmth. He said that: 'If charity were a tree, cordiality would be its fruit; … if an apple were charity, its colour would be cordiality.'[19] In 1658 he told the Daughters of Charity that friendliness and cordiality were the mid-point between two extremes, cold, gloomy, boorishness on the one hand, and an over demonstrative affection on the other. 'Friendliness is, strictly speaking, the outward effect of charity in the heart. It springs from the heart and shows how glad you are to be with a particular companion … It is joy felt in the heart when you see the person you love and it shows in your face.'[20] Speaking about the affective dimension of charity, Vincent said that another effect of Christian love is 'that we show affection. We have to let each other see that we really do love one another … We should be prompt in letting others know of our affection, not at the wrong time or in the wrong way but at a suitable moment and in a suitable way, and not overdoing it.'[21] There is nothing cold or dutiful about Vincent's conception of cordial relationships. On the contrary, he obviously believed that there should be real warmth of feeling informing community life.

- *Gentleness and compassion.* It is clear that Vincent wanted community members to relate to one another in a gentle and compassionate way. He maintained that gentleness and forbearance were necessary in and outside of the community. For example, he said: 'Gentleness not only makes us excuse the affronts and injustices we receive, but even inclines us to treat with gentleness those from whom we receive them, by means of kind words.'[22] Speaking about the need for compassion, Vincent said in a talk on charity in 1659: 'One of the effects of love is to enable hearts to enter into each other and feel what the other feels. This is far removed from the sort of people who have no feeling for the pain of those who suffer … These duties of friendship have come down to us, coming from the roots of Christianity … In line with this we ought to look on the misfortunes of others as our own.'[23]

- *Mutual respect.* A person has respect when he or she goes beyond appearances, to esteem and reverence another person, because he or she knows and believes that the other is made in God's image and likeness and has been redeemed by the blood of Jesus. Whereas 'cordiality springs from the heart', St Vincent says that 'respect has its source in the understanding for it proceeds from the knowledge of the value of the person.'[24] Speaking of the relationship between friendliness and respect Vincent said: 'Just as respect without friendliness is not true respect, so friendliness without respect is not solid but will sometimes engender familiarities that are scarcely proper and will render friendliness thin and changeable, which will not happen if friendliness is joined to respect and respect to friendliness.'[25]

- *Loving action.* Vincent said that affective love needs to find expression in effective action. In other words, the way we feel about companions should find expression in charitable deeds. For example, he stated in his talks on Christian love: 'Having charity in the heart and saying so is not the end of the affair; it must be spread out into what we do; in that way it is perfect; it has an effect, since it stirs up love in the hearts of those who experience it; it conquers the world.'[26] On another occasion he said: 'Let us love God, but let it be in the strength of our arm and in the sweat of our brow. Sentiments of love of God, of kindness, of goodwill, good as these may be, are often suspect if they do not result in good deeds.'[27]

Friendliness and friendship contrasted

In modern psychological writing a distinction is drawn between closeness and intimacy.[28] Closeness is love experienced in feelings of warmth, affection, tenderness, esteem, etc. Intimacy goes beyond closeness by engaging in deep and honest communication of all one's thoughts and feelings. In these terms St Vincent advocated closeness rather than intimacy, friendliness rather than friendship in community.

Research has indicated that in practice most men prefer closeness to intimacy. For example, the McGill report on *Male Intimacy* observes: 'To say that men have no intimate friends seems on the surface too harsh, and it raises quick objections from most men … However, only one man in ten has a friend with whom he discusses work, money, marriage; only one in more than twenty has a friendship where he discloses feelings about himself.'[29] Research also shows that when a man does form an intimate relationship, it is usually with a woman. Sadly, intimacy between men is rare.[30] So, much as they may be desirable, deep, non-exclusive friendships between men are the exception rather than the rule. However, some of us have formed friendships of this kind with people, both male and female.

In spite of the dangers and difficulties involved, these relationships can have many desirable benefits.[31] They can banish loneliness, energise one's spirit, protect chastity, heal hurting memories, increase self-awareness, develop empathic skills and mediate the presence of God. St Aelred of Rievaulx celebrated the fruits of these kinds of friendship in the *Mirror of Charity* when he wrote: 'It is such a great joy to have the consolation of someone's affection – someone to whom one is deeply united by the bonds of love, someone in whom our weary spirit may find rest, and to whom we may pour out our souls … someone whose conversation is as sweet as a song in the tedium of our daily life. He must be someone whose soul will be to us a refuge to creep into when the world is altogether too much for us; someone to whom we can confide all our thoughts … He will weep with us when we are troubled, and rejoice with us when we are happy, and he will always be there to consult when we are in doubt. And we will be so deeply bound to him in our hearts that even when he is far away, we will find him together with us in spirit ... In this life on earth we can love a few people in this way, with heart and mind together, for they are more bound to us by the ties of love than any others.'[32] As a result of friendships like these, affective and effective love flows out both to community members and the poor alike, in such a way that there is a congruence rather than a conflict between the different forms of affection in our lives. Needless to say, the same principles apply to family life, relationships in groups, e.g. prayer groups, and in ecumenical work.

Vincent on the connection between friendliness and evangelisation
There are clear indications that St Vincent related affective love in community to effective evangelisation in the world, much as St Luke had done in the Acts. There were at least two ways in which this was true.

Firstly, his God was, before all else, a God of compassion. It was out of love for suffering humanity that the Father sent his beloved Son. It was Jesus' compassionate love for the poor that motivated his preaching, works of charity and deeds of power (cf. Mt 9:36). Evangelists will be motivated by the same compassion if they have first experienced this form of Christian love in a friendly community. On one occasion Vincent stated the implications in a succinct way: 'First, the missionary should be touched to the quick and afflicted in his heart at the miseries of his neighbour. Secondly, this compassion should manifest itself exteriorly in his countenance after the example of our Lord who wept over the city of Jerusalem because of the calamities with which it was threatened. Thirdly, he should give expression to his compassion which will indicate to the neighbour that he really feels for him and shares his sufferings with him. Finally, he must bring succour and aid to the afflicted as much as possible in their needs and in their sufferings, and try to rescue them in whole or in part, because as far as is possible the hand should be conformed to the heart.'[33]

Secondly, Vincent believed that unless there was unity of mind and heart in the community, united witness to Christ would be impossible. Speaking to the missionaries who were soon to depart for Ireland, he said: 'How will we ever be able to draw souls together in Jesus Christ if you are not united among yourselves and with him? It will not be possible. Have then but one heart and one will. Otherwise you will be acting like horses who, when they are hitched to a plough, pull some in one direction, others in another, and thus they will spoil and ruin everything. God calls you to work in his vineyard. *Go then, as having one heart and one intention, and by this means you will produce fruit.*'[34]

The connection between friendship and evangelisation today
There is agreement nowadays in the Vincentian order that the community exists in order to evangelise. For example, a recent book on the religious vows included these striking words: 'The following of Jesus can be understood and lived only in friendship and fraternal relationships. True fraternal communion supports the missionary in his response to the gift of celibacy which he has received. Community life should be a privileged space for expressing the affectivity that is part of everyone's life.'[35] There is a good example of what this quotation might involve in *Spiritual Friendship*. Speaking about his own experience, St Aelred of Rievaulx wrote: 'The day before yesterday, as I was walking the round of the cloister of the monastery, the brethren were sitting around forming as it were a most loving crown ... In that multitude of brethren I found no one whom I did not love, and no one by whom, I felt sure, I was not loved. I was filled with such joy that it surpassed all the delights of this world. I felt, indeed, my spirit transfused into all and the affection of all to have passed into me, so that I could say with the Prophet: "Behold how good and how pleasant it is for brethren to dwell in unity."'[36] The 1980 version of the Vincentian Constitution, paragraph 33 stated: 'This fraternal life together, nourished continually by the mission, forms a community which promotes both personal and community good and *renders the work of evangelisation more effective.*'[37]

The same interrelationship was acknowledged in statements that tried to encapsulate the Vincentian spirit, which were produced a number of years ago. For example, the Dublin version stated: 'We Vincentians are called to experience the gentle and compassionate love of Christ in community and to share that love with those to whom we are sent.' We have already noted that reverential compassion is the quality, *par excellence*, that needs to inform our community life, our friendships and therefore our evangelisation. It is clear in Lk 6:36-39 that three attitudes are alien to such loving-kindness: judgement, condemnation, and unforgiveness. They weaken trust, quench affectionate love, and grieve the Holy Spirit. For cordiality to flourish, communities need to agree that they will abstain from these negative attitudes in thought and word. When they make such a covenant – it might be stated in the community plan and expressed at a community eucharist – they create a zone of psychological safety where mutual trust gives rise to a growing spirit of freedom, joy and peace.

SOME IMPLICATIONS FOR THE LOCAL CHURCH

Although this chapter was written with the Vincentian family, specifically, in mind, I hope it will have relevance, not only for other religious orders, but for lay people also. The following reflections are intended to suggest how the Vincentian connection between friendship and evangelisation might be lived out in the local church.

a) Relationships in the parish and evangelisation

All of us are called to the important task of spreading the Good News and effective evangelisation will not possible without structural change at the parish level. Having conducted many missions around the country, I'm convinced that each parish needs to have a parish council, one that formulates a realistic yearly plan. There are a number of requirements for its formation:

- Firstly, the parish council needs to be elected, or appointed in one way or other.
- Secondly, the council needs to formulate a mission statement. It could be defined as a succinct, public statement that sets forth the unique contribution that the group is striving to deliver. It

centres the group in the richness of its past and gives meaning to that history by saying, here is where we are going with what has been given to us.[38]

- Thirdly, in the light of that general articulation of pastoral and evangelistic goals, the parish needs to designate two or three practical steps that will be taken during the year in order to attain those goals.
- Fourthly, the plan needs to state what structural changes need to be made in the parish, while designating who will do what task, how they will be resourced, when they will be done, and how.
- Fifthly, the plan needs to include personal and collective accountability by stating when and how it will be evaluated, e.g. at mid-year and at the end of the year.

To facilitate this kind of planning the clergy need to learn how to collaborate with lay people. This requires a real, as opposed to a notional, appreciation of lay ministries, and how, as Vatican II taught, baptised men and women have a right and a duty to exercise their gifts for the common good.[39] Clergy also need to have an experiential knowledge of the dynamics of group process as well as planning, i.e. how to facilitate right relationships as a prerequisite for making right decisions. Many lay people discover that, for one reason or another, some priests find this difficult if not impossible. It is not clear whether it is a result of male individualism, an outdated clericalism or a combination of both. One way or another, it is only when parishes enjoy real unity of mind and heart, that they are empowered to engage in credible and effective evangelisation.

There are clear indications that most contemporary parishes, especially in the large towns and cities, fail to satisfy people's need for community. The numbers involved are too great and therefore relationships tend to be formal and weak. What many modern day Christians are looking for are smaller groups within the parish which can encourage personal relationships and a strong sense of belonging. There are a number of ways of satisfying that need. I will look at four examples: prayer, bible, Alpha and cell groups.

b) Prayer groups

There has been a rapid growth of prayer groups of one kind or another since the Second Vatican Council. For example, nearly every parish has a charismatic prayer group. I belonged to one for many years. I can remember a time when some of the more experienced members formed what they called a community group. It consisted of about sixteen men and women, most of whom were lay people. At our very first get-together I gave a talk on Christian community as a network of friendships. When I invited comments, a number of people said that they thought that the ideal I had described was too demanding. We prayed for a while. Then one of the members, a lorry driver, got a remarkable word of knowledge. Spontaneously he said, 'Look up Sirach 6:14-17, that is where you will discover God's point of view.' Incidentally, I'm quite sure that he had no idea what the passage was about. We opened the bible at the nominated text, only to find that it was about the joys of friendship. That ended all discussion. We felt that God was encouraging us to live after the manner of dear friends by cultivating unity of mind and heart.

I can recall how faith sharing really helped to build friendly relationships. We tended to follow a four point method.

1. In what ways were you aware of the Lord's presence, guidance or action in your life during the past week?
2. What has the Lord been teaching you in your prayer time or as a result of your scripture or spiritual reading?
3. In what ways has the Lord prompted you to serve others during the week?
4. What changes has the Lord been asking of you in order that you might be more loving in your relationship with your brothers and sisters in Christ?[40]

On one such occasion a member of the community group read Lk 6:36-39 and shared how this passage, about a merciful way of life, had inspired her. When she finished she spontaneously knelt on the floor and promised she would refrain from criticising, judging or condemning anyone in the group in thought or word. She ended by saying that if she broke her promise, in any way, she would confess the fault to the group and seek forgiveness. Her words had a remarkable effect. One by one, everyone present knelt down and made the same promise. As a result, trust levels deepened, unity of mind and heart increased, and we were granted many of the gifts of the Spirit.

As a group, we were committed to evangelisation. Besides conducting Life in the Spirit Seminars we often prayed for opportunities of spreading the Good News. I can remember how, at one time, we repeatedly asked God to prompt some priest to invite us to conduct an outreach together in his parish. After about two months, our prayers were answered when the parish priest of a rural area in the mountains of Tyrone invited all sixteen of us to conduct a mini mission. The day before we headed off, I was apprehensive about the impending visit. I prayed for guidance and was led to look up a certain page in a certain volume of the *Catholic Encyclopedia*. It contained a photograph of an ancient manuscript. I asked a colleague, who was good at languages, if it made any sense to him. He said: 'That is a passage in Hebrew, from the book of Joshua, beginning at chapter one, verse nine.' I rushed off to my room, opened my bible and read: 'I hereby command you: Be strong and courageous; do not be frightened or dismayed, for the Lord your God is with you wherever you go.' When we reached the village the following day, we assembled in the sacristy of the church to pray together. I asked if anyone had received a word of guidance for the day. One of the men answered yes, and read out Jos 1:9, the very verse I had received in prayer the day before! Then we confidently headed of in twos to visit homes. Later we had a service of reconciliation, followed by a Mass of healing. As a result, many people were reconciled to Christ and others were healed of physical and emotional ailments. That mini mission stands out in my memory because it taught me about the vital link that exists between friendship and effective evangelisation.

c) Bible groups

The scriptures play a crucial role in the formation of genuine community and the conduct of effective evangelisation. Bob Maloney says, in his book *He Hears the Cry of the Poor*, that listening to God's word is the basis of spirituality.[41] One might add that attentiveness to God's word is also the basis of evangelisation. The main reason for reading the scriptures is to get to know who God is and what God wants. In a colourful passage, Abelly, St Vincent de Paul's first biographer, noted how devoted he was to the word of God. 'He seemed to suck meaning from passages of scripture so as to be strengthened and have his soul nourished by them – and he did so in such a way that in all his words and actions he appeared to be filled with Jesus Christ.'[42] Not surprisingly, Vincent that said that the word of God never fails: 'Christ's teaching will never let us down, while worldly wisdom always will.'

In recent years there has been a rapid growth in the number of Catholic bible groups. They use different methodologies.[43] For example, Cardinal Martini of Milan has championed the cause of the Benedictine method by forming many bible groups, especially for young adults. He has described the way in which they operate in *Lectio Divina and Vocation in Life: A Process for Discerning One's Life Calling*.[44] I firmly believe that loving relationships in bible groups constitute an indispensable hermeneutical key that opens up the meaning of the scripture. The extent to which the Spirit is present in the united local group is the extent to which the same Spirit will enable the members to understand the inspired word of God. As they glean insights from the scriptures and act upon them they will strengthen the bonds of unity. So there is a reciprocal relationship between unity in community and insight into God's word.

c) Ecumenical and Alpha groups

I want to begin this section by adverting to the link between ecumenism and friendship. In the 1920s, Fr Portal, a French Vincentian, was involved in the Catholic-Anglican dialogue which was initiated by Cardinal Mercier of Melines in Belgium. He wrote: 'Let me tell the people of my time, as well as those of tomorrow, that there is a way to increase their strength a hundredfold … I am speaking of friendship. A friend, a true friend, is a gift of God, even if what we experience together is simply the sweetness of being united in joy and suffering. But if we encounter a soul who harmonises with our highest aspirations, who considers that the ideal of his whole life is to work for the Church, that is, for Jesus Christ, our Master, we become united in our inmost depths. And if it so happens that these two Christians are separated, that they belong to different churches, to different backgrounds, but desire with all their strength and might to knock down the barriers and actively work together to this end, will there be any limits to their power?'[45]

Many of those who are involved in the ecumenical movement know, from personal experience, that what Fr Portal stated is correct. Over the years Catholics and Protestants have formed what could be called interdenominational friendships. In reality, the ecumenical movement is a network of inter-connecting friendships. Not surprisingly, therefore, there is also a strong conviction in inter-church circles that evangelisation will be effective to the extent that there is genuine reconciliation and fellowship. For example, in 1998 an ecumenical document was published. It's stated aim was to call Christians – Evangelicals and Catholics – to build friendships together, so that Ireland may hear more clearly the good news of Jesus Christ. In a section entitled, 'We Witness Together,' it says: 'The Teaching of our Lord is unmistakable. The credibility of his mission in the world (and in Ireland in particular) is dependent upon the unity and love of his disciples as expressed in Jesus' prayer in Jn 17: 'May they all be one, as you Father are in me, and I in you, so also may they be one in us, that the world may believe that you sent me. The same connection between unity and witness is strongly echoed in Acts 4:32-36... All who truly believe in Jesus Christ are brothers and sisters in the Lord and must not allow their differences, however important, to undermine this great truth, or to deflect them from bearing witness together to God's gift of salvation in Christ.'[46]

The Alpha course, which originated in the Church of England, is rooted in the conviction already mentioned. It is currently being used, by Catholics and Protestants alike, as they seek to engage in basic evangelisation. Alpha is a ten week introduction to Christian faith that includes fifteen talks. A typical session begins with a meal. People who don't know one another can sit down together and chat. As they do so, relationships and even friendships are formed. Those who run Alpha courses would argue that this is the secret to their success. They link friendship and evangelisation in an attractive and enjoyable way. Following the meal, everyone listens to a talk which may be given by an invited speaker. If none is available, they watch the same talk on video. The presentations are kerygmatic in nature i.e. about the basics of Christianity such as, Who is Jesus? Why did Jesus die? How does one pray? The talk is followed by group discussion. The aim of the course is to lead non-believers, the lapsed and the alienated to freely and joyfully commit their hearts and lives to the Lord. As more and more Catholics and Protestants come into this common experience of the Good News, Alpha will contribute greatly to the on-going search for unity.

d) Cell groups

Those who run Alpha courses repeatedly run into the same problem. What advice does one give to a person who has become newly committed to the Lord? Go back to the church? Sadly, the local church often fails to notice when people either lapse or return. That, in a way, is the core of the problem. There is often a lamentable lack of fellowship and sharing in parishes. Nowadays people are looking for something more personal, experiential and dynamic. In his book, *Transforming Your Parish: Building Christian Community*, Michael Hurley has proposed one possible answer.[47] David Yonggi Cho, a Pentecostal minister in Korea, formed cell groups which flourished. As a consequence, his congregation has become the largest on earth. The idea was copied and adapted by Catholics in the US and Italy. Fr Hurley studied these initiatives and introduced an adapted version into the parish of Ballinteer in Dublin. At one point he had as many as 300 people involved in thirty-one cells. While the groups have a number of aims, good supportive relationships and friendships are a key to the success of their efforts to evangelise.

A number of years ago David Watson did much the same in his thriving parish, of two to three thousand people, in York. In his autobiography he says: 'It is significant that virtually every major movement for spiritual renewal in the history of the church has

been marked by the development of the small group.'[48] He
describes how he formed a number of area groups, each one of
which was headed up by a trained leader. The responsibilities of the
area leaders were spelt out as follows:

1. To have the pastoral care of the group.

2. To arrange regular house meeting every two weeks.

3. To encourage the group to relate to each other in depth, to
serve the whole body of Christ, and to think of witness, evangelisation and service within the area.

4. To stimulate bible and faith sharing.

5. To be sensitive to other churches in the area.

6. To come to a leaders' meeting every third Saturday at 7 am.

The groups were to be not less than eight in size, and if possible, not
more than 16-20 before they split to form two groups.[49] It is lively,
united communities of friends, like these, that will be the source of
genuine renewal and the new evangelisation called for by the
church.

Conclusion

Unity of mind and heart is the *sine qua non* for all the activities mentioned above. Any individual, whether lay or clerical, needs to deal
with those negative attitudes and feelings of envy, jealousy, judg-
mentalness, criticism, and resentment which are inimical to unity.
The extent to which they are unacknowledged and left unresolved
is the extent to which the Holy Spirit will be quenched in the community. That Spirit is the essential influence that animates our
evangelisation. As St Vincent de Paul once said: 'Neither philosophy nor theology, nor learned talks influence souls. Jesus Christ
must be united with us and we with him. We must work in him and
he in us, to speak as he did and with his Spirit.'[50] Pope Paul VI
echoed these sentiments in his encyclical on *Evangelisation in the
Modern World* when he wrote: 'Techniques of evangelisation are
good, but even the most advanced ones could not replace the gentle
action of the Spirit. The most perfect preparation of the evangeliser
has no effect without the Holy Spirit. Without the Holy Spirit the
most convincing dialectic has no power over the heart of man.

Without him the most highly developed *schemas* resting on a socio-logical or psychological basis are quickly seen to be quite value-less.'[51] That being so, conflict resolution and reconciliation are vital for the family, prayer group, religious community, or parish, that hopes to evangelise in the power of the Holy Spirit.

I was fortunate to spend eight years as a member of the Irish Vincentian Mission Team. That time on the road proved to me, if proof were needed, that the effectiveness of our efforts to evange-lise were proportionate to the quality of our cordiality and unity. The extent to which we lived after the manner of dear friends was the extent to which we experienced zest and joy in our vocation. As a result, our cordial relationships tended to counteract loneliness, hardship and discouragement. Many was the time when people told us during missions that the obvious unity and affection of the missioners, not only edified them, it added real credibility to what we had to say. It seems that in our individualistic culture increasing numbers of people are longing for the comfort and consolation that only loving communities can provide.

On one occasion, St Vincent spoke about the eschatological joy that results from such relationships, when he said to the Daughters of Charity in 1658: 'St Paul says in another place that whoever abides in charity has fulfilled the law … Our Lord teaches forbear-ance … It is a means of establishing a holy friendship among you and of living in perfect union, and in this way enabling you to make a paradise in this world; and therefore if God gives you the grace to bear with one another; your life will be a paradise begun.'[52] He echoed these sentiments when he said to the Vincentian priests and brothers in 1659: 'If God gives this grace to the missioners, what's your opinion of the Company as a whole? Their life is a life of love, the life of heaven.'

Notes

FOREWORD

1. *The Passing of King Arthur*, l. 407.
2. *The Pope in Ireland* (Dublin: Veritas, 1979), 46.
3. Andy Pollak, 'Poll Shows Church's Moral Authority in Decline,' (Mon. Dec. 16, 1996), 5.
4. Ester, Halman & de Moor, 'The Individualizing Society: Value Changes in Europe and North America,' quoted by Andrew Greely in 'Are the Irish Really Loosing the Faith?' *Doctrine and Life*, Vol. 44 (March 1994), 132.
5. Karl Rahner, 'The Situation of Faith Today,' in *The Practice of Faith: A Handbook of Contemporary Spirituality* (London: SCM, 1985), 30.
6. May 19th 1975, *Pope Paul and the Spirit*, Edward D. O'Connor (Notre Dame: Ave Maria Press, 1978), 234.
7. (London: Paladin, 1979), 171.
8. cf. Ken Wilber, 'Postmodernism: To Deconstruct the World,' *The Marriage of Sense and Soul* (Dublin: Newleaf, 1998), 116-136; Richard Tarnas, 'The Postmodern Mind,' *The Passion of the Western Mind*, New York: Ballantine Books, 1991), 395-410.

CHAPTER ONE

1. H.H. Price, *Belief*, (London: Allen & Unwin, 1969), 475.
2. 'Spirituality in the Academy', *Theological Studies* 50 (1989), 684.
3. 'Introduction', *Women's Spirituality: Resources for Christian Development* (New York: Paulist Press, 1986), 3.
4. 'Religion as a Dimension in Man's Spiritual Life' in *Phenomonology of Religion*, ed. J. Bettis (London: SCM Press, 1969), 177.
5. *The Eye of Spirit* (Boston: Shambhala, 1977), 215-216.
6. 'The Spirituality of the Future,' *The Practice of Faith: A Handbook of Contemporary Spirituality*, (London: SCM Press, 1985), 21.
7. *Confession*, 1, 1.
8. (Dublin: Veritas, 194), par. 2684.
9. cf. Aldous Huxley *The Perennial Philosophy* (London: Fontana, 1966), 157.
10. cf. Cross & Livingstone, eds., *The Oxford Dictionary of the Christian Church* (Oxford: Oxford University Press, 1985), 349, 1302.
11. (New York: Paulist Press, 1973).
12. (London: Sheldon Press, 1980).

13. (London: SCM Press, 1985).

14. (Oxford: Oneworld, 1997).

15. *Message of the Fathers of the Church*, 16 (Wilmington, Del: Glazier, 1985).

16. 'The Psychological Foundations of Belief in God' in *Toward Moral and Religious Maturity* (New Jersey: Silver Burdett Company, 1980), 118.

17. Cd Rom, 1997 edition.

18. *Models of the Church* (New York: Doubleday, 1974); *Models of Revelation* (Dublin: Gill & Macmillan, 1983); 'The Meaning of Faith Considered in Relationship to Justice' *The Faith that Does Justice* (New York: Paulist Press, 1977); *The Assurance of Things Hoped For: A Theology of Christian Faith* (New York: Oxford University Press, 1994).

19. For example, O'Grady, *Models of Jesus*, (New York: Image, 1982) and J.C. Haughey, 'Contemporary Spiritualities and the Spirit' *The Christian Conspiracy* (New York: Doubleday, 1973); D. Fleming, 'Models of Spiritual Direction', *The Christian Ministry of Spiritual Direction: The Best of the Review 3*, ed. Fleming (St Louis: Review for Religious, 1988), 106-112.

20. *Models of Revelation* (Dublin: Gill & Macmillan, 1983), 30.

21. *Second Collection*, eds. Ryan & Tyrell (Philadelphia: The Westminister Press, 1974), 101.

22. cf. Richard Tarrnas, 'The Postmodern Mind' in *The Passion of the Western Mind* (New York: Ballantine Books, 1993), 395-410.

23. cf. *Veritatis Splendor*, 1993, *Fides et Ratio*,1998.

24. (London: Picador, 1992), 11.

25. (Dublin: Dominican Publications, 1984) and *Values and Social Change in Ireland* (Dublin: Gill & Macmillan, 1994) and MRBI Poll *The Irish Times*, (Mon Dec 16th, 1996), 5, and Mc Greil, 'Religious Attitudes and Perceptions', *Prejudice in Ireland Revisited* (Maynooth: St Patrick's College, 1996), 218-223.

26. *Redemptoris Missio*, par. 42.

27. *Values and Social Change in Ireland* (Dublin: Gill & Macmillan, 1994), 44.

28. 'Contemporary Spiritualities and the Spirit', *The Conspiracy of God* (New York: Doubleday, 1973), 97.

29. cf. Sandra Hirsh & Jean Kummerow, *Life Types* (New York: Warner Books, 1989).

30. *Common Rules of the Congregation of the Mission*, V, 1.

31. From 'Meditations and Devotions' *The Essential Newman*, ed. Blehl (New York: New American Library, 1963), 337-338.

32. *Natural Symbols: Exploration in Cosmology* (London: Penguin, 1973), 64-69.

33. Louis Abelly, T*he Life of the Venerable Servant of God Vincent de Paul*, vol. 3 (New York: New City Press, 1993), 318.

34. *The Holy Spirit* (New York: Paulist Press, 1974), 199-200.

35. (London: SCM Press, 1972), 25-39.

36. (Dublin: Dominican Publications, 1982), 29.

37. Abelly, op. cit., vol. 1, 106-107.

38. *The Faith that Does Justice*, ed. Haughey (New York: Paulist Press, 1977), 13.

39. David Fleming, 'Models of Spiritual Direction' in *The Christian Ministry of Spiritual Direction; The Best Review 3*, (St Louis, Mo. Review for Religious, 1988), 106-112.

40. cf. Pat Collins, 'Models of Evangelization', *Doctrine and Life*, vol. 48 (Jan 1988), No 1, 31-41.

41. Andy Pollak, 'Poll shows church's moral authority in decline' (Mon. Dec. 16, 1996), 5.

CHAPTER TWO

1. 'Introduction' to Max Weber's, *The Sociology of Religion* (Boston: Beacon Press, 1963), xxviii.

2. *De Inventione Rhetorica*, II, 53, 161.

3. 'Psychology and Religion' *The Basic Writings of C G Jung* (New York: The Modern Library, 1959), 473.

4. Dermot Lane, *The Experience of God: An Invitation to do Theology* (Dublin: Veritas, 1981), 13; William Barry, *Spiritual Direction & The Encounter with God* (New Jersey: Paulist Press, 1992), 29-39.

5. W. Rowe, *Philosophy of Religion* (Belmont, Calif: Wadsworth Publishing Co., 1992), 57.

6. *Psychoanalysis and Religion*, (New Haven: Yale University Press, 1984),10.

7. Quoted by Avery Dulles, *The Assurance of Things Hoped For: A Theology of Faith* (New York: Oxford University Press, 1994), 45-46.

8. 'An account of the Revival of Religion in Northampton in 1740-1742, as Communicated in a Letter to a Minister in Boston,' *Jonathan Edwards on Revival* (Edinburgh: Banner of Truth, 1987), 151.

9. *The Religious Affections* (Edinburgh: Banner of Truth, 1986), 49.

10. (Cambridge: Cambridge University Press, 1991)

11. op. cit., 102.

12 *The Vision of God* (NY: Ungar, 1978), 45-50.

13. *Way to Wisdom* (New Haven: Yale University Press, 1970), 28-38.

14. 'The Christian Faith' quoted by Hans Kung, 'Friedrich Schleiermacher, Theology at the Dawn of Modernity,' *Great Christian Thinkers* (London: SCM Press, 1994), 174.

15. Quoted by Wulf in *Psychology of Religion: Classic and Contemporary Views* (New York: Wiley, 1991), 475.

16. *The Varieties of Religious Experience* (London: Fontana, 1971), 50

17. (New York: Oxford University Press, 1970)

18. *The Idea of the Holy*, 33.

19. Quoted by Wulf in *Psychology of Religion*, op. cit., 531.

20. *The Faith of a Scientist* (London: Lindsey Press, 1948)

21. Quoted by David Hay, *Religious Experience Today: Studying the Facts* (London: Mobray, 1990), 29.

22. Quoted by Hay, op. cit., 29-30.

23. (Oxford: Oxford University Press, 1983)

24. (London: Arkana, 1990)

25. Quoted by William Barry, *Spiritual Direction and the Encounter with God* (New York: Paulist Press, 1992), 37-38.

26. David Hay, *Reports of Religious Experience by a Group of Postgraduate Students: A Pilot Survey* (Nottingham: University School of Education, 1978).

27. Fogarty, Ryan & Lee, eds., (Dublin: Dominican Publications,1984).

28. C.T. Whelan, ed. (Dublin, Gill & Macmillan, 1994).

29. C.J. Jung, *Psychology and Western Religion* (London, Ark, 1988), 230.

30. *The Autobiography of St Ignatius of Loyola with Related Documents* (New York: Harper & Row, 1974), 24.

31. *Spiritual Exercises*, par. 2.

32. Madeline Birmingham and William Connelly, *Witnessing to the Fire: Spiritual Direction and the Development of Directors, One Center's Experience* (Kansas City: Sheed & Ward, 1994)

33. William Barry; William Connolly, *The Practice of Spiritual Direction* (San Francisco: Harper & Row, 1982), 8.

34. *Hom. in Ev.* 30.1 (PL 76:1220C). quoted by Bernard Mc Ginn *The Growth of Mysticism* (London: SCM, 1994), 59

35. See Pat Collins 'The Pain of Self-Discovery' *Intimacy and the Hungers of the Heart* (Dublin: Columba, 1991), 58-73.

36. 'Forms of the Implicit Love of God,' *Waiting on God* (London: Routledge and Kegan Paul, 1951)

37. *Splendor of the Truth*, par. 8.

38. Quoted by Frank Lake, *With Respect: A Doctor's Response to a Healing Pope* (London: Darton, Longman & Todd, 1982), 43-45.

39. (New York: The Free Press, 1963), 47.

40. Anthony Giddens, Introduction to *Emile Durkheim: Selected Writings* (Cambridge: Cambridge University Press).

41. Peter Gay, *Freud: A Life for our Time* (London: Papermac, 1988), 28

42. Michael Palmer, *Freud and Jung on Religion* (London: Routledge, 1997), 37.

43. Jung's view quoted in *Freud and Jung on Religion*, 90.

44. *Psychoanalysis and Religion* (New York: Bantam Books, 1967), 49

45. *Psychoanalysis and Religion*, 26.

46. *Psychoanalysis and Religion*, 36

47. *Psychoanalysis and Religion*, 48

48. *Ecstasy: A Study of Some Secular and Religious Experiences* (London: Cresset Press, 1961).

49. 'Psychology and Religion' *The Basic Writings of C.J. Jung* (New York: The Modern Library, 1959), 473.

50. Quoted by Michael Palmer, *Freud and Jung on Religion*, 116

51. Palmer, op. cit. 124

52. *A Critical Dictionary of Jungian Analysis*, eds. Samuels, Shorter, Plaut, (London: Routledge & Keegan Paul, 1987), 131.

53. *Collected Works*, vol. 8, para 528.

54. Palmer op. cit. 195.

55. 'Freud and Jung' in *Psychoanalysis and Religion*, op. cit., 20.

56 See Andrew Fuller, 'Viktor Frankl' *Psychology and Religion: Eight Points of View* (London: Littlefield Adams, 1994), 264.

57. 'A New Buddha and a New Tao' in *The Concise Encyclopedia of Living Faiths* (New York: Hawthorn Books, 1959), 403.

58. cf. Donal Leonard, 'Myth According to Joseph Campbell' *Alpha Omega*, no. 2. (May-Aug. 1998), 266-270.

59. Quoted by Barnett, *The Universe and Doctor Einstein* (New York: Bantam, 1968), 108.

60. *Foundations of Christian Faith: An Introduction to the Idea of Christianity* (New York: Crossroad, 1982), 21.

61. Quoted by Heiler in *Prayer: A Study in the History and Psychology of Religion*, (Oxford: Oneworld, 1997), xii.

62. *Love and Will* (San Francisco: Harper & Row, 1982), 89.

63. (Grand Rapids: Eerdmans, 1980).

CHAPTER THREE

1. *The Varieties of Religious Experience* (London: Fontana, 1971), 366.

2. W. R. Inge, *Mysticism in Religion* (London: Rider & Co., 1969), 31.

3. Evelyn Underhill, *Mystics of the Church*, (Cambridge: James Clarke, 1975), 9-10.

4. William Johnston, *The Inner Eye of Love* (San Francisco: Harper & Row, 1978), 20, 31, *Mystical Theology: The Science of Love* (London: Fount, 1994), 9.

5. *The Religious Consciousness: A Psychological Study* (New York: Macmillan, 1920), 339.

6. *The Religious Consciousness*, op. cit., 337.

7. cf. June Singer, *Boundaries of the Soul: The Practice of Jung's Psychology* (New York: Anchor, Doubleday, 1994), 326-329.

8. Walter Stace, *Mysticism and Philosophy* (New York: J. B. Lippincott Co., 1960), 71-72.

9. William L. Rowe, *Philosophy of Religion*, (Belmont, CA: Wadsworth, 1992) 63-64.

10. (London: Fontana, 1965), 76-77; 128.

11. Thérèse of Lisieux, *Autobiography of a Saint* (London: Harvill, 1958), 134-135;

12. S. T. Q. 43, Art 7.

13. (London: Mobray, 1990), 2-3.

14. 'The Religious Dimension of Experience', *Spiritual Direction and the Encounter with God: A Theological Enquiry* (New Jersey: Paulist Press, 1992), 35.

15. Phyllis Campbell quoted in Happold's *Prayer and Meditation*, (London: Penguin, 1971), 122.

16. 'Mystical Theology,' chapt 1, in *The Fire and the Cloud: An Anthology of Catholic Spirituality*, ed. D. Fleming, (London: Geoffrey Chapman, 1978), 57.

17. *The Story of a Soul*, 255-256.

18. *The Little Way*, (London: DLT, 1979), 53.

19. *The Little Way*, 11.

20. *The Little Way*, 53.

21. *The Little Way*, 54

22. *The Little Way* ,12

23. Quoted by David Wulf, *Psychology and Religion*, (New York: Wiley, 1991), 506

24. (London: Fontana, 1966), 9.

25. *Myth and Ritual in Christianity* (Boston: Beacon Press, 1970), 14-15.

26. *The Eye of Spirit* (Boston: Shambala, 1997), 64.

27. cf *The Marriage of Sense and Soul* (Dublin: Newleaf, 1998), 18.

28. *Myths, Dreams and Mysteries* (London: Fontana, 1970).

29. *The Hero with a Thousand Faces* (Princeton: Princeton University Press, 1990).

30. *Man and His Symbols* (NY: Dell, 1981), 99.

31. Victor White, *God and the Unconscious* (London: Fontana, 1952), 231. Cf Wis 2:12-20.

32. (New York: Dutton, 1969), 65; 81.

33. *Cosmic Consciousness*, 3.

34. *Cosmic Consciousness*, 3.

35. *Cosmic Consciousness*, 79.

36. 'Schleiermacherís Philosophy of Religion,' *The Journal of Religion*, vol., XLIV, no. 2, (April 1964), 100.

37. *Jesus Christ in Modern Thought* (London: SCM, 1989), 195; 199.

38. Cf McGinn, *The Foundations of Mysticism* (London: SCM, 1992), 307.

39. *Christ: The Christian Experience in the Modern World* (London: SCM Press, 1982), 34; 32.

40. Quoted by Harvey Egan in 'Pierre Teilhard de Chardin 1881-1955' *Christian Mysticism, The Future of a Tradition*, (New York: Pueblo, 1984), 278.

41. *Concordant Discord* (London: Oxford University Press, 1970), 436; 439.

42. See, William Meissner, *Psychoanalysis and Religious Experience*, (New Haven: Yale University Press, 1984), 151-152; and Peter Gay, *Freud: A Life for our Time* (London: Papermac, 1988), 544-545.

43. *Prayer: A Study in the History and Psychology of Religion* (Oxford, Oneworld, 1997), 283-284.

44. Quoted in Mc Ginn, *The Foundations of Mysticism*, 267-268.

45. Quoted in 'Religious Experience: Mysticism,' *Encyclopedia Brittanica* CD Version 97,

46. Quoted by Happold in *Prayer and Meditation* (London: Pelican, 1971), 21.

47. *The Practice of Faith: A Handbook of Contemporary Spirituality* (London: SCM Press, 1985), 22.

48. cf. Henry Chadwick, *The Early Church, The Pelican History of the Church*, vol. 1, (London: Pelican, 1974), 97.

49. Quoted in, *A New Catechism* (London: Burns & Oates, 1967), 33.

CHAPTER FOUR

1. The Heart of Man, (London: Fontana, 1963), 13.
2. (New York: Henry Holt, 1890), 561-562.
3. Quoted by Walter Burghardt, 'Contemplation,' Church (Winter, 1989), 15.
4. Treatise on the Love of God, Vol. 1, Book 6, chap. 3 (Rockford, Ill.: Tan, 1975), 275.
5. Waiting on God (Glasgow: Fontana, 1951), 75.
6. For more on the distinction between willfulness and willingness in contemplative knowing, see Gerald May, Will and Spirit: A Contemplative Psychology (San Francisco: Harper and Row, 1987), 5-7.
7. Quoted by James Gill in 'Empathy is at the Heart of Love' Human Development, Vol. 3, No. 3, (Fall, 1982), 29.
8. cf. Pat Collins, 'Love as Empathy' Family Matters, no. 5. (Family Life and Prayer Centre, Knock), 46-48.
9. Summa Theologiae: A Concise Translation, ed. Timothy Mc Dermott, (London: Methuen, 1991), 337.
10. From Introduction to Metaphysics, quoted by Leszek Kolakowski, Bergson, (Oxford: Oxford University, 1985), 24.
11. 'Reflections on the Unity of Love of the Neighbor and Love of God,' Theological Investigations, Vol.6, (London: DLT, 1969), 241.
12. Quoted by Grace Jantzen, Julian of Norwich: Mystic and Theologian (London: SPCK, 1987), 127.
13. Gregory of Palamas used this word. It seems to refer to the manifestations or epiphanies of God, much as a work of art is a manifestation or epiphany of the mind of the artist.
14. Julian of Norwich: Showings (London: SPCK, 1978), 56.
15. 'Concerning the use of Biblical Quotations in Matters of Science' Quoted by Mazlish and Bronowski, The Western Intellectual Tradition (London: Pelican, 1963), 153.
16. (London: Methuen, University Paperbacks, 1960), 300-301.
17. 'The Ladder of Monks' The Companion to the Catechism of the Catholic Church: A Compendium of Texts Referred to in the Catechism of the Catholic Church (San Francisco: Ignatius Press, 1994), 2654.
18. Quoted by Bernard Mc Ginn, The Growth of Mysticism: From Gregory the Great to the Twelfth Century (London: SCM, 1994), 140.

CHAPTER FIVE

1. Joseph Duffy, Patrick in His Own Words (Dublin: Veritas, 1975), 23.
2. De orat. 12: PG 11, 452C.
3. Quoted by Kenneth Leech, True Prayer: An Introduction to Christian Spirituality (London: Sheldon Press, 1980), 191.
4. 'Treatise on the first letter of St John' The Divine Office vol. 1. (Dublin: Talbot, 1974), 537.
5. Thomas Aquinas: Preacher and Friend, The Way of the Christian Mystics No. 15, (Dublin: Gill & Macmillan, 1993), 128.

6. Commentary on 1 Thess 5:2, quoted in *Thomas Aquinas: Preacher and Friend*, 129.

7. All subsequent quotations from 'Cassian's Tenth Conference on Prayer,' *The Fire and the Cloud: An Anthology of Catholic Spirituality*, ed. David Fleming, (London: Geoffrey Chapman, 1978), 28-40.

8. *The Cloud of Unknowing and Other Works* (London; Penguin Classics, 1978),

9. *The Cloud of Unknowing and Other Works*, 69-70.

10. All subsequent quotations taken from 'The Way of the Pilgrim,' *The Fire and the Cloud* op. cit., pp. 318-328.

11. 'Centering Prayer,' *The New Dictionary of Catholic Spirituality*, p. 139.

12. *Tongue Speaking: An Experiment in Spiritual Experience*, (London: Hodder & Stoughton, 1968)

13. *Sermon on Psalms* 32, 1, 7-8.

14. *Sounds of Wonder: A Popular History of Speaking in Tongues in the Catholic Tradition*, (New York: Paulist Press, 1977), 60

15. *Sounds of Wonder*, 86.

16. *A New Pentecost?* (London: Darton, Longman & Todd, 1975), 101.

17. Quoted by Kenneth Leech, *True Prayer: An Introduction to Christian Spirituality* (London: Sheldon Press, 1980), 191.

18. *Riding the Wind* (Ann Arbor: Word of Life, 1977), 49.

19. *Teach Us to Pray* (London: Darton, Longman & Todd, 1974), 20.

20. cf. George Montague, 'The Spirit and his Gifts', (New York: Paulist Press, 1974), 33.

CHAPTER SIX

1. (London: Marshell Pickering, 1991), 40.

2. (Wheaton, Ill,: Quest Books, 1997), 96-97.

3. Quoted by Aidan Nichols 'The New Age Movement' *The Month*, (March, 1992), 87.

4. *True God:An Exploration in Spiritual Theology* (London: Sheldon Press, 1985), 421.

CHAPTER SEVEN

1. *Paths in Spirituality* (London, SCM, 1972), 122-123.

2. C. Merchant, *The Death of Nature* (New York: Harper & Row, 1980), xvii.

3. *Chance and Necessity* (New York: Knopf, 1971), 122.

4. *The World is Too Much with Us*, line. 1.

5. *La Tentation de L'Occident*, 1926.

6. *Real Presences*, (London: Faber & Faber, 1989), 228.

7. Quoted by Josephson, 'Introduction,' *Man alone: Alienation in Modern Society* (New York: Dell, 1972), 16.

8. 'Alienation Under Capitalism' *Man alone*, op. Cit. 59.

9. 'For the Time Being' in *The Choice is Always Ours* eds. Phillips, Howes and Nixon, (Wheaton: Re-Quest Books, 1975), 459.

10. Josephson, *Man Alone: Alienation in Modern Society*, 14.
11. (London: Fontana, 1972), 28
12. 'Previous Attempts at Integration' Part II of *The Marriage of Sense and Soul: Integrating Science and Religion* (Dublin: Newleaf, 1998), 79-136.
13. *A New Vision of Reality:Western Science, Eastern Mysticism and Christian Faith* (London: Collins, 1989), 17
14. (New York: Harper, 1992), 54
15. See Capra, Mathus and Stendal-Rast, *Belonging to the Universe*, X-XI.
16. *Tractatus Logico-Philosophicus* (London: Routledge & Keegan Paul, 1951), 187.
17. (New York: Bantam, 1980)
18. Quoted by David Wulf, *Psychology of Religion* (New York: John Wiley, 1991), 613.
19. *A New Vision of Reality*, 54
20. *The Ages of Gaia: A Biography of Our Living Earth* (Oxford: Oxford University Press, 1988), 14
21. op. cit. (London: Century, 1990), 88-89
22. *Against Heresies*, V. vi. 1.
23. *Against Heresies*, IV, xxxviii, 2.
24. *Against Heresies*, IV, xxxviii, 3.
25. *The Letters of John Keats*, ed. M. B. Forman, (London: Oxford University Press, 1952), 334-345.
26. *Evil and the God of Love* (London: Fontana, 1968), 220-221.
27. *The Spectrum of Consciousness* (Wheaton, Il.: Quest Books, 1993), 96-97.
28. *A New Vision of Reality* (London: Fount, 1989), 98
29. *A New Vision of Reality*, 100
30. *The Religion of Teilhard de Chardin*, (New York: Desclee Company, 1967), 120.
31. *The Passion of the Western Mind* (New York: Ballentine, 1991), 441-442.
32. *The Passion of the Western Mind*, 444.

CHAPTER EIGHT

1. *De Def. Orac.* 9, quoted by William Barclay '*Splagchnizesthai:* The Divine Compassion,' *New Testament Words* (London: SCM, 1971), 279.
2. Nouwen, McNeill, Morrison, *Compassion* (London: DLT, 1982), 17.
3. c.f. William Barclay, 'He descended into Hell' chapt 10, *The Plain Man Looks At the Apostles Creed* (London: Fontana, 1975), 119-133.
4. Cf Pat Collins, 'Loving Empathy' in *Spirituality*, vol 4, no 19 (July-August 1998), 235-240.
5. *Intimacy and the Hungers of the Heart* (Dublin: Columba, 1991), 154-155.
6. Joseph Schmid, The Regensberg New Testament, *The Gospel According to Mark* (Cork: Mercier, 1968), 51-52.
7. *Jesus Before Christianity* (London: Darton, Longman & Todd, 1992), 167.
8. (New York: Avon, 1971), 75-76
9. St Thomas Aquinas, *Summa Theologiae: A Concise Translation*, ed. Timothy Mc Dermott, (London: Methuen, 1989), 360.

10. P. Coste, *Collected works*, XII 270-271.
11. Coste, Vol I, 526.
12. Coste, *Collected Works*, X, 332.
13. Abelly, Vol 3, 118.
14. See Pat Collins, *Expectant Faith and the Power of God* (Dublin: Columba, 1998)

CHAPTER NINE

1. cf. Pat Collins, *Expectant Faith* (Dublin: Columba, 1998), 13.
2. *Riding the Wind* (Ann Arbor: Word of Life, 1977), 30.
3. 'Leonardo Da Vinci and a memory of his childhood' in *SE II*, 123.
4. *Psychology and Westren Religion* (London: Ark, 1988), 204.
5. *Psychology and Western Religion*, 202.
6. Viktor Frankl, 'Group Psychotherapeutic Experiences in a Concentration Camp,' *Psychotherapy and Existentialism: Selected Papers on Logotherapy* (London: Pelican, 1967), 102.
7. 'The Two Standards,' *Meditations on Priestly Life* (London: Sheed and Ward, 1974), 174.
8. *Riding the Wind*, 36.
9. *Pass it On* (New York: Alcoholics Anonymous World Services, 1984), 121.
10. (New York: Alcoholics Anonymous World Services, 1953), 106-107.
11. *Man's Search for Himself* (New York: Norton, 1953), 241.
12. *Meister Eckhart*, trans R. B. Blackney (New York: Harper and Brothers, 1941), 204.
13. *Psychology and Western Religion* (London: Ark, 1988), 208.
14. 'Self-esteem and the Love of God' *Growing in Health and Grace* (Galway: Campus, 1992), 27-43.
15. cf. Robert Eagle, *A Guide to Alternative Medicine* (London: BBC, 1980), 17.
16. (Evesham: Arthur James,1974)
17. Pat Collins, 'Faith and Eucharistic Healing' *Finding Faith in Troubled Times* (Dublin: Columba, 1993), 150-183; 'Faith and the Anointing of the Sick' *Expectant Faith: And the Power of God* (Dublin: Columba, 1998), 141-150; 'Praying for Healing' *Maturing in the Spirit* (Dublin: Columba, 1991), 125-140.

CHAPTER TEN

1. Albert Nolan, *Jesus Before Christianity* (London: Darton, Longman & Todd, 1992), 61.
2. *Spiritual Exercises* [313]
3. Martin Israel, *Exorcism: The Removal of Evil Influences* (London: SPCK, 1997); Michael Scanlon and Randall Cirner, *Deliverance From Evil Spirits: A Weapon for Spiritual Warfare* (Ann Arbor: Servant, 1980); Cardinal Suenens, *Renewal and the Powers of Darkness* (London: Darton, Longman & Todd, 1983); Matthew and Denis Linn, *Deliverance Prayer* (New York: Paulist Press, 1981); Morton Kelsey, *Discernment: A Study in Ecstacy and Evil* (New York: Paulist Press, 1978).

4. Pat Collins, 'Faith and Deliverance From Evil' part 3, *Finding Faith in Troubled Times* (Dublin: Columba, 1993), 102-147; *Unveiling the Heart: How to Overcome Evil in The Christian Life* (Dublin: Veritas, 1995).

5. cf. Pat Collins, *Expectant Faith* (Dublin: Columba, 1998),

6 *Early Christian Writings* (London: Penguin Classics, 1968), 129.

CHAPTER ELEVEN

1. Rosemary Radar, *Breaking Boundaries: Male/Female Friendships in Early Christian Communities* (New York: Paulist Press, 1983), 24.

2. James Mc Evoy, 'Friendship and Love' *Irish Theological Quarterly* (No. 1, Vol. 50, 1983/1984), 38-39.

3. *Laelius De Amicitia*, 4. 15-5.19.

4. cf. Jerome Crowe, *The Acts*, New Testament Message 8 (Dublin: Veritas, 1979), 29; Richard J. Dillon, 'Acts of the Apostles,' *The New Jerome Biblical Commentary*, eds. Brown, Fitzmyer, Murphy, (New Jersey: Prentice Hall, 1990), 738, [44:36].

5. Cistercian Studies Series: Number Ninety-Five, (Kalamazoo, Michigan: Cistercian Publications Inc., 1988)

6. See Mary Ann Fatula, *Thomas Aquinas: Preacher and Friend*, The Way of the Christian Mystics 15 (Dublin: Gill & Macmillan, 1993)

7. (Kalamazoo, Michigan: Cistercian Publications Inc., 1977), 66; Aelred Squire, 'God is Friendship,' *Aelred Of Rievaulx: A Study* (Kalamazoo, Michigan: Cistercian Publications Inc, 1981), 98-111.

8. Quoted by E. C. Sellner in 'Soul Friendship: Sharing One's Life and Heart' in *The Furrow* (July-Aug 1998), 410.

9. *The Fire of Love* (London: Penguin, 1972), 175-176.

10. Gerald Vann, *To Heaven With Diana* (New York: Pantheon, 1960)

11 *To heaven With Diana*, 34.

12. Elizabeth Stopp, trans., & ed., *St Francis de Sales: A Testimony by Jane de Chantal* (London: Faber & Faber, 1967)

13. Translated and edited John Ryan, (New York: Harper Torchbooks, 1966), 138-150.

14. Vol 1, translated John Ryan, (Rockford, Illinois: Tan Books, 1975), 88-89.

15. Louis Abelly, *The Life of the Venerable Servant of God, Vincent de Paul*, Vol 2, (New York: New City Press, 1993), 283.

16. *Bond of Perfection*, 26.

17. John Rybolt C.M. ed., 'Codex Sarzana,' *Vincentiana* 33 (1991), 307-406.

18. Abelly, Vol. 2, 126.

19. 'On Cordiality, Respect and Special Friendships,' June 2nd. 1658, *The Conferences of St Vincent de Paul to the Daughters of Charity* (London: Collins, 1979), 1061

20. *The Conferences of St Vincent de Paul to the Daughters of Charity*, 1060.

21. 'Charity,' 30th May 1659, trans., Tom Davitt C.M., *Colloque: Journal of the Irish Province of the Congregation of the Mission* (Autumn 1993, No. 28), 234.

22. SV XII, 192, quoted by Bob Maloney C.M. 'A Further Look at "Gentleness",' *Vincentiana*, No. 4-5, (July-October 1995), 292.

23. 'Charity,' *Colloque*, 232.

24. 'On Cordiality, Respect and Special Friendships,' *The Conferences of St Vincent de Paul to the Daughters of Charity*, 1064.

25. 'On Cordial Respect' Jan 1st, 1644, *The Conferences of Vincent de Paul to the Daughters of Charity*, 129.

26. 'Charity.' *Colloque*, 234.

27. Abelly, *The Life of the Venerable Servant of God Vincent de Paul* (New York: New City Press, 1993), vol 1, 106.

28. Thomas and Patrick Malone, 'Balancing Closeness and Intimacy,' *The Art of Intimacy* (London: Simon & Schuster Ltd., 1987), 25-29.

29. Quoted by Donna Tiernan Mahoney, *Touching the Face of God: Intimacy and Celibacy in Priestly Life*, (Boca Raton, Florida: Jeremiah Press, 1991), 104.

30. cf. Daniel Levinson, *The Seasons of a Man's Life* (New York: Ballentine, 1978), 335; Lillian Rubin, *Intimate Strangers* (London: Fontana, 1985), 129-131.

31. See Pat Collins CM, 'Maturing as a Priest' *The Furrow* (Nov. 1990), 605-615.

32. Quoted by Aelred Squire, *Aelred of Rievaulx: A Study* (Kalamazoo, Mich.: Cistercian Publications, 1981), 49-50.

33. Abelly, Vol. 3, 119.

34. Abelly, Vol 2, 126.

35. *Instruction on Stability Chastity Poverty and Obedience in the Congregation of the Mission* (Vincentiana Jan-Feb. 1996), 24.

36. op. cit. p. 112.

37. Quoted by John Rybolt CM, 'As Good Friends' Reflections on the development of the Concept of Fraternal Life in the Congregation of the Mission,' *Vincentiana* (Spring, 1994), 484.

38. See Jean Alvarez 'Focusing a Congregation's Future' *Human Development* Vol 5, No. 4, (Winter 1984), 25-34.

39. See Pat Collins, *Expectant Faith* (Dublin: Columba, 1998), 13-15; 19.

40. Adapted from Bert Ghezzi, *Build With the Lord* (Ann Arbor: Word of Life, 1976), 102.

41. (New York: New City Press, 1995), 13-29.

42. Abelly, *The Life of the Venerable Servant of God Vincent de Paul*, Vol 3. (New York: New City Press, 1993), 72-73.

43. Pat Collins 'Reading and Praying the Scriptures,' *The Joy of Belonging* (Galway: Campus, 1993), 78-82.

44. *Spirituality*, Vols 3 & 4, Nov/Dec 1997, and Jan/Feb 1998.

45. Cardinal Suenens, *Ecumenism and Charismatic Renewal: Theological and Pastoral Orientations* (London: Darton, Longman & Todd, 1978), 101-102.

46. *Evangelicals and Catholics together in Ireland* (Belfast: ECT, 1998), 11-12.

47. (Dublin: Columba, 1998)

48. *You are my God*, (London: Hodder & Stoughton, 1983), 159.

Index

The Eclectic Gourmet Guide to New Orleans

Tom Fitzmorris

MENASHA
RIDGE
PRESS

Every effort has been made to ensure the accuracy of information throughout this book. Bear in mind, however, that prices, schedules, etc., are constantly changing. Readers should always verify information before making final plans.

Menasha Ridge Press, Inc.
P.O. Box 43059
Birmingham, Alabama 35243

Cover and text design by Suzanne H. Holt

Cover art by Michele Natale

ISBN: 0-89732-219-3

Library of Congress Catalog Card Number: 96-22965

Manufactured in the United States of America

10 9 8 7 6 5 4 3 2 1

First Edition

CONTENTS

acknowledgments

M y most sincere gratitude to my wife and kids for putting up with many more nights on the town than the average daddy dares to steal. I also thank the listeners to my radio show for all the tips, reports, disagreements, and feedback; it keeps me in the real world. I also thank the publisher and his associates. I only had one dinner with them, but they clearly share my mission.

About the Author

Tom Fitzmorris is New Orleans' foremost restaurant critic. His first reviews of the dining scene appeared in 1972, when he was still a student at the University of New Orleans; they have continued on at least a weekly basis ever since. This is Tom's fourteenth New Orleans restaurant guide; he is also the author of several cookbooks. He is the host of a long-running daily talk show called "Dining Around" on WSMB, 1350 AM. (You can call him for gastronomic advice during the show's hours—10 A.M. to 1 P.M. central—at (504) 260-9762.) He also publishes *The New Orleans Menu,* a quarterly review of Louisiana food, and his reviews appear widely in local and national publications. Tom and his wife Mary Ann live in Covington with their two children, Jude and Mary Leigh.

Tom was born on Mardi Gras and has never left New Orleans for more than three weeks at a time.

The
Eclectic
Gourmet
Guide to
New Orleans

Getting it Right

A lot of thought went into this guide. While producing a dining guide may appear to be a straightforward endeavor, I can assure you that it is fraught with peril. I have read dining guides by authors who turn up their noses at anything except four-star French restaurants (of which there are a whole lot fewer than people think). Likewise, I have seen a guide that totally omits Thai and Indian restaurants—among others—because the author did not understand those cuisines. I have read guides absolutely devoid of criticism, written by "experts" unwilling to risk offending the source of their free meals. Finally, I've seen those books that are based on surveys and write-ins from diners whose credentials for evaluating fine dining are mysterious at best and questionable at least.

How, then, do you go about developing a truly excellent dining guide? What is the best way to get it right?

If dining guides are among the most idiosyncratic of reference books, it is primarily because the background, taste, integrity, and personal agenda of each author are problematic. The authors of most dining guides are vocational or avocational restaurant or food critics. Some of these critics are schooled professionals, with palates refined by years of practical experience and culinary study; others are journalists, often with no background in food criticism or cooking, who are arbitrarily assigned the job of reviewing restaurants by their newspaper or magazine publisher. (Although it *is* occasionally possible to find journalists who are also culinary professionals.) The worst cases are the legions of self-proclaimed food critics who mooch their way from restaurant to restaurant, growing fat on free meals in exchange for writing glowing reviews.

Ignorance of ethnic cuisine or old assumptions about what makes for haute cuisine particularly plague authors in cities without much ethnic variety in restaurants, or authors who have been writing for years about the same old white-linen, expense-account tourist traps. Many years ago in Lexington, Kentucky, for example, there was only one Chinese restaurant in town and it was wildly successful—in spite of the fact that it was Chinese in name only. Its specialty dishes, which were essentially American vegetable casseroles smothered in corn starch, were happily gobbled up by loyal patrons who had never been exposed to real Chinese cooking. The food was not bad, but it was not Chinese either. Visitors from out of town, inquiring about a good local Chinese restaurant, were invariably directed to this place. As you would expect, they were routinely horrified by the fare.

And, while you might argue that American diners are more sophisticated and knowledgeable nowadays than at the time of the Lexington pavilion, the evidence suggests otherwise. In Las Vegas, for instance, a good restaurant town with a number of excellent Italian eateries, the local Olive Garden (a chain restaurant) is consistently voted the city's best Italian restaurant in a yearly newspaper poll. There is absolutely nothing wrong with the Las Vegas Olive Garden, but to suggest that it is the best Italian restaurant in the city is ludicrous. In point of fact, the annual survey says much more about the relative sophistication of Las Vegas diners than it does about the quality of local Italian restaurants.

But if you pick up a guide that reflects the views of many survey respondents, a *vox populi* or reader's choice compendium, that is exactly the problem. You are dependent upon the average restaurant-goer's capacity to make sound, qualitative judgments—judgments almost always impaired by extraneous variables. How many times have you had a wonderful experience at a restaurant, only to be disappointed on a subsequent visit? Trying to reconcile the inconsistency, you recall that on your previous visit, you were in the company of someone particularly stimulating, and that perhaps you had enjoyed a couple of drinks before eating. What I am getting at is that our reflections on restaurant experiences are often colored by variables having little or nothing to do with the restaurant itself. And while I am given to the democratic process in theory, I have my doubts about depending entirely on survey forms that reflect such experiences.

There are more pragmatic arguments to be made about such eaters' guides as well. If you cannot control or properly qualify your survey respondents, you cannot assure their independence, knowledge, or critical sensitivity. And, since literally anyone can participate in such surveys, the ratings can be easily slanted by those with vested interests. How many bogus responses would it take to dramatically upgrade a restaurant's rating in a survey-based, big city dining guide? Forty or even fewer. Why? Because the publisher receives patron reports (survey responses, readers' calls) covering more restaurants than can be listed in the book. Thus the "voting" is distributed over such a large number of candidate restaurants that the median number of reports for the vast majority of establishments is 120 or fewer. A cunning restaurant proprietor who is willing to stuff the ballot box, therefore, could easily improve his own rating—or lower that of a competitor.

So my mission in the *Eclectic Gourmet Guides* is to provide you with the most meaningful, useful, and accessible restaurant evaluations possible. Weighing the alternatives, I have elected to work with culinary experts, augmenting their opinions with a carefully qualified survey population of totally independent local diners of demonstrated culinary sophistication. The experts I have sought to author the *Eclectic Gourmet Guides* are knowledgeable, seasoned professionals; they have studied around the world, written cookbooks or columns, and closely follow the development of restaurants in their cities. They are well versed in ethnic dining, many having studied cuisines in their native lands. And they have no prejudice about high or low cuisine. They are as at home in a Tupelo, Mississippi, catfish shack as in an exclusive French restaurant on New York's Upper East Side. Thus the name "Eclectic Gourmet."

Equally important, I have sought experts who make every effort to conduct their reviews anonymously, and who always pay full menu prices for their meals. We are credible not only because we are knowledgeable, but also because we are independent.

You, the reader of this *Eclectic Gourmet Guide,* are the inspiration for and, we hope, the beneficiary of our diligence and methodology. Though we cannot evaluate your credentials as a restaurant critic, your opinion as a consumer—of this guide and the restaurants within—is very important to us. A clip-out survey can be found at the back of the book; please tell us about your dining experiences and let us know whether you agree with our reviews.

Eat well. Be happy.

Bob Sehlinger

dining in
NEW ORLEANS

I used to work for a New Orleans newspaper whose masthead motto quoted a French philosopher: "Localism alone leads to culture." That could serve as a slogan for Orleanians, who live lives quite different from those of other Americans. Not just on Mardi Gras, and not only among certain classes, either. The style that gave New Orleans its nickname "The Big Easy" imbues every aspect of local society.

Here's a classic New Orleans story. A guy leaves town for a better job in a more stable place. After a year or so, though, he returns to a lower salary and less promise for the future because he can't stand not being able to get gumbo or an oyster poor boy when he wants.

Food is of incalculable importance to Orleanians. The degree to which that is true can be observed in any restaurant. Conversations that seem from a distance to be about sports, politics, or business are actually, more often than not, about eating: what was eaten yesterday, where eating will occur tomorrow, and whether this place is as good as it was last time. Although a seemingly equivalent kind of gustatory consciousness has swept across the country in recent years, the interest in food in New Orleans wells up from a much deeper place, through six or seven generations of genes.

But, to return to that motto . . . The main appeal of New Orleans' food is in its localism. You'd have to travel to Europe to find its like. In just the way that French or Italian towns offer their local culinary styles to the near-exclusion of anything else, so too is New Orleans obsessed with Creole and Cajun food. And that's nothing new. Creole was America's first regional gourmet cuisine. Over a century ago, books were bring written that identified Creole cooking as both fairly comprehensive and a thing apart.

The question that everybody who gets interested in New Orleans eating wants answered is: "What's the difference between Creole food and Cajun food?" A colossal amount of discussion on this matter has transpired—usually in restaurants—and nobody, regardless of his claims to authority, has ever been allowed to nail anything down.

But I'll try. Creole is the cooking style of New Orleans proper, which has been a cosmopolis for almost 200 years. Creole cuisine is based on French cuisine, but with powerful influences from Spain and Africa (the latter by way of the Caribbean). Other nationalities have added their touches, most significantly the Germans and Italians.

The Cajuns are also French, but they're different French: Acadians expelled from Nova Scotia two centuries ago. Living in almost complete isolation and poverty on the bayous of South Louisiana for two-thirds of the time since then, they have developed a culture of survival. They had a lot of seafood and farm products, but they had to sell the best of them to stay alive, and were forced to invent a unique style of cooking to make the inferior stuff taste good. Even today, real Cajun food—as delicious as it is—looks pretty bad. Which is why it has only rarely translated in authentic form to restaurant menus.

So Creole is city food and Cajun is country. A big fillet of fish with a complicated sauce draped over it is more likely to be found in a Creole milieu; the Cajun restaurant will tend more toward its etouffees and other slow-cooked pot dishes. Okay, okay. Now let's abandon the issue. Creole and Cajun have influenced each other so much in recent years that you find the same menus and flavors throughout Southeast Louisiana, save for a few unreconstructed pockets of hyper-localism here and there. And any argument over which is better is bound to end in trouble.

Creole and Cajun cooking have one notable distinction in common: the raw materials. The cooking of Southeast Louisiana is in large part defined by its native seafoods. Principal among them are oysters, shrimp, crabs, and crawfish. And there's a large cast of finfish from local waters. While restaurants in most other cities thrive on the tide of fish delivered by fast airplanes, there's nothing quite like the freshness of seafood that came to the general vicinity of your plate by way of a beat-up old truck that only had to drive a few miles. There are restaurants in New Orleans where you can eat a fish while watching his relatives swim and jump in the waters right outside the window.

I suppose you're expecting me to define the Creole taste now. Well, I give up. I'm blinkered by having eaten Creole food all my life, which makes me think of it as totally normal. What I can tell you is what I miss in the food I eat when I travel. I find non-Creole American food lacking in salt, pepper, richness, and general intensity of flavor.

One of the explanations for this is the amount of salt, pepper, cream, butter, and other fats in classic Creole cooking. Indeed, an often-cited characteristic of New Orleans recipes is that they have a way of beginning: "First you make a roux." (Roux, a blend of flour and oil, butter, or other fat, cooked to various shades of brown, is the main active ingredient in dishes from gumbo to oysters Rockefeller.) As a result, much of Creole and Cajun cooking in the old style is high in all the things the food police tell us to stay away from.

But during the past decade there's been a revolution in Creole cooking, spurred by intense competition from the hundreds (this is no exaggeration) of new restaurants that have opened. Diners have come to expect new dishes, ingredients, and flavors, and the younger, higher-profile chefs have been happy to invent them. Most of the new Creole cuisine is incomparably lighter than the old standards. Even roux is becoming rare. Occasionally it's left out of gumbos, a state of affairs my mother—like every other old-time Creole cook—would consider heresy.

The current crop of chefs takes two different routes to their innovations. Most of them are one-worlders, importing ingredients, flavors, and techniques from exotic places. Many of them incorporate those outside influences into dishes that are still quite recognizably Creole. But more than a few are serving food that has no local connection at all—sometimes not even local ingredients. That is a completely new development in a city where diners historically haven't accepted even French or Italian food until it hybridized with Creole. At the same time, purveyors of unusual ethnic cuisines in New Orleans are finding success for the first time.

If this causes you to cock an eyebrow and wonder whether our island of culture will lose its distinctiveness, rest easy. No matter how enthusiastic even the most sophisticated New Orleans diner waxes about some new Vietnamese-Mexican fusion bistro, you can be sure that in his most relaxed moments he's still munching down poor boy sandwiches, boiled crawfish, jambalaya, and bread pudding. As will all other aficionados of Creole food from near or far. Because we all know that, like all the world's other great ethnic cuisines, great Creole and Cajun cooking is only found in the land of its birth.

a few things you should know

Because the cuisine of New Orleans is so intimately tied to the indigenous ingredients, it's important to pay attention to the seasons. Although many restaurants serve, say, crawfish year-round, there's no question that crawfish are incomparably better in the peak of their natural cycle. Here's the schedule:

Crawfish: Christmas through the Fourth of July, with the peak of quality in April and May.

Crabs, soft-shell and otherwise: April through October. The peak is unpredictable, but usually the warmer it is, the better the crabmeat.

Oysters: Good year-round, but a little off during the spawn in July and August. (In other words, forget that months-with-an-R myth.)

Shrimp: There are several species, so seasons click on and off. The best times are May through August and October through December. The only poor month for shrimp is March.

Tuna: May through September.

Pompano: July through October.

Creole tomatoes: These meaty, sweet, gigantic, sensual tomatoes have a short season, in April and May, but are worth waiting for.

The calendar is also reliable in predicting when restaurants will be at their best. Absolutely the worst time to eat in New Orleans is during the Mardi Gras season, which extends three weeks before the movable Ash Wednesday (in February or early March). The city's restaurants are stretched thin at that time of year by tourists, conventions, and Mardi Gras balls. What's more, waiters and other restaurant personnel tend to be heavy participants in Carnival hijinks and are, shall we say, not at their peaks.

The best times for a serious eater to come to town are the months of October and April. The weather is beautiful for patio dining, the food supplies are at their best, and the conventions aren't overwhelming. Also good are the summer months, especially July and September. The heat and humidity convince tourists and conventions to stay away (despite the fact that there may be no better air-conditioned city on earth), and the restaurants are eager to please.

Also of note are two superb food festivals. The New Orleans Jazz and Heritage Festival takes place on the last week of April and the first week of May, with an outdoor surfeit of music and indigenous food. Then, in late July, the New Orleans Wine and Food Experience brings you indoors for an extended weekend of special feasting with the city's best chefs and drinking with the world's best winemakers.

TOURIST pLACES

In the restaurant profiles that make up most of this book, you may notice that a few well-known or highly visible restaurants are missing. This is not an oversight. The following restaurants may come to your attention, but in my opinion they're not as worthwhile as other comparable options.

Caribbean Room
2031 St. Charles Avenue   524-0581
Once a great favorite of local diners, the dining room of the Pontchartrain Hotel has been truncated and its menu jerked around so much that it's lost its appeal.

Central Grocery
923 Decatur   523-1620
As this old emporium of imported food has allowed its floor space to become taken over by the vending of muffulettas to tourists, both the store and the muffulettas have declined.

Deanie's Seafood
1713 Lake Avenue, Bucktown   831-4141
Deanie's is immensely popular, but what brings that about is the eye-popping size of its indifferent seafood platters.

Hard Rock Cafe
440 North Peters   529-5617
Although the burgers, roasted chicken, and ribs are not bad, the New Orleans edition of the international chain is much more of a place than a restaurant.

Jackson Square Cafe
801 Decatur   523-5061
This place has a great location in the Lower Pontalba Building on Jackson Square, and its menu promises all the clichéd New Orleans food you'd ever want, but it's not very good.

Jimmy Buffett's Margaritaville Cafe
1104 Decatur   592-2565
A must for parrot heads—but only after eating somewhere else.

Kabby's

Riverside New Orleans Hilton, 2 Poydras   584-3880

Assuming a ship hasn't pulled alongside, this big restaurant offers a great view of the river, but they change the concept of the menu so often that eating here is chancy at best.

Kristal Seafood

600 Decatur   522-0336

At the top of the Jackson Brewery, with a fine view of the river and the Quarter, this place serves forgettable seafood.

La Louisiane

725 Iberville   523-4664

One of the oldest restaurants in town, La Louisiane has suffered through a series of owners who have not been able to maintain its kitchen. The current proprietor did a fine job of restoring the place, but the food is not what it should be.

Landry's Seafood House

400 North Peters   558-0038

A regional chain, Landry's has the look of a great old middle-of-nowhere Louisiana roadhouse, but the food is strictly formula and not very good.

Mulate's

201 Julia   522-1492

A mammoth place copied from the original Cajun dance restaurant in Breaux Bridge, Mulate's does indeed have good Cajun music, but the food is only occasionally interesting.

Patout's Cajun Cabin

501 Bourbon   524-4054

They occupy the space where Al Hirt plays when he's in town with gilded versions of Cajun food. Although it can be quite good, the inconsistency is so extreme as to make the place unrecommendable.

Planet Hollywood

Jackson Brewery   522-7826

This chain of rock 'n' roll glitz palaces has a New Orleans chef running its food operations, and he installed a very heavy emphasis on local food. This is admirable, but the seasoning levels are so high they're less convincing than offensive.

Ralph & Kacoo's
519 Toulouse   522-5226

It started as a fine seafood house upriver and expanded into a chain of very large, somewhat overpriced, and mediocre food factories.

NEW pLACES

On the other hand, the following are restaurants that opened too recently to be reviewed. Based on my early investigations, however, I think they will evolve into eateries worthy of your attention.

Casablanca
A Middle Eastern and Moroccan cafe of some goodness that also manages to keep strictly kosher. In Zone 10—Metairie Above Causeway.

Leano's
Creole-Italian fare. In Zone 7—Lakeview.

Lucky Cheng's
Avant-garde Asian food served by extravagant and flagrant drag queens. In Zone 1—French Quarter.

Mat & Naddie's
A Creole cottage with interesting nouvelle Creole dishes, cooked by one of the area's best caterers. In Zone 4—Uptown Above Napoleon.

Pacific Rim Grill
Exactly what the name promises. In Zone 12—North Shore (Mandeville).

Randolph's
A beautiful restaurant serving very spicy versions of contemporary Creole food. In Zone 4—Uptown Above Napoleon.

MORE RECOMMENdATIONS

◆ Best Restaurants for Sunday Brunch

Arnaud's
813 Bienville   523-5433
Bacco
310 Chartres   522-2426

Begue's
Royal Sonesta Hotel, 300 Bourbon   586-0300
Brennan's
417 Royal   525-9711
Cafe Sbisa
1011 Decatur   522-5565
Cafe Volage
720 Dublin   861-4227
Charley G's
111 Veterans Boulevard, Metairie   837-6408
Commander's Palace
1403 Washington Avenue   899-8221
Court of Two Sisters
613 Royal   522-7273
Dakota
629 North US 190, Covington   (504) 892-3712
Feelings
2600 Chartres   945-2222
House of Blues
225 Decatur   529-2583
La Gauloise
Le Meridien Hotel, 614 Canal   527-6712
Mr. B's
201 Royal   523-2078
Palace Cafe
605 Canal   523-1661
Praline Connection
901 South Peters   523-3973
Rib Room
Omni Royal Orleans Hotel, 621 St. Louis   529-7045
Sazerac
Fairmont Hotel, University Place   529-7111
Vaqueros
4938 Prytania   891-6441
Veranda
Inter-Continental Hotel, 444 St. Charles Avenue   522-5566
Windsor Court Grill Room
300 Gravier   523-6000

◆ Best Breakfasts

Bacco
310 Chartres   522-2426
Bailey's
123 Baronne   529-7111
Begue's
300 Bourbon   586-0300
Bluebird Cafe
3625 Prytania   895-7166
7801 Panola   866-7577
Brennan's
417 Royal   525-9711
Cafe Pontchartrain
2031 St. Charles Avenue   524-0581
Camellia Grill
626 South Carrollton Avenue   866-9573
Coffee Pot
714 St. Peter   524-3500
La Gauloise
614 Canal   527-6712
La Madeleine
547 St. Ann   568-9950
601 South Carrollton Avenue   861-8661
Louis XVI
730 Bienville   581-7000
Mother's
401 Poydras   523-9656
Peppermill (Riccobono's)
3524 Severn Avenue, Metairie   455-2266
Petunia's
817 St. Louis   522-6440
Tailgators Cafe
933 Metairie Road, Metairie   832-0122
Tally-Ho
400 Chartres   566-7071
Tiffin Inn
6601 Veterans Boulevard, Metairie   888-6602
Veranda
Inter-Continental Hotel, 444 St. Charles Avenue   522-5566

Windsor Court Grill Room
300 Gravier   523-6000

- ◆ Best Hamburgers

Bud's Broiler
500 City Park Avenue   486-2559
6325 Elysian Fields Avenue   282-6696
2800 Veterans Boulevard, Kenner   466-0026
3151 Calhoun   861-0906
4101 Jefferson Highway, Jefferson   837-9419
112 Sauve Road, River Ridge   738-2452
9820 Lake Forest Boulevard   244-6866
5100 Lapalco Boulevard   348-0492
Camellia Grill
626 South Carrollton Avenue   866-9573
Doug's Place
748 Camp   527-5433
Hard Rock Cafe
440 North Peters   529-5617
Hummingbird Grill
804 St. Charles Avenue   561-9229
Katie's
3701 Iberville   488-6582
Lee's Hamburgers
904 Veterans Boulevard   836-6804
Michael's Mid-City Grill
4139 Canal   488-2878
New Orleans Hamburger & Seafood Co.
1005 South Clearview Parlwau, Jefferson   734-1122
6920 Veterans Boulevard, Metairie   455-1272
817 Veterans Boulevard, Metairie   837-8580
Port of Call
838 Esplanade   523-0120
Snug Harbor
626 Frenchmen   949-0696
Straya
4517 Veterans Boulevard, Metairie   887-8873
Ye Olde College Inn
3016 South Carrollton Avenue   866-3683

◆ Restaurants with Most Unusual Architecture

Allegro
1100 Poydras   582-2350
Antoine's
713 St. Louis   581-4422
Arnaud's
813 Bienville   523-5433
Bacco
310 Chartres   522-2426
Bella Luna
914 North Peters   529-1583
Brennan's
417 Royal   525-9711
Broussard's
819 Conti   581-3866
Cafe Sbisa
1011 Decatur Street   522-5565
Christian's
3835 Iberville   482-4924
Commander's Palace
1403 Washington Avenue   899-8221
Emeril's
800 Tchoupitoulas   528-9393
Nola
534 St. Louis   522-6652
Restaurant des Familles
LA 45 at LA 3134, Crown Point   689-7834
Tavern On The Park
900 City Park Avenue   486-3333
Upperline
1413 Upperline   891-9822
Vaqueros
4938 Prytania   891-6441
Veranda
Inter-Continental Hotel, 444 St. Charles Avenue   522-5566

◆ Best Cafes for Dessert and Coffee

Angelo Brocato
214 North Carrollton Avenue   486-1465
537 St. Ann   525-9676
Cafe du Monde
800 Decatur   525-4544
Churros Cafe
3100 Kingman, Metairie   885-6516
Coffee Cottage
2559 Metairie Road, Metairie   833-3513
Coffee Rani
2324 Veterans Boulevard, Metairie   833-6343
Croissant d'Or
617 Ursulines   524-4663
La Madeleine
547 St. Ann   568-9950
601 South Carrollton Avenue   861-8661
La Marquise
625 Chartres   524-0420
Maurice's French Pastries
3501 Hessmer Avenue, Metairie   885-1526
Morning Call Coffee Stand
3325 Severn Avenue, Metairie   885-4068
Plantation Coffeehouse
5555 Canal Boulevard   482-3164

◆ Best Restaurants for Dining with Children

Assunta's
2631 Covington Highway (US 190), Slidell   (504) 649-9768
Bozo's
3117 21st Street, Metairie   831-8666
Brick Oven Cafe
2805 Williams Boulevard, Kenner   466-2097
Bruning's
West End Park   282-9395
Cafe Atchafalaya
901 Louisiana   891-5271

Cavallino's
1500 South Carrollton Avenue   866-9866
Copeland's
1001 South Clearview Parkway, Jefferson   733-7843
701 Veterans Boulevard, Metairie   831-3437
4338 St. Charles Avenue   897-2325
1700 Lapalco, Harvey   364-1575
1337 Gause Boulevard, Slidell   (504) 643-0001
Corky's
4243 Veterans Boulevard, Metairie   887-5000
Delmonico
1300 St. Charles Avenue   525-4937
Doug's Place
748 Camp   527-5433
Fausto's
530 Veterans Boulevard, Metairie   833-7121
Figaro Pizzerie
2820 East Causeway Approach, Mandeville   (504) 624-8500
7900 Maple   866-0100
Golden Lake Chinese Restaurant
1712 Lake Avenue, Bucktown   838-8646
La Gauloise
614 Canal   527-6712
Louisiana Pizza Kitchen
2800 Esplanade Avenue   488-2800
615 South Carrollton Avenue   866-5900
Mark Twain Pizza Landing
2035 Metairie Road, Metairie   832-8032
Peppermill (Riccobono's)
3524 Severn Avenue, Metairie   455-2266
Sal's Pasta Garden
1414 Veterans Boulevard, Metairie   835-3699
Semolina
3242 Magazine   895-4260
5080 Pontchartrain Boulevard   486-5581
Oakwood Mall (197 West Bank Expy.), Gretna   361-8293
3501 Chateau Boulevard, Kenner   468-1047
Sid-Mar's
1824 Orpheum, Bucktown   831-9541

Straya
4517 Veterans Boulevard, Metairie   887-8873
West End Cafe
8536 Pontchartrain Boulevard   288-0711
Ye Olde College Inn
3016 South Carrollton Avenue   866-3683

◆ Best Restaurants for Local Color

Antoine's
713 St. Louis   581-4422
Arnaud's
813 Bienville   523-5433
Bon Ton Cafe
401 Magazine   524-3386
Bozo's
3117 21st Street, Metairie   831-8666
Brigtsen's
723 Dante   861-7610
Broussard's
819 Conti   581-3866
Bruning's
West End Park   282-9395
Cafe du Monde
800 Decatur   525-4544
Cafe Sbisa
1011 Decatur Street   522-5565
Casamento's
4330 Magazine   895-9761
Clancy's
6100 Annunciation   895-1111
Coffee Pot
714 St. Peter   524-3500
Commander's Palace
1403 Washington Avenue   899-8221
Court of Two Sisters
613 Royal   522-7273
Delmonico
1300 St. Charles Avenue   525-4937

Dooky Chase
2301 Orleans Avenue   821-0600
Doug's Place
748 Camp   527-5433
Galatoire's
209 Bourbon   525-2021
Joey K's
3001 Magazine   891-0997
Liuzza's
3636 Bienville   482-9120
Mandina's
3800 Canal   482-9179
Mosca's
4137 US 90, Waggaman   436-9942
Napoleon House
500 Chartres   524-9752
Pascal's Manale
1838 Napoleon Avenue   895-4877
Praline Connection
542 Frenchman   943-3934
901 South Peters   523-3973
Rocky & Carlo's
613 West St. Bernard Highway, Chalmette   279-8323
Sid-Mar's
1824 Orpheum, Bucktown   831-9541
Tujague's
823 Decatur   525-8676
Uglesich's
1238 Baronne   523-8571

◆ Best Muffulettas

Cafe Buon Giorno
830 Third Street, Gretna   363-9111
Compagno's
7839 St. Charles Avenue   866-9313
Giovanni's Sausage Co.
1325 Veterans Boulevard, Metairie   835-4558
Italian Pie
417 South Rampart   522-7552

Joey K's
3001 Magazine   891-0997
Johnny's Po-Boys
511 St. Louis   524-8129
Katie's
3701 Iberville   488-6582
Landry's
789 Harrison Avenue   488-6476
Messina's
200 Chartres   523-9225
Napoleon House
500 Chartres   524-9752

◆ Best Restaurants with Oyster Bars

Acme Oyster House
724 Iberville   522-5973
Bozo's
3117 21st Street, Metairie   831-8666
Bruning's
West End Park   282-9395
Casamento's
4330 Magazine   895-9761
Drago's
3232 North Arnoult Road, Metairie   888-9254
Felix's
739 Iberville   522-4440
Messina's
200 Chartres   523-9225
Mike Anderson's
215 Bourbon   524-3884
Pascal's Manale
1838 Napoleon Avenue   895-4877
Remoulade
309 Bourbon   523-0377
Uglesich's
1238 Baronne   523-8571

◆ Best Restaurants for Outdoor Dining

Bayona
430 Dauphine   525-4455
Bayou Ridge Cafe
437 Esplanade   949-9912
Broussard's
819 Conti   581-3866
Cafe Degas
3127 Esplanade   945-5635
Cafe Volage
720 Dublin   861-4227
Court of Two Sisters
613 Royal   522-7273
G&E Courtyard Grill
1113 Decatur   528-9376
Louis XVI
730 Bienville Street   581-7000
Martinique
5908 Magazine   891-8495
Vaqueros
4938 Prytania   891-6441

◆ Best Pizza

Brick Oven Cafe
2805 Williams Boulevard, Kenner   466-2097
Cafe Buon Giorno
830 Third Street, Gretna   363-9111
Cafe Italiano
3244 Magazine   891-4040
Cavallino's
1500 South Carrollton Avenue   866-9866
Figaro Pizzerie
2820 East Causeway Approach, Mandeville   (504) 624-8500
7900 Maple   866-0100
Italian Pie
417 South Rampart   522-7552
Louisiana Pizza Kitchen
2800 Esplanade Avenue   488-2800
615 South Carrollton Avenue   866-5900

Mama Rosa's
616 North Rampart   523-5546
Mark Twain Pizza Landing
2035 Metairie Road, Metairie   832-8032
Mona Lisa
1212 Royal   522-6746
874 Harrison Avenue   488-0133
Mr. Roma
4421 Clearview Parkway, Metairie   455-8010
New York Pizza
5201 Magazine   891-2376
Roman Pizza
7329 Cohn   866-1166
Sweet Basil's Bistro
3445 Prytania Street   891-2227
1000 Behrman Highway, Gretna   391-0018
Tailgators Cafe
933 Metairie Road, Metairie   832-0122
Tower of Pizza
2104 Veterans Boulevard, Metairie   833-9373

understanding the ratings

We have developed detailed profiles for the best restaurants (in our opinion) in town. Each profile features an easily scanned heading which allows you, in just a second, to check out the restaurant's name, cuisine, star rating, cost, quality rating, and value rating.

Star Rating. The star rating is an overall rating that encompasses the entire dining experience, including style, service, and ambience in addition to the taste, presentation, and quality of the food. Five stars is the highest rating possible and connotes the best of everything. Four-star restaurants are exceptional and three-star restaurants are well above average. Two-star restaurants are good. One star is used to connote an average restaurant that demonstrates an unusual capability in some area of specialization, for example, an otherwise unmemorable place that has great barbecued chicken.

Cost. Below the star rating is an expense description that provides a comparative sense of how much a complete meal will cost. A complete meal for our purposes consists of an entree with vegetable or side dish, and choice of soup or salad. Appetizers, desserts, drinks, and tips are excluded.

Inexpensive	$14 and less per person
Moderate	$15–25 per person
Expensive	$26–40 per person
Very Expensive	Over $40 per person

Quality Rating. Below the cost rating appear a number and a letter. The number is a quality rating based on a scale of 0–100, with 100 being the highest (best) rating attainable. The quality rating is based expressly on the taste, freshness of ingredients, preparation, presentation, and creativity of food served. There is no consideration of price. If you are a person who wants the best food available, and cost is not an issue, you need look no further than the quality ratings.

Value Rating.   If, on the other hand, you are looking for both quality and value, then you should check the value rating, expressed in letters. The value ratings are defined as follows:

A   Exceptional value, a real bargain
B   Good value
C   Fair value, you get exactly what you pay for
D   Somewhat overpriced
F   Significantly overpriced

locating the restaurant

Just below the restaurant name is a designation for geographic zone. This zone description will give you a general idea of where the restaurant described is located. For ease of use, we divide New Orleans into twelve geographic zones.

Zone 1.   French Quarter
Zone 2.   Central Business District
Zone 3.   Uptown Below Napoleon
Zone 4.   Uptown Above Napoleon
Zone 5.   Downtown/St. Bernard
Zone 6.   Mid-City/Gentilly
Zone 7.   Lakeview/West End/Bucktown
Zone 8.   New Orleans East
Zone 9.   Metairie Below Causeway
Zone 10.   Metairie Above Causeway/Kenner/Jefferson Highway
Zone 11.   West Bank
Zone 12.   North Shore

If you are in the French Quarter and intend to walk or take a cab to dinner, you may want to choose a restaurant from among those located in Zone 1. If you have a car, you might include restaurants from contiguous zones in your consideration.

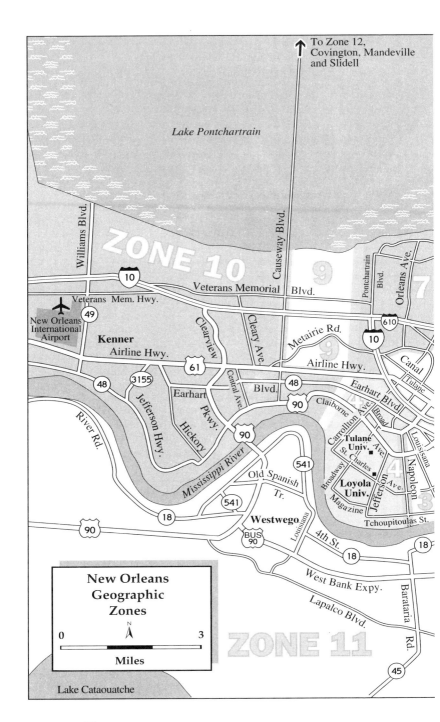

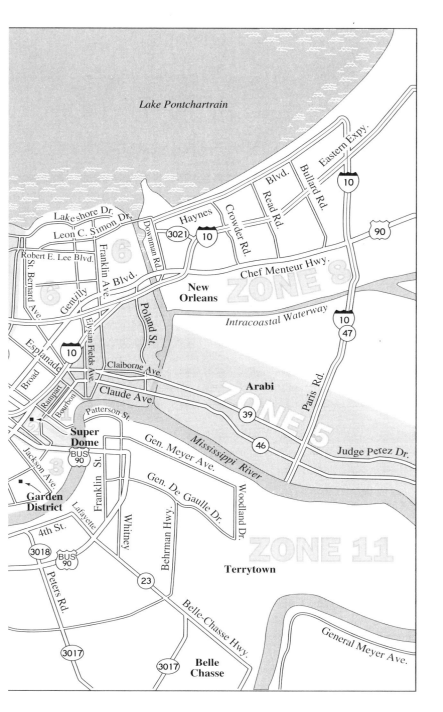

OUR PICK OF THE BEST NEW ORLEANS RESTAURANTS

Because restaurants are opening and closing all the time in New Orleans, we have tried to confine our list to establishments—or chefs—with a proven track record over a fairly long period of time. Those newer or changed establishments that demonstrate staying power and consistency will be profiled in subsequent editions.

Also, the list is highly selective. Non-inclusion of a particular place does not necessarily indicate that the restaurant is not good, but only that it was not ranked among the best or most consistent in its genre. Detailed profiles of each restaurant follow in alphabetical order at the end of this chapter.

A NOTE ABOUT SPELLING

Most diners who enjoy ethnic restaurants have noticed subtle variations in the spelling of certain dishes and preparations from one menu to the next. A noodle dish found on almost all Thai menus, for example, appears in one restaurant as *pad thai,* in another as *Paht Thai,* and in a third as *Phad Thai.*

This and similar inconsistencies arise from attempts to derive a phonetic English spelling from the name of a dish as pronounced in its country of origin. While one particular English spelling might be more frequently used than others, there is usually no definitive correct spelling for the names of many dishes. In this guide, we have elected to use the spelling most commonly found in authoritative ethnic cookbooks and other reference works.

We call this to your attention because the spelling we use in this guide could be different from that which you encounter on the menu in a certain restaurant. We might say, for instance, that the *tabbouleh* is good at the Byblos, while at the restaurant itself the dish is listed on the menu as *tabouli*.

Restaurants by Cuisine

Restaurant	Star Rating	Price	Quality Rating	Value Rating	Zone
American					
House of Blues	★★★	Mod	81	C	1
Chart House	★★★	Exp	78	C	1
Bakery Cafe					
La Madeleine	★★	Inexp	74	C	1, 4, 10
Barbecue					
Corky's	★★★	Inexp	80	B	10
Tipton County Tennessee Pit Barbecue	★★★	Inexp	80	B	4
Harold's Texas Barbecue	★★	Inexp	67	C	10
Cajun					
Bon Ton Cafe	★★★	Mod	79	B	2
Copeland's	★★★	Mod	76	C	4, 9, 10
Caribbean					
Martinique	★★★	Mod	85	B	4
Palmer's	★★★	Mod	82	A	6
Tango Tango	★★★	Mod	80	B	3
Chinese					
China Blossom	★★★★	Mod	87	B	11
Trey Yuen	★★★★	Exp	85	D	12
Mr. Tai's	★★★	Mod	83	C	9
Kung's Dynasty	★★★	Mod	82	C	3
China Doll	★★★	Mod	79	B	11
Five Happiness	★★★	Mod	78	C	4
Golden Lake Chinese Restaurant	★★★	Mod	76	B	9
Jade East	★★★	Mod	74	C	8
Coffee / Breakfast					
Cafe du Monde	★★★	Inexp	70	C	1
Continental					
Veranda	★★★	Exp	82	C	2

28

Restaurant	Star Rating	Price	Quality Rating	Value Rating	Zone
Creole					
Tujague's	★★★★	Exp	87	C	1
Doug's	★★★★	Mod	83	B	12
La Cuisine	★★★	Mod	87	B	7
Feelings	★★★	Mod	86	B	5
Gallagher's	★★★	Exp	86	C	12
Begue's	★★★	Exp	83	C	1
Delmonico	★★★	Exp	82	B	3
Cafe Rue Bourbon (Cafe Vieux Carre)	★★★	Exp	81	D	1
Gumbo Shop	★★★	Mod	80	B	1
Tavern On The Park	★★★	Exp	80	C	6
Dooky Chase	★★★	Mod	78	B	6
Frankie's Cafe	★★★	Mod	76	B	4
Court of Two Sisters	★★★	Exp	75	C	1
Riverside Cafe	★★	Mod	75	C	2
Coffee Pot	★★	Mod	71	C	1
Crescent City Brewhouse	★★	Mod	68	C	1
Windjammer	★★	Mod	67	C	7
Creole French					
Christian's	★★★★	Exp	90	B	6
Galatoire's	★★★★	Exp	90	C	1
Arnaud's	★★★★	Exp	86	D	1
Antoine's	★★★★	Exp	83	D	1
Brennan's	★★★	Very Exp	82	F	1
Cafe Volage	★★★	Mod	78	B	4
Creole Italian					
Vincent's Italian Cuisine	★★★★	Mod	90	A	10
Mosca's	★★★★	Exp	88	C	11
Sal & Judy's	★★★★	Exp	86	B	12
Pascal's Manale	★★★★	Exp	85	B	4
Bacco	★★★★	Mod	84	C	1
Smilie's	★★★	Mod	84	A	10
Barreca's	★★★	Mod	81	B	9

Restaurant	Star Rating	Price	Quality Rating	Value Rating	Zone
Creole Italian *(continued)*					
Peppermill (Riccobono's)	★★★	Mod	77	C	10
Tony Angello's	★★★	Mod	76	B	7
Salvatore's	★★	Exp	74	C	10
Sal & Sam's	★★	Mod	73	C	10
Carmine's	★★	Mod	72	B	7
Creole / Neighborhood Cafe					
Uglesich's	★★★★	Mod	86	D	3
Greco's	★★★	Exp	81	C	1
Katie's	★★★	Inexp	80	B	6
Mandich	★★★	Mod	80	B	5
Praline Connection	★★★	Mod	80	B	2, 5
Zachary's	★★★	Mod	80	B	4
Liuzza's	★★★	Inexp	79	B	6
Compagno's	★★★	Mod	76	C	4
Fury's	★★★	Mod	76	C	9
Mandina's	★★★	Mod	75	A	6
Olivier's Creole Restaurant	★★★	Mod	75	C	1
West End Cafe	★★★	Mod	74	C	7
Eddie's	★★★	Inexp	73	A	6
Galley Seafood	★★★	Mod	73	B	9
Landry's	★★★	Inexp	73	C	7
Ye Olde College Inn	★★	Mod	73	B	4
Joey K's	★★	Inexp	72	B	3
Petunia's	★★	Mod	72	B	1
Dunbar's	★★	Inexp	70	A	4
Cuban					
Garces	★★	Inexp	70	C	6
Deli					
Martin Wine Cellar Deli	★★★	Inexp	75	B	3, 9
Kosher Kajun Deli	★★	Inexp	80	B	10
Diner					
Camellia Grill	★★★	Inexp	73	C	4
Bluebird Cafe	★★★	Inexp	70	B	3, 4

Restaurants by Cuisine (continued)

Restaurant	Star Rating	Price	Quality Rating	Value Rating	Zone
Eclectic					
Pelican Club	★★★★★	Exp	96	C	1
Windsor Court Grill Room	★★★★★	Very Exp	94	F	2
Bayona	★★★★★	Exp	96	B	1
Bella Luna	★★★★	Very Exp	92	C	1
Gautreau's	★★★★	Exp	89	C	4
Mike's On The Avenue	★★★★	Very Exp	89	D	2
Jason's	★★★★	Exp	87	B	3
Graham's	★★★	Very Exp	86	D	2
Bistro at Maison de Ville	★★★	Exp	84	C	1
Gauthier's Market Cafe	★★★	Exp	84	C	12
Straya	★★★	Mod	83	B	10
Bayou Ridge Cafe	★★★	Mod	82	B	5
Semolina	★★★	Mod	81	A	3, 6, 11
Midnight Star Cafe	★★★	Exp	80	D	7
French					
La Provence	★★★★★	Exp	98	C	12
Louis XVI	★★★★	Very Exp	87	D	1
La Gauloise	★★★	Mod	86	C	2
Sazerac	★★★★	Very Exp	89	C	2
French Bistro					
Crozier's	★★★★★	Exp	93	C	10
Chez Daniel	★★★★	Mod	90	B	9
La Crepe Nanou	★★★★	Mod	87	A	4
Martinique	★★★	Mod	85	B	4
Cafe Degas	★★★	Mod	73	B	6
Greek					
Zissis	★★★★	Mod	84	C	9
Odyssey Grill	★★★	Mod	87	B	7
Hamburgers					
Port of Call	★★★	Inexp	77	B	1
Snug Harbor	★★★	Inexp	75	B	5
Michael's Mid-City Grill	★★	Inexp	71	C	6

Restaurant	Star Rating	Price	Quality Rating	Value Rating	Zone
Indian					
India Palace	★★★	Mod	83	C	10
Shalimar	★★★	Mod	82	C	1
Taj Mahal	★★★	Mod	81	B	9
Italian					
Andrea's	★★★★	Exp	87	C	9
La Riviera	★★★★	Exp	83	C	10
Irene's Cuisine	★★★★	Mod	82	B	1
Sclafani's	★★★	Mod	84	A	8
Impastato's	★★★	Exp	81	B	10
Rigatoni	★★★	Mod	80	B	3
Ristorante Carmelo	★★★	Mod	79	C	1
Brick Oven Cafe	★★★	Mod	78	B	10
Sal's Pasta Garden	★★	Mod	73	B	9
Japanese					
Shogun	★★★★	Mod	86	C	9
Ninja	★★★	Mod	84	C	4
Hana	★★★	Mod	82	C	4
Little Tokyo	★★★	Mod	82	C	9
Little Tokyo	★★★	Mod	82	C	3
Korean					
Genghis Khan	★★★	Mod	87	C	6
Mediterranean					
Petra	★★★	Exp	83	B	9
Mexican					
Vaqueros	★★★★	Mod	90	C	4
El Patio	★★★★	Mod	83	C	10
Santa Fe	★★★	Mod	87	C	1
Jalapeño's	★★★	Mod	79	B	9
Taqueria Corona	★★★	Mod	79	A	2, 4, 10
Castillo's	★★	Mod	74	C	1
Vera Cruz	★★	Mod	71	C	1, 4

Restaurants by Cuisine (continued)

Restaurant	Star Rating	Price	Quality Rating	Value Rating	Zone
Middle Eastern					
Byblos	★★★★	Mod	83	A	9
Cucina Med	★★★	Exp	79	C	12
Jerusalem	★★★	Inexp	75	A	6
Nouvelle Cajun					
K-Paul's Louisiana Kitchen	★★★★	Very Exp	91	D	1
Alex Patout's Louisiana Restaurant	★★★	Exp	84	C	1
Charley G's	★★★	Exp	83	D	9
Nouvelle Creole					
Emeril's	★★★★★	Very Exp	98	C	2
Commander's Palace	★★★★★	Exp	97	B	3
Versailles	★★★★★	Very Exp	95	C	3
Dakota	★★★★★	Exp	94	C	12
Gabrielle	★★★★	Exp	93	B	6
Brigtsen's	★★★★	Exp	92	B	4
Rib Room	★★★★	Very Exp	91	D	1
Clancy's	★★★★	Exp	90	B	4
Mr. B's	★★★★	Exp	90	C	1
Nola	★★★★	Exp	90	C	1
Upperline	★★★★	Exp	88	C	4
Broussard's	★★★★	Very Exp	84	D	1
Palace Cafe	★★★	Exp	84	C	2
Kelsey's	★★★	Mod	82	B	3
Bombay Club	★★★	Very Exp	81	C	1
Cafe Sbisa	★★★	Exp	79	C	1
Allegro	★★★	Mod	78	B	2
Traveler's Post	★★	Mod	75	C	3
Nouvelle French					
Peristyle	★★★★	Exp	94	B	1
L'Economie	★★★	Exp	80	C	2

Restaurant	Star Rating	Price	Quality Rating	Value Rating	Zone
Nouvelle Italian					
G&E Courtyard Grill	★★★★	Exp	93	B	1
Cafe Giovanni	★★★★	Exp	87	B	1
Nuvolari's	★★★★	Exp	86	B	12
Maximo's Italian Grill	★★★	Exp	81	C	1
Oyster Bar					
Acme Oyster House	★★	Inexp	71	B	1
Pizza					
Louisiana Pizza Kitchen	★★★	Mod	83	B	1, 4, 6
Brick Oven Cafe	★★★	Mod	78	B	10
Figaro Pizzerie	★★★	Mod	78	C	4, 12
Cavallino's	★★★	Mod	76	B	4
Cafe Buon Giorno	★★★	Inexp	72	B	11
Italian Pie	★★	Inexp	82	B	2
Mona Lisa	★★	Inexp	71	B	1, 7
Salvadoran					
Pupuseria Divino Corazon	★★★	Inexp	79	A	11
Sandwiches					
Mother's	★★★	Mod	83	D	2
Giovanni's Sausage Co.	★★★	Inexp	78	B	9
Cafe Maspero	★★★	Inexp	74	A	1
Napoleon House	★★	Inexp	74	B	1
Johnny's Po-Boys	★★	Inexp	73	A	1
R&O's	★★	Inexp	68	B	7
Seafood					
Bozo's	★★★★	Inexp	86	B	9
Drago's	★★★★	Mod	85	C	10
Barrow's Shady Inn	★★★	Inexp	84	B	4
Sid-Mar's	★★★	Mod	83	A	9
Mike Anderson's	★★★	Mod	80	C	1
Bruning's	★★★	Inexp	79	A	7
Middendorf's	★★★	Mod	79	B	12
Restaurant des Familles	★★★	Mod	76	C	11

Restaurants by Cuisine (continued)

Restaurant	Star Rating	Price	Quality Rating	Value Rating	Zone
Casamento's	★★★	Inexp	72	C	3
Messina's	★★	Inexp	70	C	I
Felix's	★★	Inexp	69	C	I
Southern					
Cafe Atchafalaya	★★★	Inexp	82	B	3
Spanish					
Lola's	★★★	Mod	80	A	6
Steak					
Ruth's Chris Steak House	★★★★	Very Exp	90	D	6, 10
Young's	★★★★	Mod	83	A	12
Steak Knife	★★★	Exp	86	C	7
Doug's Place	★★★	Mod	80	C	2
Beef Room	★★★	Mod	78	B	10
Crescent City Steak House	★★★	Exp	77	C	6
Charlie's Steak House	★★★	Mod	75	B	4
Crazy Johnnie's	★★★	Inexp	75	A	10, 12
Thai					
Siamese	★★★	Mod	84	C	10
Bangkok Cuisine	★★★	Mod	83	B	6
Tunisian					
Jamila's	★★★	Mod	83	A	4
Vegetarian					
Old Dog New Trick	★★	Inexp	80	C	I
Vietnamese					
Kim Son	★★★★	Mod	87	A	11

Restaurants by Star Rating

Restaurant	Cuisine	Price	Quality Rating	Value Rating	Zone
Five-Star Restaurants					
Emeril's	Nouvelle Creole	Very Exp	98	C	2
La Provence	French	Exp	98	C	12
Commander's Palace	Nouvelle Creole	Exp	97	B	3
Bayona	Eclectic	Exp	96	B	1
Pelican Club	Eclectic	Exp	96	C	1
Versailles	Nouvelle Creole	Very Exp	95	C	3
Dakota	Nouvelle Creole	Exp	94	C	12
Windsor Court Grill Room	Eclectic	Very Exp	94	F	2
Crozier's	French Bistro	Exp	93	C	10
Four-Star Restaurants					
Peristyle	Nouvelle French	Exp	98	B	1
G&E Courtyard Grill	Nouvelle Italian	Exp	93	B	1
Gabrielle	Nouvelle Creole	Exp	93	B	6
Bella Luna	Eclectic / Southwestern	Very Exp	92	C	1
Brigtsen's	Nouvelle Creole	Exp	92	B	4
K-Paul's Louisiana Kitchen	Nouvelle Cajun	Very Exp	91	D	1
Rib Room	Nouvelle Creole	Very Exp	91	D	1
Chez Daniel	French Bistro	Mod	90	B	9
Christian's	Creole French	Exp	90	B	6
Clancy's	Nouvelle Creole	Exp	90	B	4
Galatoire's	Creole French	Exp	90	C	1
Mr. B's	Nouvelle Creole	Exp	90	C	1
Nola	Nouvelle Creole	Exp	90	C	1
Ruth's Chris Steak House	Steak	Very Exp	90	D	6, 10
Vaqueros	Mexican	Mod	90	C	4
Vincent's Italian Cuisine	Creole Italian	Mod	90	A	10
Gautreau's	Eclectic	Exp	89	C	4
Mike's On The Avenue	Eclectic	Very Exp	89	D	2
Sazerac	French	Very Exp	89	C	2
Mosca's	Creole Italian	Exp	88	C	11

Restaurants by Star Rating (continued)

Restaurant	Cuisine	Price	Quality Rating	Value Rating	Zone
Upperline	Nouvelle Creole	Exp	88	C	4
Andrea's	Italian	Exp	87	C	9
Cafe Giovanni	Nouvelle Italian	Exp	87	B	1
China Blossom	Chinese	Mod	87	B	11
Jason's	Eclectic	Exp	87	B	3
Kim Son	Vietnamese	Mod	87	A	11
La Crepe Nanou	French Bistro	Mod	87	A	4
Louis XVI	French	Very Exp	87	D	1
Tujague's	Creole	Exp	87	C	1
Arnaud's	Creole French	Exp	86	D	1
Bozo's	Seafood	Inexp	86	B	9
Nuvolari's	Nouvelle Italian	Exp	86	B	12
Sal & Judy's	Creole Italian	Exp	86	B	12
Shogun	Japanese	Mod	86	C	9
Uglesich's	Creole / Neighborhood Cafe	Mod	86	D	3
Drago's	Seafood	Mod	85	C	10
Pascal's Manale	Creole Italian	Exp	85	B	4
Trey Yuen	Chinese	Exp	85	D	12
Bacco	Creole Italian	Mod	84	C	1
Broussard's	Nouvelle Creole	Very Exp	84	D	1
Zissis	Greek	Mod	84	C	9
Antoine's	Creole French	Exp	83	D	1
Byblos	Middle Eastern	Mod	83	A	9
Doug's	Creole	Mod	83	B	12
El Patio	Mexican	Mod	83	C	10
La Riviera	Italian	Exp	83	C	10
Young's	Steak	Mod	83	A	12
Irene's Cuisine	Italian	Mod	82	B	1

Three-Star Restaurants

Genghis Khan	Korean	Mod	87	C	6
La Cuisine	Creole	Mod	87	B	7
Odyssey Grill	Greek	Mod	87	B	7
Santa Fe	Mexican	Mod	87	C	1
Feelings	Creole	Mod	86	B	5

Restaurant	Cuisine	Price	Quality Rating	Value Rating	Zone
Three-Star Restaurants *(continued)*					
Gallagher's	Creole	Exp	86	C	12
Graham's	Eclectic	Very Exp	86	D	2
La Gauloise	French	Mod	86	C	2
Steak Knife	Steak	Exp	86	C	7
Martinique	French Bistro / Caribbean	Mod	85	B	4
Alex Patout's Louisiana Restaurant	Nouvelle Cajun	Exp	84	C	1
Barrow's Shady Inn	Seafood	Inexp	84	B	4
Bistro at Maison de Ville	Eclectic	Exp	84	C	1
Gauthier's Market Cafe	Eclectic	Exp	84	C	12
Ninja	Japanese	Mod	84	C	4
Palace Cafe	Nouvelle Creole	Exp	84	C	2
Sclafani's	Italian	Mod	84	A	8
Siamese	Thai	Mod	84	C	10
Smilie's	Creole Italian	Mod	84	A	10
Bangkok Cuisine	Thai	Mod	83	B	6
Begue's	Creole	Exp	83	C	1
Charley G's	Nouvelle Cajun	Exp	83	D	9
India Palace	Indian	Mod	83	C	10
Jamila's	Tunisian	Mod	83	A	4
Louisiana Pizza Kitchen	Pizza	Mod	83	B	1, 4, 6
Mother's	Sandwiches	Mod	83	D	2
Mr. Tai's	Chinese	Mod	83	C	9
Petra	Mediterranean	Exp	83	B	9
Sid-Mar's	Seafood	Mod	83	A	9
Straya	Eclectic	Mod	83	B	10
Bayou Ridge Cafe	Eclectic	Mod	82	B	5
Brennan's	Creole French	Very Exp	82	F	1
Cafe Atchafalaya	Southern	Inexp	82	B	3
Delmonico	Creole	Exp	82	B	3
Hana	Japanese	Mod	82	C	4
Kelsey's	Nouvelle Creole	Mod	82	B	3
Kung's Dynasty	Chinese	Mod	82	C	3
Little Tokyo	Japanese	Mod	82	C	9

Restaurant	Cuisine	Price	Quality Rating	Value Rating	Zone
Palmer's	Caribbean	Mod	82	A	6
Shalimar	Indian	Mod	82	C	1
Veranda	Continental	Exp	82	C	2
Barreca's	Creole Italian	Mod	81	B	9
Bombay Club	Nouvelle Creole	Very Exp	81	C	1
Cafe Rue Bourbon (Cafe Vieux Carre)	Creole	Exp	81	D	1
Greco's	Creole / Neighborhood Cafe	Exp	81	C	1
House of Blues	American	Mod	81	C	1
Impastato's	Italian	Exp	81	B	10
Maximo's Italian Grill	Nouvelle Italian	Exp	81	C	1
Semolina	Eclectic	Mod	81	A	3, 6, 11
Taj Mahal	Indian	Mod	81	B	9
Corky's	Barbecue	Inexp	80	B	10
Doug's Place	Steak	Mod	80	C	2
Gumbo Shop	Creole	Mod	80	B	1
Katie's	Creole / Neighborhood Cafe	Inexp	80	B	6
L'Economie	Nouvelle French	Exp	80	C	2
Lola's	Spanish	Mod	80	A	6
Mandich	Creole / Neighborhood Cafe	Mod	80	B	5
Midnight Star Cafe	Eclectic	Exp	80	D	7
Mike Anderson's	Seafood	Mod	80	C	1
Praline Connection	Creole / Neighborhood Cafe	Mod	80	B	2, 5
Rigatoni	Italian	Mod	80	B	3
Tango Tango	Caribbean / South American	Mod	80	B	3
Tavern On The Park	Creole	Exp	80	C	6
Tipton County Tennessee Pit Barbecue	Barbecue	Inexp	80	B	4
Zachary's	Creole / Neighborhood Cafe	Mod	80	B	4
Bon Ton Cafe	Cajun	Mod	79	B	2

Restaurant	Cuisine	Price	Quality Rating	Value Rating	Zone
Three-Star Restaurants *(continued)*					
Bruning's	Seafood	Inexp	79	A	7
Cafe Sbisa	Nouvelle Creole	Exp	79	C	1
China Doll	Chinese	Mod	79	B	11
Cucina Med	Middle Eastern	Exp	79	C	12
Jalapeño's	Mexican	Mod	79	B	9
Liuzza's	Creole / Neighborhood Cafe	Inexp	79	B	6
Middendorf's	Seafood	Mod	79	B	12
Pupuseria Divino Corazon	Salvadoran	Inexp	79	A	11
Ristorante Carmelo	Italian	Mod	79	C	1
Taqueria Corona	Mexican	Mod	79	A	2, 4, 10
Allegro	Nouvelle Creole	Mod	78	B	2
Beef Room	Steak	Mod	78	B	10
Brick Oven Cafe	Pizza / Italian	Mod	78	B	10
Cafe Volage	Creole French	Mod	78	B	4
Chart House	American	Exp	78	C	1
Dooky Chase	Creole	Mod	78	B	6
Figaro Pizzerie	Pizza	Mod	78	C	4, 12
Five Happiness	Chinese	Mod	78	C	4
Giovanni's Sausage Co.	Sandwiches	Inexp	78	B	9
Crescent City Steak House	Steak	Exp	77	C	6
Peppermill (Riccobono's)	Creole Italian	Mod	77	C	10
Port of Call	Hamburgers	Inexp	77	B	1
Cavallino's	Pizza	Mod	76	B	4
Compagno's	Creole / Neighborhood Cafe	Mod	76	C	4
Copeland's	Cajun	Mod	76	C	4, 9, 10
Frankie's Cafe	Creole	Mod	76	B	4
Fury's	Creole / Neighborhood Cafe	Mod	76	C	9
Golden Lake Chinese Restaurant	Chinese	Mod	76	B	9

Restaurant	Cuisine	Price	Quality Rating	Value Rating	Zone
Restaurant des Familles	Seafood	Mod	76	C	11
Tony Angello's	Creole Italian	Mod	76	B	7
Charlie's Steak House	Steak	Mod	75	B	4
Court of Two Sisters	Creole	Exp	75	C	1
Crazy Johnnie's	Steak	Inexp	75	A	10, 12
Jerusalem	Middle Eastern	Inexp	75	A	6
Mandina's	Creole / Neighborhood Cafe	Mod	75	A	6
Martin Wine Cellar Deli	Deli	Inexp	75	B	3, 9
Olivier's Creole Restaurant	Creole / Neighborhood Cafe	Mod	75	C	1
Snug Harbor	Hamburgers	Inexp	75	B	5
Cafe Maspero	Sandwiches	Inexp	74	A	1
Jade East	Chinese	Mod	74	C	8
West End Cafe	Creole / Neighborhood Cafe	Mod	74	C	7
Cafe Degas	French Bistro	Mod	73	B	6
Camellia Grill	Diner	Inexp	73	C	4
Eddie's	Creole / Neighborhood Cafe	Inexp	73	A	6
Galley Seafood	Creole / Neighborhood Cafe	Mod	73	B	9
Landry's	Creole / Neighborhood Cafe	Inexp	73	C	7
Cafe Buon Giorno	Pizza	Inexp	72	B	11
Casamento's	Seafood	Inexp	72	C	3
Bluebird Cafe	Diner	Inexp	70	B	3, 4
Cafe du Monde	Coffee / Breakfast	Inexp	70	C	1

Two-Star Restaurants

Restaurant	Cuisine	Price	Quality Rating	Value Rating	Zone
Italian Pie	Pizza	Inexp	82	B	2
Kosher Kajun Deli	Deli	Inexp	80	B	10
Old Dog New Trick	Vegetarian	Inexp	80	C	1
Riverside Cafe	Creole	Mod	75	C	2
Traveler's Post	Nouvelle Creole	Mod	75	C	3

Restaurant	Cuisine	Price	Quality Rating	Value Rating	Zone
Two-Star Restaurants (continued)					
Castillo's	Mexican	Mod	74	C	1
La Madeleine	Bakery Cafe	Inexp	74	C	1, 4, 10
Napoleon House	Sandwiches	Inexp	74	B	1
Salvatore's	Creole Italian	Exp	74	C	10
Johnny's Po-Boys	Sandwiches	Inexp	73	A	1
Sal & Sam's	Creole Italian	Mod	73	C	10
Sal's Pasta Garden	Italian	Mod	73	B	9
Ye Olde College Inn	Creole / Neighborhood Cafe	Mod	73	B	4
Carmine's	Creole Italian	Mod	72	B	7
Joey K's	Creole / Neighborhood Cafe	Inexp	72	B	3
Petunia's	Creole / Neighborhood Cafe	Mod	72	B	1
Acme Oyster House	Oyster Bar	Inexp	71	B	1
Coffee Pot	Creole	Mod	71	C	1
Michael's Mid-City Grill	Hamburgers	Inexp	71	C	6
Mona Lisa	Pizza	Inexp	71	B	1, 7
Vera Cruz	Mexican	Mod	71	C	1, 4
Dunbar's	Creole / Neighborhood Cafe	Inexp	70	A	4
Garces	Cuban	Inexp	70	C	6
Messina's	Seafood	Inexp	70	C	1
Felix's	Seafood	Inexp	69	C	1
Crescent City Brewhouse	Creole	Mod	68	C	1
R&O's	Sandwiches	Inexp	68	B	7
Harold's Texas Barbecue	Barbecue	Inexp	67	C	10
Windjammer	Creole	Mod	67	C	7

Restaurants by Zone

Restaurant	Star Rating	Price	Quality Rating	Value Rating
Zone 1—French Quarter				
◆ *American*				
House of Blues	★★★	Mod	81	C
Chart House	★★★	Exp	78	C
◆ *Bakery Cafe*				
La Madeleine	★★	Inexp	74	C
◆ *Coffee / Breakfast*				
Cafe du Monde	★★★	Inexp	70	C
◆ *Creole*				
Tujague's	★★★★	Exp	87	C
Begue's	★★★	Exp	83	C
Cafe Rue Bourbon (Cafe Vieux Carre)	★★★	Exp	81	D
Gumbo Shop	★★★	Mod	80	B
Court of Two Sisters	★★★	Exp	75	C
Coffee Pot	★★	Mod	71	C
Crescent City Brewhouse	★★	Mod	68	C
◆ *Creole French*				
Galatoire's	★★★★	Exp	90	C
Arnaud's	★★★★	Exp	86	D
Antoine's	★★★★	Exp	83	D
Brennan's	★★★	Very Exp	82	F
◆ *Creole Italian*				
Bacco	★★★★	Mod	84	C
◆ *Creole / Neighborhood Cafe*				
Greco's	★★★	Exp	81	C
Olivier's Creole Restaurant	★★★	Mod	75	C
Petunia's	★★	Mod	72	B
◆ *Eclectic*				
Bayona	★★★★★	Exp	96	B
Pelican Club	★★★★★	Exp	96	C
Bella Luna	★★★★	Very Exp	92	C
Bistro at Maison de Ville	★★★	Exp	84	C

Restaurant	Star Rating	Price	Quality Rating	Value Rating
◆ *French*				
Louis XVI	★★★★	Very Exp	87	D
◆ *Hamburgers*				
Port of Call	★★★	Inexp	77	B
◆ *Indian*				
Shalimar	★★★	Mod	82	C
◆ *Italian*				
Irene's Cuisine	★★★★	Mod	82	B
Ristorante Carmelo	★★★	Mod	79	C
◆ *Mexican*				
Santa Fe	★★★	Mod	87	C
Castillo's	★★	Mod	74	C
Vera Cruz	★★	Mod	71	C
◆ *Nouvelle Cajun*				
K–Paul's Louisiana Kitchen	★★★★	Very Exp	91	D
Alex Patout's Louisiana Restaurant	★★★	Exp	84	C
◆ *Nouvelle Creole*				
Rib Room	★★★★	Very Exp	91	D
Mr. B's	★★★★	Exp	90	C
Nola	★★★★	Exp	90	C
Broussard's	★★★★	Very Exp	84	D
Bombay Club	★★★	Very Exp	81	C
Cafe Sbisa	★★★	Exp	79	C
◆ *Nouvelle French*				
Peristyle	★★★★	Exp	94	B
◆ *Nouvelle Italian*				
G&E Courtyard Grill	★★★★	Exp	93	B
Cafe Giovanni	★★★★	Exp	87	B
Maximo's Italian Grill	★★★	Exp	81	C
◆ *Oyster Bar*				
Acme Oyster House	★★	Inexp	71	B

Restaurant	Star Rating	Price	Quality Rating	Value Rating
◆ *Pizza*				
Louisiana Pizza Kitchen	★★★	Mod	83	B
Mona Lisa	★★	Inexp	71	B
◆ *Sandwiches*				
Cafe Maspero	★★★	Inexp	74	A
Napoleon House	★★	Inexp	74	B
Johnny's Po-Boys	★★	Inexp	73	A
◆ *Seafood*				
Mike Anderson's	★★★	Mod	80	C
Messina's	★★	Inexp	70	C
Felix's	★★	Inexp	69	C
◆ *Vegetarian*				
Old Dog New Trick	★★	Inexp	80	C

Zone 2—Central Business District

Restaurant	Star Rating	Price	Quality Rating	Value Rating
◆ *Cajun*				
Bon Ton Cafe	★★★	Mod	79	B
◆ *Continental*				
Veranda	★★★	Exp	82	C
◆ *Creole*				
Riverside Cafe	★★	Mod	75	C
◆ *Creole /Neighborhood Cafe*				
Praline Connection	★★★	Mod	80	B
◆ *Eclectic*				
Windsor Court Grill Room	★★★★★	Very Exp	94	F
Mike's On The Avenue	★★★★	Very Exp	89	D
Graham's	★★★	Very Exp	86	D
◆ *French*				
Sazerac	★★★★	Very Exp	89	C
La Gauloise	★★★	Mod	86	C
◆ *Mexican*				
Taqueria Corona	★★★	Mod	79	A

Restaurant	Star Rating	Price	Quality Rating	Value Rating
◆ *Nouvelle Creole*				
Emeril's	★★★★★	Very Exp	98	C
Palace Cafe	★★★	Exp	84	C
Allegro	★★★	Mod	78	B
◆ *Nouvelle French*				
L'Economie	★★★	Exp	80	C
◆ *Pizza*				
Italian Pie	★★	Inexp	82	B
◆ *Sandwiches*				
Mother's	★★★	Mod	83	D
◆ *Steak*				
Doug's Place	★★★	Mod	80	C
Zone 3—Uptown Below Napoleon				
◆ *Caribbean / South American*				
Tango Tango	★★★	Mod	80	B
◆ *Chinese*				
Kung's Dynasty	★★★	Mod	82	C
◆ *Creole*				
Delmonico	★★★	Exp	82	B
◆ *Creole / Neighborhood Cafe*				
Uglesich's	★★★★	Mod	86	D
Joey K's	★★	Inexp	72	B
◆ *Deli*				
Martin Wine Cellar Deli	★★★	Inexp	75	B
◆ *Diner*				
Bluebird Cafe	★★★	Inexp	70	B
◆ *Eclectic*				
Jason's	★★★★	Exp	87	B
Semolina	★★★	Mod	81	A

Restaurant	Star Rating	Price	Quality Rating	Value Rating
◆ Italian				
Rigatoni	★★★	Mod	80	B
◆ Japanese				
Little Tokyo	★★★	Mod	82	C
◆ Nouvelle Creole				
Commander's Palace	★★★★★	Exp	97	B
Versailles	★★★★★	Very Exp	95	C
Kelsey's	★★★	Mod	82	B
Traveler's Post	★★	Mod	75	C
◆ Seafood				
Casamento's	★★★	Inexp	72	C
◆ Southern				
Cafe Atchafalaya	★★★	Inexp	82	B
Zone 4—Uptown Above Napoleon				
◆ Bakery Cafe				
La Madeleine	★★	Inexp	74	C
◆ Barbecue				
Tipton County Tennessee Pit Barbecue	★★★	Inexp	80	B
◆ Cajun				
Copeland's	★★★	Mod	76	C
◆ Chinese				
Five Happiness	★★★	Mod	78	C
◆ Creole				
Frankie's Cafe	★★★	Mod	76	B
◆ Creole French				
Cafe Volage	★★★	Mod	78	B
◆ Creole Italian				
Pascal's Manale	★★★★	Exp	85	B

Restaurant	Star Rating	Price	Quality Rating	Value Rating
◆ *Creole / Neighborhood Cafe*				
Zachary's	★★★	Mod	80	B
Compagno's	★★★	Mod	76	C
Ye Olde College Inn	★★	Mod	73	B
Dunbar's	★★	Inexp	70	A
◆ *Diner*				
Camellia Grill	★★★	Inexp	73	C
Bluebird Cafe	★★★	Inexp	70	B
◆ *Eclectic*				
Gautreau's	★★★★	Exp	89	C
◆ *French Bistro*				
La Crepe Nanou	★★★★	Mod	87	A
Martinique	★★★	Mod	85	B
◆ *Japanese*				
Ninja	★★★	Mod	84	C
Hana	★★★	Mod	82	C
◆ *Mexican*				
Vaqueros	★★★★	Mod	90	C
Taqueria Corona	★★★	Mod	79	A
Vera Cruz	★★	Mod	71	C
◆ *Nouvelle Creole*				
Brigtsen's	★★★★	Exp	92	B
Clancy's	★★★★	Exp	90	B
Upperline	★★★★	Exp	88	C
◆ *Pizza*				
Louisiana Pizza Kitchen	★★★	Mod	83	B
Figaro Pizzerie	★★★	Mod	78	C
Cavallino's	★★★	Mod	76	B
◆ *Seafood*				
Barrow's Shady Inn	★★★	Inexp	84	B
◆ *Steak*				
Charlie's Steak House	★★★	Mod	75	B

Restaurant	Star Rating	Price	Quality Rating	Value Rating
◆ *Tunisian*				
Jamila's	★★★	Mod	83	A
Zone 5—Downtown / St. Bernard				
◆ *Creole*				
Feelings	★★★	Mod	86	B
◆ *Creole / Neighborhood Cafe*				
Mandich	★★★	Mod	80	B
Praline Connection	★★★	Mod	80	B
◆ *Eclectic*				
Bayou Ridge Cafe	★★★	Mod	82	B
◆ *Hamburgers*				
Snug Harbor	★★★	Inexp	75	B
Zone 6—Mid-City / Gentilly				
◆ *Caribbean*				
Palmer's	★★★	Mod	82	A
◆ *Creole*				
Tavern On The Park	★★★	Exp	80	C
Dooky Chase	★★★	Mod	78	B
◆ *Creole French*				
Christian's	★★★★	Exp	90	B
◆ *Creole / Neighborhood Cafe*				
Katie's	★★★	Inexp	80	B
Liuzza's	★★★	Inexp	79	B
Mandina's	★★★	Mod	75	A
Eddie's	★★★	Inexp	73	A
◆ *Cuban*				
Garces	★★	Inexp	70	C
◆ *Eclectic*				
Semolina	★★★	Mod	81	A
◆ *French Bistro*				
Cafe Degas	★★★	Mod	73	B

Restaurant	Star Rating	Price	Quality Rating	Value Rating
◆ *Hamburgers*				
Michael's Mid-City Grill	★★	Inexp	71	C
◆ *Korean*				
Genghis Khan	★★★	Mod	87	C
◆ *Middle Eastern*				
Jerusalem	★★★	Inexp	75	A
◆ *Nouvelle Creole*				
Gabrielle	★★★★	Exp	93	B
◆ *Pizza*				
Louisiana Pizza Kitchen	★★★	Mod	83	B
◆ *Spanish*				
Lola's	★★★	Mod	80	A
◆ *Steak*				
Ruth's Chris Steak House	★★★★	Very Exp	90	D
Crescent City Steak House	★★★	Exp	77	C
◆ *Thai*				
Bangkok Cuisine	★★★	Mod	83	B
Zone 7—Lakeview / West End / Bucktown				
◆ *Creole*				
La Cuisine	★★★	Mod	87	B
Windjammer	★★	Mod	67	C
◆ *Creole Italian*				
Tony Angello's	★★★	Mod	76	B
Carmine's	★★	Mod	72	B
◆ *Creole / Neighborhood Cafe*				
West End Cafe	★★★	Mod	74	C
Landry's	★★★	Inexp	73	C
◆ *Eclectic*				
Midnight Star Cafe	★★★	Exp	80	D

Restaurant	Star Rating	Price	Quality Rating	Value Rating
◆ *Greek*				
Odyssey Grill	★★★	Mod	87	B
◆ *Pizza*				
Mona Lisa	★★	Inexp	71	B
◆ *Sandwiches*				
R&O's	★★	Inexp	68	B
◆ *Seafood*				
Bruning's	★★★	Inexp	79	A
◆ *Steak*				
Steak Knife	★★★	Exp	86	C
Zone 8—New Orleans East				
◆ *Chinese*				
Jade East	★★★	Mod	74	C
◆ *Italian*				
Sclafani's	★★★	Mod	84	A
Zone 9—Metairie Below Causeway				
◆ *Cajun*				
Copeland's	★★★	Mod	76	C
◆ *Chinese*				
Mr. Tai's	★★★	Mod	83	C
Golden Lake Chinese Restaurant	★★★	Mod	76	B
◆ *Creole Italian*				
Barreca's	★★★	Mod	81	B
◆ *Creole /Neighborhood Cafe*				
Fury's	★★★	Mod	76	C
Galley Seafood	★★★	Mod	73	B
◆ *Deli*				
Martin Wine Cellar Deli	★★★	Inexp	75	B

Restaurants by Zone (continued)

Restaurant	Star Rating	Price	Quality Rating	Value Rating
◆ *French Bistro*				
Chez Daniel	★★★★	Mod	90	B
◆ *Greek*				
Zissis	★★★★	Mod	84	C
◆ *Indian*				
Taj Mahal	★★★	Mod	81	B
◆ *Italian*				
Andrea's	★★★★	Exp	87	C
Sal's Pasta Garden	★★	Mod	73	B
◆ *Japanese*				
Shogun	★★★★	Mod	86	C
Little Tokyo	★★★	Mod	82	C
◆ *Mediterranean*				
Petra	★★★	Exp	83	B
◆ *Mexican*				
Jalapeño's	★★★	Mod	79	B
◆ *Middle Eastern*				
Byblos	★★★★	Mod	83	A
◆ *Nouvelle Cajun*				
Charley G's	★★★	Exp	83	D
◆ *Sandwiches*				
Giovanni's Sausage Co.	★★★	Inexp	78	B
◆ *Seafood*				
Bozo's	★★★★	Inexp	86	B
Sid-Mar's	★★★	Mod	83	A

Zone 10—Metairie Above Causeway/Kenner/Jefferson Highway

Restaurant	Star Rating	Price	Quality Rating	Value Rating
◆ *Bakery Cafe*				
La Madeleine	★★	Inexp	74	C

Restaurants by Zone (continued)

Restaurant	Star Rating	Price	Quality Rating	Value Rating
◆ Barbecue				
Corky's	★★★	Inexp	80	B
Harold's Texas Barbecue	★★	Inexp	67	C
◆ Cajun				
Copeland's	★★★	Mod	76	C
◆ Creole Italian				
Vincent's Italian Cuisine	★★★★	Mod	90	A
Smilie's	★★★	Mod	84	A
Peppermill (Riccobono's)	★★★	Mod	77	C
Salvatore's	★★	Exp	74	C
Sal & Sam's	★★	Mod	73	C
◆ Deli				
Kosher Kajun Deli	★★	Inexp	80	B
◆ Eclectic				
Straya	★★★	Mod	83	B
◆ French Bistro				
Crozier's	★★★★★	Exp	93	C
◆ Indian				
India Palace	★★★	Mod	83	C
◆ Italian				
La Riviera	★★★★	Exp	83	C
Impastato's	★★★	Exp	81	B
◆ Mexican				
El Patio	★★★★	Mod	83	C
Taqueria Corona	★★★	Mod	79	A
◆ Pizza / Italian				
Brick Oven Cafe	★★★	Mod	78	B
◆ Seafood				
Drago's	★★★★	Mod	85	C

Restaurant	Star Rating	Price	Quality Rating	Value Rating
◆ Steak				
Ruth's Chris Steak House	★★★★	Very Exp	90	D
Beef Room	★★★	Mod	78	B
Crazy Johnnie's	★★★	Inexp	75	A
◆ Thai				
Siamese	★★★	Mod	84	C
Zone 11—West Bank				
◆ Chinese				
China Blossom	★★★★	Mod	87	B
China Doll	★★★	Mod	79	B
◆ Creole Italian				
Mosca's	★★★★	Exp	88	C
◆ Eclectic				
Semolina	★★★	Mod	81	A
◆ Pizza				
Cafe Buon Giorno	★★★	Inexp	72	B
◆ Salvadoran				
Pupuseria Divino Corazon	★★★	Inexp	79	A
◆ Seafood				
Restaurant des Familles	★★★	Mod	76	C
◆ Vietnamese				
Kim Son	★★★★	Mod	87	A
Zone 12—North Shore				
◆ Chinese				
Trey Yuen	★★★★	Exp	85	D
◆ Creole				
Doug's	★★★★	Mod	83	B
Gallagher's	★★★	Exp	86	C
◆ Creole Italian				
Sal & Judy's	★★★★	Exp	86	B

Restaurants by Zone (continued)

Restaurant	Star Rating	Price	Quality Rating	Value Rating
◆ *Eclectic*				
Gauthier's Market Cafe	★★★	Exp	84	C
◆ *French*				
La Provence	★★★★★	Exp	98	C
◆ *Middle Eastern*				
Cucina Med	★★★	Exp	79	C
◆ *Nouvelle Creole*				
Dakota	★★★★★	Exp	94	C
◆ *Nouvelle Italian*				
Nuvolari's	★★★★	Exp	86	B
◆ *Pizza*				
Figaro Pizzerie	★★★	Mod	78	C
◆ *Seafood*				
Middendorf's	★★★	Mod	79	B
◆ *Steak*				
Young's	★★★★	Mod	83	A
Crazy Johnnie's	★★★	Inexp	75	A

Recommended for Late Night Dining

Restaurant	Cuisine	Star Rating	Price	Quality Rating	Value Rating	Zone
Bailey's	Creole	★★	Inexp	72	C	2
Beef Room	Steak	★★★	Mod	78	B	10
Bombay Club	Nouvelle Creole	★★★	Very Exp	81	C	1
Brick Oven Cafe	Pizza/Italian	★★★	Mod	78	B	10
Cafe du Monde	Coffee/Breakfast	★★★	Inexp	70	C	1
Cafe Maspero	Sandwiches	★★★	Inexp	74	A	1
Camellia Grill	Diner	★★★	Inexp	73	C	4
Chart House	American	★★★	Exp	78	C	1
Coffee Pot	Creole	★★	Mod	71	C	1
Crescent City Brewhouse	Creole	★★	Mod	68	C	1
Decatur House	Creole	★★	Mod	75	C	1
Hard Rock Cafe	American	★★	Mod	68	D	1
House of Blues	American	★★★	Mod	81	C	1
Hummingbird Grill	Neighborhood Cafe	★★	Inexp	70	A	2
Tiffin Inn	American	★	Inexp	66	C	10
Tipton County Tennessee Pit Barbecue	Barbecue	★★★	Inexp	80	B	4
Ye Olde College Inn	Creole/Neighborhood Cafe	★★	Mod	73	B	4

Recommended for Quiet and Romantic Dining

Restaurant	Cuisine	Star Rating	Price	Quality Rating	Value Rating	Zone
Alex Patout's Louisiana Restaurant	Nouvelle Cajun	★★★	Exp	84	C	1
Andrea's	Italian	★★★★	Exp	87	C	9
Antoine's	Creole French	★★★★	Exp	83	D	1
Arnaud's	Creole French	★★★★	Exp	86	D	1
Bacco	Creole Italian	★★★★	Mod	84	C	1
Bayona	Eclectic	★★★★★	Exp	96	B	1
Bayou Ridge Cafe	Eclectic	★★★	Mod	82	B	5
Beef Room	Steak	★★★	Mod	78	B	10

Restaurant	Cuisine	Star Rating	Price	Quality Rating	Value Rating	Zone
Begue's	Creole	★★★	Exp	83	C	1
Bella Luna	Eclectic / Southwestern	★★★★	Very Exp	92	C	1
Bistro at Maison de Ville	Eclectic	★★★	Exp	84	C	1
Bombay Club	Nouvelle Creole	★★★	Very Exp	81	C	1
Brennan's	Creole French	★★★	Very Exp	82	F	1
Brigtsen's	Nouvelle Creole	★★★★	Exp	92	B	4
Broussard's	Nouvelle Creole	★★★★	Very Exp	84	D	1
Cafe Giovanni	Nouvelle Italian	★★★★	Exp	87	B	1
Cafe Sbisa	Nouvelle Creole	★★★	Exp	79	C	1
Cafe Volage	Creole French	★★★	Mod	78	B	4
Caribbean Room	Creole French	★	Exp	72	D	3
Chez Daniel	French Bistro	★★★★	Mod	90	B	9
Christian's	Creole French	★★★★	Exp	90	B	6
Commander's Palace	Nouvelle Creole	★★★★★	Exp	97	B	3
Court of Two Sisters	Creole	★★★	Exp	75	C	1
Crozier's	French Bistro	★★★★★	Exp	93	C	10
Dakota	Nouvelle Creole	★★★★★	Exp	94	C	12
G&E Courtyard Grill	Nouvelle Italian	★★★★	Exp	93	B	1
L'Economie	Nouvelle French	★★★	Exp	80	C	2
La Provence	French	★★★★★	Exp	98	C	12
Louis XVI	French	★★★★	Very Exp	87	D	1
Mike's On The Avenue	Eclectic	★★★★	Very Exp	89	D	2
Petra	Mediterranean	★★★	Exp	83	B	9
Sazerac	French	★★★★	Very Exp	89	C	2
Tavern On The Park	Creole	★★★	Exp	80	C	6
Veranda	Continental	★★★	Exp	82	C	2
Versailles	Nouvelle Creole	★★★★★	Very Exp	95	C	3
Windsor Court Grill Room	Eclectic	★★★★★	Very Exp	94	F	2

Recommended for Dining with a View

Restaurant	Cuisine	Star Rating	Price	Quality Rating	Value Rating	Zone
Bella Luna	Eclectic/ Southwestern	★★★★	Very Exp	92	C	1
Bruning's	Seafood	★★★	Inexp	79	A	7
Mike's On The Avenue	Eclectic	★★★★	Very Exp	89	D	2
Riverside Cafe	Creole	★★	Mod	75	C	2
Riverview Restaurant	French Creole	★★	Exp	71	D	1
Tavern On The Park	Creole	★★★	Exp	80	C	6
Versailles	Nouvelle Creole	★★★★★	Very Exp	95	C	3

Recommended for Business Dining

Restaurant	Cuisine	Star Rating	Price	Quality Rating	Value Rating	Zone
Allegro	Nouvelle Creole	★★★	Mod	78	B	2
Andrea's	Italian	★★★★	Exp	87	C	9
Antoine's	Creole French	★★★★	Exp	83	D	1
Arnaud's	Creole French	★★★★	Exp	86	D	1
Bacco	Creole Italian	★★★★	Mod	84	C	1
Beef Connection	Steak	★★★	Exp	78	D	11
Brennan's	Creole French	★★★	Very Exp	82	F	1
Charley G's	Nouvelle Cajun	★★★	Exp	83	D	9
Dakota	Nouvelle Creole	★★★★★	Exp	94	C	12
Delmonico	Creole	★★★	Exp	82	B	3
Emeril's	Nouvelle Creole	★★★★★	Very Exp	98	C	2
Mike's On The Avenue	Eclectic	★★★★	Very Exp	89	D	2
Petra	Mediterranean	★★★	Exp	83	B	9
Rib Room	Nouvelle Creole	★★★★	Very Exp	91	D	1
Ruth's Chris Steak House	Steak	★★★★	Very Exp	90	D	6, 10
Sazerac	French	★★★★	Very Exp	89	C	2

Recommended for Business Dining (continued)

Restaurant	Cuisine	Star Rating	Price	Quality Rating	Value Rating	Zone
Veranda	Continental	★★★	Exp	82	C	2
Versailles	Nouvelle Creole	★★★★★	Very Exp	95	C	3
Windsor Court Grill Room	Eclectic	★★★★★	Very Exp	94	F	2

Recommended Near the Ernest N. Morial Convention Center

Restaurant	Cuisine	Star Rating	Price	Quality Rating	Value Rating	Zone
Bon Ton Cafe	Cajun	★★★	Mod	79	B	2
Doug's Place	Steak	★★★	Mod	80	C	2
Emeril's	Nouvelle Creole	★★★★★	Very Exp	98	C	2
Graham's	Eclectic	★★★	Very Exp	86	D	2
Grand Cuisine	Deli	★★	Inexp	73	C	2
L'Economie	Nouvelle French	★★★	Exp	80	C	2
Mike's On The Avenue	Eclectic	★★★★	Very Exp	89	D	2
Mother's	Sandwiches	★★★	Mod	83	D	2
Praline Connection	Creole / Neighborhood Cafe	★★★	Mod	80	B	2, 5
Riverside Cafe	Creole	★★	Mod	75	C	2
Taqueria Corona	Mexican	★★★	Mod	79	A	2, 4, 10
Windsor Court Grill Room	Eclectic	★★★★★	Very Exp	94	F	2

RESTAURANT
profiles

ACME OYSTER HOUSE

Zone 1   French Quarter
724 Iberville
522-5973

Oyster Bar	
★★	
Inexpensive	
Quality 71	Value B

Reservations:	Not accepted
When to go:	Anytime
Entree range:	$4–5
Payment:	Cash only
Service rating:	★★
Friendliness rating:	★★
Parking:	Pay lot nearby
Bar:	Full bar
Wine selection:	A few house wines
Dress:	Anything goes
Disabled access:	Limited
Customers:	Tourists, some locals; businessmen at lunch
Open:	Every day, 11 A.M.–10 P.M.

Atmosphere / setting: All the trappings of a classic oyster bar: the marble-topped counter behind which hard-working men shuck 'em, the adjacent bar for beer, the aroma of frying seafood, and a dark environment cut only by the light of neon beer signs.

Recommended dishes: Oysters on the half shell; oyster poor boy; red bean "poopa" (served in a French bread loaf).

Summary & comments: Not the quintessential oyster bar it once was (and still looks like), but still a reliable place to enjoy one of the great culinary assets of Louisiana. When records for eating oysters are set, they're set here.

Alex Patout's
Louisiana Restaurant

Zone 1   French Quarter
221 Royal Street
525-7788

Nouvelle Cajun	
★★★	
Expensive	
Quality 84	Value C

Reservations:	Recommended
When to go:	Anytime
Entree range:	$12–20
Payment:	AMEX, DC, DS, MC, V
Service rating:	★★★
Friendliness rating:	★★★
Parking:	Validated at Dixie Parking, around the corner on Iberville
Bar:	Full bar
Wine selection:	Substantial list, with emphasis on California
Dress:	Jacket recommended but not required
Disabled access:	Limited
Customers:	Tourists, some locals
Dinner:	Every day, 6–10 P.M.

Atmosphere / setting: A rather too handsome dining room for the cuisine, with a formal look and big comfortable chairs.

Recommended dishes: Homemade boudin and andouille sausages; baked oysters; gumbo; grilled fish; crabmeat imperial; crawfish etouffee; roast duck with rice dressing. Bread pudding; sweet potato pie.

Summary & comments: A collection of Cajun dishes is moved upmarket here by one of the more enthusiastic and earliest practitioners of the new Cajun style. Richness from cream and butter, smokiness, and spiciness are found in most dishes; sometimes there is a bit too much of these. The cooking is somewhat inconsistent, but when it's hot it performs well above the three-star level. More casual than the grand surroundings might indicate.

Allegro

Zone 2 Central Business District	Nouvelle Creole
1100 Poydras	★ ★ ★
582-2350	Moderate
	Quality 78 Value B

Reservations:	Accepted
When to go:	Anytime
Entree range:	$7–16
Payment:	AMEX, MC, V
Service rating:	★ ★
Friendliness rating:	★ ★ ★
Parking:	Garage in building; validated at dinner
Bar:	Full bar
Wine selection:	Decent list with good international balance
Dress:	Dressy casual
Disabled access:	Full
Customers:	Businessmen at lunch
Brunch:	Buffet on Saints game days; time varies with the start time of the game
Lunch:	Monday–Friday, 11:30 A.M.–3 P.M.; Saturday and Sunday, closed.

Atmosphere / setting: A magnificent dining room dominated by an art deco bar in its center. The tables, however, are oddly and sometimes uncomfortably placed.

Recommended dishes: Eggplant St. Charles (a sandwich with crabmeat in the center); shrimp rémoulade; eggplant and tomato soup; shrimp l'ancienne (with cream and horseradish sauce); seafood specials; lamb chops; roast duck.

Summary & comments: The chef is ambitious and talented, particularly with seafood specials, which are usually the best eats here. The only thing that might beat them would be the occasional special employing large cuts of red meat, such as lamb chops. Dinner doesn't happen here anymore, killed by the local curse on restaurants in office buildings, especially downtown. The pre-game buffet is a sort of free-for-all that's more fun than it is culinarily impressive.

Andrea's

Zone 9   Metairie Below Causeway
3100 19th Street, Metairie
834-8583

	Italian
	★★★★
	Expensive
Quality 87	Value C

Reservations:	Recommended
When to go:	Anytime
Entree range:	$10–24
Payment:	All major credit cards
Service rating:	★★★★
Friendliness rating:	★★★
Parking:	Free lot adjacent
Bar:	Full bar
Wine selection:	Substantial list, mostly Italian and French; a bit overpriced
Dress:	Jacket recommended but not required
Disabled access:	Full
Customers:	Businessmen at lunch; daters
Brunch:	Sunday, 11 A.M.–3 P.M.
Lunch/Dinner:	Monday–Thursday, 11:30 A.M.–10 P.M.; Friday, 11:30 A.M.–11 P.M.; Saturday, 4–11 P.M.; Sunday, 11 A.M.–9 P.M.

Atmosphere / setting: The collection of dining rooms has a suburban look, but the environment is sophisticated and comfortable.

Recommended dishes: Antipasto (especially marinated vegetables); oysters Andrea; vitello tonnato; pasta with smoked salmon; mussels or clams marinara; pasta fagioli soup; fresh cheese salad; fish (especially red snapper, trout, or pompano) with basilico, fresh herb, or cream pesto sauces; veal chop Valdostana; roast duck with green peppercorns; steak with three-pepper sauce; pannéed veal Tanet. Tiramisu; strawberry cake; fruit flan; chocolate mousse.

Entertainment & amenities: Strolling accordionist at Sunday brunch.

Summary & comments: Andrea's revolutionized the Italian restaurant scene when it opened in the mid-Eighties by giving Italian food the same shrift that the best French places always did. Few restaurants can match the quality and freshness of its raw materials, particularly seafood and vegetables. The menu is enormous—too big, really—and the chef offers to fix you anything that might not be on it. When it's at its best, Andrea's serves food at the five-star level, but it's a bit inconsistent. The monthly regional Italian menus are fascinating. Sunday brunch is more likely to be an off-meal than any other here.

ANTOINE'S

Zone 1   French Quarter
713 St. Louis
581-4422

Creole French	
★★★★	
Expensive	
Quality 83	Value D

Reservations:	Recommended
When to go:	Lunch and early evenings; avoid days before holidays
Entree range:	$13–26
Payment:	All major credit cards
Service rating:	★★★
Friendliness rating:	★
Parking:	Pay garages nearby
Bar:	Full bar
Wine selection:	Distinguished cellar with tremendous inventory; French-dominated; many older vintages; the wine cellar presents a great visual
Dress:	Jacket required at dinner
Disabled access:	Limited
Customers:	Tourists, some locals
Lunch:	Monday–Saturday, 11:30 A.M.–2:30 P.M.
Dinner:	Monday–Saturday, 5–9:30 P.M.; Sunday, closed.

Atmosphere / setting: The front room is fine at lunchtime, when the place is rarely busy; in the evenings, the larger annex is where the action is. But there are so many other interesting rooms that they make for a fascinating tour.

Recommended dishes: Oysters Rockefeller; oysters Foch; escargots bordelaise; shrimp rémoulade; crawfish cardinale; grilled pompano; soft-shell crabs Colbert; chicken Rochambeau; chicken bonne femme; tournedos marchand de vin; lamb chops béarnaise. Baked Alaska.

Summary & comments: The oldest restaurant in America, Antoine's was founded in 1840 by the great-great grandfather of the present proprietor. Extraordinarily old-fashioned, usually in a good way, Antoine's requires a certain taste for and patience with antiquity for fullest enjoyment. The best dishes, once common elsewhere, can only be found here now. Meat and poultry dishes tend to be better than seafood. Antoine's is at its best if you're either a regular or in the company of one.

ARNAUD'S

Zone 1 French Quarter	Creole French
813 Bienville	★★★★
523-5433	Expensive
	Quality 86 Value D

Reservations:	Recommended
When to go:	Anytime
Entree range:	$13–40 (median: $20)
Payment:	All major credit cards
Service rating:	★★★★
Friendliness rating:	★★★
Parking:	Validated (free) at garage on the corner of Dauphine and Iberville
Bar:	Full bar
Wine selection:	Distinguished cellar, good international balance; a bit pricey
Dress:	Jacket recommended but not required
Disabled access:	Full
Customers:	Tourists, some locals
Brunch:	Sunday, 11 A.M.–3 P.M.
Lunch:	Every day, 11:30 A.M.–2:30 P.M.
Dinner:	Every day, 6–10 P.M.

Atmosphere / setting: The distinctive decor of tiled floors, beveled glass, and ceiling fans are classic old New Orleans.

Recommended dishes: Shrimp Arnaud (rémoulade); oysters Arnaud (an assortment of five); turtle rilettes; shrimp Bellaire; oyster stew in cream; trout meunière; pompano David; pompano en croûte; Cornish hen Twelfth Night; rack of lamb. Crème brûlée; bananas Foster; bread pudding.

Entertainment & amenities: Strolling jazz trio at Sunday brunch.

Summary & comments: One of the great restaurants of the first half of this century, Arnaud's was in steep decline by the Sixties, and was rescued in the nick of time in the late Seventies. It was beautifully restored in both premises, and the cuisine has been remarkable ever since. The menu is encyclopedic and requires much explanation from the waiters. In the past couple of years, Arnaud's has become a bit touristy and its prices have risen steeply, but it's still a great taste of the old style.

BACCO

Zone 1   French Quarter
310 Chartres
522-2426

Creole Italian

★★★★

Moderate

Quality 84   Value C

Reservations:	Recommended
When to go:	Anytime
Entree range:	$10–20
Payment:	All major credit cards
Service rating:	★★★★
Friendliness rating:	★★★★
Parking:	Free valet parking in hotel garage
Bar:	Full bar
Wine selection:	Substantial list, mostly Italian and Californian; many interesting, offbeat bottles
Dress:	Jacket recommended but not required
Disabled access:	Full
Customers:	Mostly locals, a few tourists
Breakfast:	Every day, 7–10 A.M.
Brunch:	Sunday, 11 A.M.–3 P.M.
Lunch:	Every day, 11:30 A.M.–2:30 P.M.
Dinner:	Every day, 6–10 P.M.

Atmosphere / setting: The premises are striking, with unusual spaces shaped largely from concrete. In the rest rooms, you can learn Italian.

Recommended dishes: White cheese pizza; grilled eggplant; baked oysters; pasta "rags" with spinach and chicken; crawfish ravioli; grilled fish; grilled veal T-bone; roasted pork tenderloin; hickory-grilled duck breast. Tiramisu; homemade ice creams.

Summary & comments: An atypical restaurant for the Brennan family, Bacco started out a very authentic Italian trattoria and has become more and more Creole as time goes on. The menu is dominated by dishes prepared in a wood-burning oven; these include not only pizza, but also roasts of meat, poultry, and fish. Lots of good grilled dishes, also accomplished over burning wood. The wine list is exceptionally good, particularly for Italian wines. Breakfast is one of the best in town.

Bangkok Cuisine

Zone 6   Mid-City / Gentilly
4137 South Carrollton Avenue
482-3606

	Thai
	★★★
	Moderate
	Quality 83 Value B

Reservations:	Accepted
When to go:	Anytime
Entree range:	$8–14
Payment:	All major credit cards except Discover
Service rating:	★★★
Friendliness rating:	★★
Parking:	Free lot adjacent
Bar:	Full bar
Wine selection:	A few house wines
Dress:	Casual
Disabled access:	Limited
Customers:	Locals
Lunch:	Monday–Friday, 11:30 A.M.–2:30 P.M.
Dinner:	Every day, 6–10 P.M.

Atmosphere / setting: The premises are spacious and interestingly decorated with Thai artifacts.

Recommended dishes: Thai appetizer tray (stuffed chicken wings, fish cakes, spring rolls, and a few other items, each with its own sauce); hot and sour shrimp soup; stuffed giant squid; pad thai; green curry with chicken and eggplant; Siam whole fish with ginger; narai beef; peppermint-leaf chicken with bamboo shoots. Thai iced tea (creamy); coconut milk custard.

Summary & comments: The Semiesuke family pioneered Thai cooking in New Orleans, and they still present it more consistently than any other restaurant. Good daily specials, particularly at lunch.

70

BARRECA'S

Zone 9   Metairie Below Causeway
3100 Metairie Road, Metairie
831-4546

Reservations:	Recommended
When to go:	Anytime but the very crowded early evenings
Entree range:	$8–17
Payment:	AMEX, MC, V
Service rating:	★★★
Friendliness rating:	★★
Parking:	Valet (free)
Bar:	Full bar
Wine selection:	Limited list of ordinary wines
Dress:	Casual
Disabled access:	Limited
Customers:	Locals; businessmen at lunch
Lunch/Dinner:	Every day, 11 A.M.–10 P.M.; close at 9 P.M. on Sunday.

Atmosphere / setting: Always crowded and bustling, with two small, dark dining rooms in the front and a large, hall-like, brighter room in the rear.

Recommended dishes: Oysters d'Italia (baked with crabmeat and bread crumbs); chicken andouille gumbo; turtle soup; any seafood dish with Lafayette sauce; roast duck; veal specials. Bread pudding.

Summary & comments: Barreca's started a few years ago as a raffish neighborhood restaurant, but on every succeeding visit it has become more handsome, better served, and more polished in its cooking. They popularized the early-evening special dinner locally and are still so busy with it that, the bargain notwithstanding, you might consider coming at other times for better food and service. Ignore the printed menu; all the best dishes are on the blackboards.

Barrow's Shady Inn

Zone 4   Uptown Above Napoleon
2714 Mistletoe
482-9427

<table>
<tr><td></td><td>Seafood
★★★
Inexpensive

Quality 84   Value B</td></tr>
</table>

Reservations:	Not accepted
When to go:	Anytime
Entree range:	$10
Payment:	No credit cards
Service rating:	★★
Friendliness rating:	★★★
Parking:	Free lot adjacent
Bar:	Full bar
Wine selection:	A few house wines
Dress:	Anything goes
Disabled access:	Limited
Customers:	Neighborhood people
Lunch / Dinner:	Tuesday and Wednesday, 5–10 P.M.;
	Thursday–Saturday, 11 A.M.–10 P.M.;
	Sunday and Monday, closed.

Atmosphere / setting: It looks like a neighborhood bar with a lot of tables. Only place in town with lava lamps (originals!) as serious interior decor.

Recommended dishes: Fried catfish with potato salad (only dish available).

Summary & comments: A family-run catfish specialist since 1943, Barrow's serves the lightest, most addictive fish in town, with an interesting glow of red pepper. Also on the plate is a fine, mildly flavored homemade potato salad. That's the only menu option; its current price is posted on the walls.

BAYONA

Zone 1   French Quarter
430 Dauphine
525-4455

	Eclectic
	★★★★★
	Expensive
	Quality 96 Value B

Reservations:	Required
When to go:	Anytime
Entree range:	$14–25
Payment:	All major credit cards
Service rating:	★★★★★
Friendliness rating:	★★★
Parking:	Validated ($3) at adjacent garage
Bar:	Full bar
Wine selection:	Distinguished cellar, with many interesting, offbeat bottles; many by-the-glass selections
Dress:	Jacket recommended but not required
Disabled access:	Limited
Customers:	Mostly locals, a few tourists
Lunch:	Monday–Friday, 11:30 A.M.–2:30 P.M.
Dinner:	Monday–Saturday, 6–10 P.M.; Sunday, closed.

Atmosphere / setting: The several small dining rooms are beautifully designed. In decent weather you may also dine al fresco.

Recommended dishes: Grilled shrimp with coriander; sweetbreads (as appetizer or entree); toad in the hole (foie gras and quail egg in brioche); roasted garlic soup; salads. Shrimp curry; salmon with choucroute and Gewürztraminer sauce; pork, lamb, or veal chops; quail with dried cherries and foie gras sauce. Lemon tart; apple-almond gratin with spice ice cream; orange-scented crêpes with vanilla gelato.

Summary & comments: The personal cuisine of Susan Spicer, who likes the food of the Mediterranean, India, and France. She combines these ideas in highly creative and unerringly tasteful ways. The menu will probably underwhelm you—the concoctions are understated and subtle to begin with—but almost anything you order will come across with surprising satisfaction. The wine list is full of rare and unusual bottles, all at affordable prices.

Bayou Ridge Cafe

Zone 5   Downtown/St. Bernard
437 Esplanade
949-9912

Eclectic	
★★★	
Moderate	
Quality 82	Value B

Reservations:	Recommended
When to go:	Anytime
Entree range:	$10–18
Payment:	All major credit cards
Service rating:	★★★
Friendliness rating:	★★★
Parking:	Limited curbside; French Market pay lot three blocks away
Bar:	Full bar
Wine selection:	Decent list, with emphasis on California
Dress:	Casual
Disabled access:	Full
Customers:	Mostly locals, a few tourists
Brunch:	Sunday, 11 A.M.–3 P.M.
Lunch:	Wednesday–Sunday, 11:30 A.M.–3 P.M.
Dinner:	Wednesday–Sunday, 5:30–10:30 P.M.; Monday and Tuesday, closed.

Atmosphere / setting: An underfurnished, triangular dining room opens onto a courtyard with even more space to stretch out.

Recommended dishes: Focaccia; black bean cake with shrimp and avocado salsa; grilled quail with shiitake mushroom ragout; Caesar salad with roasted polenta croutons. Smoked shrimp on eggplant cakes with chipotle cream; herb-marinated tuna with tapenade, eggplant caviar, and tomato; crab and artichoke ravioli; veal tournedos with Fontina cheese; venison tenderloin with raspberry-balsamic demi-glace. Crème brûlée; fresh berries.

Summary & comments: The food here tends to be on the lighter side, reminiscent of the style pioneered by Susan Spicer. There's more of an emphasis on olive oil, herbs, and intensely flavored morsels of this and that than is customarily the case around New Orleans. Salads, pastas, and the simply garnished grilled dishes are the most pleasant eating here, although almost everything has its points of interest. Not, however, for those on whom subtlety is lost. The Sunday brunch, very popular among Quarterites, is less involved and less expensive than most.

Beef Room

Zone 10   Metairie Above Causeway /
           Kenner / Jefferson Hwy.
2750 North Causeway Boulevard,
   Metairie
835-8555

Steak
★★★
Moderate
Quality 78   Value B

Reservations:	Accepted
When to go:	Anytime
Entree range:	$10–22
Payment:	All major credit cards
Service rating:	★★★
Friendliness rating:	★★★
Parking:	Free lot adjacent
Bar:	Full bar
Wine selection:	Limited list of ordinary wines
Dress:	Casual
Disabled access:	Limited
Customers:	Locals, couples
Dinner:	Every day, 4 P.M.–midnight

Atmosphere / setting: The red velvet walls and wood railing dividers make for a time warp back to 1971.

Recommended dishes: Fettuccine Alfredo; baked oysters Saia; crabmeat rémoulade; filet mignon; strip sirloin; porterhouse for two; tournedos with two sauces; shrimp Anthony with pasta.

Summary & comments: Although ownership changed a few times and the place even closed for a while a couple of years ago, this has been one of the most consistently fine steakhouses in the area. The beef is obtained from scrupulous sources of USDA prime moo-cow and broiled with skill. The sauce is a sizzling, lightly browned butter that brings the flavor and especially the aroma to an exciting peak. They also prepare good grilled seafood and chicken dishes, but these take second place to the steaks. Side dishes are basic but well prepared. Everything is served in large portions.

BEGUE'S

Zone 1   French Quarter
300 Bourbon
586-0300

Creole
★★★
Expensive

Quality 83   Value C

Reservations:	Recommended
When to go:	Anytime; Friday's lunch buffet is particularly inviting
Entree range:	$12–22
Payment:	All major credit cards
Service rating:	★★★★
Friendliness rating:	★★★★
Parking:	Validated free in the Royal Sonesta garage, downstairs
Bar:	Full bar
Wine selection:	Decent list, good international balance
Dress:	Jacket recommended but not required
Disabled access:	Full
Customers:	Tourists, some locals; mostly local for Sunday brunch
Breakfast:	Every day, 7–10 A.M.
Brunch:	Sunday, 11 A.M.–3 P.M.
Lunch:	Monday–Saturday, 11:30 A.M.–2:30 P.M.
Dinner:	Every day, 6–10 P.M.

Atmosphere / setting: The principal restaurant of the picturesque and luxurious Royal Sonesta Hotel occupies the south face of its lush courtyard. Beyond that, its design is airy and fresh.

Recommended dishes: Smoked salmon; crab cake; shrimp and crabmeat rémoulade in an avocado; spinach salad; tomato and tasso bisque; seafood gumbo; baby salmon with potato cakes; sautéed shrimp with refried grits and spinach; grilled double pork chop; roasted lamb chops with spaetzle; steamed lobster on fettuccine with vanilla beurre blanc. Sorbets; ice creams; chocolate pecan pie.

Entertainment & amenities: Pianist plays throughout dinner and at Sunday brunch.

Summary & comments: They serve all three meals here, and although the menus seem at first glance to be standard hotel fare, the food here is actually quite original and good, using first-class local ingredients. Of particular note are the seafood buffet at lunch on Fridays and the Sunday brunch buffets, both of which are far better than buffets tend to be. Service is a little lackluster, but the restaurant is always a pleasure.

Bella Luna

Zone 1   French Quarter
914 North Peters
529-1583

	Eclectic / Southwestern
	★★★★
	Very Expensive
	Quality 92 Value C

Reservations:	Recommended
When to go:	Anytime
Entree range:	$14–25
Payment:	All major credit cards
Service rating:	★★★★
Friendliness rating:	★★★
Parking:	Validated free for French Market lot, immediately adjacent
Bar:	Full bar
Wine selection:	Distinguished cellar with many interesting, offbeat bottles; many by-the-glass selections
Dress:	Jacket recommended but not required
Disabled access:	Limited
Customers:	Mostly locals, a few tourists; couples
Dinner:	Every day, 6–10 P.M.

Atmosphere / setting: One of the town's two or three most striking restaurants, Bella Luna is on the second floor of a building in the French Market, and from that vantage point it offers a superb view of the Mississippi River and its activity.

Recommended dishes: The entire menu is always changing, but at last look: crab cakes with chipotle rémoulade; fettuccine with aged Reggiano; Barq's-marinated baby-back ribs; eggless Caesar salad; shrimp quesadillas; black bean soup; grilled or blackened tuna; veal T-bone; osso buco; grilled pork tenderloin with chile-ancho polenta; veal T-bone with herb-infused olive oil; any game special. Dessert assortment; fudge brownie cappuccino pie; warm apple tart with cinnamon ice cream.

Summary & comments: The food is every bit the equal of the environment. Chef Horst Pfeifer unites Italian, Southwestern, and Creole flavors into singular creations. Much grilling, roasting, and smoking of foods goes on, and plates are finished off with delightfully unexpected flavoring ingredients. The wine list is first-rate and the service usually pleasing, although they could use some work on the front-desk greeting.

Bistro at Maison de Ville

Zone 1   French Quarter
733 Toulouse
528-9206

Eclectic	
★★★	
Expensive	
Quality 84	Value C

Reservations:	Recommended
When to go:	Anytime
Entree range:	$14–21
Payment:	All major credit cards
Service rating:	★★★★
Friendliness rating:	★★★
Parking:	Several pay lots within two blocks
Bar:	Full bar; many single-malt scotches, cognacs, armagnacs, etc.
Wine selection:	Decent list; many interesting, offbeat bottles; many by-the-glass selections
Dress:	Jacket recommended but not required
Disabled access:	Limited
Customers:	Mostly locals, a few tourists
Brunch:	Sunday, 11:30 A.M.–3 P.M.
Lunch:	Monday–Saturday, 11:30 A.M.–2:30 P.M.
Dinner:	Every day, 6–10 P.M.

Atmosphere / setting: A tiny, somewhat claustrophobic, but nicely designed cafe, dominated by banquettes along one wall. There are a few tables on the small courtyard for dining.

Recommended dishes: Entire menu changes every two or three months. All of the following will be gone by the time you get there, but this is a typical menu: gravlax with dill yogurt and wasabi caviar; crawfish with spicy aïoli; tuna tartare; chicken stuffed with boursin and leek confit; seared pompano with saffron couscous; filet mignon with green-peppercorn mustard sauce; grilled sea scallops with wild mushroom galette. Crème brûlée; flourless chocolate cake.

Summary & comments: The Bistro made its name by hiring hot young chefs who established the place as a source of fascinating and good food. Trouble is, these chefs have had a way of opening their own restaurants after a year or two here, so there have been some ups and downs. At the moment the place is pretty good but, as always, the menu is utterly unpredictable. The service, wine list, and admirable list of single-malt scotches, cognacs, and other spirits, are all orchestrated by a maître d' who has survived each change in the kitchen.

Bluebird Cafe

Zone 3   Uptown Below Napoleon
3625 Prytania
895-7166

Zone 4   Uptown Above Napoleon
7801 Panola
866-7577

	Diner
	★ ★ ★
	Inexpensive
Quality 70	Value B

Reservations:	Not accepted
When to go:	Late mornings
Entree range:	$3–7
Payment:	No credit cards
Service rating:	★
Friendliness rating:	★
Parking:	Curbside (metered and scarce)
Bar:	No alcohol
Wine selection:	None
Dress:	Anything goes
Disabled access:	Limited
Customers:	Neighborhood people
Breakfast/Lunch:	Monday–Friday, 7 A.M.–3 P.M.;
	Saturday and Sunday, 8 A.M.–3 P.M.

Atmosphere / setting: Both locations of the Bluebird are somewhat spare, New-Agey cafes with counters and tables.

Recommended dishes: Huevos rancheros; omelettes; pancakes; waffles; hamburgers. Daily plate special lunches.

Summary & comments: The Bluebird's adherents keep it very busy, particularly in the morning hours and on weekends, when you can expect to wait in line at least a little while. One way of avoiding that is to sit at the rarely full counter. Although they serve typical diner food, the main attraction is breakfast.

Bombay Club

Zone 1   French Quarter
830 Conti
586-0972

	Nouvelle Creole
	★★★
	Very Expensive
	Quality 81 Value C

Reservations:	Required
When to go:	Late nights
Entree range:	$14–26
Payment:	All major credit cards
Service rating:	★★★
Friendliness rating:	★★
Parking:	Valet ($5)
Bar:	Full bar
Wine selection:	Decent list, French dominated
Dress:	Jacket required
Disabled access:	Full
Customers:	Hip, social crowd
Dinner:	Tuesday–Saturday, 6 P.M.–1 A.M.; Sunday and Monday, closed.

Atmosphere / setting: The dressiest and most stylish rendezvous in town, the Bombay Club functions first as a bar, famous for its martinis (and good for any other kind of imbibition) and its two fine pianists, who provide nonstop music.

Recommended dishes: Crawfish cakes; fried oyster cocktail; barbecue shrimp; oyster Rockefeller soup; gumbo; French Market garden salad; curried shrimp; seafood specials; rack of lamb; tournedos of beef with escargots bordelaise. Apple crisp à la mode; chocolate mousse cake.

Entertainment & amenities: Two pianists alternate from 7 P.M. to closing time nightly.

Summary & comments: The restaurant aspect of the Bombay Club is secondary to its bar scene. The quality and style of the food have jerked around dizzyingly over the years. At the moment, the menu is a collection of fairly conventional, polished Creole dishes. At its best, the dining experience here is memorable, romantic, and evocative of a more glorious age. But expect inconsistencies.

Bon Ton Cafe

Zone 2   Central Business District
401 Magazine
524-3386

Cajun
★★★
Moderate
Quality 79   Value B

Reservations:	Recommended
When to go:	Anytime
Entree range:	$12–18
Payment:	All major credit cards
Service rating:	★★★
Friendliness rating:	★★★★
Parking:	Pay lot and curbside (metered)
Bar:	Full bar
Wine selection:	A few house wines
Dress:	Jacket recommended but not required
Disabled access:	Limited
Customers:	Mostly locals at lunch, mostly tourists at dinner
Lunch:	Monday–Friday, 11:30 A.M.–2:30 P.M.
Dinner:	Monday–Friday, 5–9 P.M.;
	Saturday and Sunday, closed.

Atmosphere / setting: A brick-walled dining room full of tables with red-checked tablecloths and an easygoing style.

Recommended dishes: Turtle soup; fried catfish fingers; shrimp rémoulade; Cajun Caesar salad; crawfish dinner (crawfish four ways: etouffee, bisque, fried, and omelette). Crabmeat au gratin; redfish Bon Ton; oysters or soft-shell crab Alvin; pan-broiled oysters; shrimp etouffee. Bread pudding.

Summary & comments: It seems strange now, but for years the Bon Ton was just about the only nice restaurant in New Orleans that would serve you crawfish. The style is Cajun, but it's the rather mild Cajun cooking of the Bayou Lafourche area. It's also very old-fashioned, and you'll see touches you haven't been treated to since the early Sixties. (The service staff is definitely from that era.) Still, it's a charming, unaffected place delivering good food and value.

Bozo's

Seafood

★★★★

Inexpensive

Quality 86   Value B

Zone 9   Metairie Below Causeway
3117 21st Street, Metairie
831-8666

Reservations:	Not accepted
When to go:	Anytime except the very busy Fridays
Entree range:	$6–12
Payment:	MC, V
Service rating:	★★★
Friendliness rating:	★★★★
Parking:	Free lot adjacent
Bar:	Full bar
Wine selection:	A few house wines
Dress:	Casual
Disabled access:	Full
Customers:	Mostly locals, a few tourists
Lunch:	Tuesday–Saturday, 11:30 A.M.–3 P.M.
Dinner:	Tuesday–Saturday, 5–10 P.M.;
	Sunday and Monday, closed.

Atmosphere / setting: A little too squeaky-clean a restaurant to house a classic old-style seafood house. Lots of action at the oyster bar.

Recommended dishes: Oysters on the half shell; boiled crawfish or shrimp in season; chicken andouille gumbo; fried oysters; fried catfish; broiled shrimp; stuffed shrimp; stuffed crab; hot sausage poor boy. Bread pudding.

Summary & comments: Bozo's sets the standard for fried seafood in New Orleans. Not only is everything fresh, but everything is extraordinarily well selected. The catfish, for example, are exclusively small, wild fish from Des Allemands, which have a much more interesting flavor than bigger, farm-raised cat. They also have a great source for oysters, served raw at the bar or fried at the table. All the fried stuff is prepared to order and comes out crackly and hot. Each species of seafood is fried in a separate pot of constantly cleaned oil. The meticulousness of the kitchen can be observed through its large windows. In season, they also have great boiled crawfish here. The portions are not as gargantuan as elsewhere, but the quality is beyond reproach.

BRENNAN'S

Zone 1   French Quarter
417 Royal
525-9711

Creole French
★★★
Very Expensive
Quality 82   Value E

Reservations:	Required
When to go:	Late mornings or lunchtime
Entree range:	$20–40
Payment:	All major credit cards
Service rating:	★★★★
Friendliness rating:	★★★★
Parking:	Validated free for Omni Royal Orleans Garage, Chartres at St. Louis
Bar:	Full bar
Wine selection:	Easily the finest restaurant wine cellar in New Orleans; tremendous inventory, variety, and depth; prices are alarming on the low side
Dress:	Dressy casual
Disabled access:	Full
Customers:	Tourists; a few locals and wine buffs
Brunch:	Every day, 8 A.M.–2:30 P.M.
Breakfast/Lunch:	Every day, 7 A.M.–2:30 P.M.
Dinner:	Every day, 6–10 P.M.

Atmosphere / setting: The founding establishment of the Brennan dynasty is a magnificent, historic French Quarter building surrounding an ideal courtyard. The best rooms are downstairs, just past the bar and alongside the courtyard. Avoid the upstairs rooms.

Recommended dishes: Breakfast: oyster soup; eggs sardou; eggs Hussarde; eggs St. Charles; grillades and grits; crêpes Fitzgerald. Dinner: oysters Rockefeller; oysters casino; buster crabs with pecans; seafood crêpes Barbara; turtle soup; Jackson salad; filet mignon Stanley; filet mignon Diane; veal Kottwitz; fish Jaime. Bananas Foster; chocolate suicide cake.

Summary & comments: Brennan's is famous the world over for its breakfast, a lengthy meal whose menu includes more specialty egg dishes than you'd ever imagine existed. Brennan's is renowned among oenophiles for its wine cellar, certainly the best in New Orleans and among the best in the country. But to most locals Brennan's is notorious as a place they'd love to go more often if the prices weren't so high (they're at the top of the scale) and if the waiters didn't treat them like the tourists who make up the lion's share of the clientele. The food at dinner can be terrific but, even for regulars, it is very inconsistent.

Brick Oven Cafe

	Pizza / Italian
	★ ★ ★
	Moderate
	Quality 78 Value B

Zone 10   Metairie Above Causeway /
                 Kenner / Jefferson Hwy.
2805 Williams Boulevard, Kenner
466-2097

Reservations:	Not accepted
When to go:	Anytime
Entree range:	$8–14
Payment:	All major credit cards
Service rating:	★ ★ ★
Friendliness rating:	★ ★ ★ ★
Parking:	Valet (free)
Bar:	Full bar
Wine selection:	A few house wines, mostly Italian
Dress:	Casual
Disabled access:	Full
Customers:	Locals
Lunch / Dinner:	Every day, 11 A.M.–11 P.M.

Atmosphere / setting: It has the look of a franchise restaurant, although this is the only location. There's an actual brick oven, visible (along with the rest of the kitchen) behind the counter.

Recommended dishes: Fried calamari; eggplant rolatine; Greek salad; pizza liberta, Florentine, or primavera; chicken Vesuvio; veal piccata; veal chop liberta; penne all' amatriciana; rigatoni with eggplant; spaghetti carbonara; manicotti. Cannoli.

Summary & comments: The specialties are pizza (which is indeed baked in a brick oven) and pasta, with all the expected accompaniments. This is not the standard New Orleans style of Italian cooking where heavy red sauces predominate; you'll see lots of vegetables, white sauces, olive-oil-and-herb sauces, and seafood. The place can be very good, but the madhouse aspect occasionally brings on a certain accidental imperfection. A fun spot, particularly for younger adults. Also one of the two or three best restaurants within quick striking distance (with wheels) of the airport.

Brigtsen's

Zone 4   Uptown Above Napoleon
723 Dante
861-7610

Nouvelle Creole

★★★★

Expensive

Quality 92   Value B

Reservations:	Required
When to go:	Early evenings
Entree range:	$10–22
Payment:	All major credit cards
Service rating:	★★★★
Friendliness rating:	★★★★★
Parking:	Curbside
Bar:	Full bar
Wine selection:	Modest list, but wines well-chosen for the food
Dress:	Jacket recommended but not required
Disabled access:	Limited
Customers:	Mostly locals, a few tourists
Dinner:	Tuesday–Saturday, 5:30–10 P.M.; Sunday and Monday, closed.

Atmosphere / setting: The restaurant was built in a 150-year-old residence that was originally constructed with lumber from disassembled Mississippi River flatboats. All the rooms are small, but claustrophobia is kept in check.

Recommended dishes: Menu changes daily, so not all of this may be available: grilled rabbit tenderloin with spinach; shrimp rémoulade; sesame-encrusted foie gras. Any soup, especially gumbos or seafood bisques; pannéed rabbit; any veal special; any grilled, broiled, or pan-sautéed fish; tournedos of beef with port and blue cheese; chicken with hot and sweet peppers. Banana bread pudding; ice creams; double chocolate cake.

Summary & comments: Frank and Marna Brigtsen are the most illustrious graduates of the hot era at K-Paul's. They opened their restaurant about a decade ago, and from that day to this they've kept all the little rooms in it filled with happy eaters. The style is very Creole, but with a freshness and imagination that grabs you not only in your mouth but in your mind. It's always agony to decide what to order here, because so many dishes sound irresistible. Because the menu changes every day and because the chef loves to experiment, you'll find quite a few foods here you've never heard of before—along with a predominance of more common eats. The service staff treats you like a live-in guest. The wine list is short but good and attractively priced.

Broussard's

Zone 1   French Quarter
819 Conti
581-3866

Nouvelle Creole	
★★★★	
Very Expensive	
Quality 84	Value D

Reservations: Recommended
When to go: Anytime
Entree range: $17–26
Payment: All major credit cards
Service rating: ★★★
Friendliness rating: ★★★
Parking: Validated (free) at adjacent garage
Bar: Full bar
Wine selection: Decent list, good international balance;
                        a bit overpriced
Dress: Jacket recommended but not required
Disabled access: Full
Customers: Tourists, some locals
Dinner: Every day, 6–10 P.M.

Atmosphere / setting: Three extremely handsome dining rooms, each with a different design, surround a lovely French Quarter courtyard.

Recommended dishes: Delice ravigote (crabmeat ravigote, shrimp rémoulade, gravlax); shrimp and crab cheesecake with roasted red pepper and dill cream; daube glacé (Creole spiced cold beef); baked oyster trio; sweet potato, corn, and shrimp bisque; duckling Normandy; poussin rochambeau (with ham, and marchand de vin and béarnaise sauces); pecan-stuffed salmon; pompano Napoleon; veal filet on braised leeks; wild game grill. Chocolate pava; crêpes Broussard; bananas Foster.

Summary & comments: Broussard's is a bona fide product of the grand era of New Orleans restaurants, having opened in 1920. But among locals it's something of a mystery, so long has it catered mainly to visitors. In the past couple of years its owners have tried to do something about that by breathing some life into the menu, and they've succeeded admirably: the dishes are the ones you'd expect of a place of this vintage, but updated to current tastes and ingredients.

BRUNING'S

Zone 7   Lakeview / West End /
               Bucktown
West End Park
282-9395

Seafood	
★★★	
Inexpensive	
Quality 79	Value A

Reservations:	Not accepted
When to go:	Anytime, but Fridays are very crowded
Entree range:	$8–16
Payment:	All major credit cards
Service rating:	★★
Friendliness rating:	★★★★
Parking:	Free lot adjacent
Bar:	Full bar
Wine selection:	A few house wines
Dress:	Anything goes
Disabled access:	Limited
Customers:	Locals, families
Lunch / Dinner:	Every day, 11 A.M.–10 P.M.

Atmosphere / setting: Quite possibly the oldest fried-seafood house in the world, Bruning's opened in 1859 at West End Park, at that time a resort reachable from New Orleans only by rail or boat. Now owned by the fifth generation of the founder's family, it's still in the same old building on stilts over Lake Pontchartrain's waters. Check out the mammoth antique bar on the way in.

Recommended dishes: Oysters on the half shell; seafood gumbo; boiled crabs, crawfish, or shrimp in season; whole broiled flounder; whole fried trout; fried seafood platter; fried chicken. Bread pudding.

Summary & comments: Things change little here over the decades; the menu consists of the archetypal platters of fried seafood, mounds of boiled seafood, and one distinctive specialty: a very large whole flounder, fried or broiled. A very casual place for eating, drinking, and reveling in the New Orleans life.

Byblos

Zone 9   Metairie Below Causeway
1501 Metairie Road, Metairie
834-9773

Reservations:	Accepted
When to go:	Anytime
Entree range:	$8–14
Payment:	AMEX, MC, V
Service rating:	★★
Friendliness rating:	★★★
Parking:	Free lot adjacent
Bar:	Full bar
Wine selection:	A few house wines
Dress:	Casual
Disabled access:	Full
Customers:	Locals
Lunch / Dinner:	Monday–Saturday, 11 A.M.–10 P.M.; Sunday, closed.

Atmosphere / setting: The dining room has a lofty ceiling and a comfortable, uncluttered look.

Recommended dishes: Hummus; baba gannoujh; stuffed kibbeh; falafel; stuffed cabbage rolls; cheese pie; tabbouleh salad; beef shawarma; beef kebab; chicken kebab; kafta kebab; fried kibbeh; kibbeh nayyi. Ashta (flaky dessert pastry).

Summary & comments: This new place (opened 1994) is the best Middle Eastern restaurant we've ever had in New Orleans. The ingredients are first-class (i.e., filet mignon is used for the beef kebab), and the cooking is careful and light. The appetizer "mezza" brings forth an assortment of some 15 appetizers for 4 to 6 people—a great way to eat.

Cafe Atchafalaya

Zone 3   Uptown Below Napoleon
901 Louisiana
891-5271

Reservations:	Accepted
When to go:	Anytime
Entree range:	$6–15
Payment:	All major credit cards except Discover
Service rating:	★★★
Friendliness rating:	★★★★
Parking:	Curbside
Bar:	Full bar
Wine selection:	Modest list, but wines well-chosen for the food
Dress:	Casual
Disabled access:	Limited
Customers:	Uptowners and Mississippi expatriates
Breakfast/Lunch:	Saturday and Sunday, 8 A.M.–2:30 P.M.
Lunch:	Monday–Saturday, 11:30 A.M.–2:30 P.M.
Dinner:	Monday–Saturday, 5–9 P.M.

Atmosphere / setting: A corner restaurant for over 75 years, the rooms are utilitarian and largely unadorned.

Recommended dishes: Grillades and jalapeño cheese grits (breakfast only). Blackeye pea dip with corn chips; fried chicken livers with pepper jelly; crabcakes; coriander shrimp; grilled fish with cilantro; chicken and dumplings; boiled brisket; calves' liver and onions; daily specials; stuffed pork chops; brabant potatoes; candied yams; crowder peas. Fruit cobblers (especially blackberry); bread pudding.

Summary & comments: This unpretentious neighborhood cafe illustrates the difference between the Creole food ubiquitous in New Orleans and the cooking of the rest of the South by serving the latter. Fried green tomatoes are the signature dish, although they're really a footnote to a menu full of very good home-style southern classics. These are less spicy than typical local fare, but the ingredients used are so good and the preparation of them so careful that there's no lack of flavor. A menu of unexpectedly with-it seafood and breakfast on weekends fills out the picture. Don't miss the jalapeño cheese bread in the basket on the table.

CAFE BUON GIORNO

Zone 11 West Bank	Pizza
830 Third Street, Gretna	★★★
363-9111	Inexpensive
	Quality 72 Value B

Reservations:	Not accepted
When to go:	Anytime
Entree range:	$6–11
Payment:	All major credit cards
Service rating:	★
Friendliness rating:	★★★
Parking:	Curbside
Bar:	Beer and wine
Wine selection:	A few house wines
Dress:	Anything goes
Disabled access:	Limited
Customers:	Neighborhood people, businessmen at lunch
Lunch/Dinner:	Every day, 11 A.M.–10 P.M.

Atmosphere / setting: A modest little dining room dominated by the buffet at lunch.

Recommended dishes: Turkish salad; artichoke heart salad; muffuletta; spinach, mushroom, and feta sub; spinach lasagna; pizza (you can pick your own ingredients), especially primavera and Jean Lafitte (crabmeat, shrimp, and mushroom) varieties. Apple dessert pizza.

Summary & comments: The area near the courthouse in the old part of Gretna is charming and has the densest concentration of good restaurants on the West Bank—at least at lunchtime. This is a cheerful dining room that gets so busy at the noon meal that the buffet food winds up being as hot and fresh as if it were made to your order. Pizza, pasta, and poor boys with an Italian flavor comprise more of the menu. Half of the selections are old standards, the other half creative (i.e., the shrimp, garlic clove, and avocado pizza).

Cafe Degas

Zone 6   Mid-City/Gentilly
3127 Esplanade
945-5635

	French Bistro
	★★★
	Moderate
	Quality 73 Value B

Reservations: Accepted
When to go: Anytime
Entree range: $7–15
Payment: AMEX, DS, MC, V
Service rating: ★★
Friendliness rating: ★★★
Parking: Curbside
Bar: Full bar
Wine selection: Limited list of ordinary wines,
                       French–dominated
Dress: Casual
Disabled access: Limited
Customers: Neighborhood people
Brunch: Sunday, 11 A.M.–3 P.M.
Lunch/Dinner: Every day, 11 A.M.–10 P.M.

Atmosphere/setting: The main attraction here is the covered but otherwise open-air deck where most of the tables are located. The inside dining room is strictly for bad weather.

Recommended dishes: Onion soup gratinée; couscous and vegetable salad; baked oysters with artichokes in cream sauce; sweetbreads Grenobloise; magret of duck a l'orange; shrimp fettuccine; quails with figs. Crème brûlée; chocolate mousse.

Summary & comments: The few blocks of Esplanade around the rear entrance of the Fair Grounds have a concentration of restaurants, and this is one of the most popular. The menu is French bistro, and some of it (chicken, red meat, salads, soups) succeeds better than others (seafood and desserts). The service staff often shows unwarranted enthusiasm for the offerings.

Cafe du Monde

Zone 1   French Quarter
800 Decatur
525-4544

<table>
<tr><td></td><td>Coffee / Breakfast</td></tr>
<tr><td></td><td>★ ★ ★</td></tr>
<tr><td></td><td>Inexpensive</td></tr>
<tr><td></td><td>Quality 70   Value C</td></tr>
</table>

Reservations:	Not accepted
When to go:	Anytime
Entree range:	$0.75
Payment:	No credit cards
Service rating:	★
Friendliness rating:	★
Parking:	Curbside (metered); pay lot nearby
Bar:	No alcohol
Wine selection:	None
Dress:	Anything goes
Disabled access:	Full
Customers:	Anyone in the world
Open:	Every day (all 365 of them), 24 hours

Atmosphere / setting: The original and last surviving French Market coffee stand, the Cafe du Monde is greatly expanded beyond its original perimeters to spill out onto the sidewalks of Washington Artillery Park. Everybody winds up here sooner or later.

Recommended dishes: Café au lait. Beignets.

Summary & comments: Coffee and chicory, brewed to the appropriate blue-black potency, is mixed with hot milk to order. Squares of dough are fried by the dozen and served in threes, dusted with powdered sugar, by rushed, indifferent waiters, mostly of foreign origin. Whatever else you can say about it, coffee and doughnuts at the Cafe du Monde is a quintessential taste of the city, whether taken first thing in the morning or last thing very late at night.

Cafe Giovanni

Zone 1   French Quarter
117 Decatur
529-2154

	Nouvelle Italian
	★★★★
	Expensive
	Quality 87 Value B

Reservations:	Recommended
When to go:	Anytime
Entree range:	$14–22
Payment:	All major credit cards
Service rating:	★★★
Friendliness rating:	★★★★
Parking:	Valet (free)
Bar:	Full bar
Wine selection:	Substantial list, mostly Italian; many by-the-glass selections
Dress:	Jacket recommended but not required
Disabled access:	Full
Customers:	Mostly locals, a few tourists
Dinner:	Every day, 6–10 P.M.

Atmosphere / setting: The dining room is much too small for the crowds the chef's food has been attracting, although unless you're close to the bar or waiting at it this doesn't make for intolerable discomfort. There are plans afoot to expand the place drastically, with an atrium, even.

Recommended dishes: Oysters Giovanni; baked seafood casino with apple-smoked bacon; Sicilian wedding soup; crabmeat Siciliana salad; pasta Gambino with rock shrimp and three cheeses; pasta absolutely (with shrimp and scallops in a vodka-basil sauce); cioppino; grilled marinated seafood assortment; filet mignon Abruzzo; roast chicken with rosemary and garlic. Dessert pastries (change daily).

Summary & comments: A smallish but very good trattoria operated by Duke LoCicero, a young but well-traveled chef with a strong sense of creativity and polish. What's interesting about his style is that he eschews the currently popular Northern Italian flavor in favor of the much-maligned Sicilian culinary traditions. What results is a fascinating, unique menu full of flavors very familiar to New Orleans eaters (especially those of Italian descent) but with lots of fresh, original touches. An especially attractive option here is to let the chef feed you an assortment of small portions of the day's specials.

Café Maspero

Zone 1   French Quarter
601 Decatur
523-6250

	Sandwiches
	★★★
	Inexpensive
Quality 74	Value A

Reservations:	Not accepted
When to go:	Anytime
Entree range:	$4–6
Payment:	No credit cards
Service rating:	★★★
Friendliness rating:	★★★
Parking:	Pay lots nearby
Bar:	Full bar
Wine selection:	A few house wines
Dress:	Anything goes
Disabled access:	Full
Customers:	Tourists, some locals
Lunch/Dinner:	Every day, 11 A.M.–midnight or later

Atmosphere/setting: It looks like a hundred other French Quarter convenience-food tourist traps, with a darkish room full of unadorned wood-topped tables.

Recommended dishes: Red beans and rice; ham sandwich; corned beef sandwich; pastrami sandwich; grilled seafood sandwich; fried oyster sandwich; seafood platter.

Summary & comments: One of the best sandwich places in New Orleans—and they don't even have poor boys! Pastrami, corned beef, ham, and seafood sandwiches come forth on big, crusty, round buns with very ample fillings of fine quality. A limited number of platters are also available; fried and grilled seafood are the best of these, but you can also get a more-than-acceptable plate of red beans or jambalaya. Everything is served at prices far below French Quarter standards, which may explain why the place is always so busy.

Café Rue Bourbon (Café Vieux Carre)

Zone 1   French Quarter
241 Bourbon
524-0114

Creole	
★★★	
Expensive	
Quality 81	Value D

Reservations:	Accepted
When to go:	Anytime
Entree range:	$10–23
Payment:	All major credit cards except Discover
Service rating:	★★
Friendliness rating:	★★★
Parking:	Validated free
Bar:	Full bar
Wine selection:	Decent list, international assortment
Dress:	Dressy casual
Disabled access:	Limited
Customers:	Mostly tourists, but a few locals, particularly at lunch
Brunch:	Sunday, 11 A.M.–3 P.M.
Lunch:	Every day, 11:30 A.M.–3 P.M.
Dinner:	Every day, 6–10 P.M.

Atmosphere / setting: It looks like it's pitched to out-of-towners, but all visitors should eat this well. The premises are handsome (this was the original location of Brennan's), and there's an upstairs dining room with a balcony that overlooks the passing parade on Bourbon Street.

Recommended dishes: Escargots in a veal reduction with red wine; veal, pork, and rabbit terrine; baked oyster combination; wild country green salad; smoked duck salad with leeks; tasso and shrimp pasta; sautéed veal forestière (with mushrooms and cream); veal chop stuffed with andouille and Gruyère; sautéed rabbit scallops with morels; four-way shrimp combination; carpetbagger steak (stuffed with oysters).

Summary & comments: The cooking is gussied-up Creole in a somewhat outmoded style, but there's nothing wrong with either the raw materials or their preparation. A few dishes are in the super-spicy style that Paul Prudhomme made popular; these are to be avoided. Both prices and portions are of a size slightly beyond comfortable.

Cafe Sbisa

Zone 1   French Quarter
1011 Decatur Street
522-5565

Nouvelle Creole	
★★★	
Expensive	
Quality 79	Value C

Reservations:	Recommended
When to go:	Anytime
Entree range:	$15–23
Payment:	All major credit cards
Service rating:	★★
Friendliness rating:	★★★★
Parking:	Validated (free) at French Market lot, one block
Bar:	Full bar
Wine selection:	Decent list, French-dominated
Dress:	Jacket recommended but not required
Disabled access:	Limited
Customers:	Mostly locals, a few tourists
Brunch:	Sunday, 11 A.M.–3 P.M.
Dinner:	Every day, 6–10 P.M.

Atmosphere / setting: A century-old restaurant, Sbisa is a charming two-level parlor of dark wood fixtures and mirrors across from the French Market.

Recommended dishes: Oysters Sbisa (baked on the shells with spinach, corn, blue cheese, and tomatoes); oysters en brochette; crabcakes with chipotle pepper sauce; flatbreads (like pizza with minimal toppings); turtle soup; oyster stew with cream and fresh thyme; grilled fish, especially tuna; trout amandine; barbecue shrimp; rack of lamb. Pecan and hazelnut pie; chocolate sin cake.

Entertainment & amenities: Pianist and blues singer at Sunday brunch.

Summary & comments: This is the third incarnation of Cafe Sbisa. The last time around, the place introduced charcoal-grilled fish to the area and was otherwise an innovator. The current Sbisa has had a string of imaginative chefs, but none of them has stayed long enough for the place to gain a culinary identity. Despite that, this is usually a very pleasant place to dine, as long as you keep a safe distance from the more bizarre-sounding offerings. On Sundays, there's a lively brunch with a good singer and piano player.

Café Volage

Zone 4   Uptown Above Napoleon
720 Dublin
861-4227

Creole French	
★★★	
Moderate	
Quality 78	Value B

Reservations:	Accepted
When to go:	Anytime
Entree range:	$8–18
Payment:	All major credit cards
Service rating:	★★★
Friendliness rating:	★★★★
Parking:	Curbside (metered)
Bar:	Full bar
Wine selection:	Limited list of ordinary wines
Dress:	Casual
Disabled access:	None
Customers:	Locals, couples
Brunch:	Sunday, 11 A.M.–3 P.M.
Lunch/Dinner:	Every day, 11:30 A.M.–10 P.M.

Atmosphere / setting: A cute cottage with quaint, nicely decorated, small dining rooms and a courtyard.

Recommended dishes: Cold crawfish Volage; seafood vol-au-vent; baked oysters; fettuccine with seafood in cream sauce; chicken a la Felix (mustard-caper sauce); veal with Calvados; roasted lamb tenderloin with rosemary and garlic.

Summary & comments: Cafe Volage is the creation of Felix Gallerani, an Italian guy who's spent the past 30 years as a chef and/or maître d' in French restaurants. His menu here is mostly French Creole, with large, generally well-made versions of the local standards, plus a few original dishes. All of this is well underpriced, but in return polish is in short supply.

Camellia Grill

Zone 4   Uptown Above Napoleon
626 South Carrollton Avenue
866-9573

Diner
★★★
Inexpensive
Quality 73   Value C

Reservations: Not accepted
When to go: Late nights
Entree range: $4–6
Payment: No credit cards
Service rating: ★★★
Friendliness rating: ★★★★
Parking: Curbside (metered)
Bar: No alcohol
Wine selection: None
Dress: Casual
Disabled access: Limited
Customers: Neighborhood people, college students,
                         late nighters
Open: Sunday–Thursday, 7 A.M.–1 A.M.;
                         Friday and Saturday, 7 A.M.–2 A.M.

Atmosphere / setting: A diner, with seating limited to the twenty-odd stools at the counter.

Recommended dishes: Hamburger; Camellia Grill Special sandwich; club sandwich; omelettes; waffles. Pecan pie; cheesecake.

Summary & comments: Almost everything is still prepared before your eyes at those grills on the other side of the counter, but the snap and verve of yesteryear, like many of the fixtures here, are wearing out. Still reliable for burgers, sandwiches, plate specials, pies, and (if you like that fluffy style) omelettes. Still very busy late at night.

CARMINE'S

Zone 7   Lakeview / West End /
            Bucktown
200 Metairie-Hammond Highway,
     Metairie
833-3004

Creole Italian	
★★	
Moderate	
Quality 72	Value B

Reservations:	Not accepted
When to go:	Early evenings; it gets packed quickly here
Entree range:	$7–14
Payment:	AMEX, DC, MC, V
Service rating:	★★
Friendliness rating:	★★
Parking:	Free lot adjacent
Bar:	Full bar
Wine selection:	A few house wines
Dress:	Casual
Disabled access:	Full
Customers:	Locals
Brunch:	Sunday, 8–11 A.M.
Lunch:	Every day, 11:30 A.M.–2:30 P.M.
Dinner:	Every day, 5–10 P.M.

Atmosphere / setting: Across the street from the lakeshore in the increasingly commercial old fishing village of Bucktown, Carmine's is packed with memorabilia, not all of it local. You get to use a kitchen towel for a napkin.

Recommended dishes: Spinach bread; fried calamari; fettuccine with shrimp; fried seafood-stuffed artichoke; fried seafood platters; soft-shell crab amandine.

Summary & comments: Overwhelmed with regular customers at most hours, Carmine's sends out gigantic platters of standard and less-than-standard Italian basics, not one of which has ever impressed me. Much better is the seafood, particularly as expressed in the unusually presented whole artichoke. If they're still serving breakfast by the time you read this, stop by for the grillades and grits, which are definitive.

CASAMENTO'S

		Seafood
Zone 3 Uptown Below Napoleon		★★★
4330 Magazine		Inexpensive
895-9761		Quality 72 Value C

Reservations:	Not accepted
When to go:	Anytime
Entree range:	$7–10
Payment:	No credit cards
Service rating:	★★
Friendliness rating:	★★
Parking:	Curbside
Bar:	Beer and wine
Wine selection:	A few house wines
Dress:	Casual
Disabled access:	Limited
Customers:	Neighborhood people
Lunch:	Tuesday–Sunday, 11 A.M.–1:45 P.M.
Dinner:	Tuesday–Sunday, 5–9:30 P.M.; Monday, closed.

Atmosphere / setting: The echoing walls of the spanking-clean dining room are covered with tiles that make the place look like a giant bathroom.

Recommended dishes: Oysters on the half-shell; fried oyster loaf; soft-shell crabs.

Summary & comments: A change in generations at this old oyster bar caused a noticeable blip in the decades-old record of consistency, but it's still an essential place for a dozen or so raw oysters on the half shell or a fried oyster loaf—served distinctively on toasted, buttered "pan bread."

Castillo's

		Mexican
Zone 1 French Quarter		★★
620 Conti		Moderate
525-7467		
		Quality 74 Value C

Reservations:	Not accepted
When to go:	Anytime
Entree range:	$6–11
Payment:	AMEX, MC, V
Service rating:	★
Friendliness rating:	★★
Parking:	Pay garages nearby
Bar:	Beer and wine
Wine selection:	A few house wines; good sangria
Dress:	Casual
Disabled access:	Limited
Customers:	Tourists, some locals
Lunch:	Monday–Friday, 11:30 A.M.–2:30 P.M.
Dinner:	Every day, 5–10 P.M.

Atmosphere / setting: More than a little dumpy, but it's an honest dumpiness.

Recommended dishes: Chalupa; guacamole; caldo xochil (chicken soup with cilantro); chilmole de puerco; enchiladas de res; stewed chicken with achiote peppers and orange juice; chicken with mole poblano; huevos rancheros; enchiladas suizas. Flan; Mexican hot chocolate.

Summary & comments: The city's oldest Mexican restaurant is holding on at its somewhat inaccessible (for parking, at least) location, but it's still worth a visit. The menu is quite different from that found in the Americanized Mexican places, and features sauces, ingredients, and styles of preparation that are much more typical of real Mexican cooking.

Cavallino's

Zone 4   Uptown Above Napoleon
1500 South Carrollton Avenue
866-9866

<table>
<tr><td>Pizza</td></tr>
<tr><td>★ ★ ★</td></tr>
<tr><td>Moderate</td></tr>
<tr><td>Quality 76   Value B</td></tr>
</table>

Reservations:	Not accepted
When to go:	Anytime
Entree range:	$7–13
Payment:	AMEX, DS, MC, V
Service rating:	★
Friendliness rating:	★ ★
Parking:	Curbside
Bar:	Beer and wine
Wine selection:	A few house wines
Dress:	Casual
Disabled access:	Limited
Customers:	Neighborhood people
Lunch / Dinner:	Every day, 11 A.M.–11 P.M.

Atmosphere / setting: A large, rather plain room that hasn't changed tremendously since it was the showroom of a bicycle store.

Recommended dishes: Caesar salad; fettuccine primavera; spinach lasagna; pizza, particularly the one topped with spinach, mushrooms, and feta cheese.

Summary & comments: Even the inept service here doesn't keep Cavallino's from being one of the best of the new-style pizza-and-pasta houses. The pizza is the better part of the menu, the crust baked in a light style and topped with fresh ingredients combined in offbeat and interesting ways. Pastas are served amply and with good, fresh-tasting sauces, several with lots of vegetables or seafood.

Charley G's

<table>
<tr><td></td><td>Nouvelle Cajun</td></tr>
<tr><td>Zone 9   Metairie Below Causeway</td><td>★★★</td></tr>
<tr><td>111 Veterans Boulevard, Metairie</td><td>Expensive</td></tr>
<tr><td>837-6408</td><td>Quality 83   Value D</td></tr>
</table>

Reservations:	Recommended
When to go:	Anytime
Entree range:	$10–17
Payment:	All major credit cards
Service rating:	★★★★
Friendliness rating:	★★★★
Parking:	Free lot adjacent
Bar:	Full bar
Wine selection:	Substantial list, assembled with great pains to match the food; many by-the-glass selections
Dress:	Jacket recommended but not required
Disabled access:	Full
Customers:	Businessmen at lunch; couples and foursomes at dinner
Brunch:	Sunday, 11 A.M.–3 P.M.; menu, with blues music
Lunch:	Monday–Friday, 11:30 A.M.–2:30 P.M.
Dinner:	Every day, 6–10 P.M.

Atmosphere / setting: The split-level dining room offers more booth seating than most places, as well as a view of the open kitchen.

Recommended dishes: Menu changes rather deeply four times a year. These dishes, or things like them, will probably be around: sausage mixed grill; duck andouille gumbo; crab cakes; shrimp rémoulade salad; crabmeat or crawfish fettuccine; tuna Dupuis (marinated with seasoned olive oil and grilled); veal with grilled portobello mushrooms; wood-grilled fish. Bullwinkle (chocolate mousse) pie; almond tuile; white chocolate bread pudding.

Entertainment & amenities: Pianist at dinner Tuesday–Saturday.

Summary & comments: The second location of a very successful Lafayette restaurant, Charley G's has all the elements of a fine restaurant: an interesting, comfortable dining room, an outgoing service staff, a menu of good local specialties prepared in original (but not too original) ways, an extensive wine list (ingeniously cross-referenced to the menu!), and even live music. The best specialties are entirely satisfying, and I've never had a bad meal here. But for some reason the parts don't add up to quite the whole dining pleasure that I'm led to expect. This could have something to do with the prices, which seem a touch high.

Charlie's Steak House

Zone 4   Uptown Above Napoleon
4510 Dryades
895-9705

Steak	
★ ★ ★	
Moderate	
Quality 75	Value B

Reservations:	Accepted
When to go:	Anytime
Entree range:	$9–16
Payment:	All major credit cards
Service rating:	★ ★
Friendliness rating:	★ ★ ★ ★
Parking:	Curbside
Bar:	Full bar
Wine selection:	A few house wines
Dress:	Casual
Disabled access:	Limited
Customers:	Locals, most of them men
Lunch:	Monday–Friday, 11:30 A.M.–3 P.M.
Dinner:	Monday–Saturday, 5–10 P.M.; Sunday, closed.

Atmosphere / setting: The dining rooms are beat-up, the walls are greasy, and the Formica surfaces of the tables are browned and curled from the thousands of red-hot steak platters that have rested upon them. Not filthy, but not for the fastidious.

Recommended dishes: Fried onion rings; wedge of lettuce with Roquefort dressing; T-bone steak.

Summary & comments: Near the top of the Horrible-Looking Places with Good Food list, Charlie's presents a proposition so simple that they don't even have a menu. They have filets, strips, and (best of all) T-bones; fried or au gratin potatoes; thin fried onions rings (best in town); and wedges of iceberg lettuce. The steaks sizzle and even smoke in their butter sauce. If you can ignore the surroundings and the gruff wait style, you'll probably like the experience. They really do know how to broil a steak here, at least most of the time.

CHART HOUSE

Zone 1   French Quarter
801 Chartres
523-2015

	American
	★★★
	Expensive
Quality 78	Value C

Reservations:	Recommended
When to go:	Anytime
Entree range:	$9–25
Payment:	AMEX, DC, MC, V
Service rating:	★★★★
Friendliness rating:	★★★★★
Parking:	French Market pay lot, two blocks away
Bar:	Full bar
Wine selection:	Decent list, with emphasis on California
Dress:	Casual
Disabled access:	None
Customers:	Tourists, some locals; youngish crowd
Dinner:	Every day, 6–11 P.M.

Atmosphere / setting: The restaurant is on the second floor of a historic building on Jackson Square, the heart of the French Quarter. There's a balcony overlooking the square for cocktails.

Recommended dishes: Oysters Rockefeller; oysters casino; artichoke with aïoli; top sirloin baseball teriyaki; filet mignon pepper steak; grilled fish; grilled chicken; Alaskan king crab legs. Key lime pie.

Summary & comments: A national chain of casual steak-and-seafood places, the Chart House stands a rung or two above the likes of Houston's or TGI Friday's. The menu is simple but the food is good, from the bucket of fresh salad through some fine seafood appetizers to thick pieces of grilled beef, chicken, and fish. Service here would do credit to the best of restaurants. Not a brilliant kitchen, but all promises are delivered upon.

Chez Daniel

French Bistro
★★★★
Moderate

Quality 90   Value B

Zone 9   Metairie Below Causeway
2037 Metairie Road, Metairie
837-6900

Reservations:	Recommended
When to go:	Early evenings
Entree range:	$9–16
Payment:	AMEX, MC, V
Service rating:	★★★★
Friendliness rating:	★★★★
Parking:	Free lot adjacent
Bar:	Full bar
Wine selection:	Decent list, good international balance, attractive prices; many by-the-glass selections
Dress:	Dressy casual
Disabled access:	Full
Customers:	Neighborhood people, couples
Dinner:	Tuesday–Saturday, 5–9:30 P.M.; Sunday and Monday, closed.

Atmosphere / setting: The restaurant was carved from an old liquor store and only minimally renovated; the most memorable detail is a large mural of a French fantasy scene. It presents an engaging style; a great low-key romantic rendezvous.

Recommended dishes: Terrine of duck; celeriac rémoulade; baby string-beans and julienne of duck vinaigrette; vegetable cream soup du jour; watercress and mushroom salad; mussels normande; broiled salmon with spinach; steak au poivre; steak tartare; sweetbreads Grenobloise; roasted chicken with rosemary. Dessert pastries.

Summary & comments: Daniel Bonnot is New Orleans' most accomplished French chef. After operating fairly grand restaurants for some fifteen years, he lowered his sights and opened a cafe as close to the classic French bistro as can be done in New Orleans. While most of the food is the simple, good cooking of the modest backstreet Parisian restaurant, there's also a certain amount of Creole flavor and more than a few flights of pure fancy.

CHINA BLOSSOM

	Chinese
	★★★★
	Moderate
	Quality 87 Value B

Zone 11   West Bank
1801 Stumpf Boulevard, Gretna
361-4598

Reservations:	Accepted
When to go:	Anytime
Entree range:	$7–15
Payment:	AMEX, MC, V
Service rating:	★★★
Friendliness rating:	★★★
Parking:	Free lot adjacent
Bar:	Full bar
Wine selection:	Limited list of ordinary wines
Dress:	Casual
Disabled access:	Full
Customers:	Locals
Lunch:	Tuesday–Sunday, 11:30 A.M.–2:30 P.M.
Dinner:	Tuesday–Sunday, 6–10 P.M.; Monday, closed.

Atmosphere / setting: Despite the location in a modest strip mall, the dining rooms are understated and comfortable.

Recommended dishes: Spring roll; five-spiced cold beef; hot and sour soup; tong-cho shrimp, trout, oysters, or soft-shell crab; spicy flaming chicken; sesame chicken; wor shu op (crisp half duck); Ming steak; beef with oyster sauce. Lotus banana.

Summary & comments: When Trey Yuen closed its Jax Brewery restaurant, much of the staff got together to open this restaurant, one of the best Chinese places in the area. The menu covers many styles of Chinese cooking, but the best dishes involve fresh local seafood: oysters, shrimp, crawfish, trout, and even alligator. Many of the dishes involve interesting tableside preparations.

CHiNA Doll

	Chinese
	★ ★ ★
	Moderate
	Quality 79 Value B

Zone 11   West Bank
830 Manhattan Boulevard, Marrero
366-1111

Reservations: Accepted
When to go: Anytime
Entree range: $7–15
Payment: AMEX, MC, V
Service rating: ★ ★
Friendliness rating: ★ ★ ★
Parking: Free lot adjacent
Bar: Full bar
Wine selection: A few house wines
Dress: Casual
Disabled access: Full
Customers: Locals
Lunch / Dinner: Monday–Saturday, 11 A.M.–10 P.M.;
                         Sunday, 4–9 P.M.

Atmosphere / setting: Not very inviting from the outside, the China Doll has the interior design of a Fifties Polynesian cafe within.

Recommended dishes: Hot and sour soup; crab rangoon; Maine lobster with garlic and ginger sauce; sweet and sour soft-shell crab; scallops with snowpeas and pineapple; crawfish velvet; sesame chicken; moo shi pork; lomi-lomi (giant shrimp wrapped with bacon and pineapple).

Summary & comments: The menu is distinctive, and a few other restaurants have copied it. There's an emphasis on seafood, and you'll find some very good concoctions involving things like crawfish in spicy but suave sauces. The restaurant is very popular and remains busy throughout the afternoon. Good drinks.

CHRISTIAN'S

Zone 6   Mid-City / Gentilly
3835 Iberville
482-4924

	Creole French
	★★★★
	Expensive
	Quality 90 Value B

Reservations:	Recommended
When to go:	Early evenings
Entree range:	$12–23
Payment:	All major credit cards except Discover
Service rating:	★★★★
Friendliness rating:	★★★
Parking:	Free lot adjacent
Bar:	Full bar
Wine selection:	Substantial list, about equally French and Californian; very attractive prices
Dress:	Jacket recommended but not required
Disabled access:	Limited
Customers:	Mostly locals, a few tourists; couples; gourmets
Lunch:	Tuesday–Friday, 11:30 A.M.–2:30 P.M.
Dinner:	Tuesday–Saturday, 6–10 P.M.; Sunday and Monday, closed.

Atmosphere / setting: With a name like Christian's, the fact that this restaurant occupies a small old church may seem like a joke. Indeed, pews are used as banquettes, the cry room as the bar, and the pulpit as a waiter's stand. But the place was called Christian's before it moved in here (it's the name of the owner), and they stop well short of using the decor as a gimmick.

Recommended dishes: Oysters Roland; oysters en brochette; shrimp rémoulade; smoked salmon; smoked soft-shell crab; shrimp-and-crabmeat-stuffed fish; stuffed eggplant; braised sweetbreads with port sauce; roast duck with blackberry vinegar sauce; veal Christian; trout meunière amandine; quenelles of fish Nantua. Crème caramel; homemade ice creams.

Summary & comments: This is not only a serious restaurant, it's a very consistent and original one that offers terrific value. Proprietor Chris Ansel combines the style of his family's restaurant Galatoire's with that of classic French cooking and some new ideas from the current young chef. The result is a collection of dishes as distinctive as the premises. The service staff has an easy style, the wines are sold at bargain prices, and the early-evening special menu is almost too good to be real. Complaints: the dessert selection is uninteresting, and some diners may find the deuces along the perimeter a little too close to their neighbors.

Clancy's

Zone 4   Uptown Above Napoleon
6100 Annunciation
895-1111

Nouvelle Creole

★★★★

Expensive

Quality 90   Value B

Reservations: Recommended
When to go: Anytime
Entree range: $13–22
Payment: All major credit cards
Service rating: ★★★★
Friendliness rating: ★★★★
Parking: Curbside
Bar: Full bar
Wine selection: Substantial list, full of oddities; the owner is an
                      oenophile and buys many short-lot wines he's
                      interested in; many by-the-glass selections
Dress: Dressy casual
Disabled access: Limited
Customers: Locals, gourmets
Lunch: Monday–Friday, 11:30 A.M.–3 P.M.
Dinner: Monday–Saturday, 6–10 P.M.; Sunday, closed.

Atmosphere / setting: An old neighborhood bar that was buffed up in the early Eighties to create an only modestly gentrified cafe, populated by a highly social group of regulars.

Recommended dishes: Oysters with Brie and spinach; crabmeat ravigote; shrimp rémoulade; house salad; smoked soft-shell crab with crabmeat; smoked shrimp with ginger; seafood pasta specials; veal liver lyonnaise; veal and lamb chops; smoked duck; filet mignon with port sauce and Stilton. Crème caramel.

Summary & comments: One of the first nouvelle Creole bistros, Clancy's remains one of the best such restaurants around. It boasts a few unique specialties, an easy, engaging style, a wine list full of offbeat bottles, and enough innovation to keep the curiosity piqued. Clancy's was the first local eatery to keep a smoker as a major part of its kitchen; it still smokes foods well. Only locals eat here because only they can find the place.

Coffee Pot

Zone 1   French Quarter
714 St. Peter
524-3500

Creole	
★★	
Moderate	
Quality 71	Value C

Reservations:	Not accepted
When to go:	Anytime
Entree range:	$7–15
Payment:	AMEX, MC, V
Service rating:	★★
Friendliness rating:	★★★
Parking:	Pay garages nearby
Bar:	Full bar
Wine selection:	A few house wines
Dress:	Casual
Disabled access:	None
Customers:	Tourists, a few Quarterites
Open:	Sunday–Thursday, 8 A.M.–midnight;
	Friday–Saturday, 8 A.M.–1 A.M.

Atmosphere / setting: The parlor and carriageway of a modest Creole townhouse serve as the dining areas.

Recommended dishes: Salad Jayne; seafood gumbo; red beans and rice; fried chicken; fried seafood platter; daily blackboard specials; omelettes. Bread pudding; fruit cobblers.

Summary & comments: This Creole cafe dates back to the Forties, and although it has long catered heavily to the tourist business it remains a good place to sample the staples of local home cooking. The place is still something of a neighborhood hangout for Quarterites, who mainly come for the very good breakfasts. One thing never changes: the coffee, by New Orleans standards, is awful.

COMMANDER'S PALACE

Zone 3   Uptown Below Napoleon
1403 Washington Avenue
899-8221

Nouvelle Creole
★★★★★
Expensive

Quality 97   Value B

Reservations:	Required
When to go:	Lunch and weekday dinners
Entree range:	$15–26
Payment:	All major credit cards
Service rating:	★★★★
Friendliness rating:	★★★
Parking:	Valet (free)
Bar:	Full bar
Wine selection:	Distinguished cellar, good international balance; rare wines from France and California
Dress:	Jacket required at dinner
Disabled access:	Limited
Customers:	Half tourists, half socializing locals; couples
Brunch:	Saturday and Sunday, 11 A.M.–3 P.M.
Lunch:	Monday–Friday, 11:30 A.M.–2 P.M.
Dinner:	Every day, 6–10 P.M.

Atmosphere / setting: Dining rooms of quite different styles fill a 19th-century mansion. The upstairs Garden Room gives a view through the boughs of the mammoth live oak tree to the courtyard below. The kitchen also serves as a passageway to the bar; there's also a single table in there for serious foodies.

Recommended dishes: A very substantial number of the best dishes here are daily specials, to which I draw your attention. Regularly offered greats: shrimp rémoulade; smoked mushrooms and pasta; smoked fish cake; lyonnaise fish; sauté of crawfish; turtle soup; grilled fish; sautéed fish with pecans; veal chop Tchoupitoulas; veal Marcelle; filet mignon Adelaide; roasted strip sirloin steak; rack of lamb. Bananas Foster; bread pudding soufflé; chocolate fudge Sheba.

Entertainment & amenities: Strolling jazz trio at Sunday brunch.

Summary & comments: If there were no Commander's Palace, the dining scene in New Orleans would be much different. For the past two decades it's consistently been the favorite both of local diners and frequent visitors. Culinary substance here runs deep, and Commander's innovations have influenced almost every other Creole restaurant. The menu combines both old and new styles of Creole cooking; either route is rewarding. The wine list is strong both in French and American bottles. And Commander's is an extraordinary value: a four-course dinner can be had for $35, lunch for $14. The service is a little too methodical, but the staff is entirely responsive to special wants.

COMPAGNO'S

Zone 4   Uptown Above Napoleon
7839 St. Charles Avenue
866-9313

Creole / Neighborhood Cafe	
★★★	
Moderate	
Quality 76	Value C

Reservations:	Not accepted
When to go:	Anytime
Entree range:	$6–16
Payment:	MC, V
Service rating:	★★
Friendliness rating:	★★★
Parking:	Curbside
Bar:	Full bar
Wine selection:	A few house wines
Dress:	Casual
Disabled access:	Limited
Customers:	Neighborhood people, college students
Lunch:	Tuesday–Thursday, 11 A.M.–2 P.M.
Dinner:	Tuesday–Thursday, 5–10 P.M.
Lunch / Dinner:	Friday–Sunday, 11 A.M.–10 P.M.; Monday, closed.

Atmosphere / setting: A fine specimen of the kind of neighborhood cafes that once occupied many more corners of New Orleans than they do now, Compagno's is divided in a bar side and a dining room side by a half-wall over which all varieties of atmosphere drift.

Recommended dishes: Muffuletta; cheese ravioli; fried seafood platters.

Summary & comments: The menu is about equally divided between very good seafood platters (fried to order and served amply and hot) and old-style Italian platters (generally topped with a fine version of the New Orleans-Sicilian sweet, smooth red sauce). Good, garlicky muffulettas.

Copeland's

	Cajun
	★★★
	Moderate
	Quality 76 Value C

Zone 4   Uptown Above Napoleon
4338 St. Charles Avenue
897-2325

Zone 9   Metairie Below Causeway
701 Veterans Boulevard, Metairie
831-3437

Zone 10   Metairie Above Causeway/Kenner/Jefferson Hwy.
1001 South Clearview Parkway
733-7843

Reservations:	Not accepted
When to go:	Anytime
Entree range:	$7–13
Payment:	AMEX, MC, V
Service rating:	★★
Friendliness rating:	★★★★
Parking:	Free lot adjacent
Bar:	Full bar
Wine selection:	Limited list of ordinary wines
Dress:	Casual
Disabled access:	Full
Customers:	Locals; youngish crowd
Brunch:	Sunday, 11 A.M.–3 P.M.
Lunch/Dinner:	Every day, 11 A.M.–10 P.M.

Atmosphere / setting: The fern restaurant look of the late Seventies prevails here: fake stained glass, hanging plants everywhere, tall stools at tall tables.

Recommended dishes: Cajun popcorn; fettuccine Alfredo; Thai chicken salad; shrimp dill-icious (sorry—that's really what they call it.); shrimp carribe; ricochet catfish with pecans and sesame seeds; blackened or grilled fish; baby-back ribs; blackened pork tenderloin; red beans and rice. Mile-and-a-half-high ice cream pie; Mexican vanilla ice cream; bread pudding.

Summary & comments: A local chain of concept restaurants, Copeland's rises above the homogenization of places like TGI Friday's with a distinctly Creole flavor and fresh food prepared to order. Although many dishes share the same seasoning balances and sauces, the menu is so extensive that with some careful ordering you can avoid having everything taste the same. Service is unusually attentive. In addition to the three listed here, there are outlying Copeland's in Harvey at 1700 Lapalco Boulevard (364-1575) and in Slidell at 1337 Gause Boulevard (504) 643-0001.

Corky's

Zone 10	Metairie Above Causeway/ Kenner/Jefferson Hwy.

4243 Veterans Boulevard, Metairie
887-5000

Barbecue
★★★
Inexpensive

Quality 80   Value B

Reservations:	Not accepted
When to go:	Anytime
Entree range:	$5–11
Payment:	All major credit cards
Service rating:	★★★
Friendliness rating:	★★★★
Parking:	Free lot adjacent
Bar:	Beer and wine
Wine selection:	A few house wines
Dress:	Casual
Disabled access:	Full
Customers:	Locals
Lunch/Dinner:	Every day, 11 A.M.–10 P.M.

Atmosphere / setting: Standard concept restaurant layout, with mostly booth seating and lots of memorabilia from the Fifties and Sixties, particularly items involving rock and roll and most particularly Mr. Presley.

Recommended dishes: Fried chicken drummies; pulled pork platter or sandwich; pork ribs, wet or dry style; rotisserie chicken; New Orleans-style barbecue shrimp; cole slaw; barbecue beans. Pecan pie; apple cobbler.

Summary & comments: Corky's is one of only two or three good places to eat barbecue in New Orleans. It's the second location of a runaway success in the barbecue capital of Memphis, which is saying something. The meats are smoked slowly over wood and charcoal, and served with the best barbecue sauce I've ever encountered—full of aromatic spices. The ribs are an exception: you have the option of getting those in the unique Memphis "dry" style, liberally encrusted with a spice mix. Bread, cole slaw, beans, and other side dishes are all terrific. So is the odd New Orleans dish: barbecue shrimp.

Court of Two Sisters

Zone 1   French Quarter
613 Royal
522-7273

Creole	
★★★	
Expensive	
Quality 75	Value C

Reservations:	Recommended
When to go:	Dinner
Entree range:	$15–23
Payment:	All major credit cards
Service rating:	★★★
Friendliness rating:	★★★★
Parking:	Pay garages nearby
Bar:	Full bar
Wine selection:	Decent list, but only a few bottles of more than routine interest
Dress:	Jacket recommended but not required
Disabled access:	Full
Customers:	Tourists
Brunch:	Every day, 9 A.M.–2 P.M.
Dinner:	Every day, 6–10 P.M.

Atmosphere / setting: Oddly, the Court is the only major New Orleans restaurant with full-time service in the kind of courtyard for which the French Quarter is famous. If you ever dine under the wisteria vines out there when the weather is right and you're in the mood for some Tennessee Williams-style New Orleans atmosphere, the evening will be unforgettable.

Recommended dishes: Baked oysters mélange (two each of three different kinds); escargots in mushroom caps; crawfish Louise; seafood gumbo; Caesar salad; shrimp Toulouse; crabmeat St. Peter; trout amandine; trout Picasso; veal Fein; coq d'Orleans. Bread pudding; chocolate mousse; cherries jubilee.

Entertainment & amenities: Strolling jazz trio at brunch daily.

Summary & comments: Local diners have long consigned this truly beautiful restaurant strictly to tourists. It is in fact more than a little touristy; the menu is limited to the most familiar clichés of Creole restaurant cooking. Still, it's better than most locals think. As long as you're not expecting to eat on the cutting edge, the chances of off-notes are slim. The service staff is very accommodating.

Crazy Johnnie's

		Steak
		★ ★ ★
		Inexpensive

Zone 10   Metairie Above Causeway /
                 Kenner / Jefferson Hwy.
3520 18th Street, Metairie
887-6641

Quality 75   Value A

Zone 12   North Shore
1202 US 190, Covington
(504) 893-5678

Reservations:	Not accepted
When to go:	Early evenings or lunch
Entree range:	$8
Payment:	All major credit cards
Service rating:	★
Friendliness rating:	★ ★
Parking:	Free lot adjacent
Bar:	Full bar
Wine selection:	A few house wines
Dress:	Casual
Disabled access:	Limited
Customers:	Locals
Lunch / Dinner:	Every day, 11 A.M.–11 P.M.

Atmosphere / setting: Crazy Johnnie's started as a bar, and it still looks like one: dark, smoky, and adult oriented.

Recommended dishes: Table salad; seafood gumbo; stuffed artichoke; filet mignon; prime rib; grilled tuna.

Summary & comments: A simple but very appealing idea keeps this place more than full most of the time. They serve a thick, prime-grade filet mignon at approximately cost: at this writing, about $8. Although the cooking is not the most accurate, they're not too far off the beam, and the quality of the beef is beyond reproach. The potatoes are just okay. The salad is mammoth and as good a deal as the steak. To make money, they sell drinks: you have to buy one, and all those people waiting for tables usually have one or two. Service is very rapid, the faster to get the next customer in. Amenities are minimal.

CRESCENT CITY BREWHOUSE

Zone 1 French Quarter	Creole
527 Decatur	★★
522-0571	Moderate
	Quality 68 Value C

Reservations:	Not accepted
When to go:	Anytime
Entree range:	$6–14
Payment:	All major credit cards
Service rating:	★★
Friendliness rating:	★★
Parking:	Jackson Brewery pay lot across the street
Bar:	Full bar; this is a microbrewery with four house-made beers on tap
Wine selection:	A few house wines; this is mainly a beer place
Dress:	Casual
Disabled access:	Full
Customers:	Mix of locals and tourists
Lunch/Dinner:	Sunday–Thursday, 11 A.M.–10 P.M.; Friday and Saturday, 11 A.M.–11 P.M.; Monday, closed.

Atmosphere/setting: The copper brewing apparatus is open to view and dominates the first of the two floors of the old French Quarter building. Aside from that, it's a bierstube.

Recommended dishes: Beer-battered onion rings; sausage platter.

Summary & comments: This is a genuine microbrewery operated by a young German guy with brewmaster ancestors. Four varieties are made and served very fresh: they're quite good. The same cannot be said about the food, which is barely adequate. Most of what's served comes from the sandwich, salad, and fried-platter categories; the few essays beyond that level are hit and miss. Still, a neat place to hang out.

CRESCENT CITY STEAK HOUSE

Zone 6   Mid-City / Gentilly
1001 North Broad
821-3271

Steak	
★★★	
Expensive	
Quality 77	Value C

Reservations: Accepted
When to go: Anytime
Entree range: $15–18
Payment: All major credit cards
Service rating: ★
Friendliness rating: ★
Parking: Free lot adjacent
Bar: Full bar
Wine selection: A handful of mostly French bottles, distributed
                        on the tables as helpful suggestions
Dress: Casual
Disabled access: Full
Customers: Very few, all local
Lunch / Dinner: Tuesday–Sunday, 11 A.M.–10 P.M.;
                        Monday, closed.

Atmosphere / setting: To say the place is peculiar is an understatement. There's rarely anyone here other than the owners, a waitress who's been around for decades, and (perhaps) a few regulars. The premises are a time warp fifty years back. This is a great place to come if you don't want to be seen.

Recommended dishes: Strip sirloin steak; T-bone steak; potatoes au gratin; Brabant potatoes; broccoli au gratin. Bread pudding; café au lait.

Summary & comments: The original high-end local steak house—founded in 1933 and widely copied—makes no strong bid for your trade, and probably has never gotten it. But the steaks are of superb quality, very well aged, and cooked to sizzling. Potatoes and vegetables are okay; salads and onion rings are awful.

CROZIER'S

Zone 10 Metairie Above Causeway/
Kenner/Jefferson Hwy.
3216 West Esplanade, Metairie
833-8108

French Bistro
★★★★★
Expensive

Quality 93   Value C

Reservations:	Recommended
When to go:	Weeknights
Entree range:	$13–20
Payment:	AMEX, DC, MC, V
Service rating:	★★★★
Friendliness rating:	★★★★
Parking:	Free lot adjacent
Bar:	Full bar
Wine selection:	Decent list, French-dominated
Dress:	Dressy casual
Disabled access:	Full
Customers:	Locals, couples
Dinner:	Tuesday–Saturday, 6–10 P.M.; Sunday and Monday, closed.

Atmosphere / setting: The present dining room belies its strip-mall exterior by being charming and very French. The two dining rooms are quiet, unexpectedly elegant, and intimate.

Recommended dishes: Pâté maison; cassoulet of shrimp or crawfish; magret of duck with pink peppercorn sauce; escargots bourguignonne; onion soup gratinée; salade maison; poached pompano or salmon hollandaise; coq au vin; sweetbreads Grenobloise; veal Crozier; beef tournedos Gerard; steak au poivre; filet mignon perigourdine. Lemon tartlet; crème caramel; gâteau de pain au whiskey (bread pudding).

Summary & comments: Gerard Crozier opened New Orleans' first pure French restaurant—no Creole flavors at all. The specific style is classic bistro food from his hometown of Lyons. No nouvelle cuisine. Despite this conventionality (or perhaps because of it), Crozier's food is some of the best around. It is certainly the most consistent: the dish the chef cooked for you a decade ago tastes the same today, even though the restaurant itself has moved twice. Service and presentations are understated. Not entirely casual, although it's easy to mistake such unrelieved Frenchness for formality.

CuciNA MeD

Zone 12   North Shore
4250 LA Highway 22, Mandeville
(504) 626-8551

	Middle Eastern
	★★★
	Expensive
	Quality 79 Value C

Reservations:	Accepted
When to go:	Anytime
Entree range:	$8–16
Payment:	All major credit cards
Service rating:	★★
Friendliness rating:	★★★
Parking:	Free lot adjacent
Bar:	Full bar
Wine selection:	Decent list, good international balance
Dress:	Casual
Disabled access:	Full
Customers:	Locals
Lunch:	Every day, 11:30 A.M.–2:30 P.M.
Dinner:	Every day, 6–10 P.M.

Atmosphere / setting: The restaurant is on the small side, but comfortable. The semi-open kitchen is the center of attention.

Recommended dishes: Stuffed grape leaves; hummus; scallop shish kebab; eggplant and peppers with yogurt and garlic sauce; salad of tomato, cucumber, mint, and feta cheese; shrimp pesto with black olives; rack of lamb with potato cake; grilled salmon with walnut sauce; Middle Eastern mixed grill; islim kebab (braised lamb covered with eggplant, tomato, and peppers).

Summary & comments: Turkish cuisine, from which the cooking styles of most of the Middle East and Northern Africa descended, is served here with some claim to authenticity: the owners are Turkish. The chef, however, is an old New Orleans hand, and he turns out decent grilled fish and meat dishes and Italian food of note.

121

Dakota

Zone 12 North Shore	Nouvelle Creole
629 North US 190, Covington	★★★★★
(504) 892-3712	Expensive
	Quality 94 Value C

Reservations:	Recommended
When to go:	Weeknights
Entree range:	$13–24
Payment:	AMEX, MC, V
Service rating:	★★★★★
Friendliness rating:	★★★★
Parking:	Free lot adjacent
Bar:	Full bar
Wine selection:	Distinguished cellar, with emphasis on California; the owner is a wine buff who travels around looking for discoveries
Dress:	Jacket recommended but not required
Disabled access:	Full
Customers:	Locals, couples, gourmets
Brunch:	Sunday, 11 A.M.–3 P.M.
Lunch:	Monday–Friday, 11:30 A.M.–2:30 P.M.
Dinner:	Monday–Saturday, 6–10 P.M.

Atmosphere / setting: Dakota's two major dining rooms are furnished and decorated with uncommon attention to detail; even the way the silverware is set is distinctive. It appears from the outside to be affiliated with the motel next door; it's not.

Recommended dishes: Sweet potato nachos with lamb and Roquefort; smoked shrimp and Brie polenta cake; sea scallops with cayenne caviar; grilled rabbit tenderloin; smoked chicken gumbo; fish with smoked artichoke and roasted bell pepper butter with rock shrimp; stuffed soft-shell crab; honey and rosemary roasted chicken; cane-syrup-glazed smoked pork tenderloin with bourbon barbecue butter; mixed grill; rack of lamb. Bread pudding; dessert pastries.

Summary & comments: Dakota is rivaled only by La Provence for the honor of Best Place to Eat on the North Shore. The chef, despite his origins on the Great Plains (hence the name), cooks Creole food in its most intensely flavorful forms, and shows no shyness about using salt, pepper, cream, butter, smoke, or anything else that might make your palate say howdy. You may also taste some flavors from exotic lands in some of the dishes here. Good daily specials and a great Sunday brunch menu. Service is attentive to an almost absurd degree. The wine list is riddled with offbeat bottles, all priced reasonably. Loaded with originality and polish.

Delmonico

Zone 3   Uptown Below Napoleon
1300 St. Charles Avenue
525-4937

	Creole
	★★★
	Expensive
	Quality 82 Value B

Reservations:	Recommended
When to go:	Anytime
Entree range:	$11–20
Payment:	All major credit cards
Service rating:	★★★
Friendliness rating:	★★★★
Parking:	Free lot adjacent
Bar:	Full bar
Wine selection:	Limited list of ordinary wines
Dress:	Jacket recommended but not required
Disabled access:	None
Customers:	Mix of locals and tourists; oldish crowd; businessmen at lunch
Lunch / Dinner:	Every day, 11 A.M.–9 P.M.

Atmosphere / setting: Just turned 100 years old, Delmonico has an honest antique charm. The dining rooms, dominated by a fascinating mural of a river scene, are less formal than the exterior might suggest.

Recommended dishes: Shrimp rémoulade; oysters three ways; turtle soup; seafood gumbo; house salad; trout amandine; soft-shell crab meunière; stuffed shrimp; broiled fish with seafood stuffing; broiled chicken Delmonico. Caramel custard; bread pudding.

Summary & comments: Delmonico is a holdover from another era of dining, and it serves a style of Creole cooking rarely seen anymore. The food is a notch above that served in the better neighborhood places. The specialty is seafood, prepared in all the time-honored Creole ways. Lunches are very inexpensive and have a home-cooking aspect. At dinner, the five-course table d'hôte menu is the way to go. Good soups and salads; less interesting desserts and wine list.

Dooky Chase

Zone 6   Mid-City / Gentilly
2301 Orleans Avenue
821-0600

	Creole
	★★★
	Moderate
	Quality 78 Value B

Reservations:	Accepted
When to go:	Anytime; Friday lunch can be very busy
Entree range:	$8–14
Payment:	All major credit cards except Discover
Service rating:	★★
Friendliness rating:	★★★
Parking:	Free lot adjacent
Bar:	Full bar
Wine selection:	A few house wines
Dress:	Casual
Disabled access:	None
Customers:	Mostly locals, a few tourists; leaders of the African-American community
Lunch / Dinner:	Every day, 11 A.M.–11 P.M.

Atmosphere / setting: The dining room features several original stained-glass panels that show vignettes of African-American life in New Orleans. The entire place is comfortable and sparkling.

Recommended dishes: Shrimp Dooky; Creole gumbo; shrimp Clemenceau; stuffed shrimp; fried seafood platter; crawfish etouffee; veal grillades with jambalaya; breast of chicken a la Dooky (stuffed with oysters; marchand de vin sauce); fried chicken; red beans and rice.

Summary & comments: A social center of the African-American community for decades, Dooky's cooks up definitive versions of the kind of Creole cooking that the best local cooks used to do for their families when everybody ate at home. (A lot of the food here tastes just like my mom's.) Some of the dishes are a tad on the fancy side; others are all-but-forgotten Creole relics. All of it's at least pretty good. At lunchtime, they do a buffet of the basics. At dinner, you can order (in advance) a Creole feast that brings all the specialties and then some. The presence of security makes this less dangerous than some suburbanites might imagine.

Doug's

Zone 12   North Shore
348 Robert Road, Slidell
(504) 649-1805

Creole
★★★★
Moderate
Quality 83   Value B

Reservations:	Recommended
When to go:	Anytime
Entree range:	$11–19
Payment:	All major credit cards
Service rating:	★★★
Friendliness rating:	★★★
Parking:	Free lot adjacent
Bar:	Full bar
Wine selection:	Limited list of ordinary wines
Dress:	Casual
Disabled access:	Limited
Customers:	Locals, couples
Lunch:	Tuesday–Friday, 11 A.M.–2 P.M.
Dinner:	Tuesday–Saturday, 6–10 P.M.;
	Sunday and Monday, closed.

Atmosphere / setting: The main dining room has a bright gardenish look; other parts are on the darkish side.

Recommended dishes: Oysters Louisiane (artichokes and lemon butter); shrimp rémoulade; stuffed mushrooms; turtle soup; trout with pecans; stuffed flounder; grilled chicken and andouille; tournedos with sauce du jour; smoked baby-back ribs; pannéed veal with fettuccine. French silk chocolate pie; bread pudding with whiskey sauce.

Summary & comments: The most ambitious restaurant in Slidell is owned by a former longtime chef from Commander's Palace, Floyd Bealer. Here he puts out only slightly toned down (and much less expensive) versions of the kind of food Commander's was doing ten years ago. Which is to say distinctly Creole, original and fresh, but free of Southwestern, Chinese, and other fusion-cuisine elements. Seasonings and sauces are full-flavored and satisfying, and the presence of a large smokehouse next door has brought a number of interesting smoked dishes to the menu.

Doug's Place

Zone 2   Central Business District
748 Camp
527-5433

Steak
★★★
Moderate
Quality 80   Value C

Reservations:	Accepted
When to go:	Dinner; good scene here on gallery opening nights
Entree range:	$10–24
Payment:	All major credit cards except Discover
Service rating:	★★★
Friendliness rating:	★★★
Parking:	Lunch: curbside (metered); dinner: free lot adjacent
Bar:	Full bar
Wine selection:	Limited list of ordinary wines
Dress:	Casual
Disabled access:	Full
Customers:	Businessmen at lunch; the art crowd on gallery opening nights
Lunch:	Monday–Friday, 11:30 A.M.–3 P.M.
Dinner:	Monday–Saturday, 5:30–10:30 P.M., later on gallery opening nights; Sunday, closed.

Atmosphere / setting: The premises, located near the Warehouse District's art galleries, was for decades the recording studio where nearly every New Orleans musician from Fats Domino on laid down tracks. Aside from the memorabilia from that era, a large collection of striking folk art is on display here. The long dining room is unusually spacious, with seating in every known format.

Recommended dishes: Caesar salad; filet mignon with bordelaise sauce; double T-bone steak; hamburger; grilled salmon or tuna; grilled chicken with Marsala sauce. Cheesecake.

Summary & comments: In the middle of the long dining room is an open grill. The original specialty was first-class beefsteak sold at bargain prices; since then, chicken and fish have been added, along with a handful of other items, none of it complex but all of it pretty good.

DRAGO'S

Zone 10	Metairie Above Causeway / Kenner / Jefferson Hwy.

3232 North Arnoult Road, Metairie
888-9254

Seafood

★★★★

Moderate

Quality 85   Value C

Reservations:	Accepted
When to go:	Anytime
Entree range:	$7–16
Payment:	All major credit cards
Service rating:	★★
Friendliness rating:	★★★
Parking:	Free lot, sometimes full at lunch
Bar:	Full bar
Wine selection:	A few house wines, including a few from Croatia
Dress:	Casual
Disabled access:	Full
Customers:	Locals, families
Lunch:	Monday–Saturday, 11:30 A.M.–2:30 P.M.
Dinner:	Monday–Saturday, 5–10 P.M.; Sunday, closed.

Atmosphere / setting: Except for the flea-market art on the walls, this is a much more handsome dining room than is found in typical seafood houses.

Recommended dishes: Raw oysters; char-grilled oysters; seafood gumbo; shrimp Ruth (sautéed with herbs over fresh tomatoes); shrimp fondue; salad with feta vinaigrette; garlic-pepper shrimp; drumfish Tommy (grilled and stuffed); fried or broiled seafood platter (great tartar sauce); boiled lobster. Lunch specials.

Summary & comments: A step up from the average casual seafood restaurant, Drago's has unusually excellent oysters, which show in its raw bar and its original char-broiled oysters (grilled in the shell, basted with garlic-herb butter). Almost everything else in the way of local seafood is available here, usually in some interesting, garlic-laced preparation. For about $30 per person, there's an unending seafood feast of the best specialties. The service can bog down at times.

DUNBAR'S

Creole / Neighborhood Cafe
★★
Inexpensive

Quality 70   Value A

Zone 4   Uptown Above Napoleon
4927 Freret
899-0734

Reservations:	Not accepted
When to go:	Anytime
Entree range:	$4–7
Payment:	No credit cards
Service rating:	★★
Friendliness rating:	★★★
Parking:	Curbside
Bar:	None
Wine selection:	None
Dress:	Casual
Disabled access:	Limited
Customers:	Neighborhood people
Open:	Monday–Saturday, 7 A.M.–9 P.M.; Sunday, closed.

Atmosphere / setting: Dunbar's is a revival of the great old soul food restaurants of the Sixties, but the premises are more agreeable. Lots of church-related wall hangings.

Recommended dishes: Red beans and rice; fried fish; gumbo. Daily specials.

Summary & comments: Red beans and rice with fried chicken is served at the astonishing price of $3.95 for an all-you-can-eat portion. Most of the rest of the menu is similarly cheap. Don't expect that everything will be cooked to order; the chicken, for example, may be merely warm instead of hot and crisp.

Eddie's

Zone 6   Mid-City / Gentilly
2119 Law
945-2207

	Creole / Neighborhood Cafe
	★★★
	Inexpensive
	Quality 73 Value A

Reservations:	Not accepted
When to go:	Anytime
Entree range:	$5–11
Payment:	AMEX, MC, V
Service rating:	★★
Friendliness rating:	★★★
Parking:	Curbside
Bar:	Beer and wine
Wine selection:	A few house wines
Dress:	Anything goes
Disabled access:	Limited
Customers:	Neighborhood people
Lunch / Dinner:	Monday–Saturday, 11 A.M.–10 P.M.; Sunday, closed.

Atmosphere / setting: Somewhat difficult to find (even getting to Law Street is a challenge), Eddie's is everyone's image of a soul food restaurant: worn out and old, but warm and friendly.

Recommended dishes: Creole gumbo; fried seafood platters; red beans and rice with hot sausage; hot sausage poor boy; stuffed crab poor boy; fried chicken. Bread pudding.

Summary & comments: Eddie's is rightly famous for serving terrific versions of fried and pot food at very low prices. They've become notorious in recent years for the buffets, but the better food is ordered from the menu. More care in the preparation of things is taken than you might imagine; the late Eddie Baquet was something of a doctrinaire, and his progeny keep the flame alive. (They also opened a more accessible, presentable restaurant, Zachary's.)

El Patio

Zone 10   Metairie Above Causeway /
           Kenner / Jefferson Hwy.
3244 Georgia Avenue, Kenner
443-1188

Mexican
★★★★
Moderate

Quality 83   Value C

Reservations:	Not accepted
When to go:	Weeknights
Entree range:	$7–16
Payment:	AMEX, MC, V
Service rating:	★★★
Friendliness rating:	★★★★
Parking:	Free lot adjacent
Bar:	Full bar
Wine selection:	A few house wines, mostly Spanish
Dress:	Casual
Disabled access:	Full
Customers:	Locals, families, couples
Dinner:	Monday–Saturday, 5–10 P.M.; Sunday, closed.

Atmosphere / setting: Two rooms: one a small, T-shaped, ceramic-tiled dining room, the other an auditorium-like space with a stage and a bar.

Recommended dishes: Ceviche; nachos; croquettes; black bean soup; avocado and tortilla soup; chicken with mole sauce; cheese enchiladas with mole sauce; red snapper Veracruz style; squid stuffed with crabmeat in cream sauce; arroz con calamares; paella. Flan; bananas al fuego.

Entertainment & amenities: Strolling guitarist / singer nightly.

Summary & comments: Jorge Rodriguez and his family run this attractive cafe, whose dining room is usually full to bursting. The menu is substantially more ambitious than that of any other local Mexican place—they make mole sauce, paella, and arroz con calamares, for example—but they do the standard combo platters well, too. The consistency record is not perfect, but in its specialties the kitchen shines.

Emeril's

		Nouvelle Creole
Zone 2 Central Business District		★★★★★
800 Tchoupitoulas		Very Expensive
528-9393		
		Quality 98 Value C

Reservations:	Required
When to go:	Lunch and early evenings
Entree range:	$16–26
Payment:	All major credit cards
Service rating:	★★★★
Friendliness rating:	★★
Parking:	Valet (free)
Bar:	Full bar
Wine selection:	Distinguished cellar, with emphasis on California; lots of well-known but rarely seen bottles; many by-the-glass selections
Dress:	Dressy casual
Disabled access:	Full
Customers:	Mix of tourists and locals; hip, gourmet crowd
Lunch:	Monday–Friday, 11:30 A.M.–2:30 P.M.
Dinner:	Monday–Saturday, 6–10 P.M.; Sunday, closed.

Atmosphere / setting: The main room is in an old, interestingly renovated factory; it is noisy to incredibly noisy. At one end, on the other side of the stoves where they cook the a la minute items, is the food bar; this is a great place for the single gourmet.

Recommended dishes: Specials here are often the most interesting possibilities. Current regular items: barbecue shrimp; parfait (a salad, really) of shrimp rémoulade; smoked trout dumplings; gumbo of the day; andouille-crusted redfish; pannéed quail; "a study of duck" (breast, foie gras, leg confit, mushroom bread pudding); filet of beef with blue cheese; double-cut pork chop with green chile mole. Banana cream pie; chocolate pecan pie; chocolate Grand Marnier soufflé. Cheeses.

Summary & comments: After establishing himself at Commander's Palace for almost a decade, Emeril Lagasse opened his own dining room and kitchen five years ago. Ever since, he's presided over the dining scene as its leading innovator. Emeril's menu is grounded in Louisiana flavors, gaining distinction by concentrating hard on ingredients. Many of the meats, vegetables, and seafoods are raised especially for the restaurant; sauces and condiments that most restaurants would buy already prepared are made on the premises. The result is a palette of very big flavors in unimpeachably fine foodstuffs. The wine list is fantastic. Prices and smugness levels climb in step with the chef's fame.

Feelings

Zone 5 Downtown / St. Bernard	Creole
2600 Chartres Street	★★★
945-2222	Moderate
	Quality 86 Value B

Reservations:	Recommended
When to go:	Anytime
Entree range:	$10–16
Payment:	AMEX, MC, V
Service rating:	★★★
Friendliness rating:	★★★
Parking:	Curbside
Bar:	Full bar
Wine selection:	Limited list of ordinary wines
Dress:	Casual
Disabled access:	Limited
Customers:	Locals, mostly from the neighborhood
Brunch:	Sunday, 11 A.M.–3 P.M.
Lunch:	Friday, 11:30 A.M.–2:30 P.M.
Dinner:	Monday–Thursday, 6–10 P.M.;
	Friday and Saturday, 6–11 P.M.

Atmosphere / setting: Feelings (we all hate the name, but it's too late to do anything about it) occupies a 200-year-old building in the Marigny section, with dining rooms in the main house, the slave quarters, on the balcony, and in the covered brick courtyard.

Recommended dishes: Shrimp etouffee spread; oysters en brochette; pâté maison; house salad; red snapper moutarde; trout pecan; soft-shell crabs with avocado butter; shrimp Clemenceau (with garlic, peas, mushrooms, and potatoes); chicken Clemenceau; tournedos au poivre; veal Florentine; duck badgered (Grand Marnier sauce). Peanut butter pie; french silk (chocolate mousse) pie.

Summary & comments: Feelings' menu is rather distinctive; it's decidedly Creole, but in a somewhat precious style you won't see anywhere else. The five-course table d'hôte menu is always the way to eat here; the courses are small, but they fill every sector of your appetite. Very popular in the neighborhood, Feelings sometimes has few or no tables available immediately, but the courtyard bar is a great place to wait.

Felix's

Zone 1   French Quarter
739 Iberville
522-4440

Seafood	
★★	
Inexpensive	
Quality 69	Value C

Reservations:	Not accepted
When to go:	Anytime
Entree range:	$6–14
Payment:	AMEX, MC, V
Service rating:	★★
Friendliness rating:	★★
Parking:	Pay garage adjacent nearby
Bar:	Full bar
Wine selection:	A few house wines
Dress:	Casual
Disabled access:	Limited
Customers:	Tourists, some locals
Lunch / Dinner:	Sunday–Thursday, 11 A.M.–10 P.M.;
	Friday and Saturday, 11 A.M.–11 P.M.

Atmosphere / setting: The oldest full-menu fried seafood house in the French Quarter, Felix's is a large L-shaped restaurant that brackets the corner of Bourbon and Iberville. But the soul of it is the oyster bar, with its much-photographed sign, "Oysters R In Season."

Recommended dishes: Oysters on the half shell; oysters Rockefeller; seafood gumbo; fried seafood platters; broiled flounder.

Summary & comments: The raw oyster bar is the best part of the restaurant. At the tables, one is served—in an overbusinesslike style that recalls the Fifties—all manner of seafood platters, fried and otherwise prepared. These vary unpredictably to just okay to quite good. Oddly, some of the best food here is the most complicated—i.e., oysters Rockefeller.

Figaro Pizzerie

	Pizza
	★★★
	Moderate
	Quality 78 Value C

Zone 4   Uptown Above Napoleon
7900 Maple
866-0100

Zone 12   North Shore
2820 East Causeway Approach, Mandeville
(504) 624-8500

Reservations:	Accepted
When to go:	Anytime
Entree range:	$8–17
Payment:	All major credit cards
Service rating:	★★
Friendliness rating:	★★★
Parking:	Free lot adjacent
Bar:	Full bar
Wine selection:	Decent list, with emphasis on California and Italy; many by-the-glass selections
Dress:	Casual
Disabled access:	Full
Customers:	Locals, families
Open:	*Uptown:* Monday–Thursday, 11:30 A.M.–10:30 P.M.; Friday and Saturday, 11:30 A.M.–11:30 P.M.; Sunday, noon–10 P.M. *North Shore:* Monday–Thursday, 11:30 A.M.–2 P.M. and 5–9:30 P.M.; Friday and Saturday, 11:30 A.M.–10:30 P.M.; Sunday, 11:30 A.M.–9 P.M.

Atmosphere / setting: Both locations have both indoor and outdoor seating. A with-it family scene is obtained.

Recommended dishes: Appetizer specials. Caesar salad; mixed greens with Gorgonzola; garlic focaccia sticks with marinara sauce; stuffed Sicilian pasta shells; spaghetti and meatballs; seafood lasagna with spinach; garlic-butter pizzas, especially spinach and feta, shrimp and cilantro, smoked salmon, and quattro stagioni (four toppings in quadrants) varieties.

Summary & comments: Pizzas are prepared from scratch and baked on a conveyor-belt oven, which gives the crust an enjoyable lightness. Those made with garlic-herb butter are better than the more familiar American-style offerings. The pasta dishes are less a specialty but generally at least decent. The daily specials, in a nouvelle-Creole vein, almost seem to have come from a different restaurant.

Five Happiness

Zone 4   Uptown Above Napoleon
3605 South Carrollton
482-3935

	Chinese
	★★★
	Moderate
	Quality 78 Value C

Reservations:	Accepted
When to go:	Anytime; Saturdays and Sundays there's more dim sum
Entree range:	$6–11
Payment:	All major credit cards
Service rating:	★★
Friendliness rating:	★★★
Parking:	Free lot adjacent
Bar:	Full bar
Wine selection:	A few house wines
Dress:	Casual
Disabled access:	Full
Customers:	Locals, families
Lunch:	Every day, 11:30 A.M.–3 P.M.
Dinner:	Every day, 5–10 P.M.

Atmosphere / setting: Standard Chinese, but a bit more substantial in its design than most.

Recommended dishes: Pot stickers; shu-mai; hot and sour soup; shrimp with sizzling rice soup; savory crispy soft-shell crabs; Szechuan shrimp; chicken with sesame seeds and spicy sauce; lemon chicken; Peking duck (two hours advance notice); moo shi pork; stir-fried pork strings in hot garlic sauce; Mongolian beef.

Summary & comments: If not one of the very best Chinese restaurants in the area, the Five Happiness is unarguably well above average. Its menu is extensive and at least a little adventuresome, and the food seems to always be a touch better than the last time you ate here. They have here one of the only menus of dim sum around. And there's an emphasis on the Mandarin classics like moo shi pork. Always busy, the restaurant seems to intentionally stop short of seriously good food and service, as if these might keep you in your seat a little too long. But you could do a lot worse than to eat here.

Frankie's Cafe

	Creole
Zone 4 Uptown Above Napoleon	★★★
8132 Hampson	Moderate
866-9555	
	Quality 76 Value B

Reservations:	Accepted
When to go:	Anytime
Entree range:	$8–15
Payment:	All major credit cards except Discover
Service rating:	★★
Friendliness rating:	★★★
Parking:	Curbside (metered)
Bar:	Full bar
Wine selection:	Many by-the-glass selections
Dress:	Casual
Disabled access:	None
Customers:	Neighborhood people
Lunch:	Monday–Saturday, 11:30 A.M.–2:30 P.M.
Dinner:	Monday–Saturday, 5:30–10 P.M.; Sunday, closed.

Atmosphere / setting: A tiny, cute dining room and a claustrophobic kitchen are crammed into one room of a Riverbend cottage.

Recommended dishes: Sautéed crab fingers; turtle soup; grilled tuna salad; fettuccine Frankie (chicken or shrimp with tasso, cream sauce); pasta Milano (with scallops in a cream sauce); crawfish fajitas; catfish Carrollton (grilled with bell peppers); filet mignon; doorstop pork chop. Daily beans-and-rice specials. Roast duck (Saturdays only).

Summary & comments: In this small space they somehow turn out, at bargain prices yet, large servings of surprisingly creative cooking. Aside from pasta—which dominates the menu—there is no obvious specialty; you're as likely to have a great grilled fish as a fine pork chop, crawfish cake, or turtle soup. A lot of the food is on the rich side. Good and ever-changing daily specials. Service is something less than polished, but the British charm of Frankie Sobol tends to gloss over the glitches.

FURY'S

Zone 9   Metairie Below Causeway
724 Martin Behrman Avenue, Metairie
834-5646

Creole / Neighborhood Cafe
★★★
Moderate

Quality 76   Value C

Reservations:	Not accepted
When to go:	Anytime
Entree range:	$8–15
Payment:	All major credit cards
Service rating:	★★
Friendliness rating:	★★
Parking:	Free lot adjacent
Bar:	Full bar
Wine selection:	A few house wines
Dress:	Casual
Disabled access:	Full
Customers:	Neighborhood people
Lunch / Dinner:	Every day, 11 A.M.–10 P.M.

Atmosphere / setting: A suburban version of the New Orleans streetcorner cafe: small, clubby, and homey.

Recommended dishes: Onion rings; seafood gumbo; crabmeat au gratin; seafood platters; fried chicken; barbecue shrimp; crawfish etouffee. Bread pudding.

Summary & comments: A neighborhood seafood cafe in the old style, with all that this implies in the way of outmoded atrocities (for example, iceberg lettuce overwhelmed with dressing). These are easily ignorable, however, in view of the low prices and goodness of the basic specialties. Seafood dominates, with every imaginable combination platter, fried or broiled. But the specials are pure backstreet New Orleans cuisine, served to a clientele as regular as ever patronized a corner cafe.

G&E Courtyard Grill

Zone 1 French Quarter	Nouvelle Italian
1113 Decatur	★★★★
528-9376	Expensive
	Quality 93 Value B

Reservations:	Required
When to go:	Early evenings, Friday lunch
Entree range:	$10–21
Payment:	All major credit cards
Service rating:	★★★★
Friendliness rating:	★★★★
Parking:	French Market pay lot, one block away
Bar:	Full bar
Wine selection:	Modest list, mostly Italian and Californian; wines well-chosen for the food; many by-the-glass selections
Dress:	Dressy casual
Disabled access:	Full
Customers:	Mostly locals, a few tourists; couples; gourmets
Lunch:	Tuesday–Sunday, 11:30 A.M.–3 P.M.
Dinner:	Sunday–Thursday, 6–10 P.M.; Friday and Saturday, 6–11 P.M.

Atmosphere / setting: In an old rowhouse built by the Ursuline nuns almost two centuries ago, the G&E maintains two dining areas: a lovely parlor with an antique bar and travertine floors, and a fine little covered courtyard. The latter is in greatest demand; not only is it lush with flowers, fresh herbs, and other greenery, but the aromas from its grill and rotisserie whet the appetite.

Recommended dishes: Antipasti; mushrooms under glass; soft-shell crab roll with caviar and wasabi; fried oyster Caesar salad; oyster Rockefeller soup; turtle soup; rotisserie chicken (finished a different way every day); pasta puttanesca; pasta with Italian-style lamb sausage. Any lamb dish: rack, chops, leg o', etc. Any treatment of grilled fish. Daily specials. All desserts are daily specials, but usually pretty good.

Summary & comments: The anticipation built by the aromas in the courtyard is fulfilled in spades by the most innovative and interesting Creole-Italian cooking around. Although the chef likes to fiddle with Asian flavors here and there, the main line is the robust but fresh flavors of herbs, olive oil, and crushed red pepper. Nobody does lamb better, and anything off the rotisserie or grill (particularly thick fish steaks) will be memorable. A subtle joy.

Gabrielle

Zone 6   Mid-City / Gentilly
3201 Esplanade Avenue
948-6233

Nouvelle Creole
★★★★
Expensive

Quality 93   Value B

Reservations:	Required
When to go:	Early evenings, weeknights
Entree range:	$14–22
Payment:	All major credit cards
Service rating:	★★★★
Friendliness rating:	★★★★
Parking:	Curbside
Bar:	Full bar
Wine selection:	Modest list, mostly California; wines well-chosen for the food; many by-the-glass selections; attractive prices
Dress:	Dressy casual
Disabled access:	Limited
Customers:	Locals, couples, gourmets
Lunch:	Friday, 11:30 A.M.–2:30 P.M.
Dinner:	Tuesday–Saturday, 6–10 P.M.; Sunday and Monday, closed.

Atmosphere / setting: This minuscule restaurant is a little frantic—the triangular dining room makes movement complicated—but once you're seated things are comfortable, if a bit loud.

Recommended dishes: Menu changes weekly. Oysters Gabie (baked with artichokes and bread crumbs); sausage mixed grill; grilled rabbit tenderloin; blackened steak; blackened tuna; jerked pork chop; roasted poussin stuffed with duck sausage. Bread pudding; lemon chess pie.

Summary & comments: One of the most interesting new-style Creole bistros, Gabrielle's food is fresh and imaginative, and usually downright exciting—more so when it arrives than when you're reading about it on the menu (certainly better than the other way around). Owners chef Greg Sonnier and wife Mary run things in a highly personal but down-to-earth way. Tough to get a reservation at times; the place has lots of enthusiastic regulars, and with good reason.

GALATOIRE'S

Zone 1   French Quarter
209 Bourbon
525-2021

Creole French

★★★★

Expensive

Quality 90   Value C

Reservations:	Not accepted
When to go:	To avoid the line, go late lunch through early dinner
Entree range:	$12–24 (median: $18)
Payment:	AMEX, MC, V
Service rating:	★★★
Friendliness rating:	★★
Parking:	Pay garage nearby
Bar:	Full bar; drinks are very generously poured and modestly priced
Wine selection:	Peculiar list of French and Californian wines; very attractive prices
Dress:	Jacket and tie required at dinner and on Sunday
Disabled access:	None
Customers:	Both tourists and locals; the latter tend to be regulars who know all the other regulars
Lunch / Dinner:	Tuesday–Sunday, 11:30 A.M.–9 P.M.; Monday, closed.

Atmosphere / setting: The single long dining room, flanked on both sides by large mirrors surmounted by naked light bulbs and motionless ceiling fans, is bright, noisy, happy, and well dressed.

Recommended dishes: Shrimp rémoulade; crabmeat maison; canapé Lorenzo; oysters Rockefeller; oysters en brochette; green salad with garlic; trout meunière or amandine; grilled pompano; poached salmon or drum hollandaise; shrimp Marguery; crabmeat Yvonne; chicken Clemenceau; filet or strip steak béarnaise; lamb, veal, or pork chop. Crème caramel; crêpes maison.

Summary & comments: A truly indispensable restaurant, Galatoire's has changed more in the last five years than in the previous fifty. Although they still don't take reservations, they do now accept credit cards. And, in a shocking concession to modern modes, a fish grill was installed a few years ago. Still, the standards of simple but excellent French-Creole cooking that the founders installed here at the turn of the century remain in force. Although seafood has always been the main draw here, they cook everything deftly, to the point that every regular Galatoire's diner can recommend one or two sleeper specialties in the catalog-like menu. The old-fashioned service style includes a bit of food-slinging; try to ignore it.

Gallagher's

Zone 12   North Shore
1630 North US 190, Covington
(504) 892-1444

	Creole
	★★★
	Expensive
	Quality 86 Value C

Reservations:	Accepted
When to go:	Anytime
Entree range:	$12–20
Payment:	All major credit cards
Service rating:	★★★
Friendliness rating:	★★★
Parking:	Free lot adjacent
Bar:	Full bar
Wine selection:	Decent list, with emphasis on California
Dress:	Dressy casual
Disabled access:	Limited
Customers:	Locals, gourmets, couples
Lunch:	Monday–Friday, 11:30 A.M.–2:30 P.M.
Dinner:	Monday–Saturday, 6–10 P.M.; Sunday, closed.

Atmosphere / setting: The several small dining rooms are intimate, comfortable, and surprisingly urbane for what is still essentially a rural area.

Recommended dishes: Crab cakes; fried baby soft-shell crabs; baby-back ribs; smoked duck and andouille gumbo; charcoal-grilled tuna with smoked tomato salsa; trout Winner's Circle (topped with artichokes and lemon cream sauce); grilled quail; smoked duckling; veal St. Tammany (mushrooms and garlic); chicken Lafayette (rich sauce with tasso). Different desserts daily.

Summary & comments: A revival of the style proprietor Pat Gallagher made rather famous at two now-deceased editions of the Winner's Circle, among a few other places. The emphasis is on grilled foods, which are seasoned very nicely and cooked with excitement. The Creole basics like gumbo, seafood platters, and steaks with sauces are also prepared with verve. Now let's hope the place stays open a little longer than Pat's last few places.

Galley Seafood

Zone 9   Metairie Below Causeway
2535 Metairie Road, Metairie
832-0955

	Creole / Neighborhood Cafe
	★★★
	Moderate
	Quality 73 Value B

Reservations:	Not accepted
When to go:	Anytime
Entree range:	$6–15
Payment:	DC, MC, V
Service rating:	★★★
Friendliness rating:	★★★
Parking:	Free lot adjacent
Bar:	Beer and wine
Wine selection:	A few house wines
Dress:	Casual
Disabled access:	Full
Customers:	Neighborhood people
Lunch / Dinner:	Tuesday–Saturday, 11:30 a.m–9:30 P.M.; Sunday and Monday, closed.

Atmosphere / setting: A small, sterile dining room with an echo.

Recommended dishes: Seafood gumbo; boiled shrimp, crabs, or crawfish; fried seafood platters or sandwiches. Daily specials and soups.

Summary & comments: The proprietors are famous (justly) for the soft-shell crab poor boy at the Jazz Festival. This little place serves that year round, as well as a menu of small and large seafood platters, usually fried lightly to order. The blackboard shows off a passel of home cooking every day; the soups here are always especially good. They also boil the usual crustaceans for eating in or taking home. Very inexpensive.

GARCES

Zone 6   Mid-City / Gentilly
4200 d'Hemecourt
488-4734

Cuban
★★
Inexpensive
Quality 70   Value C

Reservations:	Not accepted
When to go:	Anytime
Entree range:	$5–11
Payment:	MC,V
Service rating:	★★
Friendliness rating:	★★
Parking:	Curbside
Bar:	Beer and wine
Wine selection:	A few house wines
Dress:	Anything goes
Disabled access:	Limited
Customers:	Neighborhood people
Lunch / Dinner:	Wednesday–Monday, 11 A.M.–10 P.M.; Tuesday, closed.

Atmosphere / setting: It started as a corner grocery serving a Latin American clientele and evolved into a fine little Cuban cafe, although it wouldn't take much for it to become a grocery again.

Recommended dishes: Black bean soup; medianoche sandwich; Cuban sandwich; empanadas; Cuban tamales. Special platters change daily; the best of them are: Ropa vieja (a shredded beef stew with rice); arroz con pollo; red beans and rice with Cuban steak. Guanabana or papaya drinks; flan.

Summary & comments: The menu starts with a half-dozen or so Cuban-style sandwiches, made much like poor boys except that they're pressed on a hot grill after being made. Other Cuban daily specials complete the offerings, all of which are inexpensive and have a home-cooked aspect. Lots of authentic Cuban drinks and desserts.

Gauthier's Market Cafe

	Eclectic
	★★★
	Expensive
	Quality 84 Value C

Zone 12   North Shore
500 North Theard, Covington
(504) 867-9911

Reservations:	Recommended
When to go:	Anytime
Entree range:	$15–20
Payment:	MC, V
Service rating:	★★★★
Friendliness rating:	★★★★
Parking:	Free lot adjacent
Bar:	Full bar
Wine selection:	Modest list, but wines well-chosen for the food
Dress:	Dressy casual
Disabled access:	Full
Customers:	Locals, couples, gourmets
Lunch:	Tuesday–Friday, 11:30 A.M.–2:30 P.M.
Dinner:	Tuesday–Saturday, 6–10 P.M.;
	Sunday and Monday, closed.

Atmosphere / setting: A very small, simple but attractive restaurant in the oldest part of Covington, Gauthier's has a certain hideout feeling.

Recommended dishes: The menu here changes almost entirely every month or so. Here's what was good at this writing: crabmeat and mango salad; garlic soup; grilled scallops; crabcakes; chicken with Thai barbecue sauce; filet mignon stuffed with boursin cheese. Pastries.

Summary & comments: Gauthier's was opened by a chef who fled New Orleans and the nouvelle-Creole restaurants he'd worked in. The style continues with food on the lighter side and full of subtleties that are at times a bit too unapparent. The appetizers are the best food here, although the drop to the entree course is not precipitous. The wine list is decent and matches the food. Service is, as it frequently is on the North Shore, a touch amateurish, but accommodating.

GAUTREAU'S

Zone 4   Uptown Above Napoleon
1728 Soniat
899-7397

Eclectic	
★★★★	
Expensive	
Quality 89	Value C

Reservations:	Recommended
When to go:	Anytime
Entree range:	$18–24
Payment:	All major credit cards
Service rating:	★★★★
Friendliness rating:	★★★★
Parking:	Valet (free)
Bar:	Full bar
Wine selection:	Modest list, but wines well-chosen for the food
Dress:	Jacket recommended but not required
Disabled access:	Limited
Customers:	Locals, couples, gourmets
Dinner:	Monday–Saturday, 6–10 P.M.; Sunday, closed.

Atmosphere / setting: The building is a former antique pharmacy, and some of the fixtures from that era remain: the pressed-tin ceiling and the wood display cabinets (now filled with wine). Smallish, but not as earsplitting as it once was.

Recommended dishes: Menu changes seasonally. Here's what was best at this writing: crisp duck confit with mustard and sage; seared sea scallops; Gorgonzola and artichoke tart; tuna carpaccio; chilled curried tomato soup; roasted grouper with braised fennel, tarragon, and crabmeat in fish broth; roasted chicken with wild mushrooms; seared beef tournedos with artichoke ragout; roasted lamb chops with truffle risotto. Crêpes with cherry fig sauce; crème brûlée.

Summary & comments: Gautreau's supplies a very loyal clientele with an exacting and highly individualistic cuisine. The menu, while not especially long, seems to have one of just about everything, whipped up in a generally nouvelle style with a light Creole influence. The best dishes tend to be the least exotic, oddly; for example, I've never had less than a wonderful filet mignon or roast chicken. Since so many of the customers are regulars, the service has a rather chummy style about it. It's often very difficult to get a table here on short notice, and there's no comfortable place to wait. It's curious that although there have been two major changes of ownership and chefs, the record of consistency is spotless.

Genghis Khan

Zone 6   Mid-City / Gentilly
4053 Tulane Avenue
482-4044

	Korean
	★★★
	Moderate
	Quality 87 Value C

Reservations:	Accepted
When to go:	Anytime
Entree range:	$8–14
Payment:	AMEX, MC, V
Service rating:	★★★
Friendliness rating:	★★★
Parking:	Curbside
Bar:	Full bar
Wine selection:	A few house wines
Dress:	Casual
Disabled access:	Limited
Customers:	Locals
Dinner:	Tuesday–Sunday, 5:30–10 P.M.; Monday, closed.

Atmosphere / setting: Looks like a standard New Orleans neighborhood restaurant, with a few extra pieces of Asian decor.

Recommended dishes: Fried mandu (dumpling); calamari tempura; kim (seaweed wafers) and rice; spinach namul; kimchee; bulgoki; whole marinated tempura-fried fish; shrimp Genghis Khan; chicken imperial; chongol hot pot (beef and shrimp in broth). Tempura banana split.

Entertainment & amenities: Live music almost every night, often performed by classical artists—of which the owner is one himself.

Summary & comments: For over two decades, classical violinist Henry Lee has operated, in a somewhat odd location, this genteel Korean restaurant. Korean food offers the same appeal that Chinese and Japanese eats do, but in its own distinctive way. Charcoal-grilled marinated beef is an essential part of the menu; so are very full-flavored, cold concoctions of leafy green vegetables. Some of the food is quite spicy. But the most popular dish here among the regulars is the whole fried fish, ample and greaseless.

Giovanni's Sausage Co.

Zone 9   Metairie Below Causeway
1325 Veterans Boulevard, Metairie
835-4558

<table>
<tr><td colspan="2" align="center">Sandwiches
★★★
Inexpensive</td></tr>
<tr><td>Quality 78</td><td>Value B</td></tr>
</table>

Reservations:	Not accepted
When to go:	Anytime
Entree range:	$4–6
Payment:	No credit cards
Service rating:	★★
Friendliness rating:	★★★★
Parking:	Free lot adjacent
Bar:	No alcohol
Wine selection:	None
Dress:	Anything goes
Disabled access:	None
Customers:	Lunchers
Open:	Monday–Saturday, 9 A.M.–6 P.M.; Sunday, closed.

Atmosphere / setting: Tiny space with a few tables and a counter crammed in.

Recommended dishes: Italian sausage and meatball poor boy; roast beef poor boy; fried shrimp or oyster (or shrimp and oyster) poor boy; muffuletta; Italian baked oyster casserole.

Summary & comments: A tiny spinoff of a very good sausage maker in Kenner, Giovanni's offers its own Louisiana and Italian sausages in its deli case. But of even greater interest are the poor boy sandwiches they make from the sausages, as well as from all the standard stuffings that go into a poor boy. Not only are the meats, cheeses, and dressing of fine quality, but they take the extra step (one that ought to be required by law) of heating the sandwich in the oven right before they give it to you. This toasts the bread and makes it smell and taste wonderful.

Golden Lake Chinese Restaurant

Chinese	
★★★	
Moderate	
Quality 76	Value B

Zone 9   Metairie Below Causeway
1712 Lake Avenue, Metairie
838-8646

Reservations:	Accepted
When to go:	Anytime
Entree range:	$6–12
Payment:	AMEX, MC, V
Service rating:	★★
Friendliness rating:	★★★
Parking:	Free lot adjacent
Bar:	Full bar
Wine selection:	A few house wines
Dress:	Casual
Disabled access:	None
Customers:	Locals, families
Lunch:	Monday–Friday, 11:30 A.M.–3 P.M.
Dinner:	Monday–Saturday, 5–10 P.M.; Sunday, closed.

Atmosphere / setting: From the outside, it looks unpromising: a standard frame house with an "open" sign in the window. Inside, however, the Golden Lake is nicely decorated and quite comfortable.

Recommended dishes: Fried dumplings; shrimp toast; spring rolls; hot and sour soup; shrimp with broccoli (better than it sounds: gigantic shrimp are heads-on and cooked dry, and the broccoli is on the side); sesame chicken; Phoenix chicken; eggplant with shrimp Szechuan style; dry-cooked string beans; moo shi pork; ma-po bean curd.

Summary & comments: A few years ago this place received the chef and cuisine of a failed—but always to my palate very good—restaurant in another part of town. The menu is a good deal different from that of most Chinese places here: there's more Mandarin and Szechuan food, and even that is offbeat within the genre. The result is one of the best inexpensive, neighborhood-style Chinese restaurants around.

GRAHAM'S

Zone 2   Central Business District
200 Magazine
524-9678

Eclectic

★ ★ ★

Very Expensive

Quality 86   Value D

Reservations:	Recommended
When to go:	Anytime
Entree range:	$11–24
Payment:	All major credit cards
Service rating:	★ ★ ★ ★
Friendliness rating:	★ ★ ★ ★
Parking:	Lunch: validated ($4) at Sheraton garage; dinner: valet ($4)
Bar:	Full bar
Wine selection:	Substantial list, good international balance; many by-the-glass selections
Dress:	Dressy casual
Disabled access:	Full
Customers:	Locals and hotel guests; gourmets; businessmen at lunch
Lunch:	Monday–Friday, 11:30 A.M.–3 P.M.
Dinner:	Monday–Saturday, 6–10 P.M.; Sunday, closed.

Atmosphere / setting: A casual-chic bistro that seems to be trying to set the record for noise, Graham's has an open kitchen, stone tabletops, tile floors, and lots of other hard surfaces. The crowd includes the well-connected, who love to dine with one another.

Recommended dishes: Menu changes every month or so, and specials are often the best choices here. Oysters Alexis (baked on mushrooms duxelles); terrine of duck livers; seared smoked tuna on crisp potato salad; lacquered duck with coffee and oranges; medallions of beef with blackberries; linguine with sweetbreads and artichokes. Crème brûlée; chocolate breathless (a hard meringue).

Summary & comments: Kevin Graham made his name during a six-year stint as executive chef of the Windsor Court Hotel. There he established a personal cuisine that worked with virtually every known cooking style in the entire world, often with very unusual ingredients. That pattern has continued now that he's opened his own place. The best food here is very good, but some of it gets strange. Just like it was at the Windsor Court.

GRECO'S

Creole / Neighborhood Cafe
★★★
Expensive

Quality 81   Value C

Zone 1   French Quarter
1000 North Peters
523-7418

Reservations:	Recommended
When to go:	Anytime
Entree range:	$9–19
Payment:	All major credit cards
Service rating:	★★★
Friendliness rating:	★★★
Parking:	French Market pay lot, one block
Bar:	Full bar
Wine selection:	Limited list of ordinary wines
Dress:	Casual
Disabled access:	Limited
Customers:	Tourists, some locals
Brunch:	Sunday, 11 A.M.–3 P.M.; menu
Lunch:	Every day, 11:30 A.M.–2:30 P.M.
Dinner:	Every day, 6–10 P.M.

Atmosphere / setting: The Red Stores was a historic part of the French Market that was torn down in the Twenties and rebuilt in the Seventies. This restaurant occupies the ground floor with a dining room that contains more marble than you'd expect. You can also grab a table in the sidewalk area near the floodwall.

Recommended dishes: Seafood beignets; shrimp rémoulade on fried green tomatoes; trio of baked oysters; mixed sausage grill; Creole gumbo; Creole tomato, smoked mozzarella, and artichoke salad; red snapper Fifi (crabmeat and anise-flavored sauce); breast of chicken Esplanade (tarragon cream sauce and portobello mushrooms); roast duck with wild rice cakes; steak au poivre with Calvados. Bread pudding; pastries.

Summary & comments: It started as a basic seafood house, but in recent years Greco's expanded its menu into the gourmet category. The food is both surprisingly creative and successful, generally in a Creole vein with some Continental polish. It would probably be even better (and certainly better known) if more locals went there, but the touristy quality of most of the French Market scares them off.

Gumbo Shop

Zone 1   French Quarter
630 St. Peter
525-1486

Creole	
★★★	
Moderate	
Quality 80	Value B

Reservations: Not accepted
When to go: Middle of the afternoon or evening
Entree range: $7–14
Payment: All major credit cards
Service rating: ★★★
Friendliness rating: ★★★
Parking: French Market pay lot, one block
Bar: Full bar
Wine selection: A few house wines
Dress: Casual
Disabled access: Limited
Customers: Tourists, some locals
Lunch/Dinner: Every day, 11 A.M.–11 P.M.

Atmosphere / setting: This best-named of all New Orleans restaurants isn't really as old as it looks, with its yellowed murals surrounding the antique dining room. But if you eat here you'll really feel as if you've dined in Old New Orleans.

Recommended dishes: Shrimp rémoulade; seafood gumbo; jambalaya; red beans and rice; crawfish pie; crawfish etouffee; redfish Florentine; blackened redfish. Pecan pie; bread pudding.

Summary & comments: If it's traditional everyday New Orleans eats you want, this is the place to get them. Gumbo and the other homestyle Creole specials are very credibly done every single day. Prices are a lot lower than they could be, given the popularity and great location of the restaurant.

HANA

Zone 4   Uptown Above Napoleon
8116 Hampson
865-1634

	Japanese
	★★★
	Moderate
Quality 82	Value C

Reservations:	Accepted
When to go:	Anytime
Entree range:	$8–13
Payment:	AMEX, MC, V
Service rating:	★★
Friendliness rating:	★★★
Parking:	Curbside (metered)
Bar:	Full bar
Wine selection:	A few house wines
Dress:	Casual
Disabled access:	None
Customers:	Neighborhood people; youngish crowd
Lunch:	Every day, 11:30 A.M.–2:30 P.M.
Dinner:	Every day, 6–10 P.M.

Atmosphere / setting: The dining room is spacious and handsome in a New Orleans way. The building is an old Creole cottage.

Recommended dishes: Gyoza; shu-mai (steamed dumplings); edamame (baked green beans); seaweed salad; sushi; sashimi; irori (skewers of various meats and seafoods, grilled at the table). Hana bento (a dinner of sushi and sashimi with many side vegetables).

Summary & comments: Hana is one of the more flagrant examples of the dichotomy that is every sushi bar: the regular customers get much better food than the average walk-in. Indeed, the chefs at Hana are capable of setting out special dinners of incomparable delicacy and beauty, as they did when they recognized me. When I came in anonymously, I got average sushi platters assembled with only routine care.

Harold's Texas Barbecue

Zone 10	Metairie Above Causeway/ Kenner/Jefferson Hwy.

3320 Houma Boulevard, Metairie
456-2832

<table>
<tr><td>Barbecue</td></tr>
<tr><td>★★</td></tr>
<tr><td>Inexpensive</td></tr>
<tr><td>Quality 67   Value C</td></tr>
</table>

Reservations:	Not accepted
When to go:	Anytime
Entree range:	$5–8
Payment:	AMEX, MC, V
Service rating:	★★
Friendliness rating:	★★
Parking:	Free lot adjacent
Bar:	Beer
Wine selection:	A few house wines
Dress:	Anything goes
Disabled access:	Limited
Customers:	Neighborhood people
Lunch/Dinner:	Monday–Thursday, 11 A.M.–10 P.M.; Friday and Saturday, 11 A.M.–11 P.M.; Sunday, closed.

Atmosphere / setting: The rough-wood-paneled dining room will make a Texan feel at home.

Recommended dishes: Beef jerky; barbecued brisket; barbecued sausage; chopped beef sandwich; baked beans; corn on the cob.

Summary & comments: Harold's is the city's oldest barbecue specialist, and as the name implies its style is that of our neighbor to the West. That means that the brisket and the sausage will be better than the chicken or the pork. All the meats are skillfully smoked, and the sauce is more than decent. Some side dishes, notably the beans and corn-on-the-cob, are exceptional.

House of Blues

	American
Zone 1 French Quarter	★★★
225 Decatur	Moderate
529-2583	Quality 81 Value C

Reservations:	Brunch only
When to go:	Lunch, and dinner when no big name is in the music room
Entree range:	$9–18
Payment:	AMEX, DS, MC, V
Service rating:	★★
Friendliness rating:	★★
Parking:	Validated (free) at adjacent garage
Bar:	Full bar
Wine selection:	Decent list, with emphasis on California
Dress:	Anything goes
Disabled access:	Limited
Customers:	Mix of tourists and locals, mostly young music fans
Brunch:	Sunday, 11 A.M.–2 P.M.
Lunch / Dinner:	Every day, 11 A.M.–11 P.M.

Atmosphere / setting: This is a mammoth old building taken over by Dan Aykroyd and his partners to create one of the first in a growing national chain of major music clubs. Big to very big acts of both local and national repute perform most nights. Food and music are segregated here; it's easier to get a table for the former.

Recommended dishes: Seafood gumbo; southwestern hummus; fried curry calamari; crawfish pizza; oyster or shrimp poor boy; smoked baby-back ribs; mahogany-roasted duck with green peppercorn sauce; honey-glazed smoked pork chop. Fried catfish dinner with greens and sweet potatoes au gratin; grilled shrimp with refried cheese grits. Crème brûlée; berry cobbler; chocolate bourbon cake.

Entertainment & amenities: Music acts (local Sunday and Monday; major acts the rest of the week) in music room nightly. Gospel acts at Sunday brunch.

Summary & comments: As with the music, some of the eats are local, some from out of town, but all are better than you might expect from a place whose main thrust is entertainment. The chef is a talented local guy who operates a real kitchen. Sunday mornings there's a brunch served to the accompaniment of live gospel singing.

IMPASTATO'S

Zone 10   Metairie Above Causeway /
           Kenner / Jefferson Hwy.
3400 16th Street, Metairie
455-1545

Italian	
★★★	
Expensive	
Quality 81	Value B

Reservations:	Recommended
When to go:	Early evenings
Entree range:	$10–20
Payment:	AMEX, MC, V
Service rating:	★★★
Friendliness rating:	★
Parking:	Free lot adjacent
Bar:	Full bar
Wine selection:	Decent list, mostly Italian
Dress:	Dressy casual
Disabled access:	Limited
Customers:	Local regulars, sports types (the Saints eat here a lot)
Dinner:	Tuesday–Saturday, 6–10 P.M.; Sunday and Monday, closed.

Atmosphere / setting: Dimly lit, intimate dining spaces tucked into miscellaneous cubbyholes. Saints souvenirs and photographs of famous customers cover the walls.

Recommended dishes: Stuffed mushrooms with crabmeat; fried calamari; oysters Norman (baked with bread crumbs and shallots, topped with a bit of cheese); crabmeat cannelloni; shrimp scampi; baked crab fingers; fettuccine Alfredo; pasta asciutta (in a light, spicy red sauce); crabmeat au gratin; veal or trout Marianna (artichokes and mushrooms); osso buco; roasted leg of lamb. Blueberry-banana pie; bananas Foster; Torroncino ice cream.

Summary & comments: Joe Impastato is one of two Italian brothers (the other one operates Sal & Judy's) who got a feel for the New Orleans palate in the kitchens of Jimmy Moran. As a result, the food here is distinctly Creole-Italian, the accent of the chef notwithstanding. But it's quite good, particularly the seafood entrees. There's one big problem here: the regular customers, of which there are many, get much and flagrantly better service and preference for available tables than you or I would. No amount of complaining will remedy this. The New Orleans Saints and other sports types hang here a lot.

India Palace

	Indian
	★★★
	Moderate
Zone 10 Metairie Above Causeway/ Kenner/Jefferson Hwy. 3322 North Turnbull, Metairie 889-2436	Quality 83 Value C

Reservations:	Accepted
When to go:	Anytime
Entree range:	$8–20
Payment:	All major credit cards
Service rating:	★★★
Friendliness rating:	★★★
Parking:	Free lot adjacent
Bar:	Full bar
Wine selection:	A few house wines
Dress:	Casual
Disabled access:	Full
Customers:	Locals
Brunch:	Sunday, 11:30 A.M.–3 P.M.; buffet with music
Lunch:	Every day, 11:30 A.M.–3 P.M.
Dinner:	Every day, 5–10 P.M.

Atmosphere / setting: The city's newest Indian restaurant is its most handsome—slick, informal, and very comfortable, with little in the way of ethnic decor.

Recommended dishes: Vegetable or chicken pakoras (fried cutlets); samosas (small pastries stuffed with meat or vegetables): tandoori chicken or prawns, roasted in charcoal-fired claypot ovens. The entire range of curries, including the very hot vindaloo curries. Saag paneer (homemade cheese in a creamed spinach sauce); lamb or chicken saagwala (sauce similar to saag paneer); yogurt-marinated lamb rack; naan (tandoor-baked bread). Cream cheese and pistachio pudding; mango sundae.

Summary & comments: If you come for lunch, you may be tempted to do the buffet, but resist this: the food is good, but is never quite as hot (either from stove or pepper) as it should be. The entire range of Indian standards is here, from the almost absurdly healthy tandoori roasts to the relatively oil-free fried foods to the curries and other stews. All are served with appropriate and first-class condiments and sauces. The staff is very helpful, if not always polished.

IRENE'S CUISINE

Zone 1   French Quarter
539 St. Philip
529-8811

Italian	
★★★★	
Moderate	
Quality 82	Value B

Reservations: Not accepted
When to go: Early evenings
Entree range: $11–19
Payment: All major credit cards except Discover
Service rating: ★★★
Friendliness rating: ★★★
Parking: Curbside
Bar: Full bar
Wine selection: Decent list, mostly Italian
Dress: Casual
Disabled access: Full
Customers: Mostly locals, a few tourists; many Quarterites
Dinner: Every day, 6–10 P.M.

Atmosphere / setting: A small, largely unadorned dining room was once the office of a paper warehouse. Borderline mysterious.

Recommended dishes: Mussels marinara; oysters Irene (baked with bacon, herbs, and Parmesan cheese); grilled shrimp and pannéed oysters with spinach; roasted chicken with rosemary, garlic, and brandy; cannelloni; veal Sorrentino (eggplant, mushrooms, prosciutto, mozzarella); roast duck with spinach and mustard; sautéed soft-shell crab and pasta; steak pizzaiola. Tiramisu; Italian ice creams.

Summary & comments: Irene DiPietro ran a few local kitchens (most notably the Brick Oven Cafe's) before opening this trattoria in the French Quarter. Although the food is quite different, the spirit of the cooking here is reminiscent of that of Mosca's: lots of roasting of simple main ingredients with generous sufficiencies of olive oil, garlic, rosemary, basil, and oregano. Although the red-sauced dishes are good here, they're in the minority and not specialties. Even though the dining room is orchestrated by former Sazerac maître d' Tommy Andrade (a co-owner), the restaurant is so small and popular that there's a certain frantic edge which, frankly, adds to the excitement of the meal.

Italian Pie

<table>
<tr><td colspan="2">Pizza</td></tr>
<tr><td colspan="2">★★</td></tr>
<tr><td colspan="2">Inexpensive</td></tr>
<tr><td>Quality 82</td><td>Value B</td></tr>
</table>

Zone 2   Central Business District
417 South Rampart
522-7552

Reservations:	Not accepted
When to go:	Anytime
Entree range:	$6–15
Payment:	AMEX, MC, V
Service rating:	★★
Friendliness rating:	★★
Parking:	Curbside (metered)
Bar:	Beer and wine
Wine selection:	A few house wines
Dress:	Anything goes
Disabled access:	Full
Customers:	Businessmen at lunch; neighborhood people at dinner
Lunch/Dinner:	Every day, 11 A.M.–11 P.M.

Atmosphere / setting: A somewhat utilitarian lunch house, with a few tables on the sidewalk.

Recommended dishes: Greek salad. Pizzas, particularly spinach and garlic pizza; artichoke, mushroom, and feta pizza; chicken pesto pizza; muffuletta pizza. Cheese calzone; spinach lasagna; manicotti; Italian special sandwich; roast beef poor boy. Tiramisu; chocolate cake.

Summary & comments: Straddling the CBD and the Poydras Plaza–City Hall area, they bring what the hurried denizens of the district have long longed for: pizza (not Domino's). It's a well-baked pie with a crust of light texture; it's topped with the ingredients currently in vogue (all those vegetarian jobs with the spinach and artichokes and feta and the like) as well as the standards. They also whip out hot, crusty poor boys with Italian accents and a plate special or two, at decent if not cheap prices.

Jade East

Zone 8   New Orleans East
7011 Read Boulevard
246-5590

Reservations:	Accepted
When to go:	Anytime
Entree range:	$8–13
Payment:	All major credit cards
Service rating:	★★
Friendliness rating:	★★
Parking:	Free lot adjacent
Bar:	Full bar
Wine selection:	A few house wines
Dress:	Casual
Disabled access:	Full
Customers:	Neighborhood people
Lunch:	Every day, 11:30 A.M.–2:30 P.M.
Dinner:	Every day, 5–10 P.M.

Atmosphere / setting: A medium-dim, typical Chinese dining room.

Recommended dishes: Shrimp toast; fried Chinese meat dumplings; shredded pork and hot cabbage soup; squirrel fish (fried fillet with bean threads); shrimp and scallops Hunan style; Szechuan chicken soong; Hunan beef; Hunan lamb; River Shiang pork; spicy bean curd with minced pork.

Summary & comments: This is one of the first local Chinese restaurants to break away from the old, boring, Cantonese-American style and serve the more complex and spicier Szechuan, Hunan, and Northern Chinese dishes. The menu has become watered down a bit over the twenty years the place has been open, but it's still an above-average restaurant, even for New Orleans East, which has quite a few good Chinese places (if little else). On Sundays, they offer a buffet, but keep your distance.

Jalapeño's

Mexican
★★★
Moderate

Quality 79   Value B

Zone 9   Metairie Below Causeway
2320 Veterans Boulevard, Metairie
837-6696

Reservations:	Accepted
When to go:	Anytime
Entree range:	$6–14
Payment:	All major credit cards
Service rating:	★★★
Friendliness rating:	★★★
Parking:	Free lot adjacent
Bar:	Full bar
Wine selection:	A few house wines
Dress:	Casual
Disabled access:	Limited
Customers:	Locals, on the young side; couples
Lunch / Dinner:	Tuesday–Saturday, 11 A.M.–10:30 P.M.; Sunday and Monday, closed.

Atmosphere / setting: The hip, breezy style of a California Mexican restaurant. The walls are covered with brilliantly executed graffiti art and neon.

Recommended dishes: Hot shrimp (stuffed with jalapeño-pepper cheese, wrapped in bacon); seafood-stuffed jalapeño peppers; tortilla (and chicken) soup; enchiladas with chili sauce; tacos al carbón; roasted pork Cuban style; chicken San Pedro (stuffed with seafood, served with chipotle pepper sauce); Cuban sandwich; fajitas. Pecan pie.

Summary & comments: The cooking is for the most part from the familiar catalog of pop-Mexican food, but there are a few specialties duplicated nowhere else around here. Some of these have a Cuban-Caribbean tilt; others are a touch on the rich side. Everything is served in mammoth portion.

Jamila's

	Tunisian
Zone 4 Uptown Above Napoleon	★★★
7806 Maple	Moderate
866-4366	Quality 83 Value A

Reservations:	Accepted
When to go:	Anytime
Entree range:	$8–16
Payment:	AMEX, MC, V
Service rating:	★★★
Friendliness rating:	★★★★
Parking:	Curbside (metered)
Bar:	Beer and wine
Wine selection:	Limited list of mostly French wines
Dress:	Casual
Disabled access:	Limited
Customers:	Locals
Lunch:	Tuesday–Sunday, 11:30 A.M.–2:30 P.M.
Dinner:	Tuesday–Sunday, 6–10 P.M.; Monday, closed.

Atmosphere / setting: A tiny cafe rather well hidden in what looks like a small office building.

Recommended dishes: Brik (shrimp or tuna baked in phyllo pastry); merguez (herbal lamb sausage); chorba (whole-wheat fish soup); soups du jour; salade Tunisienne (apples, peppers, tuna, cucumbers). Grilled fish with roasted garlic tomato sauce; stuffed calamari with shrimp and bulghur wheat; couscous royale (lamb, chicken, merguez, and vegetables). Crème brûlée; makroud (semolina cake with dates and orange blossom syrup); Turkish coffee.

Summary & comments: Jamila's serves the food of Tunisia—an interesting cuisine that blends French and Turkish flavors. The appetizers and soups tend toward the French side of the equation, with the flaky pastries of the Middle East filled with rather rich fillings. The dominant entree is couscous, steamed over the boiling broth in which the meat part of the dish is cooking. The menu covers a great deal more ground, including food familiar enough for the timid eater. This is a total family operation: Mom is the chef, Dad (who worked in numerous hotel restaurants before opening this place) runs the dining room, and the two boys are usually on hand too. A great change of pace.

JASON'S

Zone 3   Uptown Below Napoleon
3636 St. Charles Avenue
897-2598

	Eclectic
★★★★
Expensive
Quality 87   Value B

Reservations:	Recommended
When to go:	Anytime except Wednesday nights, when the place becomes a bar dispensing three-for-one drinks—a long local tradition
Entree range:	$10–22
Payment:	All major credit cards
Service rating:	★★★
Friendliness rating:	★★★★
Parking:	Valet (free)
Bar:	Full bar
Wine selection:	Substantial list, good international balance; many Australian and New Zealand wines; many by-the-glass selections
Dress:	Casual
Disabled access:	Limited
Customers:	Locals, couples, gourmets; doctors and others from the nearby hospitals
Brunch:	Sunday, 10 A.M.–3:30 P.M.
Lunch/Dinner:	Every day, 11 A.M.–11 P.M.

Atmosphere / setting: The unique L-shaped dining room feels like a patio, with windows that remain open in all but the most inclement weather. More than a little element of the bar that this place was for years remains.

Recommended dishes: Grilled portobello mushrooms; crab cake; white-bean and roasted garlic soup; roasted red bell pepper and beet salad; Caesar salad; citrus-horseradish escolar; seared salmon; pan-roasted red snapper; cornmeal-fried catfish with black-eyed peas; five-spice filet mignon; orange crème brûlée; hazelnut-chocolate sin cake; Cuervo-lime pie with coconut.

Summary & comments: The old Que Sera—more of a bar and hangout than a restaurant—changed its name (but not owners) in 1995 and became a good cafe. The two chefs (so far) took their own highly personal directions with the menu, making for some adventuresome—if inconsistent—fare. At its best, this place has served some wonderful dinners. Beware of Wednesday nights, when the bar aspect takes over again with a three-for-one drink offer and a mob.

Jerusalem

Zone 6   Mid–City / Gentilly
4641 South Carrollton Avenue
488-1450

Middle Eastern
★ ★ ★
Inexpensive
Quality 75   Value A

Reservations:	Not accepted
When to go:	Anytime
Entree range:	$4–7
Payment:	No credit cards
Service rating:	★
Friendliness rating:	★ ★
Parking:	Curbside
Bar:	No alcohol
Wine selection:	None
Dress:	Anything goes
Disabled access:	Limited
Customers:	Locals
Lunch:	Monday–Friday, 11:30 A.M.–4 P.M.; Saturday and Sunday, closed.

Atmosphere / setting: This corner cafe started out as a Palestinian grocery store with a lunch counter, but food service took over. Maps on the wall show how the partition of Israel should look from the Palestinian perspective.

Recommended dishes: Hummus; baba gannoujh; tabbouleh salad; fried kibbeh; falafel; beef shawarma; kafta kebab. Baklava.

Summary & comments: This inconspicuous place serves some of the best Middle Eastern eats around. These are for the most part the sandwiches and appetizers you've had in the Greek and Lebanese restaurants around town, with even less formality and a touch more pepper.

Joey K's

Zone 3   Uptown Below Napoleon
3001 Magazine
891-0997

Creole / Neighborhood Cafe
★★
Inexpensive
Quality 72   Value B

Reservations: Not accepted
When to go: Anytime
Entree range: $7–11
Payment: AMEX, MC, V
Service rating: ★★
Friendliness rating: ★★★
Parking: Curbside (metered)
Bar: Beer and wine
Wine selection: A few house wines
Dress: Anything goes
Disabled access: Limited
Customers: Locals
Breakfast: Saturday, 8–11 A.M.
Lunch / Dinner: Monday–Saturday, 11:30 A.M.–10 P.M.;
                      Sunday, closed.

Atmosphere / setting: An only slightly self-conscious neighborhood joint on an Irish Channel corner. The kind of place you'd expect cops to have lunch in.

Recommended dishes: Onion rings; shrimp rémoulade; vegetable soup; tuna salad; roast beef poor boy; chicken-fried steak poor boy; shrimp Magazine (artichoke hearts, ham, green onions on pasta); fried seafood platters. Daily plate specials. Carrot cake; pies.

Summary & comments: Joey K's serves the daily specials such places are supposed to have: red beans, brisket, liver and onions, and (of course) meatloaf. All these come with a starch (what an unappetizing word) and good old New Orleans overcooked vegetables. There's tremendous variation in quality from special to special, but the stuff is so cheap that one can't complain much. The all-you-can-eat catfish is a draw, although not for me.

Johnny's Po-Boys

Zone 1   French Quarter
511 St. Louis
524-8129

	Sandwiches
	★★
	Inexpensive
	Quality 73 Value A

Reservations:	Not accepted
When to go:	Anytime
Entree range:	$4–6
Payment:	No credit cards
Service rating:	★
Friendliness rating:	★★★
Parking:	Jackson Brewery pay lot, one block away
Bar:	No alcohol
Wine selection:	None
Dress:	Anything goes
Disabled access:	Full
Customers:	Locals
Breakfast/Lunch:	Every day, 8 A.M.–4 P.M.

Atmosphere/setting: Not much in the way of a dining room; most of the business looks to be take-out for Quarterites.

Recommended dishes: Roast beef poor boy; broiled ham and cheese poor boy; fried seafood poor boys; muffuletta.

Summary & comments: Without doubt the best poor boy stand in the Quarter and one of the best in town. Johnny's menu (painted on a board on the back wall) starts with a terrific roast beef (freshly cooked and juicy, with a classic poor boy gravy) and ends with things like salami and liver cheese that hardly anybody puts on a poor boy anymore.

K-Paul's Louisiana Kitchen

Zone 1   French Quarter
416 Chartres
524-7394

Nouvelle Cajun	
★★★★	
Very Expensive	
Quality 91	Value D

Reservations:	Not accepted downstairs; required upstairs
When to go:	Lunch, and during slack tourist and convention periods
Entree range:	$22–30
Payment:	AMEX
Service rating:	★★
Friendliness rating:	★★
Parking:	Jackson Brewery pay lot, one block
Bar:	Very limited bar
Wine selection:	Believe it or not, just one wine (it varies) downstairs; a little more variety upstairs
Dress:	Casual
Disabled access:	Full
Customers:	Mostly tourists, a few locals; gourmets
Lunch:	Monday–Saturday, 11:30 A.M.–2:30 P.M.
Dinner:	Monday–Saturday, 6–10 P.M.; Sunday, closed.

Atmosphere / setting: In the hypercasual downstairs dining room, small parties share tables with other small parties, and amenities are minimal. The new upstairs dining room offers everything local diners had been complaining about the lack of: tablecloths, private tables, and even reservations.

Recommended dishes: Stuffed, smoked soft-shell crawfish; chicken andouille gumbo; Cajun popcorn with sherry sauce; shrimp or crawfish etouffee; stuffed soft-shell crab Choron; blackened tuna; fried mirliton and oysters with tasso hollandaise; roast duck with pecan gravy; pan-fried veal with roasted stuffed peppers; blackened beef tenders in debris sauce. Sweet potato-pecan pie; bread pudding with lemon sauce; chocolate mocha cake.

Summary & comments: Chef Paul Prudhomme's fame as the archetypal Cajun chef allowed his restaurant to make the point that you need him more than he needs you for years. But K-Paul's has become much friendlier: it's open for lunch and on Saturdays now, which shortened the lines. And in the new upstairs dining room, he plans an entire formal dinner for you. Either way, you get the unique cooking of Chef Paul, with his consistently impressive ability to make the first-class ingredients they buy here explode with flavor—not all of which is Cajun. Also still in place: some of the town's highest prices.

KATIE'S

Zone 6   Mid-City / Gentilly
3701 Iberville
488-6582

Creole / Neighborhood Cafe
★★★
Inexpensive

Quality 80   Value B

Reservations:	Not accepted
When to go:	Anytime
Entree range:	$4–11
Payment:	AMEX, MC, V
Service rating:	★★
Friendliness rating:	★★★
Parking:	Curbside
Bar:	Full bar
Wine selection:	A few house wines
Dress:	Anything goes
Disabled access:	Full
Customers:	Neighborhood people
Lunch:	Monday, 11 A.M.–3 P.M.
Lunch / Dinner:	Tuesday–Saturday, 11 A.M.–10 P.M.; Sunday, closed.

Atmosphere / setting: The layout is a classic neighborhood joint: two big rooms, one with a bar and a jukebox, the other with a window through which the kitchen passes its work to the waitresses.

Recommended dishes: Onion rings; eggplant fingers; stuffed artichoke; roast beef poor boy; fried seafood poor boys; fried seafood platters; fried chicken; grilled liver and onions with mashed potatoes. Daily specials, especially red beans and rice on Monday. Bread pudding.

Summary & comments: In Mid-City, where there are more good old-style neighborhood restaurants than anywhere else in town, Katie's is one of the best. They not only excel at all the classics of local streetcorner cuisine (poor boys, red beans, seafood platters, etc.) but also get ambitious at times with the daily specials. The raw foodstuffs are of far greater intrinsic interest than in most such places.

Kelsey's

Zone 3   Uptown Below Napoleon
3923 Magazine
897-6722

	Nouvelle Creole
	★★★
	Moderate
	Quality 82 Value B

Reservations:	Recommended
When to go:	Anytime
Entree range:	$9–18
Payment:	All major credit cards
Service rating:	★★
Friendliness rating:	★★★
Parking:	Free lot adjacent
Bar:	Full bar
Wine selection:	Limited list of ordinary wines
Dress:	Casual
Disabled access:	None
Customers:	Neighborhood people; younger couples
Lunch:	Tuesday–Friday, 11:30 A.M.–2 P.M.
Dinner:	Tuesday–Saturday, 5–10 P.M.;
	Sunday and Monday, closed.

Atmosphere / setting: An old corner store converted—but not too deeply—into a high-ceilinged, long dining room with an antique barroom.

Recommended dishes: Eggplant delight (fried, topped with spicy shrimp); shrimp Bombay pie; rabbit tenderloin; Creole gumbo; eggplant Kelsey (stuffed with seafood and herbs); grilled fish; barbecue drum; blackened ribeye; pannéed rabbit with pasta; braised pork T-bone with apple butter. Chocolate hazelnut torte; orange poppyseed cheesecake; bread pudding.

Summary & comments: Chef Randy Barlow is a product of the new, upscale Creole-Cajun style of the early Eighties. He established his version of it in this cafe, one of the best places to eat on the West Bank. Flavors are very big, thanks to the profligate use of cream, intense seasoning blends, aromatic vegetables, and tasso—not to mention fresh seafood and vegetables. The flavors, epitomized by the eggplant with seafood in cream sauce, can get a little repetitive if you don't order carefully, but there's a lot of variety here. Desserts are a little dull. The service staff is never quite up to busy days.

Kim Son

Zone 11   West Bank
349 Whitney Avenue, Gretna
366-2489

	Vietnamese
	★★★★
	Moderate
	Quality 87 Value A

Reservations:	Accepted
When to go:	Anytime
Entree range:	$6–11
Payment:	AMEX, MC, V
Service rating:	★★
Friendliness rating:	★★★★
Parking:	Free lot adjacent
Bar:	Full bar
Wine selection:	Limited list of ordinary wines
Dress:	Casual
Disabled access:	Limited
Customers:	Locals, gourmets
Lunch:	Monday–Saturday, 11:30 A.M.–2:30 P.M.
Dinner:	Every day, 5–10 P.M.

Atmosphere / setting: A long, heavily windowed room with subtle but typical Asian decor, and a tank full of large, weird fish.

Recommended dishes: Imperial roll; spring roll; shrimp toast; Vietnamese hot and sour fish soup; charcoal-broiled beef over cold noodles; salt-baked crab; salt-baked scallops; fish cooked in clay pot; steamed whole fish with ginger and onion; shrimp (or chicken) with curry and coconut in clay pot; leaf-bound beef; beef fondued in boiled vinegar; beef on iron plate; gluten puffball (a sort of dumpling) in black bean sauce; eggplant and bean cake in clay pot.

Summary & comments: The oldest, best, and most accessible Vietnamese restaurant in the area; Kim Son's markedly underpriced menu is riddled with exciting food. The Vietnamese cuisine has a lot of the rapid wok cooking of China, but is distinctive in its very heavy use of fresh herbs—to the point that some dishes are borderline salads. The best way to do this place is to come with six to eight people, both to raise the adventure level and to get samples of all of Kim Son's specialties. These include charcoal-grilled, claypot, salt-baked, and noodle dishes along with the more familiar stir-fried jobs. Here is also the longest list of vegetarian dishes in town. The staff is very friendly and unhesitant about either explaining or serving the restaurant's more unusual creations.

Kosher Kajun Deli

Zone 10 Metairie Above Causeway / Kenner / Jefferson Hwy. 3520 North Hullen, Metairie 888-2010	Deli ★★ Inexpensive Quality 80 Value B

Reservations:	Not accepted
When to go:	Anytime except right before and during Jewish holy days
Entree range:	$4–6
Payment:	AMEX, MC, V
Service rating:	★★
Friendliness rating:	★★★★
Parking:	Free lot adjacent
Bar:	Beer and wine
Wine selection:	A few house wines, but these are strictly kosher wines from Israel and elsewhere
Dress:	Anything goes
Disabled access:	Full
Customers:	Orthodox Jews, neighborhood people
Lunch:	Sunday–Friday, 10 A.M.–6 P.M.; Saturday, closed.

Atmosphere / setting: A few tables scattered among the shelves of groceries.

Recommended dishes: Chopped liver; lox and bagel; matzo-ball soup; cole slaw; kugel; knishes; pastrami sandwich on rye; corned beef sandwich on pumpernickel; roast beef on onion roll; hot dog with sauerkraut. Pareve cheesecake; strudel; Dr. Brown's sodas.

Summary & comments: Unique in the New Orleans area, the Kosher Kajun is kosher in the strictest sense of the word. They will not serve you a pastrami-and-cheese sandwich or anything else in violation of Jewish dietary laws. What you will find is the most beautiful corned beef, roast beef, turkey, pumpernickel, rye, and pickles imaginable, all brought in from unimpeachable sources in New York and Chicago, served in very generous sandwiches. They also have delicious chopped liver, knishes, and all the rest of it, for eating on the premises or taking home. The place is also a fully-stocked store of kosher groceries, including wines and glatt meats.

Kung's Dynasty

Zone 3   Uptown Below Napoleon
1912 St. Charles Avenue
525-6669

Chinese	
★★★	
Moderate	
Quality 82	Value C

Reservations:	Accepted
When to go:	Anytime
Entree range:	$6–17
Payment:	AMEX, MC, V
Service rating:	★★★
Friendliness rating:	★★★
Parking:	Curbside
Bar:	Full bar
Wine selection:	A few house wines
Dress:	Casual
Disabled access:	None
Customers:	Mostly locals, a few tourists
Lunch:	Every day, 11:30 A.M.–2:30 P.M.
Dinner:	Every day, 6–10 P.M.

Atmosphere / setting: The building is decidedly un-Chinese: a fine old Uptown mansion, with big windows giving out onto St. Charles Avenue.

Recommended dishes: Diced boneless squab packages (in lettuce); Peking duck appetizer; crabmeat fried won ton; ruby and crystal shrimp (shrimp in two different sauces); soft-shell crab with ginger and garlic; oysters Szechuan-style; Kung's chicken (plum sauce; crispy); imperial beef in spicy orange sauce; lemon chicken; pork Hunan-style. Honey banana; almond bean curd.

Summary & comments: The food is on the ambitious side, employing very fine ingredients (especially in the seafood department) in well-made, refined sauces. The main style is Hunan, with its thick, translucent, subtly spicy-sweet sauces. Portions would be considered enormous even in places serving dishes of much lesser quality. Service is ordinary.

L'Economie

Zone 2　　Central Business District
325 Girod
524-7405

<table>
<tr><td colspan="2">Nouvelle French</td></tr>
<tr><td colspan="2">★★★</td></tr>
<tr><td colspan="2">Expensive</td></tr>
<tr><td>Quality 80</td><td>Value C</td></tr>
</table>

Reservations:	Recommended
When to go:	Anytime
Entree range:	$12–20
Payment:	All major credit cards
Service rating:	★★★
Friendliness rating:	★★★
Parking:	Lunch: curbside (metered); dinner: free lot adjacent
Bar:	Full bar
Wine selection:	Modest list, but wines well-chosen for the food
Dress:	Casual
Disabled access:	Full
Customers:	Businessmen at lunch; couples and gourmets at dinner
Lunch:	Monday–Friday, 11:30 A.M.–2:30 P.M.
Dinner:	Monday–Saturday, 6–10 P.M.; Sunday, closed.

Atmosphere / setting:　The battered sign painted on the side of this old Warehouse District building tells of "The Economy," a deceased workingman's lunchroom. The premises have not been extensively remodeled since the old days, but the furnishings create a sort of seedy chic reminiscent of the backstreet cafes of Paris, with a clientele to match.

Recommended dishes:　Much, but not all, of the menu changes daily; pan-baked oysters with spicy barbecue sauce; crawfish cakes with pepper aïoli; smoked salmon with endive and capers; mixed green salad with potato vinaigrette; pan-seared sea scallops with oriental marinade; champagne-poached salmon with mango beurre blanc; pan-seared ostrich with port sauce; veal chop with roasted shallots; pork medallions with wild rice. Desserts du jour.

Summary & comments:　It's a bistro with an adventuresome menu of food with a French accent, mostly on the nouvelle side.

La Crepe Nanou

Zone 4   Uptown Above Napoleon
1410 Robert Street
899-2670

	French Bistro
	★★★★
	Moderate
	Quality 87 Value A

Reservations:	Not accepted
When to go:	Early evenings
Entree range:	$7–16
Payment:	MC, V
Service rating:	★★★
Friendliness rating:	★★★
Parking:	Curbside
Bar:	Full bar
Wine selection:	Substantial list, French-dominated; many by-the-glass selections; attractive prices
Dress:	Casual
Disabled access:	Limited
Customers:	Uptowners, Francophiles
Dinner:	Every day, 6–10 P.M.

Atmosphere / setting: It looks as if it had been transported here from a Parisian back street, complete with mismatched everything in its collage of crowded, noisy dining spaces.

Recommended dishes: Pâté maison; mussels marinière; escargots de bourguignonne; onion soup au gratin; salad tropicale; crêpes, especially crab, crawfish, Florentine, and Provençal; grilled salmon béarnaise; roast chicken; grilled quails with mushrooms; filet mignon with green peppercorn sauce; lamb chops with cognac sauce; sweetbreads with lemon, Capers, and butter. Dessert crêpes, especially Antillaise, belle Hélène, and Calvados; baked Alaska for two.

Summary & comments: Evolved far beyond its origins as a crêpe shop, Nanou is a fix for Francophiles. Incredibly (and understandably) popular, meals here usually mean at least a short wait for a table to open; the social scene that results during the delay is a latter-day version of the Uptown cocktail party that Manale's was in the Seventies. The food is stereotypical bistro fare: fresh, very French, inexpensive, and more delicious than you anticipate. Crêpes—both entree and dessert varieties—remain a specialty that no other local restaurant can match.

La Cuisine

Zone 7   Lakeview / West End /
          Bucktown
225 West Harrison Avenue
486-7664

Creole
★★★
Moderate
Quality 87   Value B

Reservations:	Recommended
When to go:	After 8 P.M.
Entree range:	$9–20 (median: $14)
Payment:	All major credit cards
Service rating:	★★★
Friendliness rating:	★★★★
Parking:	Free lot adjacent
Bar:	Full bar
Wine selection:	Limited list of ordinary wines
Dress:	Dressy casual
Disabled access:	Limited
Customers:	Locals, mostly on the older side
Lunch:	Tuesday–Sunday, 11 A.M.–2:30 P.M.
Dinner:	Tuesday–Saturday, 5–10 P.M.; Monday, closed.

Atmosphere / setting: The two main rooms are a bit too formal for today's tastes, but everything else about the place is easygoing.

Recommended dishes: Oysters Deanna (baked with garlic and bread crumbs); oysters trois façon (baked three different sauces); shrimp rémoulade; crab soup; crawfish bisque; crawfish etouffee; crabmeat Martin (a creamy, spicy casserole); trout meunière amandine; Joe's hot shrimp (stuffed with mozzarella and jalapeños); filet mignon; boiled beef brisket; osso buco; broiled chicken bordelaise. Bread pudding; lemon ice box pie.

Summary & comments: After 25 years spent assembling a loyal audience for its familiar, very likeable Creole food, La Cuisine abruptly went out of business in 1994. The consternation of the faithful was salved when the place reopened with much of the same staff and the same old menu in 1995. The culinary style is quite out of vogue, but if you can get past the minor atrocities (iceberg lettuce salads, mushy vegetables, overuse of stuffing, and terrible wine service), you'll find a lot of honest flavor.

La Gauloise

	French
Zone 2 Central Business District	★★★
614 Canal	Moderate
527-6712	
	Quality 86 Value C

Reservations:	Recommended
When to go:	Anytime
Entree range:	$9–20
Payment:	All major credit cards
Service rating:	★★★
Friendliness rating:	★★★★
Parking:	Valet (free) at Common Street entrance of hotel
Bar:	Full bar
Wine selection:	Decent list, French-dominated; many by-the-glass selections
Dress:	Casual
Disabled access:	Full
Customers:	Hotel guests; mostly locals for Sunday brunch; businessmen at lunch
Breakfast:	Every day, 7–10 A.M.
Brunch:	Sunday, 11 A.M.–3 P.M.
Lunch:	Monday–Saturday, 11:30 A.M.–2:30 P.M.
Dinner:	Every day, 5–10 P.M.

Atmosphere / setting: The all-purpose restaurant of the luxurious Meridien Hotel is a largish, pretty room in the brasserie style. Tiled floors, polished brass, glass panels, mirrors, banquette seating, and two walls of windows (one viewing Canal Street) give a bright, comfortable environment.

Recommended dishes: Chicken curry pappadums; pecan crab cakes; French onion soup; frogs' legs persillade; seared salmon with sunflower seeds and cabbage; mixed grill; boudin blanc with morels; grilled lamb chops with fresh thyme. Chocolate profiteroles; dessert buffet.

Entertainment & amenities: Dixieland jazz quartet, balloon-blowing clown, and magician at Sunday brunch. Clown also plays Bach on water glasses.

Summary & comments: The menu is an ever-changing and surprisingly deft blending of Creole and French dishes. But few diners here look very long at the menu, choosing instead the buffets offered at breakfast, lunch, Sunday brunch, and Friday dinner. These are far more interesting than average, largely because of the wide-ranging tastes of the chef who, while French, has spent time all over the world.

La Madeleine

Zone 1 French Quarter	Bakery Cafe
547 St. Ann	★★
568-9950	Inexpensive
Zone 4 Uptown Above Napoleon	Quality 74 Value C
601 South Carrollton Avenue	
861-8661	

Zone 10   Metairie Above Causeway / Kenner / Jefferson Hwy.
3300 Severn Avenue, Metairie
456-1375

Reservations:	Not accepted
When to go:	Anytime
Entree range:	$4–10
Payment:	No credit cards
Service rating:	★
Friendliness rating:	★★★★
Parking:	Quarter: French Market pay lot, one block away; Carrollton: curbside; Metairie: free lot
Bar:	Beer and wine
Wine selection:	A few house wines
Dress:	Anything goes
Disabled access:	Limited
Customers:	Mix of tourists and locals
Open:	Every day, 7 A.M.–10 P.M.

Atmosphere / setting: The main bakery is in the historic Lower Pontalba building, which has serious French Quarter charm (how could it not, here on a corner of Jackson Square?). The other two locations are more prosaic, but still possessed of a certain Gallic air.

Recommended dishes: Breakfast pastries and breads; entree salads; soups; country-style pizza (lots of aromatic vegetables and herbs with ham). Dessert pastries and tarts.

Summary & comments: A French engineer opened this chain of French-style bakeries in Dallas, from which it spread here. It has succeeded mightily: the breads in particular are in wide demand, made as they are in the real French style (in contrast with the much lighter New Orleans French bread) and baked in a wood-burning oven. A good place for a pastry-and-coffee breakfast; later in the day they make soups, salads, pizzas, sandwiches, and a few French-cafe-style plate specials, which range from okay to pretty good. Self-service and very schlep.

La Provence

<table>
<tr><td></td><td>French</td></tr>
<tr><td></td><td>★★★★★</td></tr>
<tr><td>Zone 12   North Shore</td><td>Expensive</td></tr>
<tr><td>25020 US 190, Lacombe</td><td></td></tr>
<tr><td>(504) 626-7662</td><td>Quality 98   Value C</td></tr>
</table>

Reservations:	Required
When to go:	Sunday afternoon
Entree range:	$14–24
Payment:	AMEX, MC, V
Service rating:	★★★★
Friendliness rating:	★★★★
Parking:	Free lot adjacent
Bar:	Full bar
Wine selection:	Distinguished cellar, French-dominated; the policy on corkage is draconian
Dress:	Jacket recommended but not required
Disabled access:	Full
Customers:	Gourmets from all over the area; couples
Dinner:	Wednesday–Saturday, 6–10 P.M.; Sunday, 1–9 P.M.; Monday and Tuesday, closed.

Atmosphere / setting: If you ever discovered an unexpectedly wonderful restaurant in a small European town, you'll recognize the scene at La Provence. Isolated in a pine forest on the old east-west highway on the North Shore, this is a lovely, comfortable, somewhat rustic, classy, and fully informal place to take a meal.

Recommended dishes: Merguez (lamb sausage); boudin noir with lentils; gravlax; baked oysters three ways; Madagascar-pepper shrimp cocktail; escargots bourguignonne; quail gumbo; Greek salad; quenelles of scallops; sautéed thyme-marinated quail; involtino of rabbit saddle (rolled and stuffed); duck à l'orange; rack of lamb; tournedos bordelaise; sweetbreads braised in port wine; diplomat pudding. Dessert cart.

Entertainment & amenities: Pianist in lounge nightly.

Summary & comments: Chef-owner Chris Kerageorgiou, a beloved local character, blends his native French, ancestral Greek, and adopted Creole flavors in thrilling, original ways. You can participate not only by eating but by entering the showplace kitchen. There are occasional inconsistencies (the place gets a little too busy Saturday nights, for example), but dinner here is usually unforgettable. My favorite time to go: late Sunday afternoon in winter, with the fireplace blazing.

La Riviera

	Italian
	★★★★
	Expensive
	Quality 83 Value C

Zone 10   Metairie Above Causeway /
           Kenner / Jefferson Hwy.
4506 Shores Drive, Metairie
888-6238

Reservations:	Recommended
When to go:	Anytime
Entree range:	$9–22
Payment:	All major credit cards
Service rating:	★★★★
Friendliness rating:	★★★★
Parking:	Free lot adjacent
Bar:	Full bar
Wine selection:	Substantial list, mostly Italian
Dress:	Jacket recommended but not required
Disabled access:	Full
Customers:	Locals, couples
Lunch:	Monday–Friday, 11:30 A.M.–2:30 P.M.
Dinner:	Monday–Saturday, 6–10 P.M.; Sunday, closed.

Atmosphere / setting: The dining room is bright and formal in a dated, Metairie-anean kind of way, but the camaraderie among the customers prevents stuffiness from getting a toehold.

Recommended dishes: Crabmeat ravioli; fried calamari; fettuccine La Riviera (like Alfredo, but lighter); baked oysters Italian style; stuffed mushrooms; broiled trout; seafood-stuffed eggplant; soft-shell crab with crabmeat; spaghetti and meatballs; osso buco; veal pizzaiola; veal piccata; filet mignon with Madeira sauce. Spumoni; amaretto kiss.

Summary & comments: This was the first permanent home of true Italian (as opposed to Creole Italian) cooking in New Orleans. Chef Goffredo Fraccaro opened La Riviera 25 years ago and has since sold it, although he's still there cooking most of the time. The menu is pretty accessible—over the years, more than a few local Italian standards have crept in (for example, the best plate of meatballs and spaghetti I've found). More ambitious dishes abound, particularly among the specials. Rather popular with a devoted bunch of regulars.

Landry's

Zone 7 Lakeview / West End /
Bucktown
789 Harrison Avenue
488-6476

Creole / Neighborhood Cafe
★★★
Inexpensive

Quality 73   Value C

Reservations:	Not accepted
When to go:	Anytime
Entree range:	$4–14
Payment:	No credit cards
Service rating:	★★
Friendliness rating:	★★★★
Parking:	Curbside
Bar:	Full bar
Wine selection:	A few house wines
Dress:	Casual
Disabled access:	Limited
Customers:	Neighborhood people
Open:	Monday–Saturday, 7 A.M.–9:30 P.M.; Sunday, closed.

Atmosphere / setting: A fine little neighborhood joint with a happy feeling, blackboards of specials, and a slight tilt to everything.

Recommended dishes: Oysters on the half shell; chicken and sausage gumbo; fried seafood platters; breaded veal cutlet with spaghetti and brown gravy; red beans and rice with hot sausage; fried chicken. Daily special platters. Grilled ham poor boy; fried seafood poor boys; muffuletta. Peach cobbler.

Summary & comments: The look of the place tells the world that here will be found a great plate of beans, a nice juicy poor boy, and some good fried seafood. But also here is a raw oyster bar, some rather ambitious appetizers and soups, breakfasts, and even some tolerably good grilled fish—all at lowball prices. The staff is young and neighborly.

Little Tokyo

Zone 9   Metairie Below Causeway
1521 North Causeway, Metairie
831-6788

Japanese	
★★★	
Moderate	
Quality 82	Value C

Reservations:	Accepted
When to go:	Anytime
Entree range:	$8–13
Payment:	All major credit cards
Service rating:	★★★
Friendliness rating:	★★★
Parking:	Free lot adjacent
Bar:	Full bar
Wine selection:	A few house wines
Dress:	Casual
Disabled access:	Limited
Customers:	Local regulars
Lunch:	Monday–Friday, 11:30 A.M.–2:30 P.M.
Dinner:	Monday–Saturday, 6–10 P.M.; Sunday, closed.

Atmosphere / setting: It's a smallish place dominated by the popular sushi bar, behind which is a stack of personalized (for the regulars) wood boxes used for beverages.

Recommended dishes: Sunomono (seaweed with octopus and shrimp); tofu steak; shu mai (steamed shrimp dumplings); beef tataki; sushi; chirashi sushi (seafood on a bed of sushi rice); sashimi; una don (teriyaki eel on rice); love boat for two (combination of sushi, tempuras, and teriyakis). Red bean ice cream.

Entertainment & amenities: Late in the evening, a karaoke bar cranks up in an adjacent room.

Summary & comments: This is the flagship of a loose chain of franchises under the same name. The sushi and sashimi are among the best around, but the menu goes on to include all the various arenas of Japanese food: the sukiyaki-like boiled meat dishes, tempuras (including a giant boat that amounts to a Japanese seafood platter), and teriyakis. You receive the most enthusiastic welcome you'll ever hear when you open the door.

Little Tokyo

Zone 3   Uptown Below Napoleon
1612 St. Charles Avenue
524-8535

Japanese	
★★★	
Moderate	
Quality 82	Value C

Reservations:	Accepted
When to go:	Anytime
Entree range:	$8–13
Payment:	All major credit cards
Service rating:	★★★
Friendliness rating:	★★★
Parking:	Curbside (metered)
Bar:	Full bar
Wine selection:	A few house wines
Dress:	Casual
Disabled access:	Limited
Customers:	Mix of locals and tourists; businessmen at lunch
Lunch:	Every day, 11:30 A.M.–2:30 P.M.
Dinner:	Every day, 6–10 P.M.

Atmosphere / setting: Somewhat utilitarian, with different scenes at the sushi bar, conventional tables, and tatami rooms.

Recommended dishes: Sunomono (seaweed with octopus and shrimp); tofu steak; shu mai (steamed shrimp dumplings); beef tataki; sushi; chirashi sushi (seafood on a bed of sushi rice); sashimi; una don (teriyaki eel on rice). Red bean ice cream.

Summary & comments: The most convenient-to-downtown sushi bar is only loosely associated with the Little Tokyo in Metairie, and a bit different in its food. This cafe offers a menu only slightly smaller than its bigger competitors, but with no sacrifice of goodness. The daily lunch box brings an interesting assortment of different specialties. The sushi bar is staffed by the owner, who has a deft hand and eye. At the tables they serve the entire range of Japanese specialties, including sukiyaki and its ilk. Pleasant, helpful servers.

Liuzza's

Zone 6   Mid-City / Gentilly
3636 Bienville
482-9120

Creole / Neighborhood Cafe
★ ★ ★
Inexpensive
Quality 79   Value B

Reservations:	Not accepted
When to go:	Anytime
Entree range:	$5–14
Payment:	No credit cards
Service rating:	★ ★ ★
Friendliness rating:	★ ★ ★
Parking:	Free lot adjacent and curbside
Bar:	Full bar
Wine selection:	A few house wines
Dress:	Anything goes
Disabled access:	Limited
Customers:	Neighborhood people, families
Lunch / Dinner:	Monday–Saturday, 11 A.M.–9:30 P.M.; Sunday, closed.

Atmosphere / setting: One of the oldest of the few remaining corner cafes, Liuzza's presents the classic neighborhood "bar & rest." aspect.

Recommended dishes: French fries; Italian breaded eggplant; oyster artichoke soup; wop salad (sorry—that's really what they call it.); fried seafood platters; roast beef poor boy; hot sausage poor boy; broiled ham and cheese poor boy; fried chicken; panneéd veal and fettuccine; eggplant casserole with spaghetti and meatballs. Daily specials. Bread pudding.

Summary & comments: Liuzza's most famous product is the large, heavy, frozen glass chalices in which they serve beer and root beer. But the food's pretty good, too, starting with a fine roast beef poor boy and moving up through interesting, very homely daily specials, seafood platters, and Italian dishes. The presence of fresh-cut french fries and the small window through which the finished orders are pushed both bear witness to the well-preserved old style for which this place is beloved. Not always perfect in its food, but always very authentically backstreet New Orleans.

Lola's

Spanish

★★★

Moderate

Quality 80   Value A

Zone 6   Mid-City / Gentilly
3312 Esplanade
488-6946

Reservations:	Not accepted
When to go:	Early evenings
Entree range:	$7–14
Payment:	No credit cards
Service rating:	★★
Friendliness rating:	★★★
Parking:	Curbside
Bar:	No alcohol; bring your own
Wine selection:	Bring your own
Dress:	Casual
Disabled access:	Limited
Customers:	Locals, mostly young
Dinner:	Tuesday–Sunday, 6–10 P.M.; Monday, closed.

Atmosphere / setting: The scene here is defined by the minuscule size of the restaurant, which comes nowhere close to satisfying the demand for tables.

Recommended dishes: Pâté and cheese board; mussels vinaigrette; garlic soup; gazpacho; grilled fish with spicy sauce du jour; garlic chicken; paprika-marinated roast pork loin; paella (meat, seafood, and vegetarian versions are all fine). Daily specials.

Summary & comments: This is the rebirth of the deceased Altamira, the city's only Spanish (as opposed to Latin American) restaurant. While much of the menu is still Spanish—gazpacho and paella are two specialties—more than a few dishes are from closer to home. (Creole and Spanish have a lot in common anyway.) Extremely popular, dining at Lola's almost always involves waiting for a table. Very cheap.

Louis XVI

Zone 1   French Quarter
730 Bienville Street
581-7000

French	
★★★★	
Very Expensive	
Quality 87	Value D

Reservations:	Recommended
When to go:	Anytime
Entree range:	$18–30
Payment:	All major credit cards
Service rating:	★★★★★
Friendliness rating:	★★★
Parking:	Validated ($3) in garage behind Mr. B's
Bar:	Full bar
Wine selection:	Wines here have never been quite as interesting or various as the food, and prices are too high
Dress:	Jacket required
Disabled access:	Full
Customers:	Mostly locals, a few tourists; couples; gourmets
Breakfast:	Every day, 7–10 A.M.
Dinner:	Every day, 6–10 P.M.

Atmosphere / setting: A pleasant dinosaur, Louis XVI is very handsome and plush in a modern way. Mirrors in the small dining room reflect a geometry of indirect neon, and a wall of windows opens onto the hotel's courtyard. Tables on the covered, climate-controlled courtyard are available for dining.

Recommended dishes: Duck pâté with onion marmalade; marinated fish with peanut–ginger relish; feuillentine de crustaces (puff pastry layered with shellfish in sauce Nantua); escargots with hazelnuts and pecans; vegetable cream soup du jour; fillet de poisson Louisiane (with banana, red bell pepper, and meunière sauce); poached or grilled fish; sweetbreads with mushrooms; rack of lamb; Châteaubriand; filet mignon St. Hebert (pepper-and-currant sauce). Gâteau au noisettes; pastries.

Entertainment & amenities: Pianist in lounge nightly.

Summary & comments: First opened a quarter-century ago, this is the first local restaurant successfully to serve Escoffier-era, non-Creole French cuisine. The service, too, is French: most dishes are presented and usually administered to at tableside. Big roasts of red meats for two are carved, sauces are brought to bubbling, and desserts are flambéed before you. Corny by today's vogues, but still romantic and special. The menu is slowly updated, and there may be more than a few new dishes since your last visit, but it's still Louis XVI.

LOUISIANA PIZZA KITCHEN

Pizza
★★★
Moderate
Quality 83   Value B

Zone 1   French Quarter
95 French Market Place
522-9500

Zone 4   Uptown Above Napoleon
615 South Carrollton Avenue
866-5900

Zone 6   Mid-City / Gentilly
2800 Esplanade Avenue
488-2800

Reservations:	Not accepted
When to go:	Anytime
Entree range:	$8–14
Payment:	AMEX, MC, V
Service rating:	★★★
Friendliness rating:	★★★
Parking:	Curbside
Bar:	Full bar
Wine selection:	Modest list, but wines well-chosen for the food
Dress:	Anything goes
Disabled access:	Limited
Customers:	Neighborhood people, younger couples
Lunch / Dinner:	Every day, 11 A.M.–11 P.M.; Esplanade, 5–10 P.M.

Atmosphere / setting: Created by a French guy, the places feel like casual French cafes. The French Quarter and Esplanade locations were built into funny, misshapen, but charming spaces. Riverbend is more conventional.

Recommended dishes: Eggplant and bell pepper bruschetta; Greek salad; Caesar salad; mozzarella with basil and tomatoes. Barbecue chicken pizza; smoked salmon and cream cheese pasta; southwestern pizza with chicken and black beans; roasted garlic and spinach pizza. Angel hair pasta primavera; tagliatelle pasta with prosciutto, Gorgonzola cheese, and peas. Italian ice creams.

Summary & comments: Pizza prepared in the style of the French Riviera: very thin, almost crackerlike crusts, baked in a wood-burning oven, more often spread with olive oil than tomato sauce, topped not with layers but piles of cheese, vegetables, meats, and seafoods. Pasta is prepared in the same spirit, and is generally much lighter than in the standard local Italian restaurant. Salads, sandwiches, and daily specials continue the theme of lightness and originality. As time goes on, the menu here gets more various and interesting. Prices are a great value. Service is a little indifferent, and the place can get maddeningly busy.

Mandich

Zone 5   Downtown / St. Bernard
3200 St. Claude Avenue
947-9553

Reservations:	Accepted
When to go:	Anytime
Entree range:	$11–16
Payment:	MC, V
Service rating:	★★★
Friendliness rating:	★★★★
Parking:	Free lot adjacent
Bar:	Full bar
Wine selection:	A few house wines, arrayed with supermarket-style price tags on the bar for your choosing
Dress:	Casual
Disabled access:	Limited
Customers:	Neighborhood people
Lunch:	Tuesday–Friday, 11 A.M.–2:30 P.M.
Dinner:	Friday and Saturday, 5–9 P.M.; Sunday and Monday, closed.

Atmosphere / setting: Dated but comfortable, the dining rooms are those of a neighborhood restaurant striving for atmosphere.

Recommended dishes: Fried calamari; oysters bordelaise; seafood gumbo; red bean soup; trout Mandich (broiled with a crisp breading, with lemon butter); crabcakes; oyster platter (four different ways); stuffed shrimp; garlic chicken; sweet potato duck; pannéed veal; filet mignon. Cheesecake; bread pudding.

Summary & comments: Restaurant Mandich is a forty-year-old holdover from an era when those who worked in the then-labor-intensive port finished their days at one or two in the afternoon, then adjourned to a nearby restaurant for a substantial dinner. Mandich still serves mostly lunches, but with a bit more verve and ambition than the typical neighborhood cafe. Most of the customers are regulars, but it's a great place to take a visitor (or yourself) for a vanishing part of local culture.

Mandina's

Zone 6 Mid-City / Gentilly	Creole / Neighborhood Cafe
3800 Canal	★★★
482-9179	Moderate
	Quality 75 Value A

Reservations:	Not accepted
When to go:	Off-peak lunch and dinner hours to avoid waiting
Entree range:	$9–17
Payment:	No credit cards
Service rating:	★★
Friendliness rating:	★
Parking:	Curbside
Bar:	Full bar
Wine selection:	A few house wines
Dress:	Casual
Disabled access:	Limited
Customers:	Locals, families; businessmen at lunch
Lunch / Dinner:	Monday–Saturday, 11 A.M.–10 P.M.; Sunday, noon–9 P.M.

Atmosphere / setting: Mandina's comes closer than any other restaurant to the Orleanian's cherished ideal of the old-time neighborhood cafe. The front room is busier, with tables vying for space with the customers waiting for their turn at the bar. In the back is a utilitarian dining room that's a bit quieter. The whole place is furnished with neon, old painted signs, beer clocks, and other relics.

Recommended dishes: Shrimp rémoulade; crab fingers in wine sauce; oyster and artichoke soup; fried soft-shell crab; trout amandine; spaghetti and Italian sausage. Daily specials, especially: red beans with Italian sausage (Monday); beef stew (Tuesday); bracioline (Thursday); stuffed crab (Friday); crabmeat au gratin (Sunday). Bread pudding.

Summary & comments: The best food on any given day will be the home-style specials, with a further edge to non-seafoods. All portions are titanic, but somehow avoid grossness. The service staff has been here a long time and will not be impressed by anything you have to offer.

Martin Wine Cellar Deli

Deli	
★★★	
Inexpensive	
Quality 75	Value B

Zone 3   Uptown Below Napoleon
3827 Baronne Street
899-7411

Zone 9   Metairie Below Causeway
714 Elmeer, Metairie
896-7300

Reservations:	Not accepted
When to go:	Anytime
Entree range:	$4–7
Payment:	MC, V
Service rating:	★
Friendliness rating:	★★★
Parking:	Free lot adjacent
Bar:	Beer and wine
Wine selection:	This is the city's premier wine retailer, and you can pick absolutely anything from the shelves at retail prices to have with your sandwich. They even decant!
Dress:	Casual
Disabled access:	Full
Customers:	Locals; wine buffs; businessmen at lunch
Lunch / Dinner:	Monday–Saturday, 10 A.M.–6 P.M.; Sunday, 11 A.M.–1 P.M.

Atmosphere / setting: A few tables and some counter space are tucked into a corner of a large wine store, near the gourmet groceries.

Recommended dishes: Sandwiches: Dave's Special (roast beef, cole slaw, pâté de campagne); downtowner (cold roast beef and Jarisberg on pumpernickel); sailor (hot knockwurst, pastrami, and Swiss); lox and bagel; executive club (turkey, ham, bacon, cheese). Cheesecake. Daily specials.

Summary & comments: This annex of the city's largest wine store has a smattering of poor boys and other local sandwiches, but in most of its menu it's the closest thing you'll find around here to a New York deli. The meats, breads, and dressings are all first-class, and the sandwiches are built to a jaw-dislocating thickness. They even offer Dr. Brown sodas, cheesecake, and pickles.

MARTINIQUE

Zone 4   Uptown Above Napoleon
5908 Magazine
891-8495

French Bistro/Caribbean
★★★
Moderate

Quality 85   Value B

Reservations:	Not accepted
When to go:	Early evenings
Entree range:	$12–17
Payment:	MC,V
Service rating:	★★
Friendliness rating:	★★★
Parking:	Curbside (metered)
Bar:	Beer and wine
Wine selection:	Modest list, but wines well-chosen for the food
Dress:	Casual
Disabled access:	Limited
Customers:	Locals, couples, gourmets
Dinner:	Tuesday–Sunday, 6–10 P.M.; Monday, closed.

Atmosphere / setting: Physically minimal in a charming way. The courtyard gives a bit more cheery an atmosphere than the darkish main room.

Recommended dishes: Grilled black-bean cake with bell pepper coulis; oysters sautéed with lime and cayenne; mussels steamed in chablis and herbs; salad of lamb sausage and lima beans; chicken stuffed with goat cheese and prosciutto; pork chop grilled with coconut and balsamic vinegar; sesame seed–crusted salmon with pickled ginger; filet mignon with sautéed pecans and orange zest; scallops Provençal. Desserts of the day.

Summary & comments: After creating an unlikely hit with L'Economie, chef Hubert Sandot—who grew up in the French West Indies—moved Uptown to the former Mais Oui. The menu is a bit different from that of L'Economie: there's an emphasis on Caribbean cuisine, although everything retains a distinct French accent. All of this is on the very light side—neither cream nor butter are to be found in the recipes—but it's flavorful and fascinating. It's a coin-flip as to whether Martinique's tables or parking places nearby are harder to come by.

Maximo's Italian Grill

Zone 1 French Quarter	Nouvelle Italian
1117 Decatur	★★★
586-8883	Expensive
	Quality 81 Value C

Reservations:	Recommended
When to go:	Anytime
Entree range:	$11–23
Payment:	All major credit cards
Service rating:	★★★
Friendliness rating:	★★★
Parking:	French Market pay lot, one block
Bar:	Full bar
Wine selection:	Substantial list, mostly Italian and Californian
Dress:	Dressy casual
Disabled access:	Full
Customers:	Mostly locals, a few tourists; couples; many Quarterites
Dinner:	Sunday–Thursday, 6–10 P.M.; Friday and Saturday, 6–11 P.M.

Atmosphere / setting: From the street, it looks like another converted old French Quarter building, but the dining room is striking and contemporary: a long, long room with a single row of tables and an unlikely counter in its rear half. Behind the counter is the open kitchen, which makes for interesting viewing for food fanatics.

Recommended dishes: Antipasto; seared carpaccio; grilled portobello mushrooms; arugula and prosciutto salad; pasta Rosa (very spicy penne with shrimp, garlic, and arugula); penne arrabbiata; linguine alla pirata (clams, calamari, shrimp, and scallops in a spicy red sauce); scallops piccata; cioppino; pan-roasted veal T-bone; chicken with white beans and sausage. Tiramisu; dessert specials.

Summary & comments: A menu of aggressively Northern Italian dishes is whipped up with verve and excitement. The style relies heavily on grilling, olive oil, garlic, and fresh herbs generally, although a convincing spike of red pepper turns up in a few dishes. There is a consistency problem, but this robust food is usually as satisfying as it is distinctive, and the wines and service are always good.

MESSINA'S

Zone 1   French Quarter
200 Chartres
523-9225

Seafood	
★★	
Inexpensive	
Quality 70	Value C

Reservations:	Not accepted
When to go:	Anytime
Entree range:	$6–13
Payment:	AMEX, MC, V
Service rating:	★★
Friendliness rating:	★★★
Parking:	Pay garage nearby
Bar:	Full bar
Wine selection:	A few house wines
Dress:	Casual
Disabled access:	Full
Customers:	Tourists, some locals
Lunch:	Tuesday–Thursday, 11 A.M.–3 P.M.
Lunch / Dinner:	Friday–Sunday, 11 A.M.–9 P.M.; Monday, closed.

Atmosphere / setting: The oyster bar is the focus of a battered but sturdy room that, while serving lots of tourists, has all the authentic trappings of a local hangout.

Recommended dishes: Oysters on the half shell; shrimp rémoulade; muffuletta; pasta with seafood; fried seafood platters. Italian ice creams.

Summary & comments: A moderately good cafe with two great specialties: the oyster bar and the muffuletta. The latter is distinguished by its olive salad, the chunkiest around, with lots of different marinated vegetables in a good matrix of olive oil and garlic. The menu goes on to include all the standard seafood and Italian platters, most of which falls solidly into the "okay" category. Service can be a touch rushed.

Michael's Mid-City Grill

Hamburgers
★★
Inexpensive
Quality 71   Value C

Zone 6   Mid-City / Gentilly
4139 Canal
488-2878

Reservations:	Not accepted
When to go:	Anytime
Entree range:	$5–100 (median: $10)
Payment:	AMEX, MC, V
Service rating:	★★
Friendliness rating:	★★★★
Parking:	Curbside
Bar:	Full bar
Wine selection:	Limited list of ordinary wines,
	plus Dom Perignon
Dress:	Casual
Disabled access:	Limited
Customers:	Locals; businessmen at lunch; couples at dinner
Lunch / Dinner:	Monday–Friday, 11 A.M.–11 P.M.;
	Saturday, 5–11 P.M.; Sunday, 5–10 P.M.

Atmosphere / setting: A long dining room lined with booths. Photographs of past consumers of the Big Bucks Burger hang on the walls.

Recommended dishes: Black bean soup; chili; hamburger; filet mignon; grilled fish with jambalaya; corned beef sandwich. Bread pudding.

Summary & comments: An easygoing, unchallenging cafe serving thick, handmade burgers of first-class quality and steaks of somewhat less interest. They also have a few other grilled platters, salads, and sandwiches. Very busy at lunch. Michael's is widely known for its $100 Big Bucks Burger, alleged to be the most expensive in America; it's made with caviar and comes with a "complimentary" bottle of Dom Perignon.

Middendorf's

<table>
<tr><td>Seafood</td></tr>
<tr><td>★★★</td></tr>
<tr><td>Moderate</td></tr>
<tr><td>Quality 79   Value B</td></tr>
</table>

Zone 12   North Shore
Manchac, Akers
(504) 386-6666

Reservations:	Not accepted
When to go:	Anytime
Entree range:	$8–14
Payment:	MC, V
Service rating:	★★★
Friendliness rating:	★★★
Parking:	Free lot adjacent
Bar:	Full bar
Wine selection:	A few house wines
Dress:	Casual
Disabled access:	Full
Customers:	Daytrippers, families
Lunch / Dinner:	Every day, 10:45 A.M.–9:30 P.M.

Atmosphere / setting: There are actually two separate buildings, both with the familiar happy-noisy environment of the local fried-fish house.

Recommended dishes: Seafood gumbo; fried catfish; fried seafood platters; stuffed crab. Bread pudding.

Summary & comments: The area's most famous catfish restaurant is a 40-mile drive from town, in a rather exotic tiny fishing town in the middle of the wetlands. It's interstate all the way; the restaurant is at the base of the Manchac exit of I-55. Middendorf's is a big, busy place (when it's really hectic, they open up an entire extra restaurant) with a simple menu: all the local seafoods in every imaginable platter configuration. The fried catfish comes either in thick fillets or crisp, thin slices. Either way, it's the proverbial golden brown, greaseless, hot, and wonderful. As is all the fried seafood here.

Midnight Star Cafe

Zone 7 Lakeview / West End /	Eclectic
Bucktown	★★★
7224 Pontchartrain Boulevard	Expensive
282-6241	Quality 80 Value D

Reservations:	Accepted
When to go:	Anytime
Entree range:	$9–24 (median: $14)
Payment:	AMEX, MC,V
Service rating:	★★
Friendliness rating:	★★
Parking:	Free lot adjacent
Bar:	Full bar
Wine selection:	Decent list, with emphasis on California;
	many by-the-glass selections
Dress:	Casual
Disabled access:	None
Customers:	Couples, mostly young; neighborhood people
Lunch / Dinner:	Every day, 11:30 A.M.–11 P.M.

Atmosphere / setting: There's a dark, cool U-shaped dining room where New Age music and jazz plays, and an L-shaped porch with tables for dining or coffee-drinking.

Recommended dishes: Black bean quesadillas; escargots with leek butter on French bread; oysters casino; shrimp and artichoke al forno; Caesar salad; pasta arrabbiata; citrus grilled shrimp with red bell pepper pesto; Thai shrimp with black beans and spaghetti; grilled pork tenderloin in papaya curry sauce; grilled fish. Dessert specials.

Summary & comments: It started as a New-Age coffeehouse but, shortly after it moved from Kenner to West End, it became a full-fledged restaurant. The menu is heavy with salads and pastas, but the main part of the entree section deals with just about all the standard foodstuffs, served with interesting sauces that don't always go with the main item on the plate. Portions are uniformly too big; for example, an appetizer of oysters casino includes a dozen oysters. They love grated Parmesan cheese and butter here, and put it in lots of places you wouldn't expect. Beware of the prices of specials, which have a way of being far above those on the menu.

Mike Anderson's

Zone 1 French Quarter	Seafood
215 Bourbon Street	★ ★ ★
524-3884	Moderate
	Quality 80 Value C

Reservations:	Not accepted
When to go:	Anytime
Entree range:	$12–20
Payment:	All major credit cards
Service rating:	★ ★
Friendliness rating:	★ ★ ★ ★
Parking:	Pay garages nearby
Bar:	Full bar
Wine selection:	A few house wines
Dress:	Casual
Disabled access:	Limited
Customers:	Tourists, some locals; businessmen at lunch
Lunch / Dinner:	Every day, 11 A.M.–11 P.M.

Atmosphere / setting: The local branch of the Baton Rouge football hero's seafood restaurant is a big, long, narrow place on Bourbon Street, full of the trappings of hunting, fishing, and other Cajun stuff.

Recommended dishes: Oysters on the half shell; three-way alligator; baked oysters four ways; fried seafood platter; broiled seafood platter; crawfish, shrimp, or crab dinner; fish stuffed with crab and shrimp; jolie rouge (broiled fish topped with crabmeat).

Summary & comments: This is the best casual seafood joint in the Quarter. The best platters are assortments of several different dishes, in a total portion size so unreasonably large that, even though you might find a thing or two that's sub-par, there'll be more than enough good stuff to fill you up. The seven-way crawfish, crab, and shrimp platters are especially appealing.

Mike's On The Avenue

Zone 2   Central Business District
628 St. Charles Avenue
523-1709

Eclectic
★★★★
Very Expensive
Quality 89   Value D

Reservations:	Recommended
When to go:	Anytime
Entree range:	$14–23
Payment:	All major credit cards
Service rating:	★★★★
Friendliness rating:	★★★
Parking:	Lunch: curbside (metered); dinner: valet ($6)
Bar:	Full bar
Wine selection:	Substantial list, with emphasis on California; many by-the-glass selections
Dress:	Dressy casual
Disabled access:	Full
Customers:	Hip, social crowd; gourmets; couples; businessmen at lunch
Brunch:	Sunday, 10:30 A.M.–3 P.M.
Lunch:	Monday–Friday, 11:30 A.M.–2:30 P.M.
Dinner:	Every day, 6–10 P.M.

Atmosphere / setting: The handsome, airy, white dining room has works of art by the chef on most walls, except for the one with big windows that look out onto Lafayette Square and Gallier Hall. A second dining room—located on the other side of the hotel's lobby—is a bit plusher but less scenic.

Recommended dishes: Chinese shrimp dumplings with tahini; crawfish spring rolls; flash-fried oysters with green chili aïoli; barbecue oysters; blackened tuna Napoleon; Maytag blue cheese salad; crawfish and scallop cakes; U-12 barbecue shrimp; shellfish stew with Creole sausage and focaccia; pannéed veal with portobello mushrooms and grilled eggplant; filet mignon with chili-lime butter and mashed potatoes. Dessert assortment; sorbets; crème brûlée.

Summary & comments: Mike Fennelly came from Santa Fe, where he made a name for himself by uniting southwestern and Asian tastes into not just menus but individual dishes. He brought that act to New Orleans in 1991, adding enough other offbeat ideas of food and service to make it one of the most eclectic restaurants around. Mike's serves the culinary equivalent of abstract art: you have to think about it a lot before you really can enjoy it. Indeed, most of the dishes have a sculptural aspect. Generally the eating here is very good to exciting; some of it is just weird. Not a good choice for the traditionalist. The crowd is lively and well connected.

Mona Lisa

Zone 1   French Quarter
1212 Royal
522-6746
Zone 7   Lakeview / West End /
          Bucktown
874 Harrison Avenue
488-0133

<table>
<tr><td></td><td>Pizza</td></tr>
<tr><td></td><td>★★</td></tr>
<tr><td></td><td>Inexpensive</td></tr>
<tr><td></td><td>Quality 71   Value B</td></tr>
</table>

Reservations:	Not accepted
When to go:	Anytime
Entree range:	$5–12
Payment:	AMEX, MC, V
Service rating:	★★
Friendliness rating:	★★
Parking:	Curbside
Bar:	Full bar
Wine selection:	A few house wines
Dress:	Anything goes
Disabled access:	Limited
Customers:	Neighborhood people
Lunch / Dinner:	Every day, 11:30 A.M.–10 P.M.

Atmosphere / setting: Both locations are dark and a little seedy, but this doesn't seem to bother the regulars.

Recommended dishes: Mediterranean salad; golden white pizza (cheese, garlic, and olive oil); pizza; Mardi Gras pasta (shrimp and sausage in a cream sauce); meatball sub. Baklava.

Summary & comments: A pizza specialist with a Middle Eastern accent, this is a webby, unkempt cafe that keeps up a pretty strong corps of regulars, largely through the agency of a single dish: the white pizza, made with olive oil, fresh garlic, and cheeses. The current array of other favorite pizzas and pastas fill out the menu, with a smattering of Middle Eastern appetizers.

MOSCA'S

Zone 11 West Bank	Creole Italian
4137 US 90, Waggaman	★★★★
436-9942	Expensive
	Quality 88 Value C

Reservations:	Accepted but rarely honored
When to go:	Weeknights; closed all of August
Entree range:	$16–22
Payment:	Cash only
Service rating:	★
Friendliness rating:	★
Parking:	Free lot adjacent
Bar:	Full bar
Wine selection:	Decent list, almost entirely Italian; several Amarones
Dress:	Casual
Disabled access:	None
Customers:	Mostly locals (many of them regular customers), a few tourists; families of adults
Dinner:	Tuesday–Saturday, 5 P.M.–10 P.M.; Sunday and Monday, closed.

Atmosphere / setting: Mosca's seems to be a restaurant that a mystery novelist dreamed up. Set inconveniently past the last suburb on US 90, surrounded by marshes and their accompanying clouds of insects and armies of amphibians, the place has all the atmosphere of a roadhouse.

Recommended dishes: Marinated crabs; crab salad; chef's bean soup; oysters Italian style; shrimp Italian style. (The previous two are totally different.) Chicken grandee (pan-roasted with garlic, potatoes, and artichokes); roast chicken; roast quail or squab; Italian sausage; filet mignon. Pineapple fluff.

Summary & comments: Don't expect sympathy from the staff for the length of your repose in the bar, or exceptions to the cash-only policy, even if the check rises well into three figures. Which, for a party of six (the right size for most enjoyment here), is a certainty. But the food is great: all the olive oil, garlic, and rosemary you always wanted, scattered around roasted chickens, sausage, shrimp, and oysters. All this is served with a total lack of ceremony (indeed, service is a bit sullen), but nobody cares: it's a food orgy.

MOTHER'S

Zone 2   Central Business District
401 Poydras
523-9656

Sandwiches

★★★

Moderate

Quality 83   Value D

Reservations:	Not accepted
When to go:	Anytime except around noon and during large conventions
Entree range:	$6–14
Payment:	No credit cards
Service rating:	★★
Friendliness rating:	★★★
Parking:	Curbside; pay lot nearby
Bar:	Beer
Wine selection:	A few house wines
Dress:	Anything goes
Disabled access:	None
Customers:	Tourists, some locals; businessmen at lunch
Open:	Monday–Saturday, 5:30 A.M.–10 P.M.; Sunday, 9 A.M.–10 P.M.

Atmosphere / setting: The brick-walled, concrete-floored dining room is even smaller than it looks, a problem exacerbated by the usually long lines and the parade of cooks bringing hot food through breaks in the line to the cafeteria-style serving area up front. A long-noticed local miracle is how, when your food is ready, a space to sit will suddenly become available.

Recommended dishes: Breakfast special (eggs, grits, breakfast meat, biscuits); Mae's omelette (crusty ham, green onions, mushrooms); pancakes; ham poor boy; Ferdi poor boy (ham and roast beef debris); turkey poor boy; fried seafood poor boys; red beans and rice with Italian sausage; gumbo of the day; jambalaya; corned beef and cabbage. Bread pudding; brownies; muffins.

Summary & comments: Mother's is the most distinguished, busiest, and certainly most expensive sandwich and short-order place in town. It's a cut above most such places: absolutely everything is cooked from scratch on the premises, with no regard to any considerations other than filling you up deliciously. There's a line most of the time; if there's not, the food will be off a bit. With one exception: breakfast, which the tourists don't know about, is always wonderful. Don't come here on a diet or without at least $15 per person in cash.

MR. B'S

Zone 1   French Quarter
201 Royal
523-2078

Nouvelle Creole
★★★★
Expensive

Quality 90   Value C

Reservations:	Accepted
When to go:	Early evenings
Entree range:	$13–22
Payment:	All major credit cards
Service rating:	★★★★★
Friendliness rating:	★★★★★
Parking:	Validated (free) at adjacent garage
Bar:	Full bar
Wine selection:	Substantial list, almost entirely West Coast
Dress:	Dressy casual
Disabled access:	Limited
Customers:	Mostly locals, some tourists; gourmets; couples
Brunch:	Sunday, 11 A.M.–3 P.M.
Lunch:	Monday–Saturday, 11:30 A.M.–2:30 P.M.
Dinner:	Every day, 6–10:30 P.M.

Atmosphere / setting: The single large, somewhat dim dining room has a certain amount of bustle, yet the place manages to preserve privacy and even a bit of romance.

Recommended dishes: Coconut and beer-battered shrimp; barbecued oysters; catfish fingers; gumbo ya-ya (chicken andouille style); seasonal salads; pasta jambalaya; hickory-grilled fish; barbecue shrimp; hickory-roasted chicken with sweet garlic glaze; seafood-and-pasta specials. Bread pudding; Mr. B's chocolate cake; profiteroles and chocolate sauce.

Entertainment & amenities: Pianist at dinner nightly and at Sunday brunch.

Summary & comments: Mr. B's began a revolution when it opened in 1979: it served great Creole food in the tradition of Commander's Palace (same owners), but did so in a casual, chic environment and with an accelerated pace of innovation. (Grilling fish over burning wood was their most important new idea.) Now that casual gourmet restaurants dominate the dining scene, Mr. B's is unique no longer, but it still has consistently interesting food served in an engaging ambience. So engaging, in fact, that at both lunch and dinner the place is usually filled right up to the bar, where one might well wait for a table. (The reservation system favors walk-ins.) The service staff and the wine list are both better than you expect.

200

MR. TAI'S

Zone 9   Metairie Below Causeway
701 Metairie Road, Metairie
831-8610

	Chinese
	★★★
	Moderate
	Quality 83 Value C

Reservations:	Accepted
When to go:	Anytime
Entree range:	$8–15
Payment:	All major credit cards
Service rating:	★★★
Friendliness rating:	★★★
Parking:	Free lot adjacent
Bar:	Full bar
Wine selection:	A few house wines
Dress:	Casual
Disabled access:	Full
Customers:	Locals; businessmen at lunch
Lunch:	Monday–Friday, 11:30 A.M.–2:30 P.M.
Dinner:	Every day, 6–10 P.M.

Atmosphere / setting: Upstairs in a shopping mall is an uncommonly handsome, modern (no red velvet dragons) Chinese restaurant with waiters in tuxedos. There's even a bit of tableside service.

Recommended dishes: Fried dumplings; diced boneless quail; fried sesame fish; shredded chicken in assorted flavors sauce; Hunan beef soup; stir-fried oysters in black bean sauce; Mr. Tai's whole fish; Hunan duck; chicken with spiced pecans; chicken chunks with sesame seeds; shrimp with pine nuts; bean curd with minced pork; Mr. Tai's lo mein. Honey crisp apple; sesame-fried banana.

Summary & comments: Many of the refined dishes served here are found in no other local restaurant. The main style is Hunan, with its elegant, translucent, spicy-sweet sauces. Entrees here tend to be the main two or three ingredients and little else; no filler of onions and anonymous vegetables. The place is not as consistent or as ambitious in its menu as it once was, but it's still one of the best Chinese restaurants in the area.

Napoleon House

Zone 1   French Quarter
500 Chartres
524-9752

Sandwiches
★★
Inexpensive
Quality 74   Value B

Reservations: Not accepted
When to go: Anytime
Entree range: $6–8
Payment: All major credit cards
Service rating: ★★★
Friendliness rating: ★★★★
Parking: Jackson Brewery pay lot, one block
Bar: Full bar
Wine selection: A few house wines
Dress: Casual
Disabled access: Full
Customers: Mostly locals, a few tourists; late nighters;
                       Quarterites
Lunch/Dinner: Monday–Thursday, 11 A.M.–midnight;
                       Friday and Saturday, 11 A.M.–1 A.M.;
                       Sunday, closed.

Atmosphere / setting: "Crumbling ruin" captures the essence of the two-century-old building, in which an apartment was once reserved for Napoleon in exile. (He never took the landlord up on the deal.) The Napoleon House today is mainly a bar where classical music plays, Quarterites complain about the failure of their last show, and everybody drinks Pimm's Cups without knowing why.

Recommended dishes: Seafood gumbo; muffuletta; pastrami sandwich; corned beef sandwich; jambalaya.

Summary & comments: The Napoleon House serves a small menu of sandwiches. Topping the list is what is to my taste the city's best muffuletta, well stuffed with good meats and cheeses and dressed with a fine olive salad.

202

Ninja

Zone 4   Uptown Above Napoleon
8115 Jeannette
866-1119

	Japanese
	★★★
	Moderate
	Quality 84 Value C

Reservations:	Accepted
When to go:	Anytime
Entree range:	$7–16
Payment:	All major credit cards except Discover
Service rating:	★★
Friendliness rating:	★★★
Parking:	Curbside
Bar:	Full bar
Wine selection:	A few house wines
Dress:	Casual
Disabled access:	None
Customers:	Neighborhood people, college types
Lunch:	Monday–Saturday, 11:30 A.M.–2:30 P.M.
Dinner:	Monday–Saturday, 5–10 P.M.; Sunday, closed.

Atmosphere / setting: An Uptown cottage, with the sushi bar in one of the small rooms and tables in the other two.

Recommended dishes: Miso soup; edamame (dry-cooked green beans); nigirisushi; sushi rolls; chirashisushi; sashimi; barbecued eel over rice; teriyaki beef; teriyaki fish; tempura shrimp.

Summary & comments: One of the better sushi bars around, with good food and service all around the restaurant. The menu includes the usual array of fried and grilled dishes, but sashimi, sushi, and the like are clearly the specialties.

NoLa

Zone 1   French Quarter
534 St. Louis
522-6652

	Nouvelle Creole
	★★★★
	Expensive
	Quality 90 Value C

Reservations:	Recommended
When to go:	Anytime
Entree range:	$12–24
Payment:	All major credit cards
Service rating:	★★★★
Friendliness rating:	★★★★
Parking:	Jackson Brewery pay lot, one block
Bar:	Full bar
Wine selection:	Substantial list, with emphasis on California; many by-the-glass selections
Dress:	Dressy casual
Disabled access:	Full
Customers:	A mix of tourists and locals, with a hip, young tilt
Lunch:	Monday–Saturday, 11:30 A.M.–2:30 P.M.
Dinner:	Every day, 6–10 P.M.

Atmosphere / setting: Dining rooms are on three levels (with elevator service), and the whole place is filled with trendy fixtures, designs, sculptures, and paintings.

Recommended dishes: Menu changes frequently. At this writing: pizzas; crabcake with chili aïoli; boudin stewed in beer; sautéed shrimp over pasta with warm rémoulade sauce; slow-roasted duck with andouille spoon bread and greens; Vietnamese-style seafood salad; cedar plank-roasted fish with citrus horseradish crust; double-cut pork chop; wood-roasted lamb shank; pannéed veal with crabmeat ravioli. Coconut bread pudding; lemon chess pie; chicory coffee crème brûlée.

Summary & comments: This is the second restaurant of Chef Emeril Lagasse, one of the most celebrated of local culinary geniuses. The ingredient standards of Emeril's are applied with equal rigor here: everything's fresh and made in-house. The scene at Nola is much looser and kickier, with a distinct pitch toward the younger gourmet. They use a wood-burning oven for baking pizzas and a few other things, a wood-burning grill for thick slabs of meat and poultry, and an open kitchen for everything else. Desserts are far more numerous than you're used to; good, too.

Nuvolari's

Nouvelle Italian

★ ★ ★ ★

Expensive

Quality 86   Value B

Zone 12   North Shore
246 Gerard Street, Mandeville
(504) 626-5619

Reservations:	Not accepted
When to go:	Anytime
Entree range:	$8–25 (median: $15)
Payment:	All major credit cards
Service rating:	★ ★ ★
Friendliness rating:	★ ★ ★ ★
Parking:	Free lot adjacent
Bar:	Full bar
Wine selection:	Substantial list, with emphasis on Californian and Italian wines; many by-the-glass selections
Dress:	Dressy casual
Disabled access:	Full
Customers:	North Shore people; couples and foursomes
Dinner:	Every day, 6–10 P.M.

Atmosphere / setting: A neat old brick building in the old part of Mandeville is jazzed up with neon on the outside and made to look somewhat like a franchise concept restaurant inside. (Even the name—commemorating a famous Italian racecar driver—suggests gimmickry.)

Recommended dishes: Antipasto (really a marinated vegetable salad); mussels marinara; gnocchi; avocado stuffed with shrimp and crabmeat rémoulade; corn and crawfish chowder; escargots and crawfish tails in demi-glace sauce; cioppino; grilled fish specials; paglia e fieno (green and white pasta with shrimp); cannelloni; rack of lamb with jalapeño sauce; roast duck with Bing cherries and green peppercorns; veal piccata. White chocolate cheesecake; Bellini ice.

Summary & comments: The food is mostly Italian, with classic dishes reworked into innovative versions. These generally are part of very ample complete dinners at surprisingly low prices. Among the specials you find just about anything from the Nouvelle Creole catalog; lots of grilled fish, for example. The wine list is very good. Service is usually fine, but has been known to mysteriously disintegrate. On weekends, you will probably wait for a table.

Odyssey Grill

Zone 7   Lakeview / West End /
         Bucktown
6264 Argonne Boulevard
482-4092

Greek

★ ★ ★

Moderate

Quality 87   Value B

Reservations:	Accepted
When to go:	Anytime
Entree range:	$8–16
Payment:	All major credit cards
Service rating:	★ ★ ★
Friendliness rating:	★ ★ ★ ★
Parking:	Free lot adjacent
Bar:	Full bar
Wine selection:	Decent list, with several Greek wines among the Californians
Dress:	Casual
Disabled access:	Limited
Customers:	Neighborhood people and members of the local Greek community
Lunch:	Tuesday–Sunday, 11:30 A.M.–3 P.M.
Dinner:	Tuesday–Sunday, 5:30–10 P.M.; Monday, closed.

Atmosphere / setting: The small room, its walls covered with subtle murals, is bright and chummy; the women of the Greek community have adopted the place as a lunchroom.

Recommended dishes: Saganaki (fried, flamed cheese); fried calamari with tzatziki; hummus; spanakopita; Greek salad; Mediterranean lamb salad; pan bagnat (grilled vegetable sandwich, also good with grilled tuna); moussaka; grilled quail with Gorgonzola stuffing; whole grilled fish; grilled veal scallopine; fish baked in phyllo; couscous with seven vegetables, chicken, lamb, and sausage. Galaktoboureko (Greek custard); yogurt cheese with honey and walnuts.

Summary & comments: As the name implies, most of the food here is brought to completion on the grill. The offbeat part of that is that the Odyssey is a Greek restaurant, with all the standards of that cuisine, cooked with élan. An unexpected specialty is the grilled fish, marinated or seasoned with a Greek spice complement and cooked to excitement, often in whole form. There's also a great French grilled vegetable sandwich here, available with grilled fish in it.

Old Dog New Trick

Zone 1 French Quarter	Vegetarian
307 Exchange Alley	★★
522-4569	Inexpensive
	Quality 80 Value C

Reservations:	Not accepted
When to go:	Anytime
Entree range:	$4–8
Payment:	MC, V
Service rating:	★★★
Friendliness rating:	★★★★★
Parking:	Pay garage nearby
Bar:	No alcohol
Wine selection:	None
Dress:	Anything goes
Disabled access:	Full
Customers:	Neighborhood people; businessmen at lunch
Lunch:	Monday–Saturday, 11:30 A.M.–3 P.M.
Dinner:	Tuesday–Saturday, 5–9 P.M.; Sunday, closed.

Atmosphere / setting: A little dining room inside and a much more appealing group of tables in Exchange Alley. Occasionally the old dog himself shows up out there.

Recommended dishes: Daily soups; eggplant Napoleon with peppers and goat cheese; polenta-crust pizzas; whole-wheat crust barbecue pizza; Ben burger (rice, lentils, and other grains made into a patty and grilled); salads; soba noodles with soy and vegetables. Vegan dessert, particularly the lemon tart.

Summary & comments: New Orleans' vegetarian restaurants have rarely done well—either in commercial or gustatory terms. This little place is a noteworthy exception. The cooking is imaginative and involves very good raw materials. The flavors that result from these efforts makes one forget that all this stuff is good for you. Interesting crowd: mostly young CBD workers and Quarterites.

Olivier's Creole Restaurant

	Creole / Neighborhood Cafe
Zone 1 French Quarter	★★★
204 Decatur	Moderate
525-7734	Quality 75 Value C

Reservations:	Accepted
When to go:	Anytime
Entree range:	$8–17
Payment:	All major credit cards except Discover
Service rating:	★★★
Friendliness rating:	★★★★
Parking:	Pay garage nearby
Bar:	Full bar
Wine selection:	Limited list of ordinary wines
Dress:	Casual
Disabled access:	Full
Customers:	Tourists, some locals
Lunch / Dinner:	Every day, 11:30 A.M.–10 P.M.

Atmosphere / setting: Pleasant but unremarkable dining room with a jazz theme in the decor.

Recommended dishes: Oysters Rockefeller; pecan-breaded oysters; gumbo sampler (three versions); braised rabbit with oyster dressing; crawfish etouffee; fried seafood platter; stuffed pork chops. Bread pudding; peach cobbler.

Summary & comments: The second generation of Oliviers in the restaurant business opened this good-looking cafe in the French Quarter, which largely follows the back-o-town Creole style of the original Olivier's in presenting the dishes that most Orleanians grew up eating at home. The menu here moves a bit beyond that to include a good deal of one-thing-on-top-of-another dishes, which are also good but not as convincing as the basics—particularly the seafood and chicken. A jazzy, real New Orleans experience for a visitor.

Palace Cafe

Zone 2   Central Business District
605 Canal Street
523-1661

Nouvelle Creole	
★★★	
Expensive	
Quality 84	Value C

Reservations:	Recommended
When to go:	Anytime
Entree range:	$11–19
Payment:	All major credit cards
Service rating:	★★★★
Friendliness rating:	★★★★
Parking:	Validated (free) at Holiday Inn and Marriott garages
Bar:	Full bar
Wine selection:	Substantial list, almost entirely West Coast
Dress:	Dressy casual
Disabled access:	Full
Customers:	Locals, tourists; businessmen at lunch
Brunch:	Sundays, 11 A.M.–3 P.M.
Lunch:	Every day, 11:30 A.M.–2:30 P.M.
Dinner:	Every day, 6–10:30 P.M.

Atmosphere / setting: Occupying two floors of the historic old Werlein's building on Canal Street, the dining area here is a spacious array of dark-wood booths on tiny-tiled floors. The acoustics are lively; when the place is full, it's loud in here. The upstairs tables offer a great view of New Orleans' main street; during the Carnival season, this is a great place to watch parades. When the weather is tolerable, you can eat at sidewalk tables in a rough approximation of the Champs Elysées.

Recommended dishes: Fried oysters with creamy horseradish sauce; oyster shooters vinaigrette; shrimp rémoulade; coconut beer shrimp with andouille; blue cheese salad; catfish pecan; grilled tuna; seared fish with rock shrimp maquechoux; rotisserie chicken; rotisserie pork chops; rotisserie prime rib chop. White chocolate bread pudding; Mississippi mud pie; warm chocolate pudding cake; fruit beignets with ice cream.

Entertainment & amenities: Unusually good player piano rolls all the time.

Summary & comments: This is the most casual restaurant run by the Commander's Palace side of the Brennan family. As such, there is difficulty with identity, as in: should they serve red beans and rice or not? The efforts to bring the homecooked Creole standards to Brennan standards of panache usually end in frustration. So stay with the rotisserie dishes, of which there are many, and the unusual seafood concoctions.

209

Palmer's

	Caribbean
	★★★
	Moderate
	Quality 82 Value A

Zone 6   Mid-City / Gentilly
135 North Carrollton Avenue
482-3658

Reservations:	Recommended
When to go:	Anytime
Entree range:	$10–18
Payment:	No credit cards
Service rating:	★★
Friendliness rating:	★★★
Parking:	Curbside
Bar:	Beer and wine
Wine selection:	A few house wines
Dress:	Casual
Disabled access:	Limited
Customers:	Locals
Lunch:	Tuesday–Friday, 11:30 A.M.–2:30 P.M.
Dinner:	Tuesday–Saturday, 5:30–10 P.M.;
	Sunday and Monday, closed.

Atmosphere / setting: Spare surroundings. Not the best place to be on the hottest summertime days: the air conditioning never seems to keep up.

Recommended dishes: Ceviche; shrimp Betty (spicy sauce, fettuccine); Bahamian seafood chowder (light, mildly peppery fish soup); Jamaican pepperpot; Jamaican chicken (rich sauce with demi-glace); braised fish Caribbean; escovitch fish; Jamaican jerked fish; Caribbean roast pork with apples and potatoes; West Indian curried goat with rice and peas. Black Forest cake; sweet potato pudding.

Summary & comments: Cecil Palmer was for many years the sous chef of Willy Coln's German-Continental restaurant, and his abilities to turn out a polished plate of food are unimpeachable. But when he opened his own restaurant, it was in the style of his homeland Jamaica—including in the matter of the very minimal decor. The array of jerk, escovitch, and curried dishes share the menu with some of the suave food he used to prepare, and the blend is brilliant. The prices are embarrassingly cheap. Both the plates and the flavors on them are quite full.

Pascal's Manale

Zone 4   Uptown Above Napoleon
1838 Napoleon Avenue
895-4877

Creole Italian	
★★★★	
Expensive	
Quality 85	Value B

Reservations:	Recommended
When to go:	Anytime
Entree range:	$10–20
Payment:	All major credit cards
Service rating:	★★★
Friendliness rating:	★★
Parking:	Free lot adjacent
Bar:	Full bar
Wine selection:	Not what it should be; mostly ordinary Italian wines
Dress:	Casual
Disabled access:	Limited
Customers:	A mix of Uptown locals and tourists
Lunch/Dinner:	Monday–Friday, 11:30 A.M.–10 P.M.
Dinner:	Saturday and Sunday, 4–10 P.M.; closed Sundays between Memorial Day and Labor Day

Atmosphere / setting: This old restaurant shows its age the way an elder movie star with too many facelifts does: the attempts to hide the wear and tear are not entirely successful. But everybody feels comfortable here. Changing the concrete-floor bar, for example, might ruin the place.

Recommended dishes: Raw oysters on the half shell; stuffed mushrooms; crab and oyster pan roast; oysters Bienville; shrimp and crabmeat rémoulade; turtle soup; barbecue shrimp (baked in black pepper butter); broiled fish with crabmeat and hollandaise; veal Puccini (a very rich piccata); filet mignon; spaghetti Collins (with green onions and butter). Bread pudding; chocolate mousse.

Summary & comments: Founded in 1913, Manale's is the archetype of the Creole-Italian restaurant. It became immensely popular in the Fifties for a dish that's still its signature: barbecue shrimp. It's badly misnamed, since the shrimp are neither grilled nor smoked, and the sauce isn't anybody's barbecue sauce, but it's undeniably wonderful: gigantic heads-on jobs with a peppery butter sauce. After some problems in the Eighties, Manale's bounced back strong and has become a terrific casual place for eating some very convincing food. The prices have even become a value—a big change from a decade ago. Service remains a bit inexact, and you might have to wait for a table on weekends. Good oyster bar. Avoid red-sauce dishes.

Pelican Club

Zone 1   French Quarter
615 Bienville
523-1504

Eclectic	
★ ★ ★ ★ ★	
Expensive	
Quality 96	Value C

Reservations:	Recommended
When to go:	Anytime
Entree range:	$14–25
Payment:	All major credit cards
Service rating:	★ ★ ★ ★
Friendliness rating:	★ ★
Parking:	Validated (free) at Monteleone Hotel garage
Bar:	Full bar
Wine selection:	Substantial list, good international balance; many by-the-glass selections
Dress:	Jacket recommended but not required
Disabled access:	Limited
Customers:	A mix of locals and tourists; couples; gourmets
Dinner:	Every day, 6–10 P.M.

Atmosphere / setting: A row of handsome dining rooms flanks semi-mysterious Exchange Alley, a French Quarter walkway that even Orleanians are unfamiliar with. Depending on what part of the restaurant you're in, the ambience ranges from party-like (the first room) to romantic (the rear of the second room).

Recommended dishes: Scallop-stuffed artichoke with lemon garlic beurre blanc; beef and shrimp potstickers; escargots with crawfish, garlic, mushrooms, and puff pastry hats; Creole Caesar salad; Thai seafood salad; smoked duck and shrimp gumbo; claypot of seafood with Thai rice; Louisiana bouillabaisse; grilled fish with ginger lime glaze; filet mignon with cabernet shiitake mushroom sauce; jambalaya. Dessert specials.

Summary & comments: This extraordinarily good restaurant keeps a low profile, although it can cook and serve with the best of them. Chefs Richard Hughes and Chin Ling combine Creole, Italian, Chinese, Southwestern, and various other flavors into dishes using ingredients of unimpeachable goodness (pompano, lobster, prime beef, etc.). The result is immensely appealing, perhaps because a bit more familiarity of flavor is preserved than in similar restaurants. The dining room can get a bit noisy; many of the regulars know one another. Service is friendly, although the greeting at the door is a bit cold.

Peppermill (Riccobono's)

	Creole Italian
Zone 10 Metairie Above Causeway / Kenner / Jefferson Hwy.	★★★
3524 Severn Avenue, Metairie	Moderate
455-2266	Quality 77 Value C

Reservations:	Accepted
When to go:	Anytime
Entree range:	$8–18
Payment:	All major credit cards
Service rating:	★★★
Friendliness rating:	★★★
Parking:	Free lot adjacent
Bar:	Full bar
Wine selection:	Decent list, with emphasis on California and Italy
Dress:	Casual
Disabled access:	Limited
Customers:	Locals, many on the older side; businessmen at lunch; families
Brunch:	Sunday, 11 A.M.–3 P.M.
Breakfast/Lunch:	Every day, 7 A.M.–3 P.M.
Dinner:	Tuesday–Sunday, 3–9:30 P.M.

Atmosphere / setting: A comfortably outmoded dining room (circa 1976).

Recommended dishes: Angel hair Angelique (crabmeat, tomato cream sauce); oysters Riccobono (baked with bread crumbs and garlic); cannelloni; stuffed mushrooms; shrimp rémoulade; crawfish bisque; eggplant Parmigiana; veal with crawfish Monica; trout supreme (crabmeat and béarnaise); pannéed oysters; grilled fish (other than catfish); veal Alexander (on pannéed eggplant with meunière sauce). Caramel custard.

Summary & comments: This place evolved from a chain of formula steak-houses, although only the gimmicky menu copy suggests that ancestry now. The menu is a fifty-fifty blend of Creole and Creole-Italian specialties, of which the former are the better. (Red-sauce dishes here are strictly for kids.) The Peppermill's breakfast is finer than anything outside the major hotels and Brennan's, with a big menu of well-prepared, sometimes fancy dishes.

Peristyle

Zone 1   French Quarter
1041 Dumaine
593-9535

Nouvelle French
★★★★
Expensive

Quality 94   Value B

Reservations:	Required
When to go:	Early evenings
Entree range:	$14–21
Payment:	MC, V
Service rating:	★★★★★
Friendliness rating:	★★
Parking:	Curbside, in a mildly unsavory neighborhood, and very difficult to come by; the best idea is to take a cab
Bar:	Full bar
Wine selection:	Modest list of offbeat, well-chosen wines that match the food well; mostly French, quite a few from Provence
Dress:	Jacket recommended but not required
Disabled access:	Limited
Customers:	Gourmets, couples, mostly locals
Lunch:	Friday, 11:30 A.M.–2 P.M.
Dinner:	Tuesday–Saturday, 6–10 P.M.; Sunday and Monday, closed.

Atmosphere / setting: The place has a sort of Art Nouveau, Storyville feel, a remnant of the previous tenant. The current management has toned it down to a cool, romantic setting.

Recommended dishes: The menu changes too thoroughly and too often for any specific recommendations, but the level of goodness across the short board is uniform.

Summary & comments: After three years of brilliance, Peristyle's owner/chef died, and the restaurant was taken over by a former chef from Emeril's who applied a new culinary style. Where there was once a fascinating tinge of France in the food, now we find a very well-conceived, but more mainstream, new American palette of flavors. The dining room staff is well orchestrated in its unpretentious activities. And the wine list is selected with care and verve. There are only two problems: the neighborhood is unsavory, and parking is difficult.

PETRA

	Mediterranean
	★★★
	Expensive
	Quality 83 Value B

Zone 9   Metairie Below Causeway
541 Oaklawn, Metairie
833-3317

Reservations:	Accepted
When to go:	Anytime
Entree range:	$9–18
Payment:	All major credit cards
Service rating:	★★★★
Friendliness rating:	★★★
Parking:	Free lot adjacent
Bar:	Full bar
Wine selection:	Decent list, mostly Italian and Californian
Dress:	Dressy casual
Disabled access:	Full
Customers:	Locals
Lunch:	Monday–Friday, 11:30 A.M.–2:30 P.M.
Dinner:	Monday–Saturday, 6–10 P.M.; Sunday, closed.

Atmosphere / setting: The attractive, dim dining room features small curtained booths for very private dining.

Recommended dishes: Oysters Petra (baked on artichoke bottoms); eggplant cakes with crabmeat or crawfish; Middle Eastern mezzas (hummus, baba gannoujh, tabbouleh); polenta (topped with different sauces daily); Mediterranean seafood soup; angel hair pasta bordelaise; lamb kebab; fish Florentine (with sautéed spinach); lamb chops with mint sauce; veal Petra (mushroom sauce); seafood pastas. Tiramisu; crème brûlée.

Summary & comments: Petra (named for an ancient town in Jordan, from whence came the owner) was founded by the former maître d' of Andrea's, along with a few chefs and waiters from that restaurant. Although the place calls itself Mediterranean, in the main the menu is Italian, with a sprinkling of Middle Eastern dishes for atmosphere.

PETUNIA'S

Zone 1   French Quarter
817 St. Louis
522-6440

Reservations:	Not accepted
When to go:	Anytime except late night
Entree range:	$6–15
Payment:	All major credit cards
Service rating:	★★
Friendliness rating:	★★
Parking:	Curbside
Bar:	Beer and wine
Wine selection:	A few house wines
Dress:	Casual
Disabled access:	None
Customers:	A mix of Quarterites and locals
Open:	Sunday–Thursday, 8 A.M.–11 P.M.;
	Friday and Saturday, 8 A.M.–midnight

Atmosphere / setting: The main dining room is the former parlor of a classic Creole townhouse. The hanging and other plant life is lush.

Recommended dishes: Basic breakfasts. Omelettes; pain perdu ("lost bread"—the local variation of French toast); veal grillades and grits; oysters en brochette; gumbo du jour; crêpes (dinner and dessert); shrimp Barataria (curry and dill over rice); jambalaya; fried seafood platters; soft-shell crabs bordelaise. Daily plate specials. Bananas Foster crêpe; hot apple and rum crêpe; pecan pie.

Summary & comments: They're popular among both Quarter residents and visitors; Petunia's specializes in breakfasts, salads, crêpes (the savory versions are incredibly rich, but good anyway), and a mixture of local clichés with some original takes on Creole cooking. It's all decent food, sold at prices below those prevailing in most of the Quarter. The service staff has been known to get into a mass mood.

Port of Call

Zone 1   French Quarter
838 Esplanade
523-0120

Hamburgers
★★★
Inexpensive
Quality 77   Value B

Reservations:	Not accepted
When to go:	Anytime
Entree range:	$7–19
Payment:	AMEX, MC, V
Service rating:	★★
Friendliness rating:	★★
Parking:	Curbside
Bar:	Full bar
Wine selection:	A few house wines
Dress:	Anything goes
Disabled access:	None
Customers:	Locals, singles, baby boomers
Lunch/Dinner:	Sunday–Thursday, 11 A.M.–midnight;
	Friday and Saturday, 11 A.M.–1 A.M.

Atmosphere/setting: A bunch of dark booths in a room with a vague nautical theme and Sixties music. You wouldn't want to see the inside of this place in bright light. There's also a somewhat more formal dining room for the steak eaters.

Recommended dishes: Hamburger; filet mignon; strip sirloin.

Summary & comments: Consistently for almost 30 years, this somewhat inaccessible pub has served New Orleans' best hamburger. A thick slab of fresh, hand-pattied chuck is grilled to a crusty-and-juicy irresistibility, served on a toasted bun with grated Cheddar and a good baked potato. They also have good steaks and bad pizza.

Praline Connection

	Creole / Neighborhood Cafe
	★★★
	Moderate
	Quality 80 Value B

Zone 2   Central Business District
901 South Peters
523-3973
Zone 5   Downtown / St. Bernard
542 Frenchman
943-3934

Reservations:	Not accepted
When to go:	Late for lunch or early for dinner
Entree range:	$7–17
Payment:	All major credit cards
Service rating:	★★★★
Friendliness rating:	★★★★
Parking:	Curbside (metered)
Bar:	Full bar
Wine selection:	A few house wines
Dress:	Casual
Disabled access:	Full
Customers:	A mix of locals and tourists
Brunch:	Warehouse District only: Sunday, 11 A.M.–3 P.M.
Lunch / Dinner:	Every day, 11 A.M.–10 P.M.

Atmosphere / setting: The Marigny location is a smallish, somewhat crowded room with a lot of hustle. The Warehouse District Connection is much larger—in fact, it's a concert hall with tables. Along one wall is a row of very well done set-pieces that resemble a New Orleans street scene.

Recommended dishes: Praline Connection platter (all fried: okra, pickles, hot chicken wings, chicken livers, catfish, shrimp, and soft-shell crawfish, with two dipping sauces). Creole gumbo; red beans and rice; crowder peas; greens; fried chicken; baked chicken; shrimp Creole. Bread pudding with praline sauce.

Entertainment & amenities: At the Warehouse District location, live jazz and blues bands perform most nights. On weekends, this goes into the wee hours. On Sundays at brunch are gospel groups.

Summary & comments: If there's such a thing as a nouvelle soul restaurant, this is it. It's a celebration of Baby Boom–Era black culture; the staff looks as if it might as well be in a jazz combo as serving food. Beans and greens (many varieties of each), chicken, fish, and chops (prepared several ways), and lots and lots of pot food. While not utterly consistent, all of this is likely to be at least pretty good. More hip, popular, and expensive than the African-heritage restaurants of the previous generation.

Pupuseria Divino Corazon

Salvadoran	
★★★	
Inexpensive	
Quality 79	Value A

Zone 11   West Bank
2300 Belle Chasse Highway, Gretna
368-5724

Reservations:	Not accepted
When to go:	Anytime
Entree range:	$2–8
Payment:	MC, V
Service rating:	★★★
Friendliness rating:	★★★
Parking:	Free lot adjacent
Bar:	Beer and wine
Wine selection:	A few house wines
Dress:	Anything goes
Disabled access:	Full
Customers:	The West Bank Hispanic community, gourmets
Lunch / Dinner:	Every day, 11 A.M.–9:30 P.M.

Atmosphere / setting: In a ramshackle building it shares with a used-tire store, this cafe is a very close approximation of an authentic Central American dining experience. The dining room, decorated with images of the Sacred Heart, is clean and colorful.

Recommended dishes: Pupusas; chicken tamales; pasteles de carne (small meat pies); nacho Chihuahua; guacamole salad; faro del Pacifico combination plate. Daily specials, especially the salpicon con consommé (broiled beef in stock, Wednesdays). Flan; tamal de elote con crème (a sweet tamale with corn and sour cream).

Summary & comments: The owners (a very nice family) are from El Salvador, and the curious name means it is a vendor of the Salvadoran national dish. The pupusa is a hybrid of a tamale and a tortilla, made with masa corn meal into quarter-inch-thick disks with morsels of pork, cheese, and onions inside, then grilled. Those are good, as are the other Salvadoran specialties and the homely Mexican dishes.

R&O's

Sandwiches	
★★	
Inexpensive	
Quality 68	Value B

Zone 7   Lakeview/West End/
          Bucktown
210 Metairie-Hammond Highway,
   Metairie
831-1248

Reservations:	Not accepted
When to go:	Lunch and early evenings
Entree range:	$4–15
Payment:	MC, V
Service rating:	★★
Friendliness rating:	★
Parking:	Free lot adjacent
Bar:	Beer and wine
Wine selection:	A few house wines
Dress:	Anything goes
Disabled access:	Full
Customers:	Locals, families
Lunch/Dinner:	Wednesday–Monday, 11 A.M.–10 P.M.;
	Tuesday, closed.

Atmosphere/setting: This place started as a terrific dumpy little joint. Then it grew into a good but bigger joint, and finally into an above-average, much bigger joint. But it never seems to grow enough to accommodate all the people who want to crowd in and add to the racket.

Recommended dishes: Boiled shrimp; boiled crawfish (in season); garlic pizza; traditional thin-crust pizza; R&O special poor boy (ham, roast beef, and Swiss); Italian special poor boy (meatballs, Italian sausage, mozzarella, red sauce); fried seafood platters. Bread pudding.

Summary & comments: With each enlargement, R&O's food showed more evidence of prefabrication to me, but it's still pretty good. The specialties are (in descending order of goodness) poor boys, seafood platters, pizza, and Italian platters. Everything is served in mammoth portions at startlingly low prices.

Restaurant des Familles

Zone 11   West Bank
LA 45 at LA 3134, Lafitte
689-7834

	Seafood
	★★★
	Moderate
	Quality 76 Value C

Reservations:	Accepted
When to go:	Anytime
Entree range:	$11–17
Payment:	All major credit cards
Service rating:	★★★
Friendliness rating:	★★★★
Parking:	Free lot adjacent
Bar:	Full bar
Wine selection:	Decent list, good international balance
Dress:	Casual
Disabled access:	Full
Customers:	Locals, families, couples
Lunch:	Tuesday–Sunday, 11:30 A.M.–2:30 P.M.
Dinner:	Tuesday–Sunday, 6–10 P.M.; Monday, closed.

Atmosphere / setting: Down the highway to Lafitte (one of the ends of the earth), this handsome seafood restaurant has a distinctive setting. Large windows give out onto the lazy Bayou des Familles, as primordial a scene as an alligator ever crawled.

Recommended dishes: Crabmeat Remick; oysters Lafitte; fried seafood platter; fried soft-shell crabs.

Summary & comments: Basic to mildly ambitious Creole-Cajun seafood dominates the menu. The fried and otherwise simply prepared entrees are good enough; the more involved items, particularly those involving pasta, are less successful. To be avoided is any dish that smacks of home cooking (i.e., the shrimp meatballs). There's enough good food here to make the trip (about 20 minutes from downtown) worthwhile, especially when combined with a visit to neighboring Jean Lafitte National Park.

Rib Room

Zone 1   French Quarter
621 St. Louis
529-7045

Nouvelle Creole	
★★★★	
Very Expensive	
Quality 91	Value D

Reservations:	Recommended
When to go:	Anytime; Friday lunch is usually a full house
Entree range:	$15–26
Payment:	All major credit cards
Service rating:	★★★
Friendliness rating:	★★
Parking:	Validated (free) in Omni Royal Orleans Hotel garage
Bar:	Full bar
Wine selection:	Substantial list, good international balance; 20 by-the-glass selections
Dress:	Jacket recommended but not required
Disabled access:	Limited
Customers:	Businessmen at lunch; hotel guests at dinner
Brunch:	Sunday, 11 A.M.–3 P.M.
Lunch:	Every day, 11:30 A.M.–3 P.M.
Dinner:	Every day, 6–10:30 P.M.

Atmosphere / setting: A large room with lofty ceilings, brick walls, big windows affording a view of the passing parade on Royal Street, and big, cushy seats. A power center at lunch, a romantic spot for dinner.

Recommended dishes: Spit-roasted shrimp with Creole mustard sauce; crab cake; crab bisque; Rib Room salad; roasted salmon. Any special involving crawfish as a main ingredient. Veal Tanet (large pannéed slice of veal atop a romaine salad); rotisserie chicken; mixed grill; prime rib; rack of lamb. Dessert pastries; chocolate mousse.

Summary & comments: The Rib Room didn't start out as the flagship dining room of the top-class Royal Orleans Hotel, but it soon became that. In the center rear of this expansive cube of a room is the station where the namesake dish—prime ribs of roast beef—are carved to order. While still as good as any other around, these are now the least interesting of the offerings. Better is what's behind the carving board: a wall of rotisseries with all sorts of meat, poultry, and seafood roasting. The rest of the menu has a distinctly Louisiana flavor with a touch of continental polish. The specials, at both lunch and dinner, are usually the best eating here. Service here has never been as gracious as one might like; much of the staff has been here a little too long.

222

Rigatoni

Zone 3 Uptown Below Napoleon	Italian
3442 St. Charles Avenue	★★★
899-1570	Moderate
	Quality 80 Value B

Reservations:	Accepted
When to go:	Anytime
Entree range:	$5–16
Payment:	DC, MC, V
Service rating:	★★
Friendliness rating:	★★★
Parking:	Curbside (metered)
Bar:	Full bar
Wine selection:	A few Italian house wines
Dress:	Casual
Disabled access:	Full
Customers:	People who work at the nearby hospitals and other locals
Lunch / Dinner:	Monday–Friday, 11:30 A.M.–10 P.M.
Dinner:	Saturday and Sunday, 5–9 P.M.

Atmosphere / setting: A narrow, triangular, well-windowed building occupies the interstice of two converging streets at St. Charles Avenue.

Recommended dishes: Leonardo salad (shrimp, avocado, hearts of palm); penne with spinach and ricotta; farfalle pasta with smoked salmon; rigatoni with tomato, basil, and Fontina cheese; gnocchi with Gorgonzola; spaghetti with asparagus and corn and a cream sauce; veal pizzaiola; costoletta of breaded veal with roasted potatoes; grilled chicken with corn, beans, and raisins.

Summary & comments: This is, believe it or not, one of a chain of restaurants whose other two locations are in Florence, Italy. Among an assortment of inexpensive, simple Italian specialties—not all of them familiar—we find a passel of pasta dishes with exactly the same textures and flavors that one finds in Italy. The sauce is flavorful without being rich, and is blended with the pasta instead of dumped all over it. Despite this quality (or perhaps because of it) there's rarely a big crowd here, but don't let that dissuade you.

RISTORANTE CARMELO

	Italian
	★★★
	Moderate
	Quality 79 Value C

Zone 1   French Quarter
541 Decatur
586-1414

Reservations:	Recommended
When to go:	Anytime
Entree range:	$8–16
Payment:	All major credit cards except Discover
Service rating:	★★★
Friendliness rating:	★★★
Parking:	Pay lot nearby
Bar:	Full bar
Wine selection:	Decent list, mostly Italian; a few very unusual Italian wines
Dress:	Dressy casual
Disabled access:	Full
Customers:	Mix
Lunch / Dinner:	Every day, 11:30 A.M.–10:30 P.M.

Atmosphere / setting: A casual trattoria, with a breezy dining room dominated by a luscious display of antipasto on the first floor, and a more formal dining room lined by wine racks on the second floor.

Recommended dishes: Antipasto freddo; bruschetta with tomatoes, fresh basil, and olive oil; zuppa della casa; risotto with mushrooms; pasta aglio e olio with broccoli; penne arrabbiata; pappardelle pasta with prosciutto and peas; grilled swordfish; salmon with capers and asparagus; veal Marsala with porcini mushrooms; manicotti of eggplant. Cannoli; tiramisu.

Summary & comments: After creating the best chain of pizza stands New Orleans has ever tasted, Carmelo Chirico decided to do some real Italian food, and here it is. Parts of its menu reach the heights, mostly in the Northern Italian idiom. The seafood dishes are especially good. The wine list offers one of the most comprehensive and interesting assortments of Italian bottles hereabouts.

224

Riverside Cafe

Zone 2   Central Business District
Riverwalk (1 Poydras)
522-2061

<table>
<tr><td></td><td>Creole</td></tr>
<tr><td></td><td>★★</td></tr>
<tr><td></td><td>Moderate</td></tr>
<tr><td>Quality 75</td><td>Value C</td></tr>
</table>

Reservations:	Accepted
When to go:	Anytime
Entree range:	$8–18
Payment:	All major credit cards
Service rating:	★★★
Friendliness rating:	★★★
Parking:	Pay lot nearby
Bar:	Full bar
Wine selection:	A few house wines
Dress:	Casual
Disabled access:	Full
Customers:	Tourists, some locals
Lunch/Dinner:	Every day, 11 A.M.–10 P.M.

Atmosphere / setting: The location makes one immediately dubious: it's in the Riverwalk, a touristy mall where most of the eating is of the food court variety. But it's better than that: a sit-down cafe with a fine view of the river and decent service.

Recommended dishes: Shrimp rémoulade; seafood gumbo; fried seafood platter; stuffed crab; red beans and rice; jambalaya. Sweet potato bread pudding.

Summary & comments: While the menu doesn't break out of the bedrock foundation of Creole cuisine, the raw materials are good and fresh and the cooking is reasonably good. Seafood entrees take up most of the menu, but there's a little of everything.

Ruth's Chris Steak House

Steak	
★★★★	
Very Expensive	
Quality 90	Value D

Zone 6   Mid-City / Gentilly
711 North Broad
486-0810

Zone 10   Metairie Above Causeway /
          Kenner / Jefferson Hwy.
3633 Veterans Boulevard, Metairie
888-3600

Reservations:	Accepted
When to go:	Anytime
Entree range:	$16–26
Payment:	All major credit cards
Service rating:	★★★★
Friendliness rating:	★★★★
Parking:	Valet (free)
Bar:	Full bar
Wine selection:	Substantial list, heavily tilted toward the reds
Dress:	Dressy casual
Disabled access:	Full
Customers:	Politicians, media figures, businessmen; couples at dinner
Lunch / Dinner:	Every day, 11:30 A.M.–11:30 P.M.

Atmosphere / setting: Both locations have a simple, masculine, but very comfortable layout. There are many booths to hide out in, and many tables from which to see or be seen. Power and celebrity crackle in the air.

Recommended dishes: Shrimp rémoulade; stuffed mushrooms; house salad with Creole French dressing; filet mignon; New York strip; porterhouse for two; lamb chops; veal chops; pork chop (lunch only); salmon fillet; boiled lobster; lyonnaise potatoes; french fries in any of the four shapes; baked potato. Bread pudding; cheesecakes.

Summary & comments: The leading chain of premium steak houses in America started on Broad Street six decades ago. Ruth Fertel, now the world's most successful female restaurateur, took it over in the Sixties and has kept it moving upward ever since. The essence of Ruth's Chris is the very simple preparation—in a superheated broiler, followed by a dousing with sizzling butter—of top-class steaks and chops. In the case of the beef, it's dry-aged USDA prime strictly. Also here is big lobster and thick flanks of salmon. Side dishes are nothing especially original but are prepared very well. The a la carte prices are quite high; you can really drop a bundle here at dinner. Lunches are more affordable. Service is effective and without ceremony.

226

Sal & Judy's

Zone 12   North Shore
US 190, Lacombe
(504) 882-9443

Creole Italian
★★★★
Expensive
Quality 86   Value B

Reservations:	Not accepted
When to go:	Weeknights
Entree range:	$10–19
Payment:	MC, V
Service rating:	★★
Friendliness rating:	★★
Parking:	Free lot adjacent
Bar:	Full bar
Wine selection:	Limited list of Italian wines
Dress:	Casual
Disabled access:	Limited
Customers:	North Shore people, families
Lunch / Dinner:	Friday–Sunday, noon–10 P.M.
Dinner:	Wednesday and Thursday, 5–10 P.M.; Monday and Tuesday, closed.

Atmosphere / setting: The pink, frilly curtains notwithstanding, this looks like a minimal roadhouse both inside or out. But then we are out on the road, in a small rural village.

Recommended dishes: Fettuccine Alfredo; stuffed artichoke (with bread crumbs and garlic); fried calamari; baked oysters Cinisi (mushrooms and Italian sausage); trout Jimmy (with artichokes and lemon); soft-shell crabs; spaghetti aglio e olio with Italian sausage and roasted peppers; spaghetti with oysters. Cheesecake; gelato.

Summary & comments: It's one of the best and most popular restaurants on the North Shore, drawing from both the Slidell and Mandeville / Covington areas. Sal Impastato came here from Sicily to work for Jimmy Moran years ago; doing so, he picked up as many good Creole moves as Italian. The printed menu here looks unimpressive, but among the specials you will find a great deal of very good eating, mostly in the veal and seafood departments. Everything is surprisingly inexpensive given the goodness and quantity; the corners are cut on the frills. At any normal dining hour you're likely to wait for a table.

Sal & Sam's

Zone 10   Metairie Above Causeway/
           Kenner/Jefferson Hwy.
4300 Veterans Boulevard, Metairie
885-5566

Creole Italian
★★
Moderate

Quality 73   Value C

Reservations:	Accepted
When to go:	Anytime
Entree range:	$13–21
Payment:	All major credit cards
Service rating:	★★★
Friendliness rating:	★★★★
Parking:	Free lot adjacent
Bar:	Full bar
Wine selection:	Limited list of ordinary wines
Dress:	Dressy casual
Disabled access:	Full
Customers:	Locals, most of them regular customers approaching middle age
Lunch/Dinner:	Every day, 11:30 A.M.–1 A.M.

Atmosphere/setting: Three dining rooms, all of them on the dark side, with the feeling of the back room of a men's club.

Recommended dishes: Shrimp rémoulade; barbecue shrimp; oysters Bienville; stuffed mushrooms; fried seafood platter; sautéed fish with crabmeat or crawfish; osso buco; filet mignon. Daily lunch specials.

Summary & comments: Sal & Sam's is the archetype of a style I call Suburban Creole. These places incorporate the favorite (although not necessarily the best) dishes of the old Creole institutions in the Quarter with the homestyle Creole and Italian dishes that suburban cooks don't feel like preparing at home anymore. All of this is served in quantities that appeal to the chowhound. Of course, the place was instantly popular, and still is with the many regulars who didn't defect to the many other Suburban Creole places out there now. The food is generally good, but don't expect any subtlety. The waitresses don't wear quite enough clothes.

228

Sal's Pasta Garden

Zone 9   Metairie Below Causeway
1414 Veterans Boulevard, Metairie
835-3699

Italian	
★★	
Moderate	
Quality 73	Value B

Reservations:	Not accepted
When to go:	Anytime
Entree range:	$5–14
Payment:	All major credit cards
Service rating:	★★
Friendliness rating:	★★★
Parking:	Free lot adjacent
Bar:	Full bar
Wine selection:	Limited list of inexpensive, mostly Italian and Californian wines
Dress:	Casual
Disabled access:	Full
Customers:	Locals, families
Lunch/Dinner:	Every day, 11:30 A.M.–10 P.M.

Atmosphere/setting: A long, heavily windowed room; pleasant, but nothing special in terms of looks.

Recommended dishes: Fried eggplant sticks; fried calamari; manicotti; Italian salad; spaghetti and meatballs; rigatoni with four cheeses; lasagna; veal Parmigiana. Italian ice creams.

Summary & comments: There will always be a big audience for the most familiar of Italian dishes, particularly if they're served inexpensively and over-sufficiently. We're talking here about spaghetti and meatballs, lasagna, cannelloni, fettuccine Alfredo with pannéed veal, and on up to veal Parmigiana as the upper limit of ambitiousness. Reliably good, though, and especially appealing for families with children.

SALVATORE'S

Zone 10   Metairie Above Causeway/
                Kenner/Jefferson Hwy.
3528 18th Street, Metairie
455-2433

Creole Italian	
★★	
Expensive	
Quality 74	Value C

Reservations:	Recommended
When to go:	Anytime
Entree range:	$11–24
Payment:	All major credit cards
Service rating:	★★★
Friendliness rating:	★★★
Parking:	Valet (free)
Bar:	Full bar
Wine selection:	Decent list, mostly Italian and Californian
Dress:	Dressy casual
Disabled access:	Full
Customers:	Locals, many of them regulars; couples
Lunch/Dinner:	Monday–Friday, 11:30 A.M.–10 P.M.
Dinner:	Saturday, 5–10 P.M.; Sunday, closed.

Atmosphere / setting: The dining room is pretty, although the atmosphere is muddied a bit by the restaurant's bar, which has live music, video poker, and lounge lizards.

Recommended dishes: Oysters Salvatore (Italian style with bread crumbs and garlic); oyster artichoke soup; three-green salad; malafatta (spinach gnocchi); penne with asparagus and ham; Italian-style shrimp (pan-roasted with whole garlic); artichoke ravioli; smoked rabbit with Italian sausage; quail with risotto; chicken grandee (pan-roasted with rosemary and garlic); filet mignon; lamb chops with kiwi mint sauce. Tiramisu; peach cake.

Entertainment & amenities: Pianist Jimmy Elledge sings country blues in the lounge Wednesday–Saturday.

Summary & comments: Salvatore's is the last refuge of the cooking and service that distinguished the much-mourned Elmwood Plantation, which burned down in the Seventies. Many of the Elmwood's specialties—not to mention a few members of their staff—live on here, along with an equal amount of newer dishes. It's all a classic example of Creole-Italian: herbaceous dishes with no shortage of garlic and olive oil, yet with enough spice and seafood to give them a distinctive local flavor.

Santa Fe

Zone 1   French Quarter
801 Frenchmen
944-6854

	Mexican
	★★★
	Moderate
	Quality 87 Value C

Reservations:	Not accepted
When to go:	Early evenings
Entree range:	$9–15
Payment:	AMEX, MC,V
Service rating:	★★★
Friendliness rating:	★★★
Parking:	Curbside
Bar:	Full bar
Wine selection:	Decent list, a mix of origins; good prices
Dress:	Casual
Disabled access:	Limited
Customers:	Neighborhood people; singles and daters
Dinner:	Tuesday–Saturday, 5–11 P.M.;
	Sunday and Monday, closed.

Atmosphere / setting: A single corner room, always busy and happy, with the enticing view of the chef's great cakes in the display cases.

Recommended dishes: Nachos del mar (with seafood and beans); ceviche; sopa de mariscos (Mexican gumbo); Caesar salad with prosciutto croutons; chile relleno stuffed with seafood; seafood combination platter (tamale, enchilada, etc.); grilled tuna with sweet red pepper sauce; chicken Maximilian (stuffed with chorizo and asadero cheese); Gypsy fajitas; pork tenderloin with demi-glace, apples, and nuts. Flan; German chocolate cake; Black Forest cake.

Summary & comments: The Santa Fe is the best Mexican restaurant in the city proper. The name is a little misleading: the food here is not New Mexican. Nor Old Mexican or Tex-Mex either. It may, however, be Creole Mexican, if you'll permit me to invent a category. The German chef-owner (getting complicated, isn't it?) reworks a familiar list of Mexican dishes into just-different-enough creations. The best of these involve seafood, although you'll find delicious essays with every main-role foodstuff, including vegetarian dishes. The place is so busy that a wait for service is unavoidable, and parking is sometimes a bit tough, but in light of the food these are minor deterrents.

Sazerac

Zone 2   Central Business District
University Place
529-7111

Reservations:	Recommended
When to go:	Anytime
Entree range:	$16–26
Payment:	All major credit cards
Service rating:	★★★★
Friendliness rating:	★★★
Parking:	Validated (free) at garage across the street (University Place side)
Bar:	Full bar
Wine selection:	Substantial list, equally divided between California and France; very pricey
Dress:	Jacket recommended but not required
Disabled access:	Full
Customers:	Businessmen at lunch; couples at dinner
Brunch:	Sunday, 11 A.M.–3 P.M.
Lunch:	Monday–Friday, 11:30 A.M.–2:30 P.M.
Dinner:	Every day, 6–10 P.M.

Atmosphere / setting: The flagship dining room of the 101-year-old Fairmont Hotel is named for the world's first cocktail. Have one of those in the large, comfortable, visually arresting lounge. Then sit down to a languid, romantic dinner served in an elaborate, nearly extinct style. The tables are clothed with lace, the walls covered with red velvet, and portraits of unidentifiable dandies of centuries ago hang on the walls.

Recommended dishes: Smoked salmon; baked oysters three ways; Turban of Dover sole stuffed with crabmeat; steak tartare; lobster bisque; Fairmont salad with shrimp and crabmeat; Louisiana bouillabaisse; grilled tuna and swordfish with savory vegetables; pompano en papillote (baked with a light seafood sauce in a parchment bag); rack of lamb; Châteaubriand. Desserts here change nightly and are uniformly delicious and beautiful.

Entertainment & amenities: Piano trio plays standards and jazz nightly.

Summary & comments: The menu has enough classic, unchanging specialties for the Sazerac to coast along comfortably. And the venerable tableside-preparation service style makes for an incomparably elegant evening. But one wishes that the parade of chefs—some of them excellent—that has passed through the kitchen in recent years would come to a halt. Consistency has been a real problem here, and, at these prices, we have a right to expect it.

Sclafani's

Italian
★★★
Moderate
Quality 84   Value A

Zone 1   French Quarter
301 Dauphine, Chateau Le Moyne Hotel
524-5475
Zone 8   New Orleans East
9900 Hayne Boulevard
241-4472

Reservations:	Accepted
When to go:	Anytime
Entree range:	$6–16
Payment:	All major credit cards
Service rating:	★★★
Friendliness rating:	★★★
Parking:	Free lot adjacent
Bar:	Full bar
Wine selection:	Decent list, mostly Italian
Dress:	Casual
Disabled access:	Limited
Customers:	Neighborhood people
Breakfast:	*French Quarter:* Every day, 6:30–10 A.M.
Lunch:	*New Orleans East:* Monday–Friday, 11:30 A.M.–2:30 P.M.
	French Quarter: Every day, 11 A.M.–2 P.M.
Dinner:	*New Orleans East:* Monday–Saturday, 5–9 P.M.; Sunday, closed.
	French Quarter: Every day, 6–10 P.M.

Atmosphere / setting: A certain rambling, ramshackle quality is in evidence; the atmosphere is more that of a neighborhood cafe than a major restaurant.

Recommended dishes: Louisiana crab cake; shrimp rémoulade; stuffed mushrooms; crawfish ravioli; chicken gumbo; eggplant Belle Rose (topped with crabmeat, mushrooms, and hollandaise); pannéed veal with fettuccine.

Summary & comments: In the Forties, Sicilian immigrant Peter Sclafani opened a great trattoria in Mid-City. It moved in the Sixties to become Metairie's first major restaurant, then closed in the Seventies. Peter Sclafani, Jr. opened this place shortly thereafter, but it didn't become the best place to eat in New Orleans East until the Nineties, when Peter Sclafani, III and brother, Gino, took over the kitchen. They combine their grandfather's volume of specialties with some highly imaginative newer dishes. They never stray far from the Creole-Italian style except in the matter of ingredients. Inexpensive, good, and never as busy as it deserves to be.

233

SEMOLINA

Zone 3 Uptown Below Napoleon	Eclectic
3242 Magazine	★★★
895-4260	Moderate
	Quality 81 Value A

Zone 3   Uptown Below Napoleon
3242 Magazine
895-4260

Zone 6   Mid-City / Gentilly
5080 Pontchartrain Boulevard
486-5581

Zone 11   West Bank
Oakwood Mall (197 West Bank Expressway), Gretna
361-8293

Reservations:	Not accepted
When to go:	Anytime
Entree range:	$6–12
Payment:	All major credit cards
Service rating:	★★★
Friendliness rating:	★★★★
Parking:	Free lot adjacent
Bar:	Beer and wine
Wine selection:	Limited list of wines, most sold by the glass
Dress:	Casual
Disabled access:	Full
Customers:	Younger locals
Lunch / Dinner:	Monday–Saturday, 11 A.M.–10 P.M.; Sunday, 11 A.M.–9 P.M.; Magazine location closed Sunday.

Atmosphere / setting: All locations look as if they'd been designed by a Mardi Gras float designer in a fit of good taste. Fun and quick service are the overarching elements of the atmosphere.

Recommended dishes: Stuffed roasted pepper; marinated vegetable appetizers; baked feta marinara; semolina salad (romaine in a mustardy Caesar-style dressing); macaroni-and-cheese cake; pad thai; pasta marinara with four cheeses; pasta jambalaya; Santa Fe pasta; shrimp Bangkok pasta. Dessert specials.

Summary & comments: The subtitle of the place is "International Pasta Bar," and that about sums it up. The chain started here in New Orleans, the work of three rather accomplished chefs who call themselves "The Taste Buds." Semolina is one of the few restaurants in my experience where the more peculiar a dish sounds, the better it's likely to be. The best have an exotic ethnic provenance. What makes these go is that they suggest, not reproduce, the authentic ethnic originals. Aside from the locations listed above, there are outlying Semolinas in Kenner, Covington, and Slidell.

Shalimar

Zone 1   French Quarter
535 Wilkinson Row
523-0099

	Indian
	★★★
	Moderate
	Quality 82 Value C

Reservations:	Accepted
When to go:	Anytime
Entree range:	$8–15
Payment:	AMEX, MC, V
Service rating:	★★★
Friendliness rating:	★★★
Parking:	Jackson Brewery pay lot, one block
Bar:	Full bar
Wine selection:	A few house wines
Dress:	Casual
Disabled access:	Full
Customers:	A mix of locals and tourists
Brunch:	Sunday, 11 A.M.–3 P.M.
Lunch:	Every day, 11:30 A.M.–2:30 P.M.
Dinner:	Every day, 6–10 P.M.

Atmosphere / setting: A pretty room replete with as many Indian artifacts as can be crammed in, and Indian music playing in the background.

Recommended dishes: Mulligatawny soup; lamb samosas; vegetable pakoras; lamb-stuffed mushrooms; shrimp in a white sauce with peanuts, cashews, and almonds; marinated, grilled tuna steak with moghlai sauce; tandoori chicken or lamb sausage; biryanis (mostly rice dishes with various meats, seafoods, and vegetables); lamb with tomato-and-raisin curry; Madras-style lamb with spicy curry sauce; chicken or lamb saagwala (with creamed spinach). Rice pudding; mango mousse; fruit cup.

Summary & comments: Around back of the Upper Pontalba is the latest and loveliest Indian restaurant from Anila and Har Keswani, who pioneered the cuisine locally and have managed to keep feeding it to us even in the face of disaster (their first two attempts bit the dust). As in their other extant place (Taj Mahal), the focus is on the tandoor, a superheated claypot oven where marinated meats and seafoods, along with fresh breads, are roasted to a dry intensity. The menu also does fine things with biryanis ("Indian jambalaya," they call it, not inaccurately), curries in a wide range of pepper levels, and vegetarian dishes. Not good enough to satisfy a Brit, but great in New Orleans.

SHOGUN

	Japanese
	★★★★
	Moderate
	Quality 86 Value C

Zone 9   Metairie Below Causeway
2325 Veterans Boulevard, Metairie
833-7477

Reservations:	Not accepted
When to go:	Anytime
Entree range:	$8–20
Payment:	AMEX, MC, V
Service rating:	★★★
Friendliness rating:	★★
Parking:	Free lot adjacent
Bar:	Full bar
Wine selection:	A few house wines
Dress:	Casual
Disabled access:	Full
Customers:	Locals, singles; families at the teppanyaki tables
Lunch:	Monday–Friday, 11:30 A.M.–2 P.M.
Lunch/Dinner:	Saturday and Sunday, noon–10 P.M.
Dinner:	Monday–Friday, 5–10 P.M.

Atmosphere / setting: In this big restaurant are three distinct areas. The sushi bar is the city's largest. The standard tables are utilitarian and quick-turning. But the most popular part of the restaurant is a recent addition: they bought the teppanyaki tables from the local Benihana when it closed, and that showy steak grilling takes up half the place. (Impressive for kids; otherwise, once will last you a lifetime.)

Recommended dishes: Baked seafood appetizer; gyoza; red miso soup; any form of sushi; sashimi; tei sho ku (box) dinners; shabu shabu (thinly sliced beef quickly boiled at the table); seafood nabe.

Summary & comments: Shogun was the first restaurant to make a commercial success in New Orleans with a sushi bar. It remains the definitive local sushi restaurant (although adherents of other places will loudly contest that), while at the same time offering a vast range of other Japanese eating styles. At the tables, they serve a dizzying assortment of teriyaki, tempura, noodle, Japanese barbecue, and sukiyaki-style dishes, all arranged into complicated complete dinners. But the best food here will always be the work of the sushi chefs.

236

SIAMESE

Zone 10	Metairie Above Causeway / Kenner / Jefferson Hwy.

6601 Veterans Boulevard, Metairie
454-8752

Thai	
★★★	
Moderate	
Quality 84	Value C

Reservations:	Accepted
When to go:	Anytime
Entree range:	$7–14
Payment:	All major credit cards
Service rating:	★★
Friendliness rating:	★★
Parking:	Free lot adjacent
Bar:	Full bar
Wine selection:	A few house wines
Dress:	Casual
Disabled access:	Full
Customers:	Locals
Lunch:	Tuesday–Sunday, 11 A.M.–2:30 P.M.
Dinner:	Tuesday–Sunday, 5–10 P.M.; Monday, closed.

Atmosphere / setting: Way in the back of a confusing strip mall is this storefront Thai restaurant, which looks like it could be turned into a convenience store in a matter of hours. A bit stark but not unpleasant.

Recommended dishes: Satay of beef, chicken, or pork (on skewers with peanut sauce). Mee krob (crisp-fried noodles with shrimp and chicken); golden wings (stuffed mid-section of chicken wings); spicy and sour shrimp soup; coconut chicken soup; squid or shrimp salad with lemongrass; pad thai; chicken with eggplant and mint leaves; roasted duck with red curry and pineapple; pla song kruenng (fried pompano with curry paste); red bean curry; steamed mussels.

Summary & comments: Your education in Thai cooking is facilitated by a book of photographs illustrating most of the menu's 78 entries. It's good that's around, because making contact with either the printed menu or the service staff is a bit difficult. But don't worry about it, because the only complaint you're likely to have about the food (assuming you like the distinctive Thai flavor palette) is that they don't give you quite enough of it here. And, given the prices, that might not bother you either.

Sid-Mar's

Zone 9 Metairie Below Causeway	Seafood
1824 Orpheum, Metairie	★★★
831-9541	Moderate
	Quality 83 Value A

Reservations:	Not accepted
When to go:	Weekdays; Fridays and Saturdays are incredibly busy here
Entree range:	$4–16
Payment:	All major credit cards
Service rating:	★★
Friendliness rating:	★★★
Parking:	Free lot adjacent
Bar:	Full bar
Wine selection:	A few house wines
Dress:	Anything goes
Disabled access:	Limited
Customers:	Locals, families
Lunch/Dinner:	Tuesday–Sunday, 11 A.M.–10:30 P.M.; Monday, closed.

Atmosphere / setting: On a spit of land between the 17th Street Canal and the lake is the working part of Bucktown, an old fishing community mostly now absorbed by the suburbs. Here you find docked the boats that fetch all those crabs and shrimp we eat, their owners probably cursing to themselves. Also here is Sid-Mar's, an equally fine relic of another era. The delightfully stark interior dining room is surrounded by more tables on a screened porch.

Recommended dishes: Oyster soup; seafood gumbo; boiled crabs; boiled shrimp; boiled crawfish; wop salad (sorry, that's what they call it—a common dish name in New Orleans); roast beef poor boy; oyster or shrimp poor boy; fried seafood platters; grilled fish; fried chicken. Daily specials. Bread pudding.

Summary & comments: Most of the time every seat is occupied by somebody eating a pile of boiled crustaceans, a fried seafood platter, or a homely special. Sid-Mar's suddenly got better in 1992 when the second generation took over, bought the building, and fixed it up—but not too much.

Smilie's

Zone 10	Metairie Above Causeway / Kenner / Jefferson Hwy.

5725 Jefferson Highway
733-3000

Creole Italian	
★★★	
Moderate	
Quality 84	Value A

Reservations:	Recommended
When to go:	Lunch; Friday and Saturday nights (good specials)
Entree range:	$10–18
Payment:	All major credit cards
Service rating:	★★★
Friendliness rating:	★★★★
Parking:	Free lot adjacent
Bar:	Full bar
Wine selection:	Decent list, mostly Italian
Dress:	Dressy casual
Disabled access:	Full
Customers:	Businessmen at lunch; neighborhood people; families
Lunch:	Monday–Friday, 11:30 A.M.–2:30 P.M.
Dinner:	Tuesday–Saturday, 5:30–10 P.M.; Sunday, closed.

Atmosphere / setting: The place serves two functions at lunch: one part is a cafeteria-style workman's lunchroom, the other a comfortable bistro full of businessmen and women's lunches. The latter is used for dinner, which has a family accent.

Recommended dishes: Fried eggplant sticks; oysters Smilie (baked with bread crumbs, garlic, herbs); chicken andouille gumbo; red beans and rice; trout Smilie (crabmeat, bread crumbs, and wine); seafood au gratin; veal Parmigiana alla Florentine; roasted chicken; chicken alla grandee (pan-roasted with garlic and olive oil); boiled beef brisket; filet mignon. Bread pudding; tiramisu.

Summary & comments: Smilie's had just opened when the Elmwood Plantation burned down, and so it inherited that venerable restaurant's mantle as Virtually the Only Place to Eat in Harahan or Anywhere Around There. The menu is Creole-Italian, most of it pretty familiar (in fact, several items are direct borrowings from the Elmwood) but very well prepared. In recent times, some of the specials have waxed ambitious and a bit nouvelle, but these too are good. In the evening, the table d'hôte specials are almost absurdly cheap and very good.

Snug Harbor

Zone 5   Downtown / St. Bernard
626 Frenchmen
949-0696

Hamburgers	
★★★	
Inexpensive	
Quality 75	Value B

Reservations:	Not accepted
When to go:	Anytime
Entree range:	$7–12
Payment:	AMEX, MC, V
Service rating:	★★
Friendliness rating:	★★
Parking:	Curbside
Bar:	Full bar
Wine selection:	A few house wines, mostly sold by the glass
Dress:	Casual
Disabled access:	Limited
Customers:	Neighborhood people; singles and daters
Dinner:	Sunday–Thursday, 6 P.M.–midnight;
	Friday and Saturday, 6 P.M.–2 A.M.

Atmosphere / setting: A pub-like environment.

Recommended dishes: Schooner salad (marinated seafood); hamburger; grilled fish specials.

Entertainment & amenities: Music acts in lounge nightly.

Summary & comments: In the center of Marigny's busy restaurant row, the Snug is the bigger, cleaner sister restaurant of the Port of Call. The important datum is that the same hamburger served at the Port of Call—the best in town for at least three decades—is also served here. The menu advances farther into the realm of seafood, though, and the presence of live music in the adjacent club makes this a bit more interesting place to spend a longer time.

Steak Knife

Zone 7   Lakeview / West End /
          Bucktown
888 Harrison Avenue
488-8981

Steak	
★★★	
Expensive	
Quality 86	Value C

Reservations:	Recommended
When to go:	Weeknights
Entree range:	$15–22
Payment:	All major credit cards
Service rating:	★★★
Friendliness rating:	★★★
Parking:	Valet (free)
Bar:	Full bar
Wine selection:	Decent list, good international balance; many by-the-glass selections
Dress:	Dressy casual
Disabled access:	Full
Customers:	Neighborhood people, couples, families
Dinner:	Every day, 6–10 P.M.

Atmosphere / setting: The place used to be a bank branch, with lots of marble and good-looking wood paneling. The branch manager's former office makes a fine private dining room.

Recommended dishes: Crabmeat au gratin; Greek tidbit in the oven (a sauceless, crustless, herbal pizza); shrimp rémoulade; coconut beer-battered shrimp; cream of crabmeat soup; seraphine salad (avocado, asparagus, hearts of palm, artichokes, and greens); filet mignon; strip sirloin; lamb chops with mint demi-glace; roasted chicken with rosemary and mushrooms. Chocolate mousse; bread pudding.

Entertainment & amenities: Live piano music in the bar most nights.

Summary & comments: For twenty years, the Steak Knife has been Lakeview's upscale version of a neighborhood restaurant, complete with regulars hanging out at the bar. During most of that time it was the beef specialist that the name implies. But when it moved to bigger, nicer quarters a few years ago, the menu grew to encompass almost everything—albeit in a nonradical way. Nothing here can be said to be the best of its kind, but the main items are prepared consistently and well using fine raw materials, and some of the side dishes are inspired. Good service except during the early-evening mob scene.

STRAYA

Zone 10	Metairie Above Causeway/
	Kenner/Jefferson Hwy.

4517 Veterans Boulevard, Metairie
887-8873

> Eclectic
> ★★★
> Moderate
>
> Quality 83   Value B

Reservations:	Call right before coming to be put on the waiting list
When to go:	Weeknights, lunch, and early evenings
Entree range:	$8–16
Payment:	All major credit cards
Service rating:	★★★★
Friendliness rating:	★★★★★
Parking:	Valet (free)
Bar:	Full bar
Wine selection:	A more extensive list than you might imagine; many by-the-glass selections
Dress:	Dressy casual
Disabled access:	Full
Customers:	Locals; hip, younger crowd
Lunch/Dinner:	Sunday–Thursday, 11 A.M.–11 P.M.; Friday and Saturday, 11 A.M.–midnight

Atmosphere / setting: Active, a bit noisy, and entry-level glamorous, Straya was designed to recall places like Los Angeles' Spago. Stars (in the decor, not the crowd) are everywhere, including in the design of the unique food bar that separates the dining room from the kitchen. In decent weather, you might want to sit on the patio.

Recommended dishes: Sesame chicken noodle salad; daily soups; rotisserie chicken; fried oyster Rockefeller pizza; Jamaican shrimp curry pizza; barbecue shrimp fettuccine on pizza; chicken tortilla pasta; sesame-crusted tuna sashimi on marinated angel hair with wasabi vinaigrette; almond-crusted trout meunière; grilled amberjack amandine with fried shrimp; garlic filet mignon; baby-back ribs. Coconut pie; crêpes; tiramisu.

Summary & comments: "California Creole Cafe" is the subtitle of this latest concept from Al Copeland and his golden gut feelings for what the mainstream diner will bite for next. The California aspect is that the menu is full of salads, sushi, pizza, and pasta, usually in unaccustomed combinations. The Creole part is (we are thankful) in the taste department. The dish that most captures the restaurant is barbecued shrimp served on top of pasta, which is in turn atop a pizza. The food here takes a little warming up to, but once you get it the eating here becomes reasonably enjoyable, if not gilded.

242

Taj Mahal

Zone 9   Metairie Below Causeway
923-C Metairie Road, Metairie
836-6859

Indian	
★★★	
Moderate	
Quality 81	Value B

Reservations:	Accepted
When to go:	Anytime
Entree range:	$7–15
Payment:	All major credit cards
Service rating:	★★
Friendliness rating:	★★★
Parking:	Free lot adjacent
Bar:	Full bar
Wine selection:	A few house wines
Dress:	Casual
Disabled access:	Full
Customers:	Locals
Brunch:	Sunday, 11 A.M.–3 P.M.
Lunch:	Tuesday–Sunday, 11 A.M.–2:30 P.M.
Dinner:	Tuesday–Sunday, 5:30–10 P.M.; Monday, closed.

Atmosphere / setting: Secreted down an alley off Metairie Road is this pleasant but (to gainsay the name) rather plain little Indian restaurant.

Recommended dishes: Mulligatawny soup; lamb samosas; vegetable pakoras; katchumber salad; tandoori chicken or lamb sausage; biryanis (mostly rice dishes with various meats, seafoods, and vegetables); navratan curry (vegetarian); saag paneer (homemade white cheese in creamed spinach sauce); rack of lamb masala; foil chicken (with mushrooms, onions, and peppers); vegetarian dinner; chicken or lamb saagwala (with creamed spinach). Rice pudding; mango mousse.

Summary & comments: The main attraction is the food cooked in the tandoor, the extremely hot clay oven where long skewers of chicken, lamb, beef (yes), sausage, and seafood hang until they achieve a fascinating dry intensity of flavor. They also prepare the entire range of curry dishes and non-curry items with a wide variety of sauces. Eating vegetarian might be the best way to dine here. At lunch, there's a small buffet, but the food doesn't stand up to steam-table holding.

Tango Tango

Zone 3   Uptown Below Napoleon
4100 Magazine
895-6632

Caribbean / South American
★★★
Moderate

Quality 80   Value B

Reservations:	Recommended
When to go:	Anytime
Entree range:	$9–20
Payment:	All major credit cards
Service rating:	★★
Friendliness rating:	★★★★
Parking:	Free lot adjacent
Bar:	Full bar
Wine selection:	Decent list, with many Argentinian and Chilean bottles
Dress:	Casual
Disabled access:	Full
Customers:	Locals
Brunch:	Menu, 11 A.M.–3 P.M.
Lunch:	Tuesday–Sunday, 11:30 A.M.–2:30 P.M.
Dinner:	Tuesday–Sunday, 6–10 P.M.; Monday, closed.

Atmosphere / setting: In a handsome addition to an old brick firehouse, a greenhouse effect has been created for the dining room. Inside the older part of the structure is a combination banquet hall and nightclub.

Recommended dishes: Creole humitas (Argentinian tamales); eggplant roulade; crawfish migas (casserole with peppers, pecans, and ginger); Caribbean black bean soup; linguine with shrimp, roasted garlic, and sun-dried tomatoes; Creole bouillabaisse; lamb shank with locro (Argentinian vegetable stew) and quinoa; mixed grill (steak, lamb, pork loin, sausage, grilled on the table); grilled fish. Bread pudding.

Entertainment & amenities: Flamenco every Friday (extra charge).

Summary & comments: Tango Tango offers something original to these parts. They call their food Latin Creole, a historically accurate term that emphasizes the commonalities our local Creole cuisine have with the cooking of Latin America and the Caribbean. A major emphasis is on meat: steaks and chops are a big part of the South American diet, and here they are of fine quality and wide variety. Also here are variations on paella, tamales, meat pies, grain-and-meat stews, and other specialties from down there. Seafood and service are the weakest parts of the operation.

244

TAQUERÍA CORONA

<table>
<tr><td>Mexican</td></tr>
<tr><td>★★★</td></tr>
<tr><td>Moderate</td></tr>
<tr><td>Quality 79   Value A</td></tr>
</table>

Zone 2   Central Business District
857 Fulton
524-9805

Zone 4   Uptown Above Napoleon
5932 Magazine Street
897-3974

Zone 10   Metairie Above Causeway / Kenner / Jefferson Hwy.
3535 Severn, Metairie
885-5088

Reservations:	Not accepted
When to go:	Lunch
Entree range:	$5–9
Payment:	Cash only
Service rating:	★★
Friendliness rating:	★★★
Parking:	Curbside; free lot at Severn
Bar:	Full bar
Wine selection:	A few house wines
Dress:	Casual
Disabled access:	Limited
Customers:	Younger locals, gourmets
Lunch:	Every day, 11:30 A.M.–2:30 P.M.; Fulton location closed for lunch on Sunday
Dinner:	Every day, 5:30–10 P.M.

Atmosphere / setting: A taste of the Third World, all locations (particularly the Magazine Street original) are studies in seedy chic. The main source of atmosphere (in both senses of the word) is the grill where the meats broil.

Recommended dishes: Cebollitas (grilled green onions); gazpacho; "Tacocado" salad with chicken; grilled beef tacos; pork tacos; beef tongue tacos; shrimp tacos; cheese enchiladas. Flan; arroz con leche (rice pudding).

Summary & comments: Taqueria Corona shows you what a taco is like in the interior of Mexico. That's a flour tortilla filled with chunks of grilled meat and pico de gallo, the minced salad of onions, peppers, garlic, lime juice, and seasonings. They serve these filled with not only beef but pork, shrimp, chicken, and beef tongue, along with some great black beans and rice on a sizzling-hot plate. The menu goes on to include the cheesiest enchiladas on earth and a lot more exciting, authentic fare. Cash only, and the doors are locked at exactly closing time. The phone numbers are unlisted.

Tavern On The Park

Zone 6   Mid-City / Gentilly
900 City Park Avenue
486-3333

Creole
★★★
Expensive

Quality 80   Value C

Reservations:	Recommended
When to go:	Anytime
Entree range:	$12–24
Payment:	All major credit cards
Service rating:	★★★★
Friendliness rating:	★
Parking:	Curbside
Bar:	Full bar
Wine selection:	Decent list, good international balance
Dress:	Jacket recommended but not required
Disabled access:	Full
Customers:	Locals, tending to the older side; businessmen at lunch
Lunch:	Tuesday–Friday, 11:30 A.M.–2:30 P.M.
Dinner:	Tuesday–Saturday, 6–10 P.M.; Sunday and Monday, closed.

Atmosphere / setting: The Tavern is an extraordinarily handsome marble-and-glass restaurant in a historic building. It's across from the entrance to City Park, which affords a lovely view—particularly from the second-floor balcony, which they don't use enough.

Recommended dishes: Fried onion rings; shrimp rémoulade; baked oysters 3&3 (Rockefeller and Bienville); tomato blossom salad (with feta and Vidalia onions); turtle soup; stuffed soft-shell crab Creolaise (hollandaise with Creole mustard); Asian-Cajun duck with pepper jelly; rack of lamb; filet mignon; veal chop. Bread pudding with rum raisin ice cream; chocolate cake; pecan snowball with chocolate sauce.

Summary & comments: It started as a premium steakhouse but evolved into a general-menu Creole cafe, with an emphasis on straightforward, traditional dishes. The food here is pretty good, and at times it rises to extraordinary. The latter is more likely in the introductory courses, which are full of nice surprises. The goodness of your entree I wouldn't hazard to predict, regardless of what you order. The service staff is unusually effective and gracious. That makes the main problem here perplexing: on rare occasion, the management has been so inhospitable that a few diners have told me they'll never return.

246

Tipton County Tennessee Pit Barbecue

	Barbecue
	★ ★ ★
Zone 4 Uptown Above Napoleon	Inexpensive
5538 Magazine	
899-9626	Quality 80 Value B

Reservations:	Not accepted
When to go:	Anytime
Entree range:	$5–12
Payment:	All major credit cards
Service rating:	★ ★ ★
Friendliness rating:	★ ★ ★
Parking:	Curbside
Bar:	Full bar
Wine selection:	A few house wines
Dress:	Anything goes
Disabled access:	Limited
Customers:	Locals, Memphis expatriates
Lunch / Dinner:	Every day, 11 A.M.–11 P.M.

Atmosphere / setting: An old workingman's cafe with a long, good-looking bar becomes a barbecue joint with the addition of Elvis memorabilia.

Recommended dishes: Rib tips; barbecue pork ribs; barbecued pulled pork (sandwich or plate); pulled chicken; cole slaw; potato salad; barbecue beans. Chess pie; pecan pie.

Summary & comments: The name is accurate: this is indeed real barbecue in the style of Memphis (Tipton County is adjacent to that BBQ capital). They smoke pork and beef in the slowest possible manner here; pork ribs in particular benefit by having a fantastic, dense, fatless texture. Pulled pork is the other specialty; brisket and chicken are only slightly less interesting. The sauce is the distinctive vinegar-based douse common in eastern barbecue styles. All the side dishes and desserts are great, too. The premises are appropriately spartan, but clean and well-served. This place is never busy, but you'll run into lots of transplanted Memphisites and Carolinians here who recognize the taste.

Tony Angello's

Zone 7 Lakeview / West End / Bucktown	Creole Italian
	★★★
6262 Fleur de Lis Drive	Moderate
488-0888	Quality 76 Value B

Reservations:	Accepted, but not always honored
When to go:	Early evenings on weeknights
Entree range:	$9–19
Payment:	AMEX, MC, V
Service rating:	★★★
Friendliness rating:	★★
Parking:	Free lot adjacent
Bar:	Full bar
Wine selection:	Decent list, mostly Italian
Dress:	Dressy casual
Disabled access:	Limited
Customers:	Locals, almost all regulars; couples
Dinner:	Monday–Saturday, 6–10 P.M.; Sunday, closed.

Atmosphere / setting: The building has no obvious sign outside and is monastic in its darkness within. Be ready to wait for even a reserved table. The bar, however, has a few interesting antique console radios to look at while you're waiting.

Recommended dishes: The "Feed": a many-small-course dinner of the night's specials; lobster cup (a small casserole); artichoke soup; eggplant tuna (like lasagna but eggplant instead of pasta); oysters Bienville; osso buco; chicken cacciatore; trout Rosa (with crabmeat). Lemon ice box pie.

Summary & comments: Overpopulated by regulars who make your patronage of marginal interest, Tony Angello's serves a decent but only occasionally extraordinary Creole-Italian food. Most people order this way: "Feed me, Mr. Tony!" Even if you never see Mr. Tony in person, this starts a parade of small courses until you cry uncle. The dishes—none of which could be called an entree—often come out two or three at a time. You may see pasta thrice. The gist usually begins with essays on seafood, olive oil, and herbs, and ends with meats and red sauces. The price for this—as well as for a la carte orders—is lower than average, which is part of the attraction.

Traveler's Post

Nouvelle Creole

★★

Moderate

Quality 75   Value C

Zone 3   Uptown Below Napoleon
1032 St. Charles Avenue
529-7678

Reservations:	Accepted
When to go:	Late nights
Entree range:	$11–22
Payment:	All major credit cards
Service rating:	★★★
Friendliness rating:	★★★
Parking:	Curbside (metered)
Bar:	Full bar
Wine selection:	Decent list, with emphasis on California
Dress:	Casual
Disabled access:	None
Customers:	Late-night crowd; waiters after hours
Lunch:	Monday–Friday, 11:30 A.M.–2 P.M.
Dinner:	Monday–Saturday, 7 P.M.–midnight or later; Sunday, closed.

Atmosphere / setting: A tiny dining room in an old mansion on Lee Circle. The name is a reference to the famous landmark outside: Robert E. Lee's horse was named "Traveler."

Recommended dishes: Shrimp rémoulade; grilled shrimp with avocado cream; sausage-stuffed mushrooms with red onion marmalade; roma shrimp and artichoke salad; crawfish etouffee; fish court-bouillon; Tucson grilled fish with avocado sauce; turkey poulette (a disassembled casserole of turkey, bacon, and cheese); daily chef's special. Rum raisin bread pudding; chocolate mousse in chocolate meringue.

Summary & comments: Operated by a former Commander's Palace captain, the Post serves fairly basic New Orleans food with, here and there, an edge of creativity. The place stays open quite late at night and is populated by staff from other restaurants. Parking can be a problem at lunchtime.

Trey Yuen

Zone 12   North Shore
600 Causeway Boulevard, Mandeville
(504) 626-4476

<table>
<tr><td></td><td>Chinese</td></tr>
<tr><td></td><td>★★★★</td></tr>
<tr><td></td><td>Expensive</td></tr>
<tr><td></td><td>Quality 85   Value D</td></tr>
</table>

Reservations:	Not accepted
When to go:	Weeknights
Entree range:	$8–20 (median: $12)
Payment:	All major credit cards
Service rating:	★★
Friendliness rating:	★★
Parking:	Free lot adjacent
Bar:	Full bar
Wine selection:	Decent list, with emphasis on California
Dress:	Casual
Disabled access:	Full
Customers:	North Shore people, families
Lunch:	Wednesday–Friday, 11:30 A.M.–2:30 P.M.
Lunch/Dinner:	Sunday, noon–10 P.M.
Dinner:	Monday–Saturday, 6–10 P.M.

Atmosphere / setting: A sort of rotunda in a Chinese style, the main dining room was built using many antique Chinese pieces and well-designed modern accents. The restaurant is surrounded by ponds, waterfalls, and gardens.

Recommended dishes: Spring rolls; pot stickers; hot and sour soup; tong cho anything, but especially oysters, soft-shell crab, and wor shu op (Mandarin duck); satay squid; shrimp in a cloud; lobster with black bean sauce; scallops imperial; presidential chicken; spicy lemon chicken; steak kew. Lotus banana; ice cream.

Summary & comments: A major breakthrough: when this oriental palace opened in 1981, it was the first time that an area Chinese restaurant offered beautiful surroundings, good service, and unusual food using first-class ingredients. Trey Yuen remains one of the best and most popular Chinese restaurants around, with a menu that essays many styles of Chinese cooking. Seafood is a particular strength here, but they cook everything well, even some of the tired old fake-Cantonese standards that people insist on ordering. There's a far better list of wines and desserts than in the typical Chinese place. Service is unceremonious but good, except when the place is very busy—which it often is. Another Trey Yuen of equal goodness is in Hammond.

TUJAGUE'S

Zone 1   French Quarter
823 Decatur
525-8676

	Creole
	★★★★
	Expensive
	Quality 87 Value C

Reservations:	Recommended
When to go:	Anytime
Entree range:	Table d'hôte: $20–29
Payment:	All major credit cards
Service rating:	★★★
Friendliness rating:	★★★★
Parking:	French Market pay lot, one block
Bar:	Full bar
Wine selection:	Limited list of inexpensive wines
Dress:	Casual
Disabled access:	Limited
Customers:	Tourists, some locals; quite a few Quarterites at lunch
Lunch:	Every day, 11:30 A.M.–3 P.M.
Dinner:	Every day, 5–10 P.M.

Atmosphere / setting: Two floors of delightfully unrenovated space in a building that has been a restaurant since before the Civil War. The bar is a magnificent antique. Despite all the history, this is a very casual, easygoing place; even families fit in.

Recommended dishes· Table d'hôte dinner menu has entrees that change daily. Shrimp rémoulad· crabmeat and spinach soup; boiled brisket of beef with Creole sauce; chicken bonne femme (batterless fried half-chicken with a tremendous amount of garlic, parsley, and fried potatoes); filet mignon. Cranberry bread pudding; pecan pie.

Summary & comments: One of America's oldest restaurants, Tujague's began as a food service to the workers in the French Market and on the docks of the French Quarter, serving a table d'hôte meal of the day. In the late 1800s, this was the base for the city's first superstar chef, Madame Begue, who wrote what may have been the first Creole cookbook. Today, Tujague's serves the traditional five-course homey Creole meal, with five or so choices for the entree. One of the courses is always the restaurant's signature boiled brisket. This is a great place to come on the major holidays; they're open for all of them.

Uglesich's

Creole / Neighborhood Cafe
★★★★
Moderate

Quality 86   Value D

Zone 3   Uptown Below Napoleon
1238 Baronne
523-8571

Reservations:	Not accepted
When to go:	Avoid noon hour
Entree range:	$6–14
Payment:	No credit cards
Service rating:	★★
Friendliness rating:	★★★
Parking:	Free lot adjacent
Bar:	Beer
Wine selection:	None
Dress:	Anything goes
Disabled access:	Limited
Customers:	A mix of locals and tourists, most on the young side; lots of restaurant people
Lunch:	Monday–Friday, 11 A.M.–4 P.M.; Saturday and Sunday, closed.

Atmosphere / setting: After seven decades of slow decay, Uglesich's has given itself a paint job, the less to frighten the many visitors who enter the rough-looking neighborhood in search of the most convincing example of New Orleans culinary funk. The premises remain the shabbiest occupied by a good restaurant, but soak it in. Your clothes will: after a half-hour, you'll smell as if you've been frying seafood all day.

Recommended dishes: Oysters on the half shell; barbecued oysters; crawfish bisque; grilled fish plate; crawfish etouffee; fried oyster poor boy; roast beef poor boy; french fries; blackboard specials.

Summary & comments: Uglesich's is one of the city's grubbiest restaurants, yet the food is consistently soul-satisfying, with standards only a few very expensive restaurants could copy. The oysters on the poor boy, for example, are not only fried but shucked to order. All the sandwiches and platters are great, robust eating; take seriously any advisory that a dish may be spicy. Raw oysters at the bar are a great way to kill the long time it takes for your entree to be whipped up, and the wait for a table. No matter how busy they are, seats will magically appear when it's time.

Upperline

Zone 4   Uptown Above Napoleon
1413 Upperline
891-9822

Nouvelle Creole	
★★★★	
Expensive	
Quality 88	Value C

Reservations:	Recommended
When to go:	Anytime; the garlic festival in summer is always interesting
Entree range:	$13–20
Payment:	All major credit cards
Service rating:	★★★★
Friendliness rating:	★★★★
Parking:	Curbside
Bar:	Full bar
Wine selection:	Modest list, but wines well-chosen for the food; many by-the-glass selections
Dress:	Casual
Disabled access:	None
Customers:	A mix of locals and tourists; gourmets
Dinner:	Wednesday–Monday, 6–10 P.M.; Tuesday, closed.

Atmosphere / setting: The place rambles from one building to another, with many tables in odd, intimate corners. The front room gets a little cluttered and frantic at times.

Recommended dishes: Fried green tomatoes with shrimp rémoulade; trout and dill mousse; Creole white bean soup with tasso; duck gumbo; watercress, Stilton, and pecan salad; grilled fish with barbecue shrimp; shrimp curry with rice and Indian condiments; calf's liver à l'orange; rack of lamb with spicy merlot sauce; filet mignon with spicy garlic mushrooms; duck etouffee with pepper jelly; garlic-stuffed pork tenderloin. Pecan pie; double chocolate amaretto mousse.

Entertainment & amenities: Major folk art collection from local artists throughout restaurant, as well as on building façade.

Summary & comments: One of the first of the nouvelle Creole bistros, the Upperline's distinctiveness is due not only to its food (always good, occasionally wonderful) but to the delightfully quirky imagination of owner and genuine bohemian JoAnn Clevenger. Her most famous creation is the summer-long garlic menu, but she has also done menus based on the food in the books of Jane Austen, the movie "Babette's Feast," and the notebooks of Claude Monet. Despite that, she never hesitates to fill her regular menu with the classic Creole dishes, including a tasting menu of gumbo, beans and rice, and so on.

VAQUEROS

Zone 4 Uptown Above Napoleon	Mexican
4938 Prytania	★★★★
891-6441	Moderate
	Quality 90 Value C

Reservations:	Not accepted
When to go:	Anytime
Entree range:	$8–19
Payment:	All major credit cards except Diners Club
Service rating:	★★★★
Friendliness rating:	★★★★
Parking:	Curbside
Bar:	Full bar
Wine selection:	Modest list, but wines well-chosen for the food; many by-the-glass selections
Dress:	Casual
Disabled access:	Full
Customers:	Uptowners, gourmets, daters
Brunch:	Sunday, 11 A.M.–3 P.M.
Lunch:	Monday–Friday, 11:30 A.M.–2:30 P.M.
Dinner:	Every day, 6–10 P.M.

Atmosphere / setting: Anyone who likes the food and the style of Santa Fe should love all the stucco, tiles, and weathered wood. The rear room is a semi-open patio.

Recommended dishes: Chips and five different salsas; seafood and chicken taquitos; Navajo fry bread; venison black bean chili; corn-fried rock shrimp salad; cheese or chicken enchiladas; Santa Fe salmon cakes; Puerto Rican stuffed sopaipillas with grilled chicken and beans; duck tamales; southwestern grilled pizza; chicken al carbón with red mole sauce; fajitas. Taco galeta (a fruit-filled cookie shell); flan.

Summary & comments: Easily the most ambitious and exciting Mexican restaurant ever to open in these parts, Vaqueros explores all parts of the cuisine with imagination. In the center of the main room is a station where cooks prepare flour tortillas from scratch; these taste as good as they smell. The tortilla chips are served in a gigantic handmade platter surrounded by five different house-made salsas. Live music, interesting drinks, and occasional festivals make the place even more engaging. Tends to be rather busy; you might have to wait for a table.

VERA CRUZ

	Mexican
	★★
	Moderate
	Quality 71 Value C

Zone 1   French Quarter
1141 Decatur
561-8081

Zone 4   Uptown Above Napoleon
7537 Maple
866-1736

Reservations:	Not accepted
When to go:	Anytime
Entree range:	$7–16
Payment:	AMEX, MC, V
Service rating:	★★★
Friendliness rating:	★★★
Parking:	Curbside; French Market pay lot, one block away
Bar:	Full bar
Wine selection:	A few house wines
Dress:	Casual
Disabled access:	Full
Customers:	Quarterites, a few tourists
Dinner:	Sunday–Thursday, 6–10 P.M.;
	Friday and Saturday, 6–11 P.M.

Atmosphere / setting: Stark in an agreeable way—at least for a Mexican place. A hangout for the neighbors in both locations.

Recommended dishes: Nachos casa (skirt steak and guacamole); grilled marinated shrimp; pollo al carbón; lechoin asado (marinated roast pork); combination steak and chicken fajitas; Guadalajara enchiladas (chicken and guacamole); enchiladas al pastor (ground beef and spicy cheese sauce); India tostada; picadillo with black beans and rice. Chocolate silk pie.

Summary & comments: The two locations of this moderately hip Mexican cafe served Americanized versions of the standards—but the adaptations are made in a generally good way, i.e., the use of better-than-average fresh ingredients. Salads and grilled items are the best of the food here; combination platters have a way of becoming a mélange.

Veranda

<table>
<tr><td colspan="2" align="center">Continental</td></tr>
<tr><td>Zone 2   Central Business District</td><td align="center">★ ★ ★</td></tr>
<tr><td>444 St. Charles Avenue</td><td align="center">Expensive</td></tr>
<tr><td>522-5566</td><td align="center">Quality 82   Value C</td></tr>
</table>

Reservations:	Recommended
When to go:	Anytime; Oktoberfest and Cinco de Mayo festival are peaks here
Entree range:	$12–22
Payment:	All major credit cards
Service rating:	★ ★ ★
Friendliness rating:	★ ★ ★
Parking:	Valet (free)
Bar:	Full bar
Wine selection:	Substantial list, good international balance
Dress:	Jacket recommended but not required
Disabled access:	Full
Customers:	Businessmen at lunch; hotel guests at dinner; locals at Sunday brunch
Breakfast:	Every day, 7–10 A.M.
Brunch:	Sunday, 11 A.M.–3 P.M.
Lunch:	Monday–Saturday, 11:30 A.M.–2:30 P.M.
Dinner:	Every day, 6–10 P.M.

Atmosphere / setting: An expansive, courtyard-like space in an atrium with a glass roof.

Recommended dishes: Crawfish beignets; crabcakes with Creole mustard sauce; smoked duck and wild mushroom strudel; barbecued oysters; potato-crusted fish; Louisiana bouillabaisse; grilled tuna with black beans and roasted corn; fried soft-shell crab meunière; pannéed rabbit; braised veal shank for two; filet mignon with peppercorn crust. Black Forest cake; bahrenjaeger (almond-and-honey cake).

Entertainment & amenities: Strolling jazz trio at Sunday brunch. During second two weeks of October, there's a highly amusing pair of German musicians accompanying the Oktoberfest menu.

Summary & comments: Most Orleanians know this as the home base for chef Willy Coln, who once operated the only really good German restaurant hereabouts. These days, he orchestrates an above-average hotel restaurant, with a good breakfast and lunch buffet and a more interesting dinner menu, the dishes showing tastes from the Creole, southwestern, Italian, and continental palettes. Coln's own signature dishes appear as specials. On Sundays, they have a popular but just-okay brunch buffet. Service is a bit amateurish, and this can impact the food.

Versailles

Zone 3   Uptown Below Napoleon
2100 St. Charles Avenue
524-2535

Nouvelle Creole	
★★★★★	
Very Expensive	
Quality 95	Value C

Reservations:	Recommended
When to go:	Anytime
Entree range:	$16–24
Payment:	All major credit cards except Discover
Service rating:	★★★★★
Friendliness rating:	★★
Parking:	Valet (free)
Bar:	Full bar
Wine selection:	Substantial list; good international balance, including more German wines than most places
Dress:	Jacket required
Disabled access:	Full
Customers:	Mostly locals, tending to the older side; gourmets; a few tourists
Dinner:	Monday–Saturday, 6–10 P.M.; Sunday, closed.

Atmosphere / setting: Low-key to a fault, the Versailles has dining rooms and a service style that seem to have been designed to facilitate slumber at table. (Romance is also possible.) The main room has windows that allow one to monitor the movements of the St. Charles Streetcar.

Recommended dishes: Terrine of lump crabmeat on nori with caper mayonnaise; smoked saddle of venison; gravlax with grilled shrimp; cappuccino-style mirliton chowder with crabmeat; sautéed fish Marcus (artichokes and capers); salmon steamed in rice paper; bouillabaisse; filet mignon of veal; roast duck with port sauce; filet mignon on seared onion with peppercorn sauce. White chocolate meringue with Campari-cherry syrup; diplomat bread custard; crème brûlée.

Summary & comments: If ratings were expressed as a ratio of culinary excellence to razzamatazz, this place would look like the best restaurant in town. The food, growing from Continental roots grafted to Creole ingredients, is buffed to a high polish both in visual and gastronomic terms. The kitchen here is inventive, but they never go too far afield of the classic catalog. Their offer of a familiar brand of deliciousness is hard to refuse. The wine list is assembled by the maître d', who can tell you all about it. The a la carte menu is a touch pricey, but its monthly table d'hôte menu is quite affordable.

Vincent's Italian Cuisine

Zone 10	Metairie Above Causeway/
	Kenner/Jefferson Hwy.
4411 Chastant Street, Metairie	
885-2984	

Creole Italian
★★★★
Moderate

Quality 90   Value A

Reservations:	Required
When to go:	Weeknights and lunch
Entree range:	$9–19
Payment:	All major credit cards
Service rating:	★★★★
Friendliness rating:	★★★★
Parking:	Free lot adjacent
Bar:	Full bar
Wine selection:	Decent list, mostly Italian
Dress:	Casual
Disabled access:	Limited
Customers:	Locals; couples and foursomes
Lunch:	Monday–Friday, 11:30 A.M.–3 P.M.
Dinner:	Monday–Saturday, 6–10 P.M.; Sunday, closed.

Atmosphere / setting: A neighborhood cafe in every physical measure.

Recommended dishes: Eggplant sandwich (two pannéed rounds with spicy mozzarella and Italian sausage); veal meatballs on garlic toast; corn and crab bisque en croûte; veal cannelloni in a crêpe; soft-shell crab with tomato garlic sauce; pannéed fish with crab cream sauce; garlic chicken; braciolone; veal Florentine; osso buco. Tiramisu; chocolate mousse cake; Torroncino ice cream.

Summary & comments: After a long career as a bartender and waiter, Vincent discovered that he could cook as well as any of the chefs who screamed at him. So he set about serving some of the most impressive food ever sold at prices this low. The style is mostly homestyle New Orleans Italian, but many dishes show what the chef learned at some of those fancy places in his past. He has a particularly skillful hand with seafood, saucing it with great versions of either red or white sauce. A few dishes are not only great eating but highly original. The salad, vegetable, and dessert courses, as well as the wine list, lack something. But everything else could be served in the grandest restaurant in New Orleans.

West End Cafe

Zone 7	Lakeview / West End / Bucktown
8536 Pontchartrain Boulevard	
288-0711	

Creole / Neighborhood Cafe

★★★

Moderate

Quality 74   Value C

Reservations:	Not accepted
When to go:	Anytime
Entree range:	$7–15
Payment:	All major credit cards
Service rating:	★★★
Friendliness rating:	★★★★
Parking:	Free lot adjacent
Bar:	Full bar
Wine selection:	A few house wines
Dress:	Casual
Disabled access:	Limited
Customers:	Locals, families, singles
Open:	Every day, 8 A.M.–11 P.M.

Atmosphere / setting: The guys who opened this place had a taste in their mouths for the ideal backstreet neighborhood hangout, and they combined that idea with that of the casual lakefront seafood house. What resulted was pretty good, and even on those occasions when the food hasn't matched your ideas of the ultimate, you can't deny that you're having a good time.

Recommended dishes: Stuffed mushrooms; boiled shrimp (or crawfish in season); crabmeat au gratin; stuffed crabs; fried seafood platters; seafood fettuccine; broiled chicken. Daily specials. Bread pudding; West End pie (a rich variation on pecan pie). Breakfast: beignets; pain perdu (rich French toast); omelettes.

Summary & comments: With the exception of what seem like impossibly over-ambitious special menus (those are actually quite successful), you're better off staying away from the more complex dishes. The daily specials, especially the soups, are always good. Boiled seafood emerges hot every afternoon.

WindJAMMER

Zone 7   Lakeview / West End /
          Bucktown
8550 Pontchartrain Boulevard
283-8301

	Creole	
	★★	
	Moderate	
Quality 67		Value C

Reservations:	Accepted
When to go:	Anytime
Entree range:	$9–24
Payment:	All major credit cards
Service rating:	★★★
Friendliness rating:	★★★★
Parking:	Free lot adjacent
Bar:	Full bar
Wine selection:	Limited list of ordinary wines
Dress:	Casual
Disabled access:	Full
Customers:	Locals, most of them middle-aged regulars
Lunch / Dinner:	Every day, 11 A.M.–11 P.M.

Atmosphere / setting: Two airy, handsome dining rooms with a nautical theme—naturally, since the city's principal private-boat marina is across the street.

Recommended dishes: Oysters Bienville; oysters Rockefeller; crabmeat-stuffed mushrooms hollandaise; red beans and rice with pickled pork; boiled beef brisket; steamed Maine lobsters; trout Timothy (mushrooms, artichokes, lemon butter); trout supreme (crabmeat atop one fillet, hollandaise shrimp on the other); filet mignon. Bread pudding; chocolate mousse cake.

Summary & comments: The Windjammer operates for a loyal bunch of regulars who have come to love the food here. Some of it is genuinely lovable: the daily specials, the unstuffed seafood, the steaks, and the lobster. Other dishes are Seventies-era kitsch (veal Oscar comes to mind). The waitresses are a bit underdressed for anyone not quite old enough to have taken *Playboy* seriously, but they're good servers anyway.

Windsor Court Grill Room

Zone 2   Central Business District
300 Gravier
523-6000

Eclectic
★ ★ ★ ★ ★
Very Expensive
Quality 94   Value F

Reservations:	Required
When to go:	Wednesday through Friday nights
Entree range:	$18–34
Payment:	All major credit cards
Service rating:	★ ★ ★ ★ ★
Friendliness rating:	★ ★ ★ ★
Parking:	Valet (free)
Bar:	Full bar
Wine selection:	One of the town's best wine cellars
Dress:	Jacket recommended but not required
Disabled access:	Full
Customers:	Locals, hotel guests, and tourists; gourmets
Breakfast:	Every day, 7–10 A.M.
Brunch:	Sundays, 11 A.M.–3 P.M.
Lunch:	Monday–Saturday, 11:30 A.M.–2:30 P.M.
Dinner:	Every day, 6–10 P.M.

Atmosphere / setting: A sybarite's dream dining room: big, heavy tables, extra-wide, comfortable chairs and banquettes, a couple million dollars' worth of original art on English themes, a Lalique crystal table, and other rich furnishings.

Recommended dishes: Menu changes frequently. These dishes may still be around: Kumamoto oysters with ginger ice; smoked salmon; seared foie gras with caramelized bananas; turtle soup; Windsor Court salad; Chinese smoked lobster; grilled tuna Rossini; any grilled fish or red-meat chop; rack of lamb; smoked venison loin with cheese grits cake.

Entertainment & amenities: Live chamber music in lounge.

Summary & comments: The Grill Room brooks no compromise in its quest for the best of surroundings, service, food, and wine; most of the time, a great meal results. The chefs here have always included in their ever-changing menus a substantial array of unheard-of savories, prepared in original styles that elude category. This sometimes results in confusing, eccentric food, but less often than was once the case. The safest offerings proceed from the grill of the name; these are ideal for purists. The circa-$70 tasting menu of the night's specials is the ultimate meal here. The wine list was built from private collections and is replete with rare vintages from all over.

Ye Olde College Inn

Zone 4   Uptown Above Napoleon
3016 South Carrollton Avenue
866-3683

Creole / Neighborhood Cafe
★★
Moderate

Quality 73   Value B

Reservations:	Not accepted
When to go:	Anytime
Entree range:	$5–14
Payment:	MC, V
Service rating:	★★★
Friendliness rating:	★★★
Parking:	Free lot adjacent
Bar:	Full bar
Wine selection:	A few house wines
Dress:	Casual
Disabled access:	Limited
Customers:	Neighborhood people, largely on the older side
Lunch / Dinner:	Every day, 11 A.M.–11 P.M.
Dinner:	Every day, 6–10 P.M.

Atmosphere / setting: A relic of the Fifties, the College Inn is purely a utilitarian neighborhood convenience restaurant.

Recommended dishes: Shrimp rémoulade; vegetable soup; gumbo; roast beef poor boy; fried oyster poor boy; hamburger; red beans and rice; fried seafood platters. Daily lunch and dinner specials. Bread pudding.

Summary & comments: The menu lists millions of dishes in teeny-tiny type: sandwiches, meat-and-two-vegetables lunches and dinners, and fried seafood. The trick here is to take the place at its own terms and to ferret out the really good dishes from the mere accommodations. Unfortunately, that process may take years. All the regulars have it figured out, though, so listen to them.

Young's

<table>
<tr><td colspan="2">Steak</td></tr>
<tr><td colspan="2">★★★★</td></tr>
<tr><td colspan="2">Moderate</td></tr>
<tr><td>Quality 83</td><td>Value A</td></tr>
</table>

Zone 12   North Shore
850 Robert Boulevard, Slidell
(504) 643-9331

Reservations:	Not accepted
When to go:	Waits for a table are unavoidable except right at opening time
Entree range:	$14–18
Payment:	No credit cards
Service rating:	★★★
Friendliness rating:	★★★
Parking:	Free lot adjacent
Bar:	Full bar
Wine selection:	Decent list, with emphasis on California; very attractive prices
Dress:	Casual
Disabled access:	Limited
Customers:	Neighborhood people
Dinner:	Tuesday–Thursday, 5–10 P.M.; Friday and Saturday, 5–11 P.M.; Sunday and Monday, closed.

Atmosphere / setting: Looks like a steakhouse, once you're inside.

Recommended dishes: House salad; grilled fish; crabmeat and mushrooms sautéed in butter; filet mignon; strip sirloin; prime rib.

Summary & comments: The first time you open the front door of this genuinely great steakhouse in Slidell, you'll steel yourself for the possibility that you might be entering someone's den: the place doesn't look like a restaurant and there's no sign or even address anywhere. The sight of the crowd waiting in the bar will both assure and exasperate you. Not the place to come in a hurry. When the steak (or grilled chicken or fish) emerges, though, the preamble will be justified. They put a great crust around those thick, juice-bulging cylinders of tenderloin (or whatever cut you like), and the prices almost seem like a mistake. Good appetizers and salads, if there's room; no desserts, reservations, or credit cards.

ZACHARY'S

Creole / Neighborhood Cafe

★ ★ ★

Moderate

Zone 4	Uptown Above Napoleon
8400 Oak	
865-1559	

Quality 80   Value B

Reservations:	Accepted
When to go:	Anytime
Entree range:	$10–17
Payment:	AMEX, MC, V
Service rating:	★ ★ ★
Friendliness rating:	★ ★ ★ ★
Parking:	Curbside
Bar:	Full bar
Wine selection:	Limited list of ordinary wines
Dress:	Casual
Disabled access:	Limited
Customers:	Locals
Lunch:	Every day, 11:30 A.M.–2:30 P.M.
Dinner:	Every day, 6–10 P.M.

Atmosphere / setting: A big house, whose rooms have been transformed into echoing dining rooms. Even a crowd can't fill this place up.

Recommended dishes: Shrimp rémoulade; oyster stuffing bread; Creole gumbo; crabmeat au gratin; trout Baquet (with crabmeat and lemon-butter sauce); fried seafood platter; pork chop with bordelaise sauce; fried chicken; roast beef brisket. Cheesecake; bread pudding.

Summary & comments: A more accessible spinoff of the classic soul restaurant Eddie's, operated by the late Eddie Baquet's children. Although some of the food is gussied up a bit, this is a restaurant where the best food will always be the kinds of dishes most Orleanians (of any color) grew up with at home. Even the seafood is served very generously, and the side dishes are straight from mama's repertoire.

Zissis

	Greek

Zone 9　　Metairie Below Causeway
2051 Metairie Road, Metairie
837-7890

Greek
★★★★
Moderate

Quality 84　　Value C

Reservations:	Accepted
When to go:	Anytime
Entree range:	$12–20
Payment:	All major credit cards
Service rating:	★★★★
Friendliness rating:	★★★★
Parking:	Free lot adjacent
Bar:	Full bar
Wine selection:	Decent list, mostly Californian in origin with quite a few Greek wines
Dress:	Casual
Disabled access:	Full
Customers:	Neighborhood people; the Greek community
Lunch:	Monday–Saturday, 11:30 A.M.–2:30 P.M.
Dinner:	Monday–Saturday, 6–10 P.M.; Sunday, closed.

Atmosphere / setting:　A spacious dining room with large murals of Greek seaside scenes. Quiet enough for a date.

Recommended dishes:　Tiropita; spanakopita; lamb carpaccio; appetizer assortment; avgolemono soup; Greek pizza (lunch only); rack of lamb; lamb souvlaki; kotopita (chicken baked in phyllo pastry); grilled fish; psari spanakopita (salmon and spinach baked in pastry). Baklava; galaktoboureko.

Summary & comments:　They cook the Greek standards and then some, all with a style and polish at a level of the better nouvelle bistros. Fresh herbs and a generally lighter touch are evident; most dishes prepared to order, which is also unusual. Good specials. The service staff is intelligent and professional. There are even some decent wines—some of them are even Greek.

Eclectic Gourmet Guide to New Orleans
Reader Survey

If you would like to express your opinion about your New Orleans dining experiences or this guidebook, complete the following survey and mail it to:

Eclectic Gourmet Guide Reader Survey
P.O. Box 43059
Birmingham, AL 35243

	Diner 1	Diner 2	Diner 3	Diner 4	Diner 5
Gender (M or F)	_____	_____	_____	_____	_____
Age	_____	_____	_____	_____	_____
Hometown	_____	_____	_____	_____	_____

Tell us about the restaurants you've visited . . . .

You're overall experience:

Restaurant	👍	👎
_____	_____	_____
_____	_____	_____
_____	_____	_____
_____	_____	_____
_____	_____	_____
_____	_____	_____
_____	_____	_____

Comments you'd like to share with other diners:

_____
_____
_____
_____
_____
_____
_____
_____
_____
_____